PLATO'S *CHARMIDES*

Plato's *Charmides* is a rich mix of drama and argument. Raphael Woolf offers a comprehensive interpretation of its disparate elements that pays close attention to its complex and layered structure, and to the methodology of reading Plato. He thus aims to present a compelling and unified interpretation of the dialogue as a whole. The book mounts a strong case for the formal separation of Plato the author from his character Socrates, and for the *Charmides* as a Platonic defence of the written text as a medium for philosophical reflection. It lays greater emphasis than other readings on the centrality of eros to an understanding of Socratic procedure in the *Charmides*, and on how the dialogue's erotic and medical motifs work together. The book's critical engagement with the dialogue allows a worked-out account to be given of how temperance, the central object of enquiry in the work, is to be conceived.

RAPHAEL WOOLF is a professor of philosophy at King's College London. He has published widely on Greek and Roman philosophy, including many articles on Plato. Recent books include *Rereading Ancient Philosophy: Old Chestnuts and Sacred Cows* (co-edited with Verity Harte, 2017); *Cicero: The Philosophy of a Roman Sceptic* (2015); and *Aristotle: Eudemian Ethics* (co-edited and translated with Brad Inwood, 2013).

CAMBRIDGE STUDIES IN THE DIAL OGUES OF PLATO

Series editor: Mary Margaret McCabe

Plato's dialogues are rich mixtures of subtle argument, sublime theorising and superb literature. It is tempting to read them piecemeal – by analysing the arguments, by espousing or rejecting the theories or by praising Plato's literary expertise. It is equally tempting to search for Platonic views across dialogues, selecting passages from throughout the Platonic corpus. But Plato offers us the dialogues to read whole and one by one. This series provides original studies in individual dialogues of Plato. Each study will aim to throw light on such questions as why its chosen dialogue is composed in the complex way that it is, and what makes this unified whole more than the sum of its parts. In so doing, each volume will both give a full account of its dialogue and offer a view of Plato's philosophising from that perspective.

Titles published in the series:

Plato's Cratylus
David Sedley

Plato's Lysis
Terry Penner and Christopher Rowe

Plato's Meno
Dominic Scott

Forthcoming titles in the series:

Plato's Crito
Brad Inwood

Plato's Euthydemus
Mary Margaret McCabe

Plato's Euthyphro
Lindsay Judson

Plato's Timaeus
Dorothea Frede

Plato's Symposium
Robert Wardy

PLATO'S *CHARMIDES*

RAPHAEL WOOLF
King's College London

Shaftesbury Road, Cambridge CB2 8EA, United Kingdom

One Liberty Plaza, 20th Floor, New York, NY 10006, USA

477 Williamstown Road, Port Melbourne, VIC 3207, Australia

314–321, 3rd Floor, Plot 3, Splendor Forum, Jasola District Centre, New Delhi – 110025, India

103 Penang Road, #05–06/07, Visioncrest Commercial, Singapore 238467

Cambridge University Press is part of Cambridge University Press & Assessment, a department of the University of Cambridge.

We share the University's mission to contribute to society through the pursuit of education, learning and research at the highest international levels of excellence.

www.cambridge.org
Information on this title: www.cambridge.org/9781009308182
DOI: 10.1017/9781009308175

© Raphael Woolf 2023

This publication is in copyright. Subject to statutory exception and to the provisions of relevant collective licensing agreements, no reproduction of any part may take place without the written permission of Cambridge University Press & Assessment.

First published 2023
First paperback edition 2025

A catalogue record for this publication is available from the British Library

Library of Congress Cataloging-in-Publication data
NAMES: Woolf, Raphael, author.
TITLE: Plato's Charmides / Raphael Woolf, King's College London.
DESCRIPTION: First edition. | Cambridge, United Kingdom ; New York, NY, USA : Cambridge University Press, 2023. | Series: Cambridge studies in the dialogues of Plato
IDENTIFIERS: LCCN 2022062059 (print) | LCCN 2022062060 (ebook) | ISBN 9781009308199 (Hardback) | ISBN 9781009308182 (Paperback) | ISBN 9781009308175 (epub)
SUBJECTS: LCSH: Plato. Charmides. | Ethics–Early works to 1800. | KNowledge, Theory of–Early works to 1800.
CLASSIFICATION: LCC B366 .W66 2023 (print) | LCC B366 (ebook) | DDC 184–dc23/eng/20230405
LC record available at https://lccn.loc.gov/2022062059
LC ebook record available at https://lccn.loc.gov/2022062060

ISBN 978-1-009-30819-9 Hardback
ISBN 978-1-009-30818-2 Paperback

Cambridge University Press & Assessment has no responsibility for the persistence or accuracy of URLs for external or third-party internet websites referred to in this publication and does not guarantee that any content on such websites is, or will remain, accurate or appropriate.

For Jane
ἧκε γάρ

Contents

Acknowledgements		*page* ix
1	Introduction: Content, Methodology, Structure	1
	1.1 An Outline of the *Charmides*	1
	1.2 Two Methodological Principles	4
	1.3 The Principle of Agnosticism	5
	1.4 The Principle of Separation	11
	1.5 The Structure of the *Charmides*: Vertical and Horizontal	16
	1.6 Vertical Structure: My Reading of the *Charmides*	17
	1.7 Vertical Structure: A Puzzle of Interpretation	19
	1.8 Vertical Structure: Addressing the Puzzle	25
2	The Stance of Enquiry: Five Examples	30
	2.1 The Perspective of Socrates	30
	2.2 Testimony and Self-Knowledge	39
	2.3 Abstract and Concrete	45
	2.4 Nature and Nurture	50
	2.5 Fiction and History	53
	2.6 Conclusion	58
3	Charmides, Eros and the Unity of the Dialogue	60
	3.1 Charmides' Entrance	61
	3.2 Humour and Perspective	63
	3.3 Subjecthood, Conversation and Truth	65
	3.4 From Body to Soul	68
	3.5 Eros, Looking and Talking	73
	3.6 Temperance and the Turn to Medicine	80
	3.7 Practical Knowledge	90
	3.8 The Treatment of Charmides	97
	3.9 Beauty at Bay	109
	3.10 Interpreting Critias	124
	3.11 Eros as Unifier	132
	3.12 Temperance as a Form of Attention	138
	3.13 Conclusion	144

4	Interpreting Temperance	145
	4.1 A Merely Verbal Disagreement?	146
	4.2 A Question of Status	152
	4.3 Reading the Mind of God	155
	4.4 Knowing What One Believes	161
	4.5 Knowledge and Method	164
	4.6 The Socratic Turn	169
	4.7 Socrates' Challenge I	173
	4.8 Socrates' Challenge II	179
	4.9 The Role of Aporia	182
	4.10 Knowing That and Knowing What	186
	4.11 The Case of Medicine	192
	4.12 Knowledge, Benefit and Utopia	197
	4.13 Benefit without Utopia	202
	4.14 Conclusion	207
5	The Art of Self-Realisation	208
	5.1 Knowing What One Thinks	210
	5.2 The Structured Self	218
	5.3 Temperance and Self-Care	222
	5.4 Socrates and Self-Realisation	226
	5.5 The Life of Temperance	230
	5.6 Temperance and Discipline	233
	5.7 The Good of Self-Realisation	236
	5.8 The Return of Eros	245
	5.9 Plato versus Socrates	252
6	Conclusion: The *Charmides* as a Written Work	253

References 257
Index of Ancient Passages 268
General Index 270

Acknowledgements

This book, though relatively quick in the writing, has been long in gestation. More years ago than either of us would probably care to remember, M. M. McCabe invited me to contribute a volume on the *Charmides* for her then incipient series on the dialogues of Plato; she has awaited the result with the patience of a saint. Although, having read not one but two versions of the manuscript and presented me with a wealth of helpful comments along the way, she is responsible for none of the book's flaws, it is fair to say that it would not exist without her encouragement and advice, even more so without the example set in her own work of how to read, write and think about Plato. For all this I owe MM an irredeemable debt.

I am much indebted also to Verity Harte and Fiona Leigh, friends of long standing, who took the time to read, respectively, a complete draft of the book and its first three chapters and whose comments helped me enormously in the revision process. My thanks too to an anonymous reader for Cambridge University Press, whose searching comments prompted a fresh round of rewriting.

I have had the opportunity to air my ideas about the *Charmides* at a number of venues, foremost among them the wonderful London ancient philosophy graduate seminar, which was kind enough to devote time to reading the whole of the dialogue over the course of a Covid-hit 2020. My thanks to the participants – colleagues and students alike – for stimulating discussion.

Versions of what became part of this book were read at: the 2019 Cambridge Graduate Conference in Ancient Philosophy; a session of the 2020 Lyceum Society Summer Work-in-Progress seminar; the 2021 Trinity Plato Centre conference on Eros and Philia in Plato and Aristotle; a meeting of the King's College London philosophy department staff seminar in 2021; and the 2022 Tartu-Stanford Workshop in Ancient Philosophy. I benefitted greatly from discussion at all these events.

Special thanks for conversations about the *Charmides* to Merrick Anderson, Joachim Aufderheide, Rachel Barney, Amber Carpenter, Niels Christensen, David Ebrey, Branislav Kotoc, Fiona Leigh, M. M. McCabe, Taichi Miura, Jessica Moss, Vasilis Politis, Frisbee Sheffield, Sol Tor, Jorge Torres and Voula Tsouna, whose *Plato's* Charmides: *An Interpretative Commentary* appeared in print as this book was taking its final form.

Last but not least, my thanks to Michael Sharp and his colleagues at Cambridge University Press for their tact and patience in shepherding the book through its various stages of production.

CHAPTER I

Introduction
Content, Methodology, Structure

1.1 An Outline of the *Charmides*

The *Charmides* is a short dialogue but a rich and intricate one. Its interpretation, like that of any Platonic work, is bound to a greater or lesser degree to be controversial. So I begin this first chapter by setting out, as neutrally as I can, an outline of the dialogue's content. In the remaining sections of the chapter I turn to more substantive issues concerning my own methodological approach to interpreting the *Charmides*, and the rather complex way in which the work is structured.

The outline that follows attempts to cover the main contours of the narrative of the work and some of the detail, but it does not aspire to be exhaustive. For the purposes of exposition, and with no intent to beg any interpretive questions, I divide the work into three main sections, which I label respectively the 'Charmides section', the 'Critias section' and the 'Final section'.

Outline of the Charmides section (153a1–162e6):

- Socrates returns to Athens from encampment at Potidaea and a recent battle there. He recounts the battle to his companions in the palaestra before asking how philosophy is going and which of the young are outstanding in wisdom, beauty, or both (153a1–d5).
- Critias says that regarding the beautiful ones it is Charmides who stands out; the latter enters causing much consternation (153d5–154d6).
- Socrates says he would prefer to look at Charmides' soul rather than his body; Critias suggests to Socrates a plan to lure Charmides over by Socrates claiming to know a cure for Charmides' headache (154d7–155b8).
- Charmides comes over; Socrates is dumbstruck by his beauty, but recovers to tell Charmides that according to one of the Thracian doctors of Zalmoxis whom he met on campaign the good condition of

the body depends on that of the soul, which must be treated first (155b9–157a3).
- The soul is treated with a 'charm' of beautiful words that instil temperance. If Charmides does not have temperance, the charm must be administered before the headache remedy can be applied (157a3–c6).
- Critias interjects that Charmides is the most temperate of his contemporaries. Socrates replies that he should be, given that he comes from such a distinguished family; he asks Charmides whether he agrees that he does have temperance (157c7–158c4).
- Charmides replies that he does not know what to say. Socrates proposes that if Charmides has temperance then he will have a perception of it from which he will be able to form a belief about its nature and report that belief. They agree to proceed by Charmides reporting what temperance strikes him as being (158c5–159a10).
- Charmides proposes that temperance is a kind of quietness; Socrates refutes the account and bids Charmides examine himself and try once more (159b1–160e1).
- Charmides proposes that temperance is the same thing as shame; Socrates refutes the account (160e2–161b2).
- Charmides asks Socrates what he thinks of a proposal that he heard from someone else, that temperance is doing one's own things; Socrates says that he finds the proposal puzzling and explains why (161b3–162b8).
- Charmides implies that he heard it from Critias, who expresses anger at Charmides' handling of it and agrees to Socrates' suggestion that he take over discussion of it from Charmides (162b9–e6).

Outline of the Critias section (162e7–175d5):

- Socrates reiterates his critique of the proposal that temperance is doing one's own things; Critias defends it, but agrees at Socrates' urging that he means by it that temperance is the doing of good things (162e7–163e11).
- Socrates points out that this would mean one can be temperate while unaware that one is temperate; Critias proposes instead that temperance is knowing oneself (164a1–165b4).
- Socrates asks what the object of this knowledge is that, as with other branches of knowledge, is distinct from it; Critias accuses Socrates of mischievously treating knowledge of oneself on a par with other branches of knowledge, in order to refute him. He says that temperance is in fact knowledge of itself and of the other branches of knowledge (165b5–166c6).

1.1 An Outline of the *Charmides* 3

- Socrates says he is just seeking to find out how things are; Critias is assuaged and returns to his proposal that temperance is knowledge of itself and of the other branches of knowledge, but agrees, at Socrates' bidding, that it is knowledge of lack of knowledge too (166c7–e9).
- Critias agrees with Socrates that this means that one with temperance will know what one knows and does not know and can examine what others do and do not know; and that they should investigate if such a thing is possible, and if is it beneficial (167a1–b5).
- On its being possible, Socrates argues that it is at best anomalous, at worst impossible, for something to have itself as its own object (167b6–169d5).
- On its being beneficial, Socrates argues that having knowledge of knowledge will mean not that one knows what one knows and does not know, but only that one knows that oneself and others have some knowledge or not, without knowing what the knowledge is of (169d5–171c10).
- And what is the benefit of that? Knowing what oneself and others do and do not know seems highly beneficial, whereas merely knowing that oneself and others have some knowledge seems less so (171d1–172c3).
- But is even the former so beneficial? It seems as if being able to ensure, through knowing what people do and do not know, that only people with knowledge are allowed to practise must be beneficial (172c4–173d7).
- But what knowledge is it exactly that would bring a good life about? Surely knowledge of good and bad. So it is not temperance if temperance is merely knowledge of knowledge and of lack of knowledge, even if one allows that to mean knowledge of what one does and does not know (173d8–175a8).
- Socrates sums up how the enquiry has failed, concluding that it has made temperance turn out to be of no benefit (175a9–d5).

Outline of the Final section (175d5–176d5):

- Socrates tells Charmides that he is sorry about the outcome on the latter's behalf but remains convinced that temperance is a great good and that Charmides is blessed if he has it. He asks Charmides again to see if he does have it and so does not need the charm (175d5–176a5).
- Charmides says he does not know but thinks he does need it and is free to be charmed by Socrates for as long as Socrates deems sufficient. Charmides gains Critias' approval for this plan and indicates that Socrates must not oppose it; Socrates says he will not (176a6–d5).

1.2 Two Methodological Principles

Once one moves from a description of content, however cryptic that may seem in bare outline, to the challenge of interpreting a Platonic work, there are not many uncontroversial statements one can make. But let me try one nonetheless: Plato's works are extremely difficult to interpret. Why they are so is itself not a straightforward question, but one reason, I take it, is the following: Plato does not use his works to give us direct access to his own views. He never speaks in his own name within them.[1] All the talking is done by characters who are not Plato, largely though not wholly through the medium of conversation. We are thus immediately faced with the problem of how (or perhaps even whether) to try to figure out what Plato himself means to convey in a given work.

There are, moreover, quite a large number of works – nearly thirty in all – that are considered authentically Platonic.[2] This raises an additional hard problem: how to interpret a given work in relation to other works in the corpus. Needless to say, in focussing here on the *Charmides*, I shall not attempt to address, let alone resolve, these interpretive problems in any remotely comprehensive way. Nonetheless, given the distinctive challenges raised by the interpretation of a Platonic work, it seems to me important to set out as explicitly as one can, in relation to any particular work, the basic principles one uses in interpreting it.

What follows therefore is a sketch of two methodological principles that I shall attempt (no doubt imperfectly) to cleave to in my reading of the *Charmides*. These principles correspond roughly, albeit in reverse order, to the two interpretive problems I identified above, namely Plato's indirectness and the relation of his works to one another. I do not claim, even with regard to the *Charmides*, that the two principles are the only or best that could be adopted. I set them out in the hope that they may provide a perspicuous framework for constructing a reading of this compact but enigmatic dialogue. Readers should feel free to contest both the principles themselves and the consistency with which I adhere to them. In the end their selection must be judged by the extent to which they help illuminate the structure and meaning of the work to which they are applied.

---

[1] I exclude for these purposes the Letters, which if authentic would promise more direct access to Plato's thoughts. However, all but one, the Seventh, whose authenticity remains doubtful, are now generally regarded as spurious.

[2] A rather larger number than this has come down to us as comprising the Platonic corpus. In addition to those deemed genuine, there remains debate about the authenticity of several further works, with the rest agreed to be spurious.

1.3 The Principle of Agnosticism

The first principle I dub *the principle of agnosticism*. This principle states that one should not assume, in advance of reading the *Charmides*, that one has knowledge of the aims and methods at work therein of either Plato or his main character Socrates. Now in a sense this might seem uncontentious. For is it not obvious that in advance of reading a work one cannot know the aims and methods of its author, let alone, where applicable, its characters? But perhaps this is not so obvious. Maybe the author has other writings that describe, explicitly or implicitly, various aims or methods to be followed, by the author or by one or more of the characters, that need not be taken as restricted to the particular work in which such descriptions appear. In the case of Plato, one character in particular – namely Socrates – plays a leading role in a number of different works. Thus one might, in advance of reading the *Charmides*, either have read, or look to read, other works of Plato in which Socrates says and does various things. These sayings and doings could then, arguably, be used to help figure out what Socrates' aims and methods are in the *Charmides*.

It is this idea that the principle of agnosticism resists,[3] and for two main reasons. The first is the danger of question-begging. Let us say that we are trying to determine Socrates' aims and methods in the *Charmides*. In order to help with this, one might read a variety of other Platonic works, draw certain conclusions about the nature of Socrates' aims and methods in those works, and allow such conclusions to help us decide what Socrates is up to in the *Charmides*. To the extent that one's readings of those other dialogues influence our reading of the *Charmides*, there is a risk that we come to see in the *Charmides* what we (think we) have seen elsewhere in Plato, and that as a result we do not determine with sufficient independence what is in the *Charmides* itself.

This can result, further, in a kind of circularity, whereby our conclusions about the *Charmides*, read in part through the lens of other dialogues, then serve to reinforce our conclusions about those other dialogues. I do not claim that such a circle is necessarily vicious. Nor do I wish to deny that any comprehensive treatment of a particular work of Plato should take into account, albeit with care, the content of other works. Since no

---

[3] Herein, I think, lies a substantial difference between the methodological approach adopted here and that to be found in Thomas Tuozzo's fine study of the *Charmides*. Tuozzo's first chapter, 'Methodological Preliminaries' (2011, 3–51), focusses mainly on appeal to other works in the Platonic corpus to help illuminate the *Charmides*.

individual reading of a Platonic work can aspire to be comprehensive, however, I content myself, in regard to the *Charmides*, with adopting an agnostic approach, in order to try to reach a view about what is going on in that work that is as independent as possible of what is to be found in other works of Plato. The subsequent drawing of comparisons and connections with other works has, it seems to me, the best chance of achieving mutual illumination rather than unhelpful circularity if such an approach is adopted.[4]

This does not mean that I shall wear a hair shirt and never mention any other Platonic work. Occasionally I shall cite other works in order to corroborate, or qualify, findings about the *Charmides* that (I hope) have been arrived at independently. And it is important to emphasise that the principle of agnosticism is a *methodological* one. I have myself read the other Platonic dialogues and naturally, in some cases a least, have formed a view about what is going on in them. No doubt interpreters cannot but be influenced, even if unconsciously, by what they have read in other parts of the corpus when they come to read the *Charmides*, or any other individual work of Plato. What is more, some of the dialogues seem written to encourage their being read in conjunction with others (a point I return to below). But it seems to me that even here, in order to minimise the risk of begging questions about the nature and scope of such interrelations, it is a matter of good method at least to attempt, as an element of an overall interpretive strategy, to form a view of a given work that does not rest, or rests minimally, on one's readings of other works.

One might seek to deflate the value of the agnostic approach by, for example, insisting that, in terms of a charitable reading of Plato's literary art, one should expect to find some sort of reasonably unified account of the character Socrates across the various dialogues in which he appears, though here too some qualifications are needed. The Socrates who is portrayed in the Platonic corpus ranges from a youth (*Parmenides*) to a septuagenarian on the day of his death (*Phaedo*) and his interlocutors range from close associates to hostile opponents and differ variously in age, opinion, social status and intellectual attainment. In view of these factors,

---

[4] The principle is thus not an example of what Rowe (2007, 3) somewhat tendentiously calls 'retreat into interpreting each dialogue on its own', which he connects with a stance whereby one 'decides in advance that he [Plato] is (e.g.) a dramatist rather than a philosopher' (ibid., n. 5). While it hardly needs saying that one should not decide *in advance* (of reading his works?) that Plato is dramatist, philosopher, or both, consideration of the structure of the *Charmides* reveals it to have the form of a drama regardless of how one chooses to classify Plato; see further Section 1.4.

one might expect a correspondingly broad variety of engagement and approaches from Socrates across the dialogues.[5]

In relation to the hypothesis of a unified character, I am, certainly, unsympathetic to the view championed most influentially by Vlastos,[6] who argues that one group of Platonic works contains a Socrates intended to represent more or less faithfully the views of the historical figure, another group a Socrates who has mutated into a mouthpiece for Platonic doctrine. But while I agree that the idea of a less fragmented Socrates is appealing,[7] the most robust way of substantiating (or refuting) the idea is by careful examination of how Socrates is presented in each of the individual works in which he appears. Attempting the latter task with respect to the *Charmides* is one of the motives for this book.

My second reason for deploying the principle of agnosticism is related more specifically than the first to the *Charmides* itself (though no doubt it may apply to other works too). Many Platonic dialogues, as I noted above, are written in a way that invites their readers to consider them in conjunction with others.[8] Among a number of examples, one might cite the sequence *Theaetetus–Sophist–Statesman*, which is explicitly written as continuous stages of a discussion, albeit with different permutations of discussants. Or there is the sequence *Apology–Crito–Phaedo*, covering respectively the periods of Socrates' trial, imprisonment and death.[9] Whatever one is supposed to do with such sequencing, it would certainly seem intended to allow or even encourage the reading of one member of a given sequence in the light of others. Again, there are passages within the dialogues that seem to involve clear reference to other works. A notable example is *Phaedo* 73a–b with its apparent recollection of the Theory of Recollection in the *Meno*.

The *Charmides* is not, it seems to me, of this sort on either count. It is not part of any obvious dialogical sequence. Nor does it contain references to the content of other works of the same overt character as that of the

---

[5] On the challenge of reading what she calls the 'many figures of Sokrates', see Blondell (2002, 8–11).
[6] The fullest statement is Vlastos (1991, 45–80).
[7] Socrates emphasises his own consistency in a number of places. See e.g. *Gorgias* 482a–c, *Phaedo* 100b1–3, and, in the *Charmides* itself, 170a2.
[8] I would not therefore say quite so starkly, with Press (1993, 110), that 'each of the genuine [Platonic] dialogues can be read sensibly without knowing anything about the content or action of any other dialogue'. *Timaeus* 17c–19b, for example, would be rather mysterious without the *Republic* in mind (whether or not it is intended as a summary of the latter work).
[9] These are of course just examples that can be extended and connected in further ways. Thus, the main action of the *Theaetetus* is set on the day on which Socrates is to attend the preliminary hearing of the charges against him; the *Euthyphro* is set later that same day, just before the hearing.

Phaedo to the *Meno*.[10] That being so, there is correspondingly less encouragement for us to read the *Charmides* by reference to other works in the corpus. This is not to deny that allusions within the *Charmides* to other dialogues can be teased out. It seems plausible, for example, that Critias' reference at 164d–e to the Delphic inscription 'Know thyself' may be intended by Plato to put us in mind of the story of Chaerephon's trip to the Oracle recounted by Socrates at *Apology* 21a,[11] though what such an allusion amounts to is of course a further question.[12]

Another example that has been suggested, by David Sedley, is of an 'authorial self-allusion' in Socrates' reference at *Charmides* 169a1–2 to 'some great man' (*megalou tinos andros*) being needed to adjudicate which reflexive relations (if any) are possible, 'significantly including', as Sedley puts it, '"self-moving motion" – a forward allusion to Plato's metaphysics of soul in *Phaedrus* and *Laws* X',[13] where the soul is characterised as self-moving.[14] In a work as concerned with reflexive relations as the *Charmides*, it seems a happy thought that in one of its key passages on the topic may be found an example of authorial self-reference. Moreover, the allusion can be read also as backward-facing (here I go beyond Sedley). For, according to Socrates earlier in the dialogue, no one is said to have been a 'greater man' (*meizōn anēr*, 158a3) than Charmides' uncle Pyrilampes, which brings the family of Plato, historically Charmides' nephew, directly into the 'great man' equation and offers a tempting picture of Plato congratulating himself on having taken over the mantle of greatest in family from his uncle's uncle.

---

[10] The Homeric line 'the presence of shame is no good for a man in need' is cited by Socrates both at *Charmides* 161a4 (discussed in Sections 2.1 and 3.9) and *Laches* 201b2–3. On possible affinities between the two works, see Dieterle (1966), Altman (2010); and on thematic relations between the *Charmides* and other Platonic works more broadly, Tsouna (2022, 40–51).

[11] One might further compare, on testing for self-knowledge, the wording at *Charmides* 167a1–5 with that of *Apology* 21c2–d8, though the latter excerpt classifies self-knowledge as belonging to wisdom, the former to temperance. Nor is there any sign in the *Apology* of the *Charmides*'s intense critique of the concept of self-knowledge, a difference that can be accounted for by, if nothing else, the fact that in the *Apology* Socrates is defending himself before a jury of ordinary Athenian citizens, not conversing with a close associate. For an argument that the *Charmides* critique marks only a limited undermining of the *Apology* claims, see Benson (2003). Mahoney (1996) is an example of a reading of Socrates' main discussion with Critias in the *Charmides* viewed substantially through the lens of the *Apology*. See also Rasmussen (2008).

[12] See Section 4.3.

[13] Sedley (2019, 48 n. 8). Notwithstanding Sedley's reference to 'forward' allusion, I take no view for the purposes of this book on the chronology of Plato's works, except to note that their order of composition need not reflect the order, if any, in which Plato might have expected them to be read.

[14] See *Phaedrus* 245c–e; *Laws* 10.894a–896b. I leave aside for present purposes the question of whether these texts offer a *solution* to the problem of how (in at least one case) reflexive relations are possible or proceed by not raising the problem.

1.3 The Principle of Agnosticism

In a dialogue that is also, at least on the surface, thoroughgoingly aporetic, it seems fair to point out, however, that were we to take Socrates' plea for a great man as a case of anticipatory Platonic boastfulness in the way Sedley urges, it would fall significantly short on its own terms. The *Phaedrus* and *Laws* discuss self-motion specifically, whereas Socrates' stated need in the *Charmides* is for one who will 'in all cases' (*kata pantōn*, 169a2) – including presumably the many that Socrates discusses at 167–8 in addition to self-motion – determine where reflexivity is possible and where it is not. If there is forward allusion here, it looks as if the great man ends up delivering substantially less than Socrates was seeking.

A further possible candidate for allusion to other works is to be found in the concept of 'doing one's own things' (*prattein ta heautou*), which serves in the *Charmides* as a (problematised) proposal, which includes an example in a civic context (161e–162a), for what temperance (*sōphrosunē*) is,[15] but also surfaces in *Republic* 4 as the official characterisation there of justice. Insofar as problems are identifiable independently of their solutions, the principle of agnosticism as applied to the *Charmides* is compatible with, but does not entail, a 'proleptic' reading of the dialogue whereby it is seen as anticipatory of other dialogues in raising problems to be addressed in those works – though it should be noted that Charles Kahn, the leading proponent of a proleptic reading of Plato, rejects the presence of 'doing one's own' as a case of prolepsis in the *Charmides*.[16]

Let us in any event grant that allusions from the *Charmides* to other Platonic works can be argued for. In the nature of the case it is hard to say whether their presence either demands, or makes desirable, that the dialogue be read in the light of them.[17] Indeed, to the extent that one

---

[15] I adopt, without wishing to beg any questions about the substance of its referent, 'temperance' as what is still a fairly standard translation of this key term. On the substance see esp. Section 3.12 and Chapter 5; and, on further issues concerning its rendition, Section 5.6.

[16] See Kahn (1988, 542), which instead opts for the work's discussion of knowledge of good and bad as proleptically significant in relation to the *Republic*. For the proleptic reading of Plato more generally see Kahn (1996). On elements of the *Charmides* anticipatory of the *Statesman*, see Schofield (2006, 146).

[17] In terms of specific allusions *to* the *Charmides* in other Platonic works, there seems to me only one that is close to indubitable: *Symposium* 222b, which I discuss in Section 5.8. At *Timaeus* 72a4–6, 'doing one's own things' reappears, together with 'knowing oneself', as features that Timaeus calls 'well and venerably said' (*eu kai palai legetai*, a4) to belong to the temperate person alone; but since this wording seems designed to frame the features as stock attributions long in currency, I am not sure whether the claim of Sedley (2019, 62 n. 30; cf. Solère-Queval 1993, 62) that the passage represents 'qualified approval … [of] two of the *Charmides*' rejected definitions of *sōphrosunē*' establishes conscious allusion to that work. On references to temperance elsewhere in the corpus, of varying degrees of closeness to elements found in the *Charmides*, see Vorwerk (2001, 36–9); and for a case study of issues in determining in which direction intertextual allusions in Plato flow, McCabe (2002).

finds their status elusive or contestable, as I have argued with regard to the 'great man' case, that only serves to highlight a feature of the *Charmides* that comes across with great vividness: its presentation of a self-contained world, lovingly detailed and richly characterised. Set several decades before its composition, its most pointed allusions seem to be not 'sideways' to other works of Plato but, as we shall see, backwards and forwards to significant historical events before and after the goings-on depicted in the work itself.[18] This aspect of the way the work is written offers further incentive to investigate it on its own terms.

The *Charmides* is, of course, fiction not history. So before turning to my second principle of interpretation, let me pause briefly to situate the principle of agnosticism in relation to the historical context of the work. Set around the time of Plato's birth, the *Charmides* is a product of Plato's creative imagination, not reportage. However, its status as fiction needs an important qualification. Its four speaking characters are not simply fictional but fictionalised. The lives of Socrates, Critias, Charmides and Chaerephon are all independently attested.[19] The historical Charmides was, as mentioned above, Plato's uncle – a lineage that the dialogue's references to Charmides' family allow us to trace. Charmides was also, as the work tells us, the younger cousin of Critias as well as his ward. Moreover Critias, like Plato, was an author of whose works a number of fragments survive.[20]

Plato's choice to populate the work with fictionalised characters rather than wholly fictional ones means, I think, that we are expected to have in mind at least some basic features of their historical counterparts' lives:[21] above all, perhaps, given the apparent allusions at the end of the dialogue to the short-lived but bloody rule of the oligarchic regime known as the Thirty (or Thirty Tyrants) – established at Athens in 404 BCE after the latter's defeat by Sparta in the Peloponnesian War – the participation of Critias and Charmides in that regime. Critias was one of its leading figures, while Charmides served it as a member of the so-called Ten who

---

[18] The apparent symmetry of this will need some qualification; see Section 2.5.
[19] On the historical evidence see Nails (2002).
[20] On the historical Critias as author of both prose and verse, and possible resonances of his writings in the *Charmides*, see Tuozzo (2011, 70–85); cf. Gottesman (2020).
[21] While one must certainly avoid assimilating the historical figure with the fictionalised character, I doubt that Kahn (1996, 202) can quite be right to say that the [Platonic] '*persona* of Socrates enjoys an independent life, free from any historical or chronological limitations'. If that were literally true, it is hard to see why Plato would have selected a character with such historical resonances in the first place. On Plato's use of the relation between fiction and history, see McCabe (2019a, 109).

administered the Piraeus. Both died fighting the democratic opposition at the Battle of Munychia, which led to the overthrow of the Thirty and the restoration of democracy in 403. Four years into that restoration, in 399, Socrates himself was tried and executed.

I will thus regard it as legitimate, even mandatory, to keep in mind such historical resonances in interpreting the dialogue.[22] Indeed I take it to be not merely a contingent fact about the *Charmides* that it uses fictionalised, rather than straightforwardly fictional, characters.[23] Their ambivalent status as both abstracted from and connected to history is, I think, carefully chosen by Plato to serve his purposes.[24] I shall argue in Chapter 2 (Section 2.5) that the irruption of history at the end of the work, in the form of allusion to the future (relative to the work's dramatic date) regime of the Thirty,[25] is supposed to raise an important question, centring on the figure of Socrates, about the extent to which it is possible or desirable to detach oneself from the spatiotemporal world.

1.4 The Principle of Separation

The second methodological principle governing my interpretation I call the *principle of separation*. This lays it down that we should not assume that what is said or done by any of Plato's characters is necessarily endorsed by Plato himself, or identifiable with Plato's own views or motivations. The core idea underlying the principle is that Plato, as we noted above, writes dramatic works in which he never himself features as a speaking character. He is on only three occasions explicitly mentioned at all: twice by Socrates in the *Apology* (34a, 38b) as

---

[22] I shall adopt a similar (non-agnostic) approach with regard to literary resonances in the work, in particular of Homer's *Odyssey*. See Section 2.1.
[23] Critias and Charmides also appear in the *Protagoras*, the latter non-speaking, the former in a small speaking role (336d–e) advocating a non-partisan approach to the question of whether Protagoras and Socrates should conduct their debate via speeches or rapid-fire question-and-answer; see Moore (2020b). If the Critias who appears in the *Timaeus* in a significant speaking role, and in the (unfinished) *Critias* as its major speaker, is our Critias (it is possible that it is his grandfather), then his remarks in the *Protagoras* would be appropriate for one evidently presented by Plato as willing to take on either format.
[24] It seems to me implausible to regard the inclusion of Critias in the work as unconnected with the political role of his historical counterpart, as claimed by Müller (1976, 133).
[25] Technically the *Charmides* has two dramatic dates: the date of its narrated events and the date at which those events were narrated by Socrates to an anonymous companion. The narration could have taken place at any time between that first date (most likely during 429 BCE) and Socrates' death in 399, hence possibly after the short-lived reign of the Thirty in 404–403. I am not sure, however, if the 'innocence' of Socrates' narration fits well with that possibility. Schultz (2013, 40) observes that this uncertainty over the date of narration 'forces the reader to confront a certain level of aporia, a certain level of not knowing, at the very outset of the dialogue'.

present at Socrates' trial, in the latter case as additionally willing to stand surety for Socrates; and once by Phaedo in the *Phaedo* (59b) as absent through illness from being with Socrates on his final day. Such allusions surely do show someone called Plato presented as in some sense a supporter of Socrates; and it is no great stretch to infer that the author Plato wished to present himself by these means as, at least around the time those works were set, such a supporter, albeit a pointedly absent one on Socrates' last day.

Let us, then, for argument's sake, bypass the principle of agnosticism and stray outside the *Charmides* to take account of Plato's writing himself in as present in support of Socrates in the *Apology* and as someone only prevented by illness from attendance, presumably therefore as part of Socrates' close circle, at the latter's last day and execution in the *Phaedo*. While this plausibly suggests that Plato the author is thereby representing himself as an admirer of Socrates, it would be rash to deduce that he took himself to be an uncritical admirer, since he would arguably fail thereby to be true to Socrates' own example, as Plato portrays it, of critical scrutiny of persons and their views. It at least leaves open the possibility that Plato was prepared both to regard and to portray Socrates warts and all.

Readers who find the principle of agnosticism uncongenial as an aid to interpreting the *Charmides* may thus care to keep in mind that its removal does not straightforwardly license a reading of the character Socrates as recipient, in his sayings and doings, of Platonic endorsement. Part of the point of that principle is, nonetheless, to caution us against reading in from other Platonic works a prejudgement that Socrates must be Plato's hero,[26] with the potential that has for distorting how we read the Socrates whom we find in the *Charmides*. Let us note in this regard that the conversation depicted in the *Charmides* has a likely dramatic date of 429 BCE, around or a little before Plato's birth, its author thereby placing its setting comfortably before the time that he came to know Socrates. This should leave us wary, when we read the *Charmides*, of projecting back onto its content any particular view we may have about a relationship between Socrates and Plato that was by some distance yet to materialise, and is only mentioned in dialogues set at the end of Socrates' life.

---

[26] In contrasting, less unfavourably than many have, Critias with Socrates in the *Charmides*, Tuozzo (2001, 324) still feels the need to assure us that 'Socrates is the philosopher-hero of the Platonic dialogues'. I have little quarrel with such assessments if the concept of 'hero' employed therein is supposed to be (as perhaps the ancient Greek conception was) compatible with the hero exhibiting flawed character or behaviour. However, this does not seem to be the sense in which Tuozzo and some other modern commentators deploy the term with regard to Plato's Socrates; see also Section 2.1 n. 5. For a sceptical view of Socrates as 'philosophical superhero' see G. Scott (2007, xiii–xiv).

1.4 The Principle of Separation

We should not, then, assume uncritical endorsement by the author Plato of the character Socrates, even though in the *Charmides* the latter is – as in many, though not all, of Plato's other works – the leading character. Indeed it is worth observing that had Plato himself featured as a speaking character in his works, we would even then not be entitled simply to read off the views of Plato as author from such views as were put into the mouth of Plato the character:[27] self-dramatisation need not be so one-dimensional.[28] Still less, it seems to me, are we entitled to read off Plato's views or motivations straightforwardly from the views or motivations we can discern in his characters who are not Plato, Socrates included.

Because Plato's works in general have this dramatic structure, involving the depiction of characters doing and saying things and interacting with one another, rather than the author writing directly in his own name, we should be wary of identifying the views or motives of any of Plato's characters with those of Plato himself. The principle of separation bids us take seriously, in order to account for the presence of this structure, the distinctness of author from characters. Given the ubiquity of the structure in Plato, we should likewise be wary of approaches that seek to apply the principle to one dialogue rather than others. An example of such selectivity is to be found in David Sedley's (2004) interpretation of the *Theaetetus*. Despite his fruitful use of the principle in reading that work, Sedley nonetheless maintains that 'The default assumption' regarding the relationship between Plato and a given dialogue's main speaker 'remains author-speaker identity' (2004, 7).[29] Sedley does not say why identity should be our default assumption; the formal separation, throughout the corpus, of Plato as author from his speakers should make the *default* the contrary of what Sedley claims.[30]

---

[27] Contra Frede (1992, 203–4), who nonetheless rightly emphasises how the formal features of Plato's works leave open whether he endorses any given argument within them.

[28] Though I cannot argue the point here, the use by Cicero in his philosophical dialogues of a character named 'Cicero' seems to me a good example of this kind of complexity.

[29] For a (still) less qualified identity thesis with regard to the relation between Plato the author and Socrates his character, see Rowe (2007, 19); and on the question of Plato's relationship with his leading characters more generally, Press (2000).

[30] Sedley (2003) maintains, partly by appeal to a belief on Plato's part that the structure of thought is itself dialogical, that the dialogues 'can legitimately be read by us as *Plato thinking aloud* ... They are an externalisation of his own thought-processes' (ibid., 1–2; Sedley's emphasis). There are two ways of reading this idea. One is a truism: the content of Plato's dialogues is the product of Plato's mind. The other, not entailed by the first, is a substantive thesis: the content (or some of it) is intended to represent Plato's own views. Invoking 'externalisation' cannot speak in favour of the substantive thesis without an explanation of why Plato would choose to represent his views by attributing them to characters who are not Plato.

As with the principle of agnosticism, the principle of separation is, as I deploy it, methodological. It does not forbid us from ultimately identifying the views of a character in a Platonic work with those of Plato himself. Rather, it instructs us in a certain methodological caution, born of the way Plato's works are constructed. We may (or may not) end up finding it plausible that the, or some, views or motives discernible in Socrates, or any other character, are to be identified with those of Plato the author. But that identity has to be argued for, not simply, even if only by default, assumed.

Indeed, with regard to the character Socrates (though the point applies in principle to other characters) there is one very basic way in which the dramatic structure of the *Charmides* (as of many other Platonic works) invites us to sustain separation: Socrates, as depicted therein, goes about his business by talking to people; Plato the author goes about his business by composing a written work. How Plato uses this aspect of his character Socrates to engage with his readers is a further important question. But in portraying, as author of a written work, a character who proceeds by oral discussion, Plato already, on the face of it, signals a certain divergence in approach between himself as author and Socrates as character. Thus, to preview a major way in which the principle of separation will influence my reading: I shall argue, particularly in Chapter 4, that the difference between the written and the oral is itself a prominent theme of the dialogue, centred on a marked difference in approach to interpretation, especially of written texts, displayed by Socrates and Critias (real-life author of written texts) respectively.

There is, moreover, a feature of the *Charmides* which, while not unique to that work in the Platonic corpus, seems to me to sharpen the applicability of the principle of separation to it. The *Charmides* is narrated in the first person (to an anonymous companion) by the character Socrates, in contrast to some Platonic works which directly lay out alternating dialogue between characters.[31] Thus the *Charmides* offers an overtly *perspectival* take on the events it purports to depict. This means, from a formal point of view, that we do not simply have here separation mandated by the fact of an author depicting the sayings and doings of certain characters. We have, in addition, rather than a formally neutral 'X says, Y says ...' pattern, a first-person narrative take on proceedings that are thereby presented as being from one particular viewpoint. This feature alerts us to the idea that

---

[31] On Plato's motives for composing narrated works, see further Schofield (2013); and on Socrates as narrator, Bowery (2007).

the viewpoint we are given may be open to challenge from other viewpoints and in this regard does not necessarily represent one that the author endorses, or expects the reader to endorse, uncritically.

To this it might be objected that, on the contrary, the presentation of a particular character's viewpoint from a first-person perspective privileges that character's viewpoint. I think that this is right, but that we need to be careful to distinguish the formal from the normative in assessing what this privileging amounts to. Presenting the sayings and doings of the *Charmides* through Socrates' eyes does indeed formally privilege Socrates' viewpoint in that it makes it the way in which matters are shown to the reader.[32] But what follows from that?

One might reasonably say that such selection of viewpoint is a sign that the author intends us to take it as the focus of our attention as readers. But from this it does not in the least follow that we are supposed to take the viewpoint as one that the author is recommending to us as, say, particularly admirable or truthful. For all that formal privileging tells us, it could be that the author finds the character particularly dangerous or deceiving and wants us to focus on him for that reason: Socrates as anti-hero to be repudiated rather than hero to be embraced. On this scenario Plato would be maintaining a strong critical distance between himself and his character, and thereby presumably would wish to allow his readers the liberty to do likewise. Or one can imagine, on a more nuanced (perhaps more plausible) scenario, that Plato is fascinated by Socrates without his necessarily regarding him as flawless or beyond criticism. My point is that all these options are compatible with the formal privileging given by the presentation of Socrates from a first-person perspective.

Again, to say this is not to argue that Plato does or does not identify himself with the views, aims and methods of his character Socrates.[33] It is, rather, to make a point about what the author's presentation of a narrative through the eyes of a character does and does not entail. It seems to me that, formally, it entails and (through the perspectival device) highlights the separateness of author from character. It thus allows for critical distance between the two, and by the same token legitimates critical exploration by readers of that character's sayings and doings.

---

[32] Cf. Finkelberg (2019, 31).
[33] For a thesis (with particular reference to the *Meno*) that he does not, see Rowett (2018, 69–70), though Rowett muddies the waters slightly by both insisting on the fictional status of the *Meno* (69) and referring to the Socrates from whom Plato must be distinguished as the latter's 'mentor' (70).

At this point there is some convergence between the principles of agnosticism and of separation, which I hope gives my approach to reading the *Charmides* a certain methodological unity. The principle of agnosticism cautions us against using as a starting point, to read what Socrates is up to in the *Charmides*, what (we think) he is up to in other Platonic works. The principle of separation disbars automatic identification of what Socrates says with what Plato thinks. On these grounds too we must therefore come to the dialogue with an open mind, prepared to look carefully and critically at Socrates' aims and methods as depicted therein, before drawing any conclusions about his status as role model, anti-hero, or somewhere in between.

Even if we are disinclined to reach any such moralised conclusions about Socrates, the principle of separation does at least license us to consider the possibility that Plato's own aims and methods might simply be *different* from those of his leading character. I shall in fact argue for an interpretation of the *Charmides* somewhat along those lines. But before turning to my more substantive proposals, let me remain a little longer at the relatively formal level and move on from the methodological principles that underpin my reading of the *Charmides* to an analysis of the basic structure of the dialogue itself. Examination of this structure will, I hope, begin to show more concretely how the methodological principles earn their keep.

1.5 The Structure of the *Charmides*: Vertical and Horizontal

In considering the way the *Charmides* is structured there are, it seems to me, broadly two main elements to take into account. The first is its horizontal structure. By this I mean the sequence of conversations and events that the work portrays: Socrates' return from battle, his being greeted by Chaerephon, and so on, up until the three-way exchange between Socrates, Critias and Charmides with which the work ends. The second main element is its vertical structure. By this I mean the way in which that sequence of conversations and events is embedded within a series of compositional levels. What are those levels? At the top level, so to speak, we have Plato composing a written work, the *Charmides*. That work, however, presents its sequence of conversations and events as narrated in the first person by a character, Socrates, to an unnamed companion. So we have altogether three layers of vertical structure: Plato writing a work that shows Socrates reciting to a companion in the first person a monologue that, in turn, depicts a sequence of conversations and events in which Socrates took a leading part.

One thing this vertical structuring might immediately suggest is that we are not necessarily to identify, on the one hand, the purposes with which Socrates interacts with the other characters in the *Charmides* and, on the other hand, the purposes that Plato may have, with regard to his potential readership, in writing the *Charmides*.[34] This structural feature thus meshes naturally with the principle of separation. In discussing that principle, I argued that the first-person narrative can be seen as formally privileging Socrates' viewpoint while at the same time allowing for critical distance between Plato the author and Socrates the character. In structural terms it is Socrates' narration, even as Plato sits atop the work as its composer.

1.6 Vertical Structure: My Reading of the *Charmides*

As a preliminary way of putting this structure to work, let me set out in brief one further element of my interpretation that is grounded on the principle of separation, concerning a difference in viewpoint between Socrates and Plato. I shall argue that Socrates is presented in the *Charmides* as motivated chiefly by erotic desire (eros):[35] his goal is to discover (or instil) beauty, the proprietary attitude towards which is erotic desire; and he is consistently portrayed in the work as in pursuit of things that he believes are or might be beautiful. We may thus refer to the *Charmides* as an erotic dialogue,[36] not in the sense that, as in the *Symposium* and *Phaedrus*, eros is itself a principal topic of discussion, but in the sense that erotic pursuit is presented as Socrates' main underlying motivation for acting as he does, together with the fact that Socrates' own erotic engagement is shown in some detail and from his perspective.[37]

---

[34] Cf. Tigerstedt (1977, 98) on the 'double dialogue' in Plato, though it does not of course follow from the depiction of dialogue within a Platonic work that dialogue with his readers was Plato's aim.

[35] Note on terminology: 'eros' serves here, in approximation to one of its standard English senses of 'erotic desire', to render the Greek *erōs*. This, I think, captures more closely than a term such as 'love' the core sense of the term in the *Charmides*. I translate, for the most part, the Greek *kalon* (and cognates) as 'beautiful' (and cognates), rather than using a flatter rendition such as 'admirable' or 'fine', in order to display perspicuously the status outlined in the *Charmides* of what is *kalon* as proper object of eros. Kosman (2010) includes an interesting discussion of the problem of translating *kalon*, in the *Charmides* and elsewhere, which, however, seems to me to make rather too much of the alleged difficulties of rendering the term univocally as 'beautiful' (here I side with Lear 2010).

[36] See here Gordon (2013, 1), Schofield (2013, 90–1).

[37] Schmidt (1985, 11) picturesquely but not inaccurately describes Socrates as narrating 'ein Liebesabenteuer'.

Plato, on the other hand, uses his portrayal of Socrates' pursuit to instil in his readers what I shall call the stance of enquiry. By this I mean an attitude that does not take ideas or arguments on trust but engages reflectively and critically with them.[38] I shall argue moreover that Plato uses his written text to try to bring it about that, by engaging with the text, we as readers find ourselves occupying that stance and are revealed to ourselves as occupiers of it. The dialogue is thus aimed at achieving a certain kind of self-knowledge in its readers, of ourselves as critical enquirers oriented towards discovering the truth. In this regard, I shall argue, Plato would have us see such enquiry as valuable, by seeing ourselves as actively engaged in it through our occupation of the critical stance. The dialogue does not, therefore, simply show a search for truth, in the form of critical enquiries undertaken by Socrates with his interlocutors, with readers invited to look in on it from the outside. It also endeavours to have us see ourselves, from the inside, as undertaking that search in response to the way the dialogue is written.

In this regard, there is an important difference between how Socrates is portrayed as a critical enquirer and how Plato would have us, his readers, see critical enquiry. Socrates, I shall argue, is shown throughout the dialogue as undertaking his enquiries for the sake of his search for beauty. Specifically, his critical enquiries into temperance do not have as their ultimate goal the discovery of the truth about temperance. Rather, that goal is subordinate to his desire to attain a vision of beauty. It is because temperance is a beautiful thing that Socrates is moved to seek it in Charmides' soul; his enquiry is in the service of his erotic drive.

Plato, by contrast, does not, I think, seek to encourage his readers to undertake an erotic quest for beauty of the kind that Socrates is shown pursuing. We as readers are of course invited to engage with that aspect of Socrates' portrayal; but Plato does not aim at our emulating Socrates' quest (so if Socrates is a role model, he is only a partial one). We are, rather, to come to regard ourselves as valuing critical enquiry by coming to see ourselves, through our engagement with the text, as pursuing such enquiry.

At the same time, the dialogue's vertical structure allows that the aporetic outcome – the lack of a positive answer and the accumulation of various problems – of the discussion between (in particular) Socrates and Critias about the nature of temperance need not rule out there being an account of temperance that Plato might wish, through his written text,

---

[38] On the *Charmides* as a 'prime example of how the dialogue form generates reflection by the reader', see McCabe (2011, 166).

to encourage his readers to formulate by critically engaging with the work. I shall argue in Chapter 5 that we can discern such an account, one that I call 'temperance as self-realisation' and that is inspired by Socrates' own practice of critical examination. Moreover, it is an account that brings with it, in a certain way, the pursuit of beauty at its core. But that is an idea that emerges from detailed (and controvertible) interpretation of Plato's text. It is not a matter of straightforward inference from the way that Socrates' own practice is depicted.

Closely connected, I shall claim, with the way that Socrates pursues his quest is the presence in the dialogue, as one of its prominent themes, of the idea of knowledge as involving *know-how* or practical skill of some kind, with medicine in turn featuring as the most prominent exemplar of this kind of knowledge. I shall argue that the dialogue encourages us to think about Socratic procedure there in the light of this conception of knowledge, and that in fact two distinct branches of knowledge of this kind are, in addition to temperance itself, suggested to help illuminate the procedure and its objectives. Let me briefly preview each of these.[39]

First is the art of (what I shall call) erotics, whose existence is implied by the reference, at 155d4–5, to Cydias the poet being, in Socrates' view, wisest in erotic matters. The principal subject-matter of this art is erotic desire; and its principal aim is securing success in erotic pursuit, in particular, in the Socratic case, success in exposing to view a soul that one has reason to think is, or can be made, beautiful. Secondly, there is a discernible connection between Socratic procedure in the *Charmides* and the art of (what I shall call) soul-medicine, whose existence is suggested by Socrates' narration of his encounter with a Thracian doctor at 156d–157c. The subject-matter of this art is the soul, rather than (as in the case of medicine) the body, and its aim is to bring souls into good condition – that is, the condition of being temperate – just as the aim of medicine is to bring bodies into good condition in the form of physical health. In line with my claim that erotic pursuit is Socrates' overriding motive in the *Charmides*, I shall further show how soul-medicine is subordinate in the dialogue to erotics, such that the goal of the latter is served by the practice of the former.

1.7 Vertical Structure: A Puzzle of Interpretation

Whatever the merits of these specific proposals, one reason for distinguishing the vertical from the horizontal aspect of the dialogue's structure is that

---

[39] They will be set out in more detail in Chapter 3. See especially Sections 3.6 and 3.7.

doing so, I contend, helps tackle a puzzle about the sequence of events that the *Charmides* depicts. The horizontal structure of the work can certainly seem puzzling, as scholars sometimes, if on occasion unwittingly, recognise. Consider the title of a 1969 paper by Adamietz: 'Zur Erklärung des Hauptteils von Platons *Charmides* (164a–175d)'. What is striking for present purposes is that what Adamietz refers to as the 'main part' (Hauptteil) of the *Charmides*, namely (as he sees it) 164a–175d, is a segment that does not begin until the work, which starts at 153a, is nearly halfway over and that encompasses barely half its total length. Stalley identifies what he calls the work's 'main argument' as beginning still later, at 164c–165a.[40] The apotheosis of this sort of characterisation may be found in an approving remark of Chen, with its apparent indifference towards questions of compositional unity, that the passage 165c–175d 'can be studied separately from the rest of the dialogue'.[41]

If these scholars are right, then the horizontal structure of the *Charmides* is puzzling indeed. Why does it take Plato around half the work to get going? And how do we account for the substantial presence of what precedes the (supposedly) main business, especially if the latter is (supposedly) independent of what has gone before? The discussion of temperance with Critias, near the beginning of which these scholars identify the main part of the work as getting underway, has a level of technical sophistication and complexity – especially once Critias proposes at 165b that temperance is knowing oneself – that is markedly different from what preceded it. This difference, however, itself needs accounting for.

Likewise, in inviting Critias to take over the discussion of temperance with him from Charmides, Socrates avers that, because of his age and interest, Critias will probably be in a better position than Charmides to undertake such a discussion (162e). Indeed, what follows seems to confirm Critias as a considerably more sophisticated discussant than Charmides. But if so, then why was Socrates so interested in Charmides in the first place? If, again, we answer this by pointing to Charmides' youthful beauty and Socrates' interest in it, then why is Charmides abandoned by Socrates for the complex discussion of temperance with Critias that follows? From either direction, an account of the relation between the two sections is required.

---

[40] Stalley (2000, 270).
[41] Chen (1978, 13). More aporetically, Effe (1971, 208) cites the relation between the Charmides and Critias sections as raising a problem about the unity of the dialogue. It should be noted that Chen (1978, 13) also maintains the (in my view) more defensible position that 165c–175d is best read without importation of 'thoughts from other dialogues'.

1.7 A Puzzle of Interpretation

Some views of what the work is concerned with, while not resolving the puzzle of why it should apparently get started so late, do begin to suggest a diagnosis. Santas states baldly that 'The *Charmides* is a search for a definition of temperance.'[42] Now the first attempt to say what temperance is is given by Charmides at 159b. Admittedly, this is now only about a quarter of the way through the work. But that still means passing over a significant portion – ingenuously described by one commentator as a 'long and entertaining introduction'[43] – that does not seem to be as Santas describes it. Even if (as I shall deny) everything in the *Charmides* ultimately serves its search for a definition of temperance, some recognition is needed that not everything in the work consists in such a search.

Irwin, in more nuanced fashion, refers to the question of what temperance is as '[i]n the *Charmides* Socrates' primary question ... introduced in a discussion of whether Charmides himself is temperate.'[44] This formulation suggests that at least one other question, in addition to 'What is temperance?', is of interest to Socrates at any rate, namely the question of whether Charmides is temperate,[45] although the description of the former question as 'primary' for Socrates presumably means that Irwin regards 'What is temperance?' as the dialogue's main question.

Now in a sense this is undeniable, and progress with the puzzle seems to have been made. The dialogue spends its greater part in pursuit of the question of what temperance is, while also being concerned, both earlier on and towards its close, with the question of whether Charmides is temperate. But Irwin's way of putting things nonetheless invites consideration of how the two questions are related in the work. The fact that Socrates spends most of his time in the *Charmides* in pursuit of the 'What is temperance?' question (the question being 'primary' in that sense) does not exclude the possibility that addressing that question is, for him, subordinate (so in that sense 'secondary') to discovering whether Charmides is temperate.[46] Socrates might, for example, wish to discover what temperance is in order to ascertain whether it is in Charmides' soul,

---

[42] Santas (1973, 105). [43] Luz (2001, 100). [44] Irwin (1995, 21).
[45] Politis (2015, 101–2; 149) argues that the question whether Charmides knows whether he is temperate is also prominent in the dialogue, though the question Politis refers to (158c2–4) in fact has Socrates ask whether Charmides *agrees* with Critias (not: knows) that he is temperate, and this in turn seems to serve the more basic question of figuring out whether Charmides *is* temperate (159a9–10).
[46] Thus Rademaker (2005, 327 n. 41) regards the question 'as a preliminary to see whether Charmides is indeed σώφρων [temperate]'. See also Dancy (2004, 31), who speaks of the *Charmides*' 'overarching question, to which the task of defining is subordinated ... explicit in the case of Charmides ...: is this person temperate?'

since, if it is, Charmides would be beautiful in soul and thus fit to satisfy Socrates' erotic desire.

In fact, there is little need to speculate on this. At 154d1–3 Chaerephon secures Socrates' agreement that Charmides is exceedingly fair of face, and goes on to assure Socrates that, were Charmides willing to strip, Socrates would suppose him to have no face, so 'totally beautiful' (*pankalos*, d5) is he in physical form. Socrates then observes that Charmides will indeed be 'irresistible' (*amachon*, d7) if he also turns out to be naturally well-endowed in respect of his soul. When Critias replies by advertising Charmides as being 'beautiful and good' in respect of those qualities too (154e4), Socrates immediately proposes (e5–6) that they therefore strip his soul and look at it rather than at Charmides' body.

What reason there may be for Socrates to prefer soul over body I shall explore later.[47] Not in doubt, however, is that Socrates is attracted by the prospect of Charmides being beautiful in soul. Since temperance will be consistently held up by Socrates (especially in his discussions with Charmides) as a beautiful thing, finding out whether Charmides possesses it fits Socrates' express motive of getting to see whether Charmides, in line with Critias' claim, does have a beautiful soul to behold.[48] So when Socrates goes on, at 158e–159a, to propose that Charmides, by attempting to say what temperance is on the basis of what he perceives to be within himself, will help them ascertain whether he has temperance in him, it seems safe to infer that, in this context, Socrates' reason for wanting to discover what temperance is is that it serves his quest for beauty, with Charmides the object of that quest.

More of course needs to be said on this. For one thing, we have to consider how Socrates' quest relates to his presentation of himself to Charmides as a doctor who needs to figure out whether Charmides has temperance in order to proceed with the treatment of Charmides' headache: if Charmides lacks temperance, he will need to be 'charmed' by Socrates until he has it. In terms of the division of labour set out at the close of the previous section, we should see the delivery of the charm as a task for 'soul-medicine'; and I shall return to this theme in Chapter 3. For present purposes, such further complications only seem to make it more

---

[47] See Section 3.5.
[48] Critias used the stock aristocratic phrase 'beautiful and good' (*kalos kai agathos*) to describe Charmides in respect of his qualities of soul. But since it is the talk of Charmides' beauty at 154d5 that occasioned the idea of stripping and looking, it seems fair to conclude that this aspect is the more salient in context. On the relation between beauty and goodness with regard to temperance, see Section 5.2.

likely that regarding 'What is temperance?' as the dialogue's sole or even, in the sense of non-subordinate, primary question may be a distortion.

On the other hand, such scholarly views do suggest, as I hinted above, a diagnosis of the tendency to treat the dialogue as not properly getting started until around halfway through. If we think, say, that Socrates is a character who engages, in various Platonic works, in a 'search for definitions', and if we suppose (not unreasonably) that in the *Charmides* this search does not begin in earnest until Socrates has moved on from Charmides to Critias, then we will naturally find ourselves with the view that the real business of the *Charmides* is not to be found until a substantial portion of the dialogue is already done.

Now the principle of agnosticism cautions us against importing from other dialogues a view about what Socrates' general interests therein may or may not be. But this methodological caution does not by itself resolve the puzzle of the *Charmides*'s horizontal structure. For I do not wish to suggest that those scholars who do not take the dialogue to get properly underway until nearly its halfway point are simply misled by prejudice or ideology built on extraneous importation. There is, I think, a strong sense, generated in part by the stark difference in tone and complexity between the long discussion of temperance that Socrates undertakes with Critias and the material that precedes it, that the core of the work is to be found in that discussion. Press expresses this sense well, while also rightly problematising it, when he contrasts the 'extreme abstraction' of parts of the discussion with Critias, with (among other things) the 'long, detailed dramatic opening' and 'Socrates' playful *elenchos* with Charmides'.[49]

In acknowledging that sense of importance with regard to the section with Critias, our problem remains. We need to account for the place of the material that precedes the discussion with Critias in a way that illuminates its relation with that upcoming discussion. Note, however, that, for all this acknowledgement, to ask what the first half (roughly speaking) of the *Charmides* is doing there might still be getting things the wrong way round. To suppose that the puzzle is reducible to the question why that first part exists is perhaps to remain too much under the spell of Socrates as above all concerned with a search for definitions. We are, after all, *given* the first part and told much therein about Socrates' motives. It features a

---

[49] Press (2002, 253 with n. 3). As Verity Harte points out to me, the *Parmenides* is also a work whose two main parts vary considerably in their degree of abstraction. It is interesting in the case of the *Parmenides* that the more abstract (second) part is in turn described as an 'exercise' (*gumnasia*, 135d7; cf.135d4, 136a2, c5) for addressing the problems raised in the first part.

Socrates who is clearly very interested in exploring Charmides' soul. What happens eventually is that Socrates turns away from Charmides and engages instead in a long discussion with Critias, before bringing Charmides back near the end. That being the order of events, we might equally well ask why Socrates ends up talking with Critias, in whom he shows nothing like the erotic interest that he manifests for Charmides.

One way of explaining this order does not, I think, go far enough, though it has the merit of attending to Socrates' motivations in his own words. When it is Socrates' turn to question his companions after relating to them details of the battle from which he has returned, he asks how philosophy is going, and who among the young are outstanding in beauty and wisdom (153d). Now one might be tempted to say that this two-part question maps onto Socrates' respective discussions with Charmides and with Critias: in talking with Charmides Socrates engages with the young man considered most outstanding in regard to beauty and wisdom; in talking with Critias he gets a sense of the state of philosophy. True, this will invert the order of Socrates' questions, but that order need not indicate a preference about which is to be dealt with first;[50] and it is, after all, Critias who seizes immediately on the second question (154a3–4) and attempts, at least partially, to address it by reference to the imminent arrival of Charmides.[51]

Unfortunately, even allowing for this, the mapping is not as neat as the attempt makes out. Critias will declare at 154e8–155a1 that Charmides is philosophical; the latter is the only character referred to in this way in the dialogue. So while one need not deny that Socrates' conversation with Critias also pertains to finding out about the state of philosophy, there seems no reason why the discussion with Charmides should not itself cover all elements of Socrates' request. True, Socrates does include Critias among the 'wise' (*sophoi*) at 161b8–c1.[52] But, as we shall later see, that appellation is distinctly equivocal in its context; and besides, Socrates' interest in the state of wisdom was expressed as part of his question about the young – and so we are back to Charmides. Thus we are left again with having to explain why Socrates moves on to talking with Critias after his conversation with Charmides, while at the same time continuing to wonder about the place of the material that precedes the long discussion with Critias, given that the latter seems eventually to constitute the meat of the work.

---

[50] Contra Hyland (1981, 30).   [51] Cf. Rutherford (1995, 88).
[52] One should not, however, take 'wisdom' and 'philosophy' in Socrates' question to be synonymous; see Section 2.3 n. 26.

1.8 Vertical Structure: Addressing the Puzzle

Taking account of the work's vertical layering, and in so doing further availing ourselves of the principle of separation as of significance for the interpretation of the *Charmides*, can help address both sides of the puzzle of its horizontal structure. We are enabled by means of this layering to differentiate what Socrates is up to with his interlocutors from what Plato is up to with his readers. The principle of agnosticism also makes a contribution here, insofar as it tasks us with uncovering Socrates' methods and motives in the *Charmides* without assuming that we know in advance, from elsewhere, what these are. Starting, then, with Socrates, I now sketch a little more elaborately than before what I think he is up to (with further elaboration to come in Chapter 3).

Socrates seeks beauty, principally of soul rather than body. In Charmides he has a youth who provides plenty of evidence of the latter and, insofar as Charmides is said by Critias (157d6–7) to be considered the most temperate of his contemporaries, ample promise of the former. Socrates then endeavours to discover whether Charmides is beautiful in soul by recruiting him to say what he thinks temperance is based on what he finds within his soul. But Charmides soon flags in this task and defaults to an account of temperance that he heard from Critias, discussion of which Socrates then continues with Critias.

Why does Socrates continue with Critias, despite there being a lack of similar evidence that Socrates has an interest in Critias' soul? I think there are two reasons one might adduce, both consistent with Socrates' erotic quest. Firstly, temperance is itself a supremely beautiful object, so that in seeking with Critias to discover temperance, Socrates is continuing his pursuit of beauty. But secondly, the *Charmides* ends with Socrates bringing Charmides back into the discussion and re-inviting him to consider whether temperance is in his soul. This reintroduction of Charmides by Socrates is itself more puzzling than has sometimes been allowed. After all, if pursuing the question of what temperance is is Socrates' true goal, then reverting to Charmides looks like a regressive step. Despite the aporetic outcome of the discussion with Critias, the latter has proven himself considerably better equipped for such discussion, as Socrates had advertised him to be at 162e, than young Charmides, for all his potential, currently is.

On the other hand, Charmides is clearly impressed by the conversation he has witnessed between Critias and Socrates, and pledges to be charmed by Socrates for as long as the latter sees fit. My suggestion, then, is that (in ways I shall expand upon) Socrates uses his discussion with Critias to seduce Charmides into baring his soul once more. Given Charmides' acknowledgement of his need to be charmed, Socrates' task is now to create a beautiful soul, rather than merely find one already there, by attempting to instil temperance in Charmides.

If that is so, then we should take the search for temperance in the discussion with Critias as ultimately subordinate to Socrates' interest in getting to see beauty in the soul of Charmides. For firstly, we know already, from the first part of the dialogue, that Socrates is interested in finding out whether there is temperance in Charmides' soul; and in the dialogue's closing scene he asks Charmides again whether he thinks he has it. Secondly, while the beauty of temperance is repeatedly marked by Socrates in his conversations with Charmides,[53] it is mentioned only once, towards its end (175a11–b1), in the main discussion with Critias, not long before Charmides rejoins the debate. The focus of that discussion is much more on temperance as good (chiefly in the sense of beneficial).[54] And this seems to imply that the idea of an erotic quest with temperance itself as its object is not to the forefront during the discussion with Critias.

I think, therefore, that at the level of Socrates' interactions with his interlocutors one can give a unified account of the dialogue's horizontal structure in terms of Socrates' quest for beauty in the soul of Charmides, for which the central discussion with Critias plays an important but supporting role, that of winning Charmides back to exposing his soul. At the level of Plato's interaction with his readers, on the other hand, the impression that the discussion with Critias, which I discuss in detail in Chapter 4, constitutes the main focus of the dialogue is not a misleading one. That discussion manifests a rigorous scrutiny on Socrates' part of various attempts to say what temperance is. Socrates appears here as an exemplar, if not necessarily an unimpeachable one, of the critical stance aimed at pursuing the truth. I have argued that for Socrates this pursuit is subordinate to his erotic quest. For Plato in relation to his readers, I think not so. Plato's aim in writing the dialogue is to bring about in us, and to reveal us to ourselves as manifesting, the critical stance. That is his tribute to Socrates.

How, then, do we account, at the Platonic (as opposed to the Socratic) level, for the presence of the material that precedes the discussion with Critias? One immediate answer may suggest itself: the earlier material is

---

[53] See 159c1, d8, d11, 160d1–2, e6–7, e13; cf. 160b8–9.
[54] See 169b4, c1, 172b1, c1–2, d3, d7, 173a1, 175a6–7.

1.8 Addressing the Puzzle

there to prepare us for the later, fiercer, discussion. Its erotic shimmer and relatively gentle argumentation serve to set us up for the more daunting philosophical explorations to come. Indeed, invocation of the dialogue's vertical layering might suggest an attractive parallel to corroborate this reading: Socrates lures Charmides into philosophical conversation by engaging him with the pleasing tale of Zalmoxis and the Thracian doctors.[55] As Socrates draws in Charmides, so Plato tempts his readers into philosophy by way of Socrates' flirtatious and relatively undemanding exchanges with Charmides.

This response is, I think, too quick. For the question presses: how exactly is such gentle exercise supposed to make us ready for the rigours to come? The response threatens to restore a version of the original puzzle, namely how two such different parts of the dialogue are supposed to cohere. Mere appreciation of the pleasant landscape of the first part seems as likely to alienate us from the harsher terrain of the second as to conciliate us to it. What needs showing, in order to connect the two parts in a way that will have the first plausibly prepare us for the second, is that the first already has resources to help elicit occupation of the critical stance in its readers.

That it does so I shall attempt to show in Chapter 2. Let me here, by way of illustrating how such a stimulus may work, offer a case from the second part. The critical stance, I have argued, is something that Socrates is shown exemplifying in the course of the dialogue, albeit ultimately in service of his erotic quest. But it is important, and indicative of the way the *Charmides* is vertically structured, that presenting the character Socrates as exemplifying a certain stance does not, in and of itself, mean that Plato aims to instil that stance in his reader – any more than showing any given character's stance in a written work thereby necessarily has the authorial purpose that the reader adopt that stance.

One way of coming at this point is to consider the figure of Charmides himself. The latter is present, listening silently, throughout Socrates' dense explorations with Critias of the nature of temperance that occupy the longest section of the work, before returning briefly to a speaking role in the dialogue's short final section. Now it may be the case (as I shall argue) that Charmides was impressed, even dazzled, by those discussions –

---

[55] I discuss this tale further in Chapter 3, but one thing immediately worth noting is that it is explicitly referenced again by Socrates at 175e2–5 when Charmides rejoins the conversation at the end of the work. So the text implies that we are not simply supposed to read the Thracian tale as a prelude to the main business, which then drops away, but as part of an overall unified structure. See Petre (2007, 50).

enough to make him keen to reconnect with Socrates. But that does not mean that he engaged seriously and critically with them in an attempt to determine the truth about temperance.

In his portrayal of Charmides, then, it may be that Plato already aims to indicate that in principle various responses to the presentation of critical enquiry are possible by those to whom it is presented. Thus we readers too might be dazzled by the brilliance of the dialogue without critically engaging with it. But one thing that the separation achieved by vertical structuring allows Plato to do is present to his reader this very issue of response via the depiction of Charmides (and, at one level up, the anonymous companion) as silent auditor. In that way, the reader is enabled to pick up on the question of how one should relate to philosophical discussion and begin to explore it for oneself. The act of noticing Charmides' extended silence is already an act of questioning; and occupation of the critical stance is underway.

Charmides is, of course, very young and so perhaps not yet capable of such critical engagement as Socrates and Critias; or he is deferential in the face of such engagement. But even for those who are neither incapable nor deferential, including as it may be readers of the *Charmides*, there may still be a temptation simply to look admiringly on at the discussion rather than engage critically with it. I shall argue in Chapter 3 that a contrast, embedded in the opening scene with Charmides, between looking and conversing allows us further opportunity to become aware of these options. By using the dramatic structure to encourage a critical stance in his readers, Plato seeks to have us emulate, rather than simply admire, the critical approach. And this may of course include adopting a critical stance towards some of the viewpoints and arguments that Socrates himself is shown exhibiting in the course of the work.

Moreover, in considering the relationship between Plato the author and his character Socrates, we must remind ourselves again of perhaps its most fundamental aspect: Plato is composing a written work that can be read, while Socrates is depicted engaging in live oral discussion with his companions. This may suggest that, even in seeking to encourage a critical stance in his readers, Plato may not be adopting an uncritical stance with regard to the way in which Socrates undertakes his own critical enquiries. We might think, for example, that, if properly undertaken, engagement with a written work is likely to be more reflective and thoughtful than live back-and-forth discussion, perhaps producing more genuine philosophical progress, with less of a sense of hasty agreement or disagreement, or of simply being trapped in the headlights.

This does not of course mean that we are to neglect engaging critically with the written text itself. But it may mean that Charmides' and the anonymous companion's own stance of apparently uncritical listening is not necessarily to be dismissed as no more than that. If (a big if perhaps) the listening is done not just to admire the fireworks but to consider the content carefully and thoughtfully, then it may be that Plato's portrayal of this approach is supposed to present us with a choice between passive consumption and active engagement that is deliberately under-determined by the stretches of silence with which Charmides and (more radically) the companion are shown to respond.

In noting the display of the work's vertical structure via its depiction of the anonymous companion's silent engagement with Socrates' narrative, and, at one level down, of Charmides' silent engagement with Socrates' central discussion with Critias, we are thus invited to reflect upon what our own engagement with the written work should be. In Chapter 2 I look in more detail at how the dialogue makes good on that invitation, with particular reference to its first part. I review a number of examples that, I shall argue, facilitate our occupation of the critical stance and serve, insofar as the examples are drawn from that first part, to prepare us for what follows. I shall try to show, through these examples, how Plato's written text not only sets out to induce a stance of enquiry in its readers but orients that enquiry by suggesting a series of thematic connections between its parts. In this way, we shall see how the first part of the dialogue both informs and is informed by the subsequent material.

CHAPTER 2

The Stance of Enquiry
Five Examples

In order to flesh out my claim about how the first part of the dialogue (the Charmides section) is written so as to induce its readers to occupy the stance of enquiry, and thus help prepare us to engage with its second part (the Critias section), I shall in this chapter focus on a series of examples, discussed respectively in Sections 2.1–2.5, the first four of which are taken from the first part. In discussing them I try to draw out some of the principal themes of that part and to show how, rather than falling away once the main discussion with Critias is underway, they serve to inform our understanding of the dialogue as a whole. The fifth example considers the function of the final part, featuring Charmides' return to the conversation, since that part has, I argue, a distinct role to play in relation to the reader's occupation of the stance of enquiry. In offering these examples, I also hope further to illustrate the interpretive benefits of delineating the work's horizontal and vertical structures.

2.1 The Perspective of Socrates

Let me begin by circling back to the question of the vertical structure of the *Charmides*, in particular the relation between Socrates as first-person narrator and Plato as author. Here are the dialogue's opening lines:

> We came from Potidaea out of camp on the previous day at evening and having returned after such a long time I gladly went to my usual haunts. (153a1–3)

We learn from the dialogue's first word (*hēkomen*, 153a1: 'we came' from Potidaea) that we have a first-person narrative, grammatically here first-person plural, though this swiftly changes to first-person singular in the second line (*ēia*, 153a2: 'I went' to my customary haunts, in this case the palaestra). The switch is perhaps an early indicator of Socrates' distinctiveness: a number return, but it is Socrates who chooses a visit to the palaestra

2.1 *The Perspective of Socrates*

to mark his return.[1] By the dialogue's tenth line, when Chaerephon addresses him by exclaiming 'Socrates' (153b4), we know that Socrates is the narrator. So we can see from the start, and are surely meant to see, given how transparently this is displayed, that there is a narrative voice (Socrates) formally distinct from that of the author (Plato).

In its possession of such a structure, the *Charmides* thus ostensibly presents a particular narrative perspective, namely that of the character Socrates. We are given a series of events and conversations as experienced and described by him. By constructing the work as perspectival in this fashion, Plato invites us to notice that feature and, as I have argued, to maintain as a result a certain critical stance towards Socrates' perspective – in the first instance just because it is simply one perspective among (potentially) many. Now we might, of course, have independent reasons for thinking that Socrates' perspective is privileged, not merely in the formal sense that it is his perspective that we are given, but in the normative sense that his take on proceedings is supposed to be especially insightful or commendable, and to that extent endorsed by Plato. It is important, however, not to equate the two senses.

There is, I think, sometimes a tendency in interpreting Plato to assume, just because Socrates is, even when not actually first-person narrator, then at least the leading character, that we are in such cases to privilege his outlook normatively. But that move is simply fallacious. We do not, I suppose, nor should we, feel compelled to regard Lear's viewpoint in *King Lear*, or that of Patrick Bateman in Bret Easton Ellis's *American Psycho*, as especially laudable simply because they are featured as respectively leading character and first-person narrator in those works.[2] There may be plenty of reasons for an author to place a character who is, for example, deluded or wicked in such roles. So we should not, in noticing that Plato has Socrates in the role of narrator and has him play, moreover, a leading role within that narration, jump to the conclusion that we are to

---

[1] Cf. Murphy (2007, 214).
[2] This does not entail dissent from the claim made by Burnyeat (1985, 33) that 'Plato's distancing of himself from his characters is quite different from Shakespeare's', though it should be noted that Burnyeat's apparent illustration of the claim in regard to the *Republic* – 'Plato uses the distance between himself and the character of Socrates not to conceal his opinions, but to show their efficacy in action' (ibid.) – needs qualifying both because the efficacy shown (Glaucon and Adeimantus are so persuaded by Socrates that they undertake to persuade others) is fictional and because, from an author's depicting a character as effective at persuading others, nothing follows about whether the author endorses the views in respect of which the character is depicted as persuasive.

regard Socrates as the good guy, the enlightened one, or the hero.³ That may of course be Plato's ultimate intent.⁴ But we cannot simply read that off from the formal role that Plato assigns to him.⁵

While I am thus sympathetic to the view considered by Waugh (2002, 282) that 'one can only get the philosophical point of the [Platonic] dialogue by reading it as literature in which Socrates is but one character among others', it is important not to make one's interpretive approach depend on the classification of the dialogues as literature. The hypothesis of critical distance derives not from the (always contestable) *genre* of the *Charmides*, but – as I have been emphasising – from its objective *structure*, in which Socrates as both character and narrator is formally distinct from Plato as author.⁶

The point is unaffected by Socrates' featuring as a *recurrent* leading character in the corpus. I take it no one would argue that such characters represent, in virtue of their recurrent status, paragons for their authors; often enough they represent the opposite. Irwin (2019, 81), who observes that 'If we were to criticize Shakespeare for holding the views of Hamlet or Othello . . . we would misunderstand Shakespeare', nonetheless goes on to state that 'If . . . we find that a reasonably coherent philosophical outlook and a reasonably intelligible line of philosophical development can be ascribed to the Platonic Socrates, we have some grounds for claiming to

---

³ One may alternatively bite the bullet in the style of Rowe (2007, 15): '[I]t is hard to credit that Socrates' voice is not *in general* Plato's: why else would it always – or very nearly always – be his opponents, rather than Socrates, that are variously defeated, humiliated or made to think again?' (Rowe's emphasis). It is striking that Rowe sees the regular infliction by a main character of defeat or humiliation as evidence that that character speaks with his author's voice; and Rowe seems to see no irony in adducing the phenomenon of being made to think again as support for a claim of shared outlook between author and main character. Gerson (2013, 36) labels as 'desperately hard' a stance that 'requires us not to "privilege" the arguments of Socrates over those of his interlocutors, even when Socrates' argument is a refutation of the views of those interlocutors'. But the difficulty that Gerson sees arises only if one presupposes endorsement by Plato of Socrates' refutations, which is to beg the question at issue. One cannot rule out the possibility of endorsement by an author of a character seen by their author as flawed, but perhaps it is best to say that good authors tend to have a complex relationship with complex characters; cf. Section 2.5.

⁴ Such intent cannot, however, be deduced from observing that, had he so wished, 'Plato could have written into his works clear signals to the reader that the arguments of Socrates do not work, and that his interlocutors are foolish to accept them' (Kraut 2017). Assume for the sake of argument that we do not get such signals from Plato. Kraut's remark only has force if one presupposes the natural state of affairs to be endorsement by authors of what their (main) characters say.

⁵ It is testament to the grip that this approach to the character Socrates has nonetheless had on commentators that even McKim, who rightly emphasises the non-identity between Plato and his character Socrates, failure to recognise which he labels as responsible for 'the preconception of Socrates as Plato's ideal hero' (McKim 1985, 65), still feels obliged to assure us in advance that 'Socrates is of course a paragon of virtue by comparison to everyone else in the dialogues' (64).

⁶ On questions of genre in Plato see further Nightingale (1995).

2.1 The Perspective of Socrates

have found Plato's views.' I doubt, however, that many authors would agree with the notion that success in endowing a recurrent leading character with a coherent outlook and intelligible development licenses a claim of identity between the character's views and those of the author.[7]

On the contrary, the deliberate presentation of a series of events as seen through one person's eyes (Socrates' in our case) might be designed to make us notice the perspectival viewpoint and be correspondingly cautious about what it reports and our responses to it.[8] There may be other features in such contexts that further encourage a sceptical stance towards a narrator. The narrator may be 'unreliable', in the sense that they may be deliberately curating their narration, through selectivity or distortion, in order to present a certain view of proceedings. Alternatively, though not incompatibly, the narrator may simply have a very peculiar take on the proceedings, not now because, inevitably, they represent just one perspective among many possible, but because they possess a very distinctive character and to that extent take a very distinctive view of the proceedings in question.

I shall not for now explore the idea of Socrates as an unreliable narrator (though I shall return to it below). I do think, however, that there is reason to take him as a somewhat peculiar character. For this we need look no further than the dialogue's opening scene. Socrates starts, as we saw, by relating his return to Athens, after a long period away, from the army camp at Potidaea. He then tells us that he proceeded to the palaestra (wrestling school) of Taureas where he is greeted by Chaerephon, who, says Socrates:

> mad creature that he is (*hate kai manikos ōn*), leapt up from the throng and rushed towards me, seizing me by the hand and asking 'Socrates, how did you survive the battle?' A short time before our departure [continues Socrates] a battle had taken place at Potidaea, which the people here [in Athens] had just heard about. (153b2–6)

Notice that it is Chaerephon who first mentions the battle. Socrates had not hitherto cared to reference it in narrating his return from camp. Moreover, he is positively nonchalant in his response to Chaerephon's question about how he survived it: after narrating casually that there had indeed been a battle, he tells Chaerephon that he survived it 'in just the state that you see' (153b7–8). When Chaerephon further says that it has been reported that the battle was fierce and that many acquaintances had

---

[7] Is the word 'philosophical' doing the work for Irwin here? If so, we need an account of why.
[8] Cf. McCabe (2019a, 109).

died (153b9–c1), Socrates maintains his nonchalance, acknowledging that 'that has been pretty much correctly reported' (153c2). Perhaps because of this startling level of nonchalance Chaerephon checks with Socrates that he was actually at the battle (c3), and when Socrates replies that he was, he relates that he was seated by Chaerephon next to Critias and recounted the details, answering the various questions that were asked, though without divulging what was said in the discussion.

How should we think about the way in which Socrates is presented here – the way he presents himself – on the occasion that he is revealed as narrator? It is once again, I think, easy to fall into the trap of regarding him, just because he is the narrator, as presenting a view that we are supposed to take as authoritative: morally, epistemically, or both. The temptation is perhaps even greater if we are predisposed, perhaps on the basis of the formal privileging of Socrates in other dialogues as well as this one, to think that Plato means to offer up this character to us as some kind of paradigm.[9]

In particular, we will soon learn that Socrates takes a particular interest in the question of whether the young Charmides has a soul blessed by temperance; and eventually the dialogue will come to be dominated by an attempt to investigate the nature of temperance. We may then be inclined to wonder retrospectively whether, whatever becomes of the attempt to articulate its nature, Plato at least intends to portray Socrates as exemplifying temperance in his behaviour and thus as some kind of guide as to what being temperate comprises.

There may indeed seem scant reason for scepticism about this being what Plato has in mind, and therefore about concluding that Socrates' status as an exemplar of temperance is far less uncertain than the dialogue's view of what temperance is. Doubt, it is true, may emerge when we learn that temperance is something that is to be found in a person's soul, and that figuring out whether it is there in a given instance might require some fairly complex enquiry: could such an attribute even in principle be conveyed by a relatively brief description of behaviour?

To this an objector might retort: on the contrary, we have a clear contrast offered in the dialogue's opening lines between crazy, impulsive Chaerephon on the one hand and cool, calm, collected Socrates on the

---

[9] Despite noting that in his dialogues Plato never intervenes, in the manner of Xenophon, to attribute virtues to Socrates, Dorion (2004, 31) nonetheless finds it 'hard to believe' that Plato does not hold out Socrates as a model of temperance in the *Charmides*, and of each virtue in the respective dialogue devoted to it (piety in the *Euthyphro* and so on). See also Gonzalez (1995).

other, the latter an impressive study in restraint and moderation in the face of the traumas of battle. Case closed. But let us remember through whose viewpoint we are offered this contrast: it is that of Socrates himself. In particular, it is he who characterises Chaerephon as that 'crazy' guy.

The objector is not done. In describing Chaerephon in this way to his anonymous companion, Socrates must surely be relying on a shared view about Chaerephon's character. To this it seems fair to respond that the companion's anonymity makes it hard to pin any view onto him. Whether Socrates assumes, rightly or wrongly, a shared perspective on behalf of his companion is quite a different matter and one that does not decide the question of how we are to evaluate Socrates' own view.

Now I am not suggesting that Socrates be taken as deliberately exaggerating Chaerephon's character, in order (for example) to make himself come out looking admirable in contrast. We need not regard Socrates as doing anything other than giving his sincere view of Chaerephon here. Nor am I suggesting that Socrates intends the appellation in anything other than a friendly or affectionate manner;[10] it is not a clinical diagnosis. But the perspectival construction cautions us against assuming, even with these qualifications, that it is either the only possible or even the most likely way in which one might choose to describe one's friend's response to one's return from a fierce battle in these circumstances.[11] If Chaerephon's reaction to Socrates' homecoming is supposed to be evidence of a madcap personality, the evidence seems questionable.

Indeed we might ask what exactly *is* 'crazy' about Chaerephon's evident combination of excitement and anxiety at seeing a friend unexpectedly return, apparently safe, after a long time away with the army, in the immediate aftermath of such a battle. Socrates' saying it about Chaerephon doesn't make it so.[12] Inclined though we may be, by the way Socrates characterises Chaerephon, to map the two of them onto the

---

[10] Cf. Moore (2013, 289) who, however, does not consider what difference it might make to our assessment of Chaerephon that it is Socrates who characterises him.
[11] A further objection might come from one unimpressed by the principle of agnosticism: is Chaerephon not described elsewhere in the Platonic corpus as an 'intense' fellow (*sphodros*, *Apology* 21a3)? So he is, but there too by Socrates. My point is not to deny that Chaerephon is presented as a certain sort of character – Socrates even claims that the Athenian jury 'know' (*iste*, ibid.) that Chaerephon is like this – but to note that the presentation is made through the eyes of another, very singular, character.
[12] An example of the approach I am resisting is that of Schultz (2013, 44–5) who, despite emphasising that we are given a Chaerephon whom 'Socrates presents', is able to read Chaerephon straightforwardly as a case of immoderation to be contrasted unfavourably with Socrates. So too Tsouna (2022, 59).

respective pair 'sensible; crazy', we might yet continue to wonder what exactly Socrates' nonchalance, depicted so emphatically in the text, shows about him. Perhaps it shows that he is a moral exemplar of some sort. But other options seem available: that his response to the battle and the deaths of his comrades is cold and unfeeling, for example. Or, if we wish to avoid hopping from Socrates-as-hero to Socrates-as-villain, that the response is at any rate strikingly out of the ordinary and, as such, if not outright objectionable, then not straightforwardly admirable either.

As I say, these are options. My purpose here is not to decide which, if any, is correct or endorsed by the author. Rather, I have tried to draw attention to some of the corollaries that arise when we consider how to interpret a piece of text in which we are pointedly shown matters filtered through one person's perspective.[13] The use by Plato of the first-person narrative device should already put us on alert as to the status of what is reported thereby, just because it is (shown as) perspectival. And this thought about the formal aspect of the device is reinforced by the fact that, as we have seen, there seems reason to hold that Socrates' perspective is not just formally particular but, in substance, pretty peculiar.

It is worth mentioning at this point another narrative of return that may lie at the back of the depiction of Socrates' return from battle abroad to Athens. We are perhaps prompted here to compare Socrates in this context not so much with the figure of that name who appears in other Platonic dialogues as with Homer's Odysseus and the latter's return from Troy, the central theme of the *Odyssey*, to his homeland of Ithaca. As various scholars have noted, there is sufficient weight of reference in the *Charmides* to put us in mind of the *Odyssey* and to make it thereby likely that we are meant to read Socrates' return in the light of that of Odysseus.[14]

Two of the most prominent references occur, firstly, at 161a4, in which Socrates, as part of his refutation of Charmides' proposal that temperance is the same thing as shame, cites *Odyssey* 17.347: 'the presence of shame is no good for a man in need', uttered in its original context by Odysseus' son Telemachus for the swineherd Eumaeus to pass on to Odysseus, who has returned to Ithaca disguised as a beggar, though he has by this point revealed himself to Telemachus. The theme of disguise discloses another Odyssean resonance in the *Charmides*, since Socrates also, as we shall see, wears a disguise in the dialogue (that of a doctor). Indeed it has been

---

[13] For some salutary remarks to this effect regarding Plato's Socrates as narrator see Morgan (2004, 364).
[14] See e.g. Lampert (2010, 150–3); Burger (2013); Raymond (2018, 40–3).

2.1 The Perspective of Socrates

argued that we should read Charmides' role in his encounter with Socrates as modelled on the story of Telemachus.[15]

If that is right, then the relationship implied between Socrates and Charmides is along the lines of father to son. That reading, however, seems not altogether unproblematic, given that Socrates feels erotic desire for Charmides. I wonder, then, if there is at least an equal case to be made that the Odyssean analogue of Charmides is not (or not only) Telemachus, but Odysseus' own heart's desire, his dear wife Penelope. There is indeed already some connection between the quotation about shame and Penelope, since the latter utters a variant of it, also in connection with the disguised Odysseus – 'shame is bad in a wanderer' – at *Odyssey* 17.578.

This brings us to the second prominent reference to the *Odyssey* in the dialogue. At 173a7–8 Socrates introduces his worry that the idea of living knowledgeably as being sufficient for happiness is ill-founded by telling Critias: 'Hear, then, my dream, whether it has come through horn or through ivory.' This is an allusion to the passage near the end of *Odyssey* 19 in which Penelope explains to the beggar (Odysseus in disguise) about a dream she has had that seemed to foretell Odysseus' return to slay the suitors and reinstall himself as head of the household and king of Ithaca. With admirable, though as it turns out excessive, epistemic caution, Penelope tells the beggar that deceptive dreams pass through gates of ivory, true dreams through gates of horn, and she does not think that hers has come via the latter route (19.562–9).[16]

With Penelope in the mix, let me then make a suggestion about Socrates' return that brings out his exceptionality even in comparison with the wily hero of Homeric legend. Recall again the opening lines of the dialogue and the way in which the grammar of the first person switches there from plural to singular in Socrates' narration: 'We came' from the camp at Potidaea; but 'I went' gladly to my usual haunts, in this case the palaestra.

The switch from grammatical plurality to singularity serves to highlight the substantive singularity of Socrates. (One may note that the *Odyssey* also contains a substantial section narrated in the first person by its leading character.) He returns alright, but not in the way of the Odyssean hero. The contrast with Odysseus' plight is poignant indeed. While Odysseus,

---

[15] See Raymond (2018, 40–3). A less likely candidate for the role of Telemachus is Chaerephon. Lampert (2010, 151) argues for the correspondence by claiming a parallel between Socrates' reply to Chaerephon at 153b7–8 ('in just the state that you see', *houtōsi hōs su horais*) and *Odyssey* 16.205, which Lampert renders 'Here I am, such as you see', but the 'you see' is not in Odysseus' exclamation to Telemachus (*hode egō toiosde*), making the parallel rather more remote.

[16] I discussion the allusion further in Sections 5.3 and 5.7.

back in Ithaca, longs quite literally to be home, fully reunited with his wife and son, but unable immediately to bring this about, Socrates, with no apparent bar to returning to his home and family, chooses instead to hang out with the beautiful boys at the palaestra.[17] Perhaps, after all, what Socrates describes *is* his return home. Not to his actual home, to be sure, but to the place where his heart's desire is to be found.

One should, strictly speaking (and always with an eye on epistemic propriety), say that we don't *know* that Socrates did not, in the everyday sense, go home; rather, he doesn't mention that he did. He relates, also in the dialogue's opening line, that the return from Potidaea took place 'on the previous day at evening' (153a1). Perhaps, then, he had a night's sleep – must one assume at home? – before making a beeline for the palaestra. But even if he did go home first, in making no mention of this he would seem to have curated his narrative to indicate exactly what importance he attaches to a home visit after a lengthy absence on campaign: none at all. Either way, this notable unconventionality, revealed to outflank standard heroic mores when thrown into relief by the Odyssean echoes, leaves us with a Socrates whose values, whether they elicit admiration or repulsion, have been impressed upon us as quite out of the ordinary and, as such, demanding to be interrogated.

The interrogative attitude with which we may then confront what we are presented with in these opening pages is, I have tried to indicate, something that Plato aims to engineer in us. The first-person narrative device, together with the characterisation of the narrator, invites us to question the perspective we are offered, and thereby to think about alternative perspectives from which to assess it. The structure that Plato deploys, and the way he deploys it, discourages us from simply taking what we are given at face value. It nudges us away from a stance of passive acceptance of a narrative towards one of more active investigation. We are moved to ask: is what is narrated all that might have been said? Once prodded into asking that question, we have begun to occupy the stance of enquiry, and epistemic progress has been made.

At this point we can see how the vertical and the horizontal structure of the *Charmides* interact to help achieve this shift. Crucial here, in regard to the role of the horizontal aspect, is the idea that events and discussions later in the sequence may colour the way we view events and discussions earlier. We cannot literally journey back in time, but we can travel along the

---

[17] Brann (2004, 72) is so struck by Socrates' rapid decamping to the palaestra that she speculates – in a way that I suspect misses the point – that 'he probably has no family yet'.

dialogue's horizontal dimension in either direction. In the course of reading it forward, we are able to see how what we are reading now may shed light on what we had read before.[18]

Thus when, on a first reading, we come upon Socrates' initial exchange with Chaerephon, we might notice a certain oddness about Socrates' character as embodied in his eerily calm reaction to the battle in which he took part. But it is not until the nature of temperance emerges as one of the dialogue's main themes that we are specifically enabled to ask what we should make of that behaviour in relation to the question of what temperance is. Conjoining this with the distancing that the vertical structure of the dialogue permits, we crystallise a new and more specific question about what, ethically, to make of Socrates. Consideration of that question in turn offers a reference point for assessing the more abstract discussion of temperance in the second part of the dialogue.

2.2 Testimony and Self-Knowledge

That we are supposed to adopt a questioning stance towards Socrates is itself made more plausible by the emphasis placed in the opening pages of the *Charmides* on people and things that are known or not known, and on ways of knowing or attempting to know them. Socrates says that when he first arrived at the palaestra, he came upon a large number of people there, 'some unknown (*agnōtas*) to me, but most known (*gnōrimous*)' (153a5–6). Many who were 'known' (*gnōrimōn*), Chaerephon says, have been reported to have died in the battle (153b9–c1). Those in Athens have 'ascertained' (*pepusmenoi*) that there was a battle (153b6) but according to Chaerephon 'have not yet ascertained everything clearly' (*ou ... pō panta saphōs pepusmetha*, c5–6).

Socrates is questioned about the events at Potidaea (153c9–d1) and then, perhaps not overly enthused by such matters (certainly not enough to narrate them to his anonymous companion in any further detail), states that when they had had enough of them, he questioned his companions in

---

[18] I am indebted here to discussion with MM McCabe of her notion of reading a Platonic dialogue backwards. See also Burnyeat (1997, 4), though despite its ancient pedigree one should resist as artificial the division of a Platonic work, as sketched by Burnyeat, into 'prologue' and 'philosophical content' (ibid.). Of note in this connection is that the most prominent application of the prologue or prelude in Plato associates its use with the supply of rational, indeed philosophical, content (*Laws* 4.719e–720e, 721d–723b, 9.857c–e, 10.888a). Burnyeat himself, while noting that a musical analogy is given to illustrate a prelude at *Laws* 4.722d–e (Burnyeat 1997, 4 n. 7), does not consider how the analogy is put to work in the target case.

turn about affairs at Athens, in particular as to how things were with regard to philosophy; and with regard to the young men, which of them were proving outstanding in wisdom, beauty, or both (d2–5).

Critias now speaks for the first time, his opening words being: 'regarding the beautiful ones, I think you will soon know (*eisesthai*)' (154a3–4), since, he adds, the young man considered most beautiful is about to enter. 'Who is he and whose [son]?' asks Socrates. 'I presume you know (*oistha*)', replies Critias, revealing that it is Charmides. 'I do know (*oida*)', agrees Socrates (154b3), albeit he will have grown from boy to youth since he last saw him; 'soon you will know (*eisei*)' how he has developed, Critias declares (b6).

Alongside this profusion of terminology of enquiring and knowing, we are also presented, in performance, with various ways of knowing and coming to know. Thus we have the first-hand testimony from Socrates about the battle, contrasting perhaps with the second-hand reporting implied by Chaerephon's remarks at 153b9–c1 and c5–6, where in response to the first Socrates confirms that the reports about the battle were true and that he was there; and in response to the second he recounts what happened, given that his companions had not yet ascertained everything clearly.

The second of Chaerephon's remarks shows that one can be aware that one does not (yet) have good testimony, but in a sense that is the more straightforward part. Unclarity and confusion in testimony are perhaps relatively easy to detect. It is harder, but all the more necessary, to maintain a critical stance when testimony seems clear and coherent: as testimony, it is still intrinsically perspectival. In this regard, Socrates' companions in the palaestra provide a miniature model of how to handle even first-hand testimony: they question Socrates (153c9–d1), apparently to the eventual satisfaction of all (d2). At the same time, the narration *by* Socrates to his anonymous companion *of* his narration to his companions in the palaestra means that we can notice for ourselves some potential complications in regard to the giving and receiving of testimony.

In particular, we can see that Socrates is *curating* his narration for his anonymous companion. For he fails to report in this phase the content either of the questions asked by his companions in the palaestra or the answers he gave to them – in terms of a later distinction that Socrates draws (cf. 170b–c), one might say that we know that Socrates knows something, but not what he knows. We see, then, that testimony can be unreliable, not necessarily because the testator does not himself know, but because of what he chooses, perhaps because of his own perspective and interests rather than any attempt at deception, to omit.

2.2 *Testimony and Self-Knowledge*

The silence of the anonymous companion is, in this regard, deafening. He could choose to question Socrates about the content of his narration, but apparently refrains from doing so. We cannot ourselves question Socrates about the battle, but we can question the narrative that we have, namely the content of the *Charmides*. If we are sensitive to, or even irked by, Socrates' omission and his companion's indulgence, we will again be encouraged to adopt a critical stance towards the material that is available.

One further way in which testimony may go awry, and at the same time one further potential source of knowledge that the dialogue highlights, is memory. Socrates' own memory comes into play at 154a8–b5, where Critias reminds him that he does know Charmides, and Socrates agrees that he does – that is, he has memories of Charmides, which is to say of being directly acquainted with him (knowing him in that sense), since he is able to recall that Charmides was no mean specimen even as a boy (154b3–4). Critias' remark that Charmides was not yet of age when Socrates left Athens (154a8–b1) and Socrates' speculation that Charmides must now be quite a youth (154b4–5) emphasise the distance of time over which memory here operates. Charmides too will later say that he remembers (*memnēmai*, 156a7) from his boyhood Socrates associating with Critias, having also remarked that Socrates has no small reputation (*logos*) among Charmides' own peers (a6–7). So here in turn we have direct acquaintance of Socrates contrasted with (mere) testimony about Socrates, testimony that is about to be corroborated by reacquaintance.

Socrates' own narration to his companions in the palaestra is only shortly after the battle (cf. 153b5), so his memory of events is at that stage likely to be fresh and, to that extent, accurate, especially given the remarkably unflustered state, as he at any rate self-attributes, in which he survived the battle. Nonetheless Socrates could in theory be narrating the events of the *Charmides* to his anonymous companion many years later. Given the fluency of his narration it seems that Socrates' powers of memory may also be remarkable;[19] but as noted above, in its capacity to carry conviction fluency can be a dangerous thing, in the face of which it may be especially important to keep up one's critical guard.

We can therefore see that the opening pages of the *Charmides* contain rich material on epistemic matters. The elegant naturalness with which Plato writes these scenes – potentially another example of dangerous

---

[19] As Fiona Leigh reminds me, one can overdo this assessment: the dialogue depicts a culture of oral discourse central to which was good memory (cf. 159e9); and for all we are told Socrates may already have been a practised narrator of the events in the palaestra that he recites.

fluency? – means that we do not necessarily notice, on a first reading, quite how much is being said about the variety of sources of knowledge, on the one hand, and the need for corroboration and the adoption of a critical stance in assessing such sources, on the other.

Certainly, the dialogue's later treatment of knowledge, and particularly self-knowledge, as itself an object of critical scrutiny allows us to look back at, and refocus on, the examples of knowledge terminology and knowledge performance in the dialogue's opening scene. Nonetheless, I contend, the narration of these early pages is itself constructed so as to make us scrutinise it. We are prompted, by the way their perspectival structure is displayed and manipulated, to reflect that we do not necessarily get an unimpeachable version of events even from a source who, within the fiction, was a first-hand witness of, and participant in, those events: at one level, in regard to the details of the battle that (so Socrates reports) he narrated to his companions in the palaestra; at another level, in regard to the events of the *Charmides* that he narrates to his anonymous companion. The latter's role as silent recipient of testimony is surely also, in the very bareness of its presence as a distinct element in the dialogue's vertical structure, there to be noticed and interrogated.

The text thus prompts us both to observe and to question the special nature of first-hand testimony. As Socrates deploys his privileged perspective to report on the battle to his friends in the palaestra, we are confronted with the substantive peculiarity as well as the formal particularity of his outlook. The substantive aspect is no mere dramatic flourish: while not to be conflated with the formal, it helps bring the latter more vividly to our attention. And thereby hangs an epistemic lesson: even first-hand testimony must be weighed carefully, since testimony, as we are made to see, is intrinsically perspectival. There is no exemption in such cases from a critical stance. Indeed, in being led by the dialogue's use of structural devices to question Socrates' presentation in the ways I have indicated, we recognise the need to occupy that stance. We are, to that extent, provoked into a certain sort of self-knowledge, of ourselves as subjects who do not know and need to enquire further in order to get closer to the truth.

These opening pages, in terms of their content, both thematise and illustrate knowledge and enquiry; but the narrative structure that frames them allows us as readers to actualise those themes by becoming aware of ourselves as questioners of the narrative. One example that I offered in support of this thesis is the way in which Socrates' and Chaerephon's respective attitudes are characterised by Socrates. In their interaction, filtered as it is through the Socratic lens, an indispensable epistemic role for Chaerephon, whose presence we might otherwise have considered a mere dramatic ornament, is revealed, his alleged craziness creating the space for a critical perspective on Socrates' uncanny coolness.

We are, in sum, oriented in this section to the idea of there being value in enquiry, and in a certain sort of self-knowledge, not by *argument* that we should value these, but insofar as our response to the perspectival structure and its dramatic content reveals us to ourselves as enquiring subjects; as subjects, moreover, who can reflect on this revelation and consider where it leaves us, epistemically speaking, in relation to a possible alternative state (if we note, for example, the prima facie attitude of Socrates' silent companion) of mere acquiescence in what we are told. We are thus equipped to critically engage with, rather than passively register, the forthcoming discussion.

When the idea of self-knowledge is itself eventually problematised – the scope of enquiry, one might say, going all the way up[20] – we have been given a motive for supposing that move to be itself worth critically investigating. This, I think, is one way in which the earlier part of the dialogue prepares us for the later discussion with Critias: by being not an entertainment to be passively enjoyed but a provocation that brings us to occupation of the critical stance and to self-recognition as enquiring subjects, ready therefore to bring that stance to a second part in which the investigation of self-knowledge becomes a prominent theme.

Alongside the dialogue's illustration of subjects who themselves occupy, to a greater or lesser extent, an enquiring stance (Socrates and Chaerephon among them), we are also prompted to notice, and so contrast, a stance of passive acceptance. As we have noted, this can be seen in the person of Socrates' mysterious anonymous companion, who, we can now see, also has a specific function in the dialogue's structural economy. For while Socrates explicitly addresses his companion on three occasions (154b8, 155c5, d3) – Plato thereby signalling that Socrates' narration is to that person – we are not told anything about them, nor do they say anything in response. The companion, on the face of it, does nothing but passively consume what is being narrated by Socrates.[21] In noticing that, we are

---

[20] Cf. Barker (1995, 27–8).
[21] See Schultz (2013, 43). Tsouna (2015, 5) remarks of the companion that Socrates' main discussion with Critias 'would have been impossible to follow by the noble listener, unless he were deeply familiar with Socrates' way of thinking'. But that is to imply, what we are not permitted to know, that the companion (who is never addressed by Socrates in the course of his relating that discussion) was able to follow it.

placed in a position to reflect on possible modes of engagement between listener and speaker – and ultimately, between reader and author.

The companion's apparent lack of critical curiosity thus means that it would be a mistake, in my view, to seek to identify them with a particular individual, including Plato the author. The latter identification might be tempting, and not just because there is a certain appeal in imagining Plato thereby inserting himself elusively into his own text. The companion's absorption of the narrative might also then be seen as a way for Plato to represent Socrates as having, in view of the young man's future fate, 'failed' with Charmides (as well as with Critias) but 'succeeded' in inspiring Plato to write the *Charmides*.[22]

That the historical Socrates *was* an inspiration for the work (as for other Platonic works) need not be denied. But this, I think, would be an odd way to commemorate it, since it would imply, in order that the result be the *Charmides*, a Plato who does no more than write down what Socrates reports to him orally. The task of writing might of course explain why the companion could not engage more interactively with what is reported to him. But that still seems like the wrong kind of tribute for Plato to pay: Socrates as inspiring a scribe rather than an active philosopher. In keeping the roles of author and anonymous addressee distinct, with the author standing firmly outside his fiction, we give Plato his due as maker of a creative work, rather than recipient of a report.

Even on this account, it might be objected, Plato still portrays himself writing down what was said to the companion. Not so, I think. In restricting himself to the role of author Plato remains one (vertical) level up from the fiction, representing himself as doing no more than write a work known as the *Charmides*. Only if he inserts himself into the fiction, for example by identifying also as the companion, does he become part of it.

Notice, then, that at one point writing almost, but not quite, itself becomes part of the drama:[23] at 156a1–2 Charmides says that he will 'make a written copy' (*apograpsomai*) of the charm that Socrates has claimed will help treat his headache. The charm never does get written down; orality, including delivery of the charm, continues (within the drama) to reign. But we have had our attention lightly drawn to the question of the status of the written word: a theme that, so I shall argue, is to loom large later in the dialogue.[24]

---

[22] Lampert (2010, 235–6) argues along these lines.   [23] Cf. Szlezák (1985, 142).
[24] See esp. Sections 4.1 and 4.3.

In any event, the identification of author with anonymous companion would imply a certain structural sloppiness on Plato's part. Socrates, from his particular and peculiar perspective as first-person narrator, plays a distinct structural role. If the companion were Plato, we would merely have an awkward duplication of the latter's anonymous presence. Plato, after all, is a real person, however elusive his authorial persona, while the anonymity of the companion is, I contend, the point: lacking any overt response or reaction to what Socrates is narrating, the companion is presented as a non-person,[25] with whom one may then contrast the vividly (if tendentiously) characterised Chaerephon, who not only has a name but is the first explicitly named character in the work (153b2).

Indeed, with Chaerephon so fully a person, his eager, anxious questioning may suggest a corresponding connection between personhood and the stance of enquiry: 'I ask therefore I am' as an alternative to the familiar (to us) Cartesian motif. What might be the grounds for positing such a connection? Perhaps the following: one's engagement, in questioning mode, with the perspective of another implies that one occupies one's own perspective, which can be recognised (including by oneself) as distinct from that other perspective to which one's questions are directed. At the same time this questioning stance acknowledges, as mere assertion by oneself as speaker need not, the existence of the perspective of that other. We have thus, in this mutual recognition of personhood, the start of, and basis for, conversation characterised by question-and-answer: a phenomenon that the *Charmides* both illustrates lavishly and reflects upon, and to which I shall return.

2.3 Abstract and Concrete

Socrates, as we noted, is eager to move on from fielding questions about the battle to finding out about the current state of philosophy – literally, love of wisdom – at Athens, and the beauty and wisdom of its young men. When contrasted with the plethora of 'knowing' terminology that surrounds it, Socrates' invocation of wisdom is perhaps meant to stand out. Wisdom, we might infer, by contrast with some cases of knowledge, does

---

[25] Thus I am inclined also to reject as misguided attempts to identify the companion with particular individuals other than Plato, such as Theodorus as suggested by Benardete (2000, 231), though it is possible that Benardete, in speaking cautiously of the companion as 'a' Theodorus, intends only to refer to a type. Were I tempted down this speculative path myself, I would proceed from Tsouna's observation that in the whole corpus 'Plato does not mention him at all' (2015, 3) to wager on Xenophon as candidate for Socrates' silent addressee.

not take as its object concrete items like battles or people, but things that are more abstract.

One reason for supposing this to be a distinction underlying Socrates' introduction of wisdom into the conversation is that wisdom is itself an abstract item, as is of course Socrates' other favourite mentioned here, beauty. If we look more closely at the structure of Socrates' opening two-part question at 153d, we can see that this in turn seems to be written so as to bring out a possible contrast between abstract and concrete, highlighted by the way each part opens with a declaration of its subject-matter:

> I in turn questioned them about matters here: concerning philosophy (*peri philosophias*) how things are currently going, and concerning the young men (*peri te tōn neōn*) whether any have turned out distinguished in wisdom (*sophia*) or beauty or both. (153d2–5)

In the sentence's construction there seems a carefully drawn balance between abstract (philosophy) and concrete (the young men).

One must of course be wary of basing the metaphysical on the grammatical. 'Philosophy', 'wisdom' and 'beauty' may grammatically be abstract nouns, but there is certainly no explicit drawing of, or theorising about, a metaphysical distinction between abstract and concrete here. Indeed, given that Socrates asks how things are currently going with it, 'philosophy' seems in this context to name a pursuit or activity,[26] something that essentially takes place in a temporal setting. Nonetheless, we should not, I think, dismiss the idea that the text, in its careful balance of the two parts of Socrates' question, does intend to draw attention to some such distinction as that between abstract and concrete. As we have seen in the case of enquiry and self-knowledge, much in this part of the *Charmides* is set up to show rather than tell.

Notice, then, that alongside the web of knowledge references, there is emphasis in the text that precedes Socrates' two-part question on what one might call the realm of the concrete, that is to say, the spatiotemporal aspects of the world. Consider again just the richly written opening sentence, which brims with references to time, location and change:

> We came from Potidaea out of camp on the previous day at evening and having returned after such a long time (*hoion ... dia chronou*) I gladly went to my habitual haunts. (153a1–3)

---

[26] See Hazebroucq (1997, 99–100); Moore (2020a, 224). Cf. *Gorgias* 484c for the sense. While the etymological connection of *philosophia* and *sophia* suggests a relation between the two (e.g. the first being the activity whose successful pursuit results in the second), Socrates seems not, *pace* Martens (1973, 19), to be using 'philosophy' and 'wisdom' as synonyms when he asks his question.

2.3 Abstract and Concrete

Socrates then specifies, at the start of the next sentence, that it was to the palaestra of Taureas that he headed, noting its location opposite the temple of Basile, and going on to talk about those he came across there (a3–6).

Scholars have been keen to identify which battle is subsequently referred to, whether that at Potidaea in 432 BCE or another at nearby Spartolus in 429, each marking an important moment in respectively the run-up to and early prosecution of the Peloponnesian War. Christopher Planeaux (1999) argued succinctly, against what he called 'the general consensus among scholars' (72), for the latter battle as referent.[27] Planeaux points out (75–6) that preference for the more problematic (from the point of view of the internal consistency of the *Charmides*) former option rested on the idea that the *Charmides* must refer to the same battle that Alcibiades describes, at *Symposium* 220d–e, as himself having been through with Socrates:[28] an example, perhaps, of how attention to a principle of agnosticism may help remove unnecessary barriers to interpretation.

Yet it is important to point out that, whatever difficulties there may be in identifying a determinate reference at the start of the *Charmides* to a historical battle,[29] this would not undermine the claim that there is emphasis here on the concrete spatiotemporal realm. To reiterate an obvious point: though Socrates' reference means that the *Charmides* is not untethered from a historical background, it is not a work of history – if it were, the details of Socrates' Q&A about the battle would surely not have been withheld – but of fiction, in which the characters discuss a battle that Socrates reports he has taken part in. *That* battle is, within the fiction, a determinate one; it is not made less so by being hard to match unequivocally with one or other historical battle.

As we noted in Section 1.3, however, the *Charmides* is more strictly described as fictionalised than fictional. While this, naturally, does not discourage reflection on historical facts, the status of its content, falling somewhere between the concreteness of history and the abstraction of fiction, seems well-suited also to encouraging reflection on the metaphysical categories of abstract and concrete themselves. The historical resonances of the fiction remind us, in turn, not simply that abstract thinking such as that represented therein does not take place in a vacuum, but that such thinking may have effects, for good or ill, on the course of history.

---

[27] In this he was in fact anticipated by Luckhurst (1934). See also McAvoy (1996, 80–1 n. 37).
[28] So too Luckhurst (1934, 207).
[29] Heitsch (2000, 8 n. 2) argues that the dramatic date of the dialogue cannot be precisely determined.

It is history that returns with a vengeance at the end of the dialogue. Moreover, cycles of birth, development, decline (if that is how we are to read the foreshadowing of the futures of Critias and Charmides) and death are prominently woven into the text throughout. In terms of Socrates' own interests, by contrast, we have to be careful not to jump to the conclusion that his preference is straightforwardly for the abstract over the concrete. As noted above, the way his two-part opening question is phrased suggests a balance. The topics he is interested in are philosophy and the young, albeit in the latter case regarding their manifestation of wisdom and beauty.

Now it is true that the first part of Socrates's question is about philosophy, and the second about the young. On the other hand, it is the second that is ostensibly taken up first, more specifically Socrates' enquiry about beauty, with Critias telling Socrates that he will soon find out 'about the beautiful ones' (*peri men tōn kalōn*, 154a3) given that Charmides is on his way. It is Critias who thus puts the question of the beauty of the youth first on the agenda; but recall that Socrates had already informed us that places like the palaestra are among his habitual haunts. He would hardly frequent such places did he not expect to find there, and find engaging, displays of youthful beauty. Furthermore, even the question about philosophy comes attached with a temporal referent – how is philosophy going 'currently' (*ta nun*, 153d3) – which reinforces the idea, noted above, that philosophy is conceived here as an activity occurring at determinate times and places.

Without, then, being given a decisive sense of a Socratic preference for engaging with abstract over concrete, we have been presented with sufficient material in this opening part of the dialogue to notice a contrast between concrete and abstract, parsed respectively as what is constitutively connected with existence in space and time and what is not: any battle, or human individual, in order to exist at all, will have (had) spatiotemporal location; wisdom and beauty, on the other hand, arguably need not, in order to exist, be instantiated in space and time.

Consider, in this regard, a suggestive example from the *Charmides* itself: a charm, consisting of beautiful words, that one may recite to treat the soul (157a3–5). The charm is an abstract object whose beauty may, but need not, be instantiated at particular times and places (when recited, say, over a particular soul). Consider similarly the wisdom of a proverb, such as that of Cydias, wisest in erotic matters, that Socrates quotes at 155d6–e1. Neither the proverb itself nor its wisdom depends on particular dated utterances for its existence. Then there is temperance, something (as Socrates insists) that must be beautiful, which Socrates says can 'come to be' in souls (157a5–6) and which one can have a 'share' of (158c3–4), formulations that at least leave open the possibility that it can exist independently of souls. As the dialogue's own enquiries into temperance will illustrate, while one might look for it in (say) Charmides' soul – the metaphysics of the soul will, as we shall see later,[30] cause some extra complications – one can also intelligibly seek it independently of any particular instantiation.

This independence perhaps then gives a reason why one might seek to pursue the abstract rather than the concrete: by being constitutively tied to the spatiotemporal world, concrete objects are subject to change. That can mean growth and development, but also decline and, eventually, destruction. All good things (bad things too) that are concrete come to an end. Better, one might think, to seek out what is not subject to these eventualities than what is.[31]

As we shall see, given that Socrates has expressed his interest in investigating the young for their wisdom and beauty, his interest in them seems largely restricted to their ability to (come to) instantiate these qualities: young Charmides, for example, will be quite brusquely (though, note, temporarily) abandoned when he ceases to cooperate in the task of showing whether he instantiates beauty in the form of temperance, and the discussion will turn to an investigation of what temperance is independently of its instantiation in that (or any particular) individual. So the depiction of Socrates' erotic quest itself prompts questions not just about the nature of enquiry but about the metaphysical status of its objects.

This may also have implications for reading what we have already seen to be a key structural feature of the *Charmides*, namely the difference in tone and difficulty between the Charmides and the Critias sections. When Charmides is abandoned and Critias engaged in his place, the overt focus changes, from the search for a concrete individual who would manifest temperance, to temperance itself, an abstract object. This is brought out clearly by the way in which Socrates repeatedly characterises the enquiry into temperance with Charmides, but only with Charmides, as having the objective of investigating whether or not the subject possesses temperance (158d8–e1), or whether or not it is 'in' him (159a9), or, more elaborately, what sort of person the presence of temperance makes him (160d6–7).

---

[30] Section 3.4.
[31] The relation between desire and temporality is of course a complex one. For some pertinent reflections that take the outlook of the Platonic Socrates as their starting point, see Hägglund (2012).

These latter two passages immediately precede, respectively, Charmides' first and second answers as to what temperance is. No parallel motive for the enquiry is given expression by Socrates once Critias takes over. It is not, then, simply that the Critias section is drier and more difficult (though it is). Such differences seem to reflect an underlying categorical difference in the primary object of investigation – though, as I shall argue in Chapter 3, Charmides remains, importantly but indirectly, Socrates' quarry even during the main discussion with Critias.

The pages of the *Charmides* that precede the main Critias section have prompted us to reflect on the kinds of objects of enquiry that there are. So when Socrates switches early on from the role of questioned to questioner, at the point where, according to him at least, they had had enough of talking about the battle, this does not represent simply a turning away from nasty things (battles) to nice things (wisdom and beauty), though no doubt that is an element in the switch. Already indicated is a switch from concrete towards abstract, from enquiry into items that are constitutively connected to the spatiotemporal world to enquiry into those that may not be.

Detached from family connections, even as (we shall shortly see) he draws attention to them in the case of Charmides; apparently lacking affect in relation to the fierce battle in which he has taken part; keen to move on from regaling his companions with discussion of the details of that battle to enquiring about the state of philosophy: the narrative seems to this extent to offer a Socrates who represents a move away from the concrete towards the abstract. As I have been at pains to argue, one should be cautious in regarding such Socratic moves as intended by Plato to command our uncritical assent. Moreover, given the quite complex way in which abstract and concrete seem to be meshed in Socrates' opening two-part question, and in his subsequent enquiries, we do not have to see Socrates himself as straightforwardly privileging one category over the other as topic of interest. Rather, I have argued that, without theorising them as such, the text encourages us to notice the categories and be alert, as the Critias section comes into view, to their possible role and significance.

2.4 Nature and Nurture

Socrates' two-part question, examined above in relation to the contrast between abstract and concrete, is phrased precisely, in the part concerning the young, as whether 'any among them have come to be (*tines en autois ... engegonotes eien*) distinguished' (153d4–5) in wisdom, beauty,

2.4 Nature and Nurture

or both. This idea of development is further brought out when Socrates notes at 154b that Charmides, no mean figure even when he last saw him as a boy, would now be quite a lad, with Critias endorsing the sentiment in terms of how Charmides 'has turned out' (*gegonen*, 154b6). Emphasis is also placed on Charmides' family relationships (154e–155a, 157d–158a), with mention of Solon as ancestor (155a3) and his distinguished maternal uncle Pyrilampes (158a2). And as we learned at 154b2, Critias and Charmides are themselves related as cousins.

Several passages in this section of the dialogue – 154e1–3, 155a2–3, 157d9–158a7 – suggest a view, expressed with particular reference to Charmides himself, that whether one has (or develops) a quality is importantly related to whether one is a descendant of those who had such qualities. Yet there is also much to suggest, beginning with the dialogue's setting in the institution of the palaestra, that Charmides' outlook is formed as well by his social environment.[32] Without wishing to overdo this terminology, one might see here both a 'vertical' picture of the formation of the individual, given by that individual's genetic ancestry, and a 'horizontal' dimension, given by their social environment, with immediate family perhaps constituting an area of overlap between the two.

Socrates' various qualifications – 'fitting' (*prepei*, 154e1); 'right' (*dikaion*, 157d9); 'likely' (*eikos*, 157e3, 158a7) – regarding the 'vertical' conception indicate that the view of these passages is not one of simple genetic determinism such that one's (good) qualities are entirely a matter of inheritance. One might hold, more weakly, that without the right ancestors one cannot develop well, or again that having the right ancestors merely makes it more likely (more 'fitting' even) that one will turn out well.

It may also be that questions of nature versus nurture are not so easily distinguished. If being counted as having the 'right' ancestors, for example, depends on the application of a set of particular conventional norms, then the concept of good or bad nature will itself be laden with social convention: Socrates' oddly qualified talk at 157e7–158a1, in the context of

---

[32] If one looks ahead to how Critias 'catches' aporia at 169c, it may be that even one's states of self-awareness are developed in a social context. It is interesting that Socrates himself speaks towards the end of the dialogue of their having failed to discover that to which the 'lawgiver' (*nomothetēs*, 175b4) applied the term 'temperance', *nomos* being the Greek term for law or convention; and intriguing to note that the historical Critias is recorded as having been given the title *nomothetēs* by the Athenians (B48 DK). If Socrates' use of the term here reflects an assumption that the usage of terms was a matter of legislation (cf. Sedley (2003), 69–71), he would be mistaken to infer from this that it does not matter which terms one uses to express one's meaning. See further Section 4.1.

Charmides' family background, of excelling in beauty and virtue (*aretē*) and 'the rest of what is called (*legomenē*) happiness', suggests a certain scepticism, on his part, about such norms.[33]

Socrates' own seeming indifference to family, made vivid by the Odyssean contrast, and his distance from conventional notions of self-development, prompt us to reflect critically not just on the relationship between one's genetic inheritance and one's social environment but on how well-formed we should take the underlying contrast between nature and nurture to be. Even in the terms suggested by that contrast, and before taking his future political role into account, there are indications that the intricate web of social convention in which Charmides is embedded should strike us as problematic, with 158c–d implying that it prevents him from answering a basic question posed by Socrates about Charmides' state of development, namely whether he is sufficiently temperate or not.[34]

On the nature side of the equation, the historical Charmides was, as we know, an uncle of Plato's, which, together with the dialogue's apparent foreshadowing, in its closing scene, of the role of Critias and Charmides in the regime of the Thirty, offers a chronological sweep beyond the dialogue's own boundaries. It is, I think, in these family connections if anywhere that Plato inserts himself into the work, in effect offering himself to the reader as one who stands in a complex relation to the idea that the great are begotten by the great. If Charmides in the end failed to live up to the promise of his ancestors, Plato perhaps goes on to exceed them. That might tell us that the connection between how one turns out and who one is descended from is far from straightforward.

Yet it seems to me that we are not thereby prompted to plump straightforwardly for the following alternative scenario: association with Socrates, with its radical break, in regard to self-development, from the standard elite nexus of nature and nurture, delivers the goods. It hardly seemed to do so for Charmides; and if it did for Plato, then that might in fact suggest, to account for his difference from Charmides – both after all came under Socrates' wing – a significant developmental part played by nature after all. It might equally suggest that association with a figure who is shown to be as much of an outlier, relative to conventional norms, as Socrates, can have catastrophically bad as well as stratospherically good outcomes.

---

[33] Is this why temperance is never itself described as a virtue in the dialogue?
[34] See further Section 3.8.

What I have argued already thus seems to me to apply here too. Plato does not push us to favour one particular permutation in the matrix of nature versus nurture and Socratic outlook versus elite convention. Rather, he allows us to discern and reflect upon a set of complex contrasts. If we find ourselves compelled to investigate these contrasts further – they do, after all, encapsulate vital questions about human possibility, including our own – then we come to occupy the stance of enquiry, emulating Socrates in that way, without necessarily endorsing – and certainly not uncritically endorsing – all that Socrates is shown to be.

2.5 Fiction and History

In this regard it is salutary to note, again, the Odyssean background that invites us to compare Socrates not just with the elite norms of his day but with those of an epic hero, and to notice startling differences in each case. In its juxtaposition of the Socratic narrative with the tale of Odysseus, the *Charmides* emphasises its own status as fiction. Homer gives us an Odysseus who may be a hero but is surely no saint. Only mediocre fiction, one might think, seeks to prescribe a particular ethical response or to offer characters who are one-dimensionally good (or evil). In considering the ways in which the text encourages us to assess, in critical fashion, the character of Socrates, we are steered away from an approach that would rank Plato as author of mediocre fiction.

Nonetheless, one contrast, from among those between the character and behaviour of Socrates and that of Odysseus, which might seem from an ethical point of view to tell unequivocally in Socrates' favour, is that in order to bring his homecoming to final fruition Odysseus slays Penelope's suitors. Only then, his disguise shed and having overcome some lingering doubt about his identity on Penelope's part, can he be reunited with her. Socrates, on the other hand, in his guise as a doctor, fulfils his own plan and seems to succeed in winning round Charmides by the end of the dialogue, Charmides declaring that he is ready to be charmed by Socrates for as long as Socrates deems sufficient (176b2–4). But while, aside from the glancing mention of death in battle at 153c1–2, there is no slaughter within the work, its ending, with its references, overtly light-hearted and therefore all the more chilling, to Critias and Charmides plotting together (176c5–6), to the use of force (c7–8, d2), and to Charmides obeying Critias' orders (c1–2, c8), points towards the violence of the rule of the Thirty and the respective roles of Critias and Charmides within it.

It is noteworthy that, in contrast with any measure of historical indeterminacy in Socrates' reference to a battle at Potidaea with which the dialogue begins, its characters do not refer even indeterminately at the dialogue's end to a coming reign of terror – they could not do so without breaking the fictional conceit, since, whatever the precise dramatic date of their conversation, that reign is at least twenty-five years in the future. Instead, it is the reader who ruptures the conceit by picking up on the delicate but decisive clues that Plato sprinkles over the final scene to bring about a confrontation with what is, from the outside, already history when the *Charmides* was written.

To spell out this point, one should note that while there may be an appearance of symmetry between the opening and closing phases of the dialogue – the former a looking back to history in the form of the battle, the latter a looking forward to history in the form of the reign of the Thirty – this appearance is somewhat illusory. As already noted, the battle is looked back on by Socrates *within* the fiction. To that extent, although the battle might make us think of one or other historical battle, the battle Socrates refers to is part of the fiction, existing within the dialogue's created world as referent of a first-hand report by one of its characters.

The looking forward to the reign of the Thirty is, by contrast, no part of that fictional world. Assuming they are not prophets,[35] the characters are not themselves hinting at coming events; *Plato* is hinting at them through what he has his characters say. What this means in turn is that, unlike the references to the battle, the referencing of those events can only be to history, or the historical future. So here there is a genuine break: once we pick up on the hints, fiction ruptures and history floods in as the dialogue closes.

One reason for this, to return to an earlier theme, is that it is only in this way that we are made to confront a real contrast between abstract and concrete. The *Charmides* itself is an abstract object (my copy of its text a concrete instantiation); and what it depicts – the characters, events, and conversations – is to that extent also an abstraction or a series of abstractions. But what it foreshadows is brute, concrete reality. One might thus say that only at this point are we compelled to contrast abstract with concrete; but of course, since we can read the *Charmides* backwards as well as forwards, the sense of that contrast as something raised by, and within, the fiction is validated too.

---

[35] Note, however, that prophecy, as knowledge of what is to come, does feature towards the end of the dialogue (173c3–4; cf. 173e10–174a1).

2.5 Fiction and History

This then provides some filling in of how Plato's provocation of the reader into a stance of enquiry carries right through to the dialogue's end. I argued above, in the context of the earlier scenes with Charmides, that such provocation was Plato's aim. So it seems consistent with that aim that the final provocation occurs when Charmides has returned to the conversation, won round to the prospect of re-engagement with Socrates. It also raises unavoidably the question of whether the provocation signals that we are to reflect on the future fate of the historical Charmides specifically in the light of his counterpart's depicted association in the *Charmides* with the character Socrates. In one way it seems implausible to deny, given the foreshadowing, that this is being asked of us. On the other hand, such an exercise may at the same time seem incongruous, a comparison of apples with oranges, Plato asking us to compare and contrast abstract (fiction) with concrete (history). These are different metaphysical categories.

So there is a twofold jarring in the way the dialogue ends: the irruption of a concretely brutal future over the urbane closing exchanges; and the incongruity of the invitation to compare fiction with history. The jarring effect suggests in turn that we are supposed to notice both elements. The foreshadowing of the Thirty perhaps means we cannot avoid asking the concrete question: was Socrates a bad influence on Charmides? I stress Charmides rather than Critias, notwithstanding work by modern interpreters of the *Charmides* to 'rehabilitate' the latter,[36] in terms both of his role in the dialogue and his historical career, as a more nuanced and equivocal figure than the cartoon villain found in some of our ancient sources.[37] For it is Charmides who is presented early in the dialogue as exemplifying the future promise of Athens: the golden boy who if he develops properly will make an outstanding member of Athenian society to rival or even surpass his distinguished ancestors. It is Charmides too who is shown as the principal object of Socrates' interest at the start and Charmides whom the dialogue shows at its end preparing to submit to treatment by Socrates on an ongoing basis.

It is, then, Charmides more than Critias whose future is presented as being at stake.[38] In fact there is reason (which I shall discuss later),[39]

---

[36] See e.g. Barker (1995, 29–31); Tsouna (1997), (2015, 11–15); Dušanić (2000); Notomi (2000); Tuozzo (2011, 54–66); Danzig (2014). For a less charitable reading of Critias in the *Charmides* see Wolfsdorf (2008, 217–33).
[37] See especially Xenophon, *Hellenica* 2.3.15–16, *Memorabilia* 1.2.12.
[38] As Beversluis (2000, 157) observes, Socrates expresses concern for Charmides, not for Critias, in the dialogue's closing section.
[39] Section 5.8.

internal to the way Charmides is portrayed, to suppose that he is unlikely to have withstood treatment at Socrates' hands for very long. Assuming this to be the case, should we then say that Charmides would not have had such a disappointing future career, as servant of the Thirty, if he had stuck with Socrates? The career of Critias, whose association with Socrates is depicted as both enduring (156a7–8) and intellectually intense,[40] suggests we may not even have that consoling option, assuming that even a rehabilitated Critias does not present a character (regarded by Plato as) of unspotted distinction.[41]

We may see at this point some importance in the characters of the *Charmides* being fictionalised rather than simply fictional. That status gives enough continuity, as merely juxtaposing fiction and history would not, to allow us to consider the relation between what we are shown within the work and Charmides' eventual fate. Yet it also allows us to notice the rather odd terms on which we are considering it. Indeed by now it seems possible to step back and ask: is such speculation really where Plato wants our focus to lie? Even as we indulge in it, we are able to notice that any basis for the speculation seems blunted by the incongruity of comparing the fictional, or even fictionalised, with history.

I suggest, then, that it is those terms themselves on which Plato may ultimately want us to reflect. To develop this thought, let us return to the question of how to assess the extraordinary character of Socrates as depicted in the dialogue, in light of the foreshadowing of historical reality with which the work closes. Grant him hero status if you will; but let us deem our hero flawed or, if one prefers, distinctive in the following way: given that he seems sufficiently indifferent to the spatiotemporal world to

---

[40] The relationship with Critias, together with Charmides' professed keenness at the end of the dialogue (with Critias' enthusiastic endorsement, 176b5–8) to re-engage open-endedly with Socrates, renders puzzling Irwin's claim (1996, 348), which he does not try to substantiate and which apparently serves as an argument that the pair 'cannot fairly be cited as examples of Socratic followers who turned out badly', that 'the dialogue does not suggest that they took a very serious interest in Socrates'. The dialogue manifestly shows them, above all at its close, taking such an interest. How much we can infer from this about its future course is a further question, but one that cannot be settled by denial. Irwin also claims Critias and Charmides as probable examples of 'wayward friends' upon whom 'Socrates' influence . . . is shown to be powerful but not lasting; in the end these characters go astray' (Irwin 1996, 347 n. 18). Putting aside the question of how to square being powerfully influenced by Socrates with not taking a very serious interest in him, one wonders on what basis Irwin concludes (without simply begging the question) that the pair's going astray means that Socrates' influence on them did not last.

[41] Brisson (2021, 64) nonetheless claims that in the *Charmides* Plato 'shows to what extent Socrates' influence on Critias and Charmides could have been beneficial, if they had been persuaded by Socrates to know themselves', the rather desperate conditional illustrative of the effort required to present a Socrates whom Plato, as Brisson sees it, 'wished to exculpate' (63).

be pretty much unaffected by the deaths of his comrades in battle, there is little reason to think he would be any more affected by the havoc wreaked by the Thirty and by Charmides' subsequent fate.[42]

To be sure, I have already sketched a thesis, to be developed in Chapter 3, that Socrates wishes, for the satisfaction of his erotic desire, to make a beautiful soul out of Charmides. That is the goal of the art of soul-medicine. But, like medicine, soul-medicine may not always succeed in healing its patient; and like medicine, it may in any case not be able to work without the patient's cooperation. If Charmides is not in the end suitable material, that need not be cause for undue concern. Socrates is, after all, an indiscriminatory 'white stick', someone to whom pretty much every boy of a certain age appears beautiful (154b8–10), notwithstanding that Charmides appeared remarkably so to him (154b10–c2). There are plenty more fish in the sea. And if none of those youthful fish proves suitable, there is the beauty of temperance itself to seek.

After all, it is not the beauty of bodies in which Socrates' real interest lies. If we find something rebarbative, in his indifference to the horrors of battle and to the beauty of bodies alike, about his heroic detachment from the spatiotemporal realm, then the irruption of history, only hinted at yet resoundingly loud, with which Plato takes his authorial leave of us in the work, may be there to suggest that, for better or worse, emulating such detachment is not a real option for us. Concrete reality has a habit of intruding, whether one likes it or not. (In the form of what lay beneath Charmides' cloak, it almost got Socrates.) We cannot, so we might think, forsake the concrete for the more abstract in the way in which Socrates is shown to do.

This is more than a question of Socrates' relation to politics. To be sure, the dialogue shows him as a close associate not just of Critias, the (future) keen oligarch, but of Chaerephon, the (future) keen democrat, the lives of whose historical counterparts were wholly in the past, and therefore relatively clear in retrospect, when the *Charmides* was written. So while the opposed political stance of that pair is not prominent within the dialogue, it will be called to mind by any informed reader, who may wonder in turn what to make of the political disinterest on Socrates' part thereby implied. One might ask whether a degree of Socratic indifference

---

[42] A rather different sort of Socratic response – cool defiance in the face of an order from the Thirty that he considered unjust (participation in the arrest of Leon of Salamis) – is recorded at *Apology* 32c–d, immediately preceded, as if to emphasise a certain sort of political neutrality on his part, by his account of resistance to an illegal procedure during the subsequent democracy (32b–c).

to the currents of contemporary politics (as opposed to a fancy for utopian visions) in turn signals a wider indifference to the ebbs and flows of the material world.[43]

Yet in considering whether Socrates' detachment from that world can be a realistic option for us, we necessarily find ourselves reflecting on abstract questions such as: what is the relation between abstract and concrete, and to what extent should we care about each? Whatever answers we give, the abstract turns out to be a topic of interest for us. In line with what I have maintained is Plato's overall strategy in relation to his readers, its proper place in our lives is for us to explore, not for him to determine on our behalf. But if we are so much as prompted to find interest in these questions, then we are able to see ourselves as subjects who engage in abstract enquiry. In our development as enquirers of this sort, the character of Socrates allows us – as we may speculate the historical figure allowed Plato – to share an extraordinary perspective to which we may not otherwise have had access, and to confront questions we may not otherwise have thought to raise. It is, I think, our asking of such questions, rather than the making of historical judgements, that the fictionalised character Socrates is there to provoke.

2.6 Conclusion

In this chapter I have tried to show how the first part of the *Charmides* (what I have called the Charmides section) prepares us for the second part, the intense discussion with Critias about temperance, by encouraging us to occupy the stance of enquiry and to see ourselves as doing so. The relation between these two parts is itself two-way. As the first part sets us up for the second by encouraging us to engage critically, from the start, with the dialogue's material, so the second part, with its more overtly abstract character and epistemological focus, brings more sharply to our attention some of the themes of the first part. The finale, I have argued, in confronting fiction with history, presents us with the question of how far detachment from concrete reality is possible, the question made more urgent, as soon as we consider it, by its revealing us to ourselves as, unavoidably, abstract enquirers.

If we consider again the dialogue's structure, there is nothing paradoxical in earlier sections helping prepare us for later ones, while later ones

---

[43] One cannot help but see, in this regard, a faintly mocking tone to Socrates' praise of Pyrilampes' ambassadorial exploits at 158a.

illuminate earlier. As we have noted, one can move in both directions, forwards and backwards, along its horizontal dimension. There is no reason to regard the *Charmides* as a one-way street, to be read from beginning to end and then we stop. It is, rather, virtuously circular that earlier stretches, having prepared us for what is ahead, are then given extra significance when re-read in the light of later material. Our engagement with the *Charmides* is, or can be, a reinforcing loop rather than an unretraceable line.

In terms of its vertical structure, I have tried to illustrate in this chapter how, at the level of Plato's relation to his readers, the dialogue seeks, particularly in its first part, to provoke us into occupying a critical stance that will equip us to engage as fully as possible with the second part. I have thus attempted to vindicate the unity of the dialogue at this level. In Chapter 3, I go back to the question of Socrates' relation to his interlocutors and, by focussing in particular on the role of eros, seek to show in more detail how unity obtains at that level too.

CHAPTER 3

Charmides, Eros and the Unity of the Dialogue

In the last of the examples discussed in the previous chapter, we previewed Charmides' reappearance at the end of the dialogue. We are now almost ready for a closer look at his first appearance. Since my particular focus in this chapter is on how Socrates' relations with Charmides are to be read across the work, let me first specify how, at the level of Socrates' motives as presented within the drama, I intend in broad terms to follow the winding path of his initial encounter with Charmides and what follows it.

I shall argue that Socrates' primary motive for engaging with Charmides is an erotic one, and that this explains why Charmides is abandoned in favour of Critias only to be brought back into discussion near the work's close. By contrast, Socrates shows no erotic interest in Critias. He never makes any mention of Critias being beautiful in either body or soul.[1] Indeed, in stark contrast to how he relates to Charmides, Socrates never mentions Critias' soul or expresses any desire to examine it.[2]

Why, then, does Socrates switch from Charmides to Critias? There are two distinct elements to be accounted for here. The first is Socrates' cessation of discussion with Charmides; the second is his then carrying on discussion with Critias. The first element does not entail the second. My explanation of the first is that Socrates suffers erotic disappointment with Charmides when the latter, disinclined to allow further access to his soul, turns to an account of temperance not based on what he takes to be in his soul but that he heard from someone else. My explanation of the second is that the switch to Critias allows the continuation of Socrates' erotic pursuit of Charmides by other means.

---

[1] The closest he gets is perhaps his remark to Critias at 155a2–3 attributing 'this beautiful thing' (namely a poetic gift) all the way back to ancestral kinship with Solon. But although the 'you' (*humin*) to whom Socrates attributes it is second-person plural, the context of the remark is Critias' reporting of praise for Charmides' poetic aptitude at 154e8–155a1.
[2] I consider some objections to the claim that Socrates shows no interest in Critias' soul in Section 3.10.

In investigating what temperance is, Socrates' overriding aim in the *Charmides* is not the discovery of what temperance is. Rather, the investigation serves Socrates' quest for beauty in Charmides' soul. His long discussion with Critias seduces Charmides into preparedness to make his soul available for inspection once more; his closing conversation with Charmides shows that the seduction has, at that point, been successful. In this way the dialogue can be read as a dramatically unified whole.

For the seduction of Charmides, I shall argue, Socrates avails himself of two arts that I label respectively the art of erotics and the art of soul-medicine, the latter here bearing a relation of subordination to the former. While the goal of the latter is to make a soul temperate, and thus beautiful, the goal of the former is, in Socrates' practice, to secure the availability of a beautiful, or prospectively beautiful, soul for the practitioner to behold. In elaborating Socrates' use of these two arts, I endeavour to make the case in detail that the theme of eros (erotic desire) gives the dialogue dramatic unity across its horizontal dimension.

In methodological terms, fidelity to the principle of agnosticism will enable Socrates' way of proceeding in the *Charmides* to be analysed without prejudice and on its own terms. It will be obvious that, in line with the principle, I resist any tendency to presuppose some uniformity of Socratic procedure across a given group of dialogues. By the same token, adherence to the principle of separation calls for the drama of the dialogue to be treated as a distinct but integral element in its construction that requires its own analysis and interpretation. I begin by considering Charmides' first appearance and its effects. By the end of the chapter, in vindicating the dialogue's dramatic unity, I hope also to have shed light on the connections it draws between eros and temperance and outlined some key elements in the way that temperance is there conceived.

3.1 Charmides' Entrance

To highlight the vividness of the moment that Charmides comes on the scene, recalled to his anonymous addressee as if happening in the moment, Socrates switches to the historic present: 'Charmides enters' (154b7). He confesses that Charmides struck him as wondrous in stature and beauty (154c1–2) but goes on to narrate:

> Indeed all the others seemed to me to feel eros (*eran*) towards Charmides – so shaken and confused were they – when he entered. (154c2–4)

By using the third-person plural Socrates reminds us that it is, formally, his narration, while seemingly marking himself out from the others as not subject in the same way as they to the erotic power exerted by Charmides. Although Socrates goes on implicitly to include himself in the response, he qualifies this as well:

> And the reaction of us men (*to men hēmeteron to tōn andrōn*) was not so surprising; but I focussed on the boys too, how not one of them, even the youngest, looked elsewhere, but they all gazed at him [Charmides] as if he were a statue. (154c5–8)

Socrates, according to his own account, *is* looking elsewhere than at Charmides, principally paying attention to the reaction of others to the vision rather than to the vision itself.[3] So even in this case there remains a contrast between the attitude of Socrates and the breathless engagement of the rest. The text prompts us to notice the distinctiveness of Socrates without necessarily either approving or disapproving.

When a still excitable Chaerephon asks Socrates how Charmides looks to him, Socrates agrees that he is indeed fair of face – 'outstandingly so' (154d3).[4] Yet just as Socrates and Chaerephon were portrayed as opposites in their response to the battle (with Socrates attributing Chaerephon's response to his 'crazy' character), so too Chaerephon cannot resist adding here that, if Charmides were willing to strip, it would seem as if he had no face, so 'totally beautiful' (*pankalos*) is his body (154d4–5). Socrates seems so far to have displayed, in regard to Charmides' physical attributes, a good deal more detachment.

The scene re-emphasises the presentation of events as viewed through a particular perspective. Socrates' apparent detachment from the bodily beauty of Charmides operates at both a formal and substantive level. As narrator of the events in question, he stands separated from those events in virtue of his occupation of that formal role: we have the narrator, on the one hand, and the narrated events on the other. But Socrates is also a participant in those events, and in that role he presents himself as detached in a more substantive sense, his initially cool response to Charmides' physical appearance standing in contrast to the excited reaction of Chaerephon and the others.

---

[3] Cf. Morris (1993, 56).
[4] There is no need to take this response, with Bloch (1973, 19), as ironic. Socrates is happy to acknowledge Charmides' outstanding facial beauty. How much weight he gives such beauty in reckoning the beauty of Charmides is a further question.

3.2 Humour and Perspective

There is, however, a striking vignette that Socrates goes on to offer (here I travel slightly ahead in the order of the text, with the gap to be filled in later) which uses perspective to implicate the reader as critical participant. I refer to Socrates' description of what follows Critias' summoning over of Charmides to join Socrates and him.[5] What happened next, narrates Socrates, is that:

> He [Charmides] came and created much laughter; for each of us who were seated tried to make room for him to sit next to them by shoving their neighbour vigorously, until the person sitting at one end had to stand up, and the person at the other end fell off sideways. (155b9–c4)

The scene is noteworthy for its vivid physicality: we are immersed in the world of bodies, not now simply that of Charmides but, in ridiculous fashion, of those scrambling to have their own body next to his. Since we are invited to laugh at this – the text does not say who at the scene did the laughing that was created – we might suppose that we are at the same time invited to make an adverse value-judgement of the behaviour on display, and by implication to regard an attitude of restraint in such circumstances as more admirable. But this is too simple.[6]

Socrates, we may note, includes himself ('each of *us* (*hēmōn*) who were seated') in the jostling behaviour, though it is not clear how much he thereby purports to implicate himself in its absurdity. After all, Critias was summoning Charmides with the express purpose, in response to Socrates' request, that Charmides talk to Socrates. Socrates' making room for Charmides to sit next to him might then be perfectly reasonable rather than funny. It is, on this account, in the pushing and shoving of all the rest that the absurdity lies.

If so, we seem to retain a picture of a Socrates less affectively engaged in the world of concrete things – of bodies specifically – than his companions. But, as with the opening scene in respect of the battle, so too here, there is a certain way of responding that comes filtered through the Socratic perspective. In that earlier scene, it was the labelling of Chaerephon by Socrates that presented a sensible Socrates in contrast with a crazy Chaerephon. In the business with the pushing and shoving, it is Socrates' selection of that scene for description in some detail, and his

---

[5] Compare the account of this episode in McCabe (2019b, 194–7).
[6] As Verity Harte suggests to me, one possible complexity is that the text leaves it unclear whether anyone was laughing at themselves.

distancing comment that it provoked laughter, that invites us to evaluate one way of responding to Charmides – with cool detachment – as sensible, the opposite way as ridiculous.

As before, the structure of the *Charmides* is set up so as to prevent easy identification of the worldview that Socrates offers with some kind of official endorsement on Plato's part. Plato, of course, is writing all the words; but it is Socrates whom he writes as narrating the dialogue's scenes from a first-person perspective. As I have already argued, once we notice this perspectival construction, we are encouraged to adopt what I have labelled the stance of enquiry and interrogate the picture with which we are presented. The admirability or otherwise of Socrates' way of engaging with the spatiotemporal world is for us to consider critically.

That said, it cannot be denied that Socrates as narrator, and thus Plato as author, do a rather effective job in making the response to Charmides come across as funny. The humour must work in part because we can identify with the perspective of Charmides' hapless admirers. Many of us, no doubt, have at times acted ridiculously in (and because of) the presence of a person to whom we are attracted. Yet the complexity of the humorous response means that it also works by creating a critical distance between us and the admirers. Without that, such a scene would, to the extent that we identify with it, make us uncomfortable rather than mirthful. In inviting us to look at the behaviour from the outside, the comedy aligns us with the Socratic perspective of detached observer. The difference is that, because Plato shows us the events as filtered through Socrates' narration, we as readers can in turn distance ourselves from the Socratic perspective.

If the humour has done its job, we will at any rate find ourselves seeing erotic attraction as having a funny side. In this way the power of humour is itself in part epistemic: it is an enabler of self-knowledge in that it reveals us to ourselves as taking a certain evaluative attitude, albeit quite a complex one, towards its subject-matter. In the case at hand, we find the admirers both ridiculous and, to a degree, sympathetic. We recognise ourselves in them even as we hold ourselves detached from them. The phenomenon of self-knowledge is thus once more exemplified in advance of its later turning up as an explicit theme. In coming to see self-knowledge function as part of our mental economy, we care about its status when it eventually becomes subject to critical scrutiny.

In contrasting the way in which the others are erotically drawn towards Charmides, the dialogue encourages us to regard Socrates' apparently more detached perspective *as* a particular perspective, and thereby to gain distance from it ourselves. Appearances, as we shall see, can be misleading.

But we should not suppose that in refraining from identifying ourselves with Socrates' perspective, we are somehow meant to end up occupying no perspective at all. One lesson perhaps suggested by the dialogue's complex use of perspective is that the view from nowhere cannot have a claim on us since it is not a view that we as human subjects can come to occupy.[7] The text's use of Socrates in the first-person role makes vivid that we inevitably see things from some perspective, even if the perspective from which we see things does not have to be that of Socrates.

Arguably, part of what it is to be able to care about a thing at all is to see ourselves as occupying a perspective from which that thing is accessible to us. So too, conversely, in at least a range of cases, with accessibility comes, for creatures like us, perspective. Sometimes, as in the case of our response to the pushing and shoving scene, being made to see that we occupy a certain perspective is what reveals our evaluative attitude to us – we would not find things so funny were we among those fighting to create an extra space. This does not of course mean that we could not come to laugh at ourselves for having been a participant in the mad scramble; but that in turn would indicate a shift in perspective (and no doubt a gain in self-knowledge) on our part.

3.3 Subjecthood, Conversation and Truth

The way the scene works suggests a connection between the subjecthood endowed by perspective on the one hand and concreteness, in the sense of spatiotemporality, on the other. Embodied subjects are formally distinct from one another insofar as each has a distinct perspective. As the pushing and shoving playfully reminds us, no more than one such subject can occupy the same portion of space at a given time. Thus my perspective on, say, a particular table cannot be exactly the same as that of another embodied subject at that time.

One reason this matters is that, in order to reach agreement or find truth as something over and above mere perspective, one may need to find a way to transcend perspectival difference. Now the formal distinctness of subjects as concrete entities is only the most basic element of this difference. One immediate corollary of the formal distinctness is that each subject will have a different history over time in virtue of which each will see things somewhat differently from the others. Difference in personal history, with which, as the *Charmides* seems keen to remind us,

---

[7] But see Moore (1997) for a contemporary challenge to this idea.

we may conjoin difference in hereditary origin, thus marks a further, substantive, source of difference between subjects. Again, agreement on, or acquisition of truth about, how things are may require the overcoming of such differences.

Moreover, each subject will be somewhat differently equipped from the other in terms of the whole range of a subject's mental and physical attributes; and this will be both producer and product of differences in personal history. One may then add a final source of perspectival difference: while many subjects may be broadly similar in terms of their qualities, and to that extent share a broadly similar perspective, we may also find a subject who seems radically different in their outlook from the majority. We have seen some evidence, not least in the pushing and shoving scene itself, that Socrates is presented in this way in the *Charmides*. This is the kind of subject who is apt to make us *notice* perspectival difference and thereby make us aware that there are questions to be asked and critical judgements to be exercised in order to determine which perspective (if any) has the greater claim on being correct.

But there is paradox here. Formally, one transcends differences of perspective by coming to agree on some potentially disputed point. Yet one cannot do this, it seems, by coming to occupy no perspective at all. How, then, do we navigate a way, given our constitution, between the poverty of mere subjectivity – the idea that all we have are differences of perspective – and the impossibility of the view from nowhere? Socrates' presentation by Plato in a scene such as the one we have been examining may offer a clue.

There is, perhaps, a certain comfort in resting with the idea that mere subjectivity is the only game in town. But awareness of difference of perspective can equally be disruptive of such comfort. For we can be made to see, through the availability of the kind of radical difference in perspective that, for example, Socrates is shown to occupy, that it is possible to occupy such a perspective and therefore, in principle, possible for us. Seeing this depends in turn on being persuaded that such a perspective *can* credibly be occupied by a subject. Plato's dramatic art thus plays an important epistemic role. If a radical perspective is occupied by a (nonetheless) convincing character – Socrates, we may care to agree, is brought to life remarkably convincingly by Plato – then we are jolted into the necessity of comparison and critical evaluation. The occupation of such a perspective by an apparently credible subject means one has to reckon with it and consider it seriously as an alternative to one's own.

3.3 Subjecthood, Conversation and Truth

Conversation is about to feature centrally in Socrates' forthcoming engagement with Charmides;[8] and conversation, whether the one provoked in our own heads by the dialogue's dramatic presentation, or the one displayed between characters in the drama, in turn seems important, since it enables perspectives to be shared and assessed and thereby offers some possibility of discovering where (if anywhere) truth lies. In the *Charmides*, one main route to the discovery of truth is characterised in terms of reaching agreement through conversation. This is most explicit in the Critias section. At 165b–c Critias pledges that he will give an account of his proposal that temperance is knowing oneself, if Socrates does not agree that it is (b3–4). Socrates does not reject Critias' offer, but says that because he does not have knowledge, he will say whether or not he agrees with the proposal once he has examined it (b5–c2).[9] There follows the long critical discussion of the proposal between Socrates and Critias. By implication, if Socrates comes to agree (as in fact he will not), it would be agreement based on sufficient examination of the proposal to constitute knowledge of its truth.

One should note that the notion of agreement at work here does not bear the attenuated sense claimed for it in the Platonic corpus by Lesley Brown, such that, where an interlocutor is asked to agree (*homologein*), 'the use of the term does not imply any other person who shares the belief in question'.[10] Critias' question at 165b3–4 is evidently whether Socrates agrees with *him* that temperance is knowing oneself; and that is how Socrates takes it (cf. *homologēsontos soi*, 'that I will agree with you', b7). Moreover, the passage from the *Charmides* that Brown herself cites (2018, 26 n. 28) in support of her thesis seems to tell against it: when Charmides replies at 158c7–d1 that he does not know whether to agree or deny what he has been asked,[11] the question that he was asked by Socrates, at 158c3, was 'whether you agree with this individual [Critias]' (*poteron homologeis tōide*) about being sufficiently temperate.

The *Charmides* thus offers a robust conception of agreement. One reason for this may be that the work's emphasis on perspectival difference makes it natural to conceive of arriving at truth in terms of overcoming such difference, via conversation of a particular norm-governed kind, to reach a shared perspective. This may, however, also have implications for the kind of thing in respect of which one can arrive at the truth. It might be argued that this would have to be of something not itself essentially

---

[8] See Section 3.5.   [9] I discuss this passage further in Sections 4.4 and 5.1.
[10] Brown (2018, 31).   [11] On this passage see further Section 3.8.

embedded in the spatiotemporal world. A particular battle or particular body is, in virtue of its metaphysical status, not accessible other than from particular perspectives; and it is not clear, in terms of reaching truth, whether one can say more than that, even if conversation provides a means for sharing or enlarging perspectives.

An abstract object such as temperance, by contrast, does not seem essentially perspective-bound, and thus one may have reason to believe that there is truth to be found in investigating it. This is not to say that different discussants (or often enough the same discussant) will not have different perspectives on what temperance is, as the *Charmides* amply demonstrates. But it does mean that in principle one can transcend particular perspectives and reach an agreement that certifies truth about temperance, just because, by contrast with concrete objects, access in such cases does not seem essentially tied to perspective. That may be one reason why, in connection with a search for the truth (cf. 166d4–6), and regardless of whether discovery of truth is Socrates' ultimate aim, an object such as temperance features in the main investigation that the work depicts.

3.4 From Body to Soul

Socrates' principal aim, as I shall try to show, is the discovery of beauty in Charmides' soul. So it will be necessary for me to spell out how that relates to the investigation into the nature of temperance that he conducts with Critias. For now, we remain in the concrete world of bodies. With regard to eros as the proprietary psychological attitude towards beauty (as Socrates will formally propound it to be at 167e7–8),[12] what we have been made to focus on thus far is the body beautiful: specifically, the beautiful body of Charmides. The pushing and shoving scene, despite its comic tone, reinforces this picture of the body as the centrepiece of the portrayal of eros and its effects. Here, however, the physical aggression occasioned by Charmides' approaching the seated Socrates and his companions, triggered as it is by physical attraction to Charmides, points additionally to a relation between body and soul that, in typical fashion for the dialogue, is shown as much as told.

---

[12] Responding to Critias' suggestion that temperance is knowledge of itself, Socrates presents a series of purported analogies designed to show that self-directed states are problematic, with Critias agreeing in the course of this to Socrates' putting it to him that there is no such eros that is 'of nothing beautiful, but rather of itself' (167e8), implying that eros takes as its standard object something (or someone) beautiful. For more on these analogies see Section 4.7.

3.4 From Body to Soul

One might, in the aggression, glimpse the tragedy of war, hinted at in the dialogue's opening scene, reprised as comedy.[13] Eros can of course be the occasion for war. Given the Odyssean resonances in the *Charmides* it seems apt to recall Helen's beauty as alleged cause of the Trojan war. Since the pushing and shoving represents eros as cause of physical aggression and thus physical harm, we may have here a loose and comic illustration of how the good condition of the body depends on the temperate condition of the soul, a claim that Socrates will shortly make on behalf of the Thracian model of medicine that he narrates to set up his own model for how to engage with Charmides.[14] We shall thus have cause to consider in some detail, in interpreting Socrates' motives for that engagement, the question of how the medical and erotic motifs are related. Meanwhile, a note of unease about the body as focal point of eros has been introduced.

Crucially, then – here is the portion of text that I skipped over in Section 3.2 – Socrates has already presented the idea that eros can be directed towards souls as well as bodies. In this shift of focus, Socrates echoes the phrasing of Chaerephon, revealing a degree of alignment with the latter's outlook, despite the purported contrast between them. When Chaerephon suggests that, if Charmides were willing to strip, Socrates would not even think he has a face, so totally beautiful is his figure, Socrates replies that Charmides will be truly invincible just so long as he also turns out to be well developed (*eu pephukōs*) in respect of his soul (154d4–e1). After Critias' reply that Charmides is 'very beautiful and good' in that regard too (154e4), Socrates says:

> Then why don't we strip this very [part] of him and look at that before his [physical] form?' For he is certainly, I presume, at his age now willing to have a conversation (*dialegesthai*). (154e5–7)

The terminology of 'stripping' reminds us that while eros can be ridiculous it can also (and not incompatibly) be assertive, even aggressive. What we might have considered language typical of the excitable Chaerephon is now co-opted by Socrates in considering the prospect of examining Charmides' soul. If anything, his approach is more brutal than that of Chaerephon,

---

[13] Aggression was also lightly suggested in the description of Charmides' cohort of admirers 'joshing' (*loidoroumenous*, 154a1–2) with one another as they entered.
[14] On the Thracian picture it is the condition of one's own body that is dependent on the condition of one's soul, whereas here it is, in the first instance, one's eros occasioning aggression against one's neighbour's body; but the mutual pushing and shoving readily suggests exposure of oneself to bodily harm in return.

such that one may wonder whether an assessment of Socrates in the *Charmides* as 'a man of exemplary gentleness in disposition' quite captures the figure that we find in its pages.¹⁵ Chaerephon, after all, showed sufficient restraint to state matters conditionally: 'if he [Charmides] were willing' (*ei etheloi*, 154d4) to strip, whereas Socrates simply presumes that at his age Charmides 'is certainly willing' (*pantōs ... ethelei*, e6–7) to converse, straight after declaring: then why don't we undress his soul.¹⁶

This suggests that what differentiates Socrates is less the intensity of his eros – cool, detached Socrates versus hot and bothered Chaerephon and the rest – than the kind of object towards which his eros is principally directed: beautiful souls rather than beautiful bodies. I claimed in Section 2.3 that Socrates' switch from discussion of the battle to discussion of the state of philosophy and the beauty and wisdom of the young can be seen, with due qualification, as indicating interest in the abstract over the concrete. The switch of focus from Charmides' body to his soul suggests a parallel, with further qualifications, to that earlier move.

The soul in question is that of an individual, Charmides. And, as previously in regard to beauty and wisdom, so now there is no theorising in the text about the metaphysics of the soul: about whether we should, for example, consider it an entity constitutively connected to existence in space and time. Nonetheless, in the redirection of the 'stripping' language, we surely do not expect the unclothing of Charmides' soul to result in exposure of something spatially present to us in the way that Charmides' body would be. The application of the language separately to body and to soul indicates at any rate that Socrates does not regard souls as corporeal, so we should probably rule out souls on this conception as occupying space (even if they do, in some sense, have a location).

On the other hand, souls do seem, given the descriptions concerning an individual's ethical development, to be taken to be subject to change over time. Souls we might then dub, indifferently, as semi-concrete or semi-abstract. If, as I shall argue, Socrates' ultimate interest is in the individual (beautiful) soul, then his turning away from the spatiotemporal world

---

¹⁵ The assessment is Smith's (2021, 127), in the context of *Charmides* 155d–e. Smith goes on to say that we should nonetheless not assume that Socrates is 'completely invulnerable to the ways in which *others* [my emphasis] can not only do mischief, but actually do real moral harm to those they victimize' (2021, 127). The idea that Plato might depict Socrates as himself a figure capable of mischief or moral harm seems beyond the pale.

¹⁶ A similar assertiveness is indicated by Socrates' peremptory 'just let him come' (*monon elthetō*, 155b7) in his assenting to Critias' suggestion that he claim to be a doctor to lure Charmides over. Charmides' own willingness to adopt the language of force at the end of the dialogue suggests that at that point eros on his part for Socrates has become salient; see further Section 5.8.

3.4 From Body to Soul

needs to be correspondingly qualified. The soul's temporality is immediately emphasised in the present context when Socrates unpacks, as we previewed above, what it actually means to speak of looking at a soul, as opposed to a body, by saying that Charmides is certainly old enough that he is now (*ēdē*) willing to have a conversation (154e6–7). The contrast and connection between looking and conversing is one to which I shall return.[17]

Charmides, implies Socrates, has reached a stage in his development (he surely does not mean bodily development) where he will not consider it inappropriate to converse with Socrates. The temporal aspect is reinforced when Socrates goes on to proclaim, after urging Critias to summon Charmides over and present him, that even if Charmides had still been younger, it would not have been improper for him to have a conversation with Socrates given the presence of Critias as Charmides' cousin and guardian (155a3–7).

This explicit connecting by Socrates of looking at a soul with having a conversation will allow us to piece together an account of why Socrates might prefer to undertake examination of someone's soul rather than their body. In terms of the erotic context, we need to explain why Socrates expresses more erotic interest when, at least as advertised, there is a beautiful soul in prospect than when there is a beautiful body. Later, we will need to consider not just what distinguishes these cases of beauty, but what unites them, such as to justify the application of the same term 'beautiful' (*kalon*), grounding their status as objects of eros, in respect of each.[18]

First, however, we need to pick up a further thread regarding Socrates' attitude to the body. Immediately after narrating the comic scene of pushing and shoving, he reveals that Charmides' physical beauty did after all have an effect on him. He tells his companion that when Charmides sat between him and Critias:

> I was, my friend, now at a loss (*ēdē ēporoun*), and the former confidence I had that it would be quite easy to have a conversation with him [Charmides] had evaporated. (155c5–7)

---

[17] See Section 3.5. On this relation in Plato see also McCabe (2017).
[18] See Section 3.12. Although I speak of a beautiful body and beautiful soul, it is worth noting that it is Charmides himself whom the text describes as beautiful in various respects, such as physical form (154d5) and qualities of soul (154e4). Neither soul nor body are directly described anywhere in the text as beautiful. Thus we seem encouraged, when it comes to persons at least, to regard *kalon* as a unified concept.

When Critias then tells Charmides, in accordance with the plot that Critias had hatched with Socrates, that it is Socrates who knows (*epistamenos*, 155c8) the remedy for Charmides' morning headache, Socrates narrates that Charmides looked at him in some unfathomable way and stirred so as to ask him a question, with everyone else pouring round them in a circle (155d1–3). He continues:

> It was then, noble one, that I saw the things inside his [Charmides'] cloak and I was aflame and was no longer in my own place and thought that Cydias was wisest in erotic matters for having said, when advising another on the subject of a beautiful boy, 'take care not to come as fawn before lion, and be seized as his portion of flesh'; for I thought that I had been caught by such a creature. (155d3-e2)

The scene contends in vividness of description with the pushing and shoving scene that immediately preceded it. But its tone is markedly different. While this is no doubt in part because of the different kind of reaction described in each case – pushing and shoving, as opposed to Socrates' becoming at the same time aroused and flustered – the substance is not so different. In both cases we are talking about the discombobulation that Charmides' proximity engenders. The key contrast is that in the first case, although Socrates nominally includes himself in the pushing and shoving, the focus is on the whole line of seated people. So we see it from the outside, as it were, and can therefore find it amusing.

In the second case, Socrates tells us what happens specifically to him and narrates it from the inside. We are thus drawn into occupying his position and feeling the discomfort that he felt. The narrative of first-person experience here reduces our distance from the scene and creates an identification with what Socrates undergoes. We could, I suppose, find his experience funny, but because of the way the scene is written, we don't. What, then, to make of the experience in the context of what seemed to be Socrates' ability to detach himself from the spatiotemporal world? What is fascinating about this moment is that it indicates Socratic self-recognition of a failure to occupy what he evidently takes to be his proprietary stance. His comment that 'I was no longer in my own place' (*ouket' en emautou ēn*, 155d4) tells us not only that he has been dislocated but that he is aware that he has been.

The text presents this dislocation as a brute fact. We need not doubt the sincerity of Socrates' previous assertive preference to seek for beauty in Charmides' soul rather than his body. Indeed, Socrates' awareness that Charmides, without even opening his mouth, has taken him away from the place of his own self, corroborates that preference. Such a phrase would have considerably less point were Charmides' physical attributes all or mainly what he was interested in (even if their effect on him may otherwise not have been that different). We have here, then, a further complex example of self-knowledge: Socrates' knowing what his own place is while (and partly because) he is at the same time aware that he is no longer occupying it.

In this regard Socrates' being at a loss when confronted with Charmides has an epistemic dimension. It is not just that Charmides' proximity, and the peek inside his cloak, dumbfounds Socrates; the effect is, further, that in a certain way Socrates doesn't understand his own reaction. The language of no longer being in his own place indicates that. In his awareness of being outside that place, he fails not certainly to experience, but rather to identify with, the strength of his erotic response to Charmides' body. Insofar as the response fails to align with his preference for investigating Charmides' soul,[19] eros is revealed, intensely if briefly, as a force not wholly subject to (his) rational control.

This does not mean that we should not see Socrates' drive to examine Charmides' soul as itself an erotic one. Given his interest in the beauty of the young, his co-option of the language of 'stripping' in relation to that soul, and that (as we learn at 167e) eros is regarded by Socrates as the proprietary psychological attitude towards what is beautiful, we should indeed read Socrates as erotically motivated at the prospect of the beauty to be found, as advertised by Critias, in Charmides' soul. What we will eventually see Socrates do, in attempting to recover from his confusion, is succeed in realigning his erotic drive with his own considered view of where the greater beauty is potentially to be found: in souls rather than bodies.

3.5 Eros, Looking and Talking

To put Socrates' approach to his recovery into context, let us get a little more to grips with his reasons for preferring to examine souls over bodies. One thing that dented Socrates' earlier confidence at the prospect of an 'easy conversation' (*rhadiōs autōi dialexomenos*, 155c7) with Charmides was

---

[19] As McCabe (2007a, 13) points out, Socrates does not say just what he saw inside Charmides' cloak, and if Charmides' soul is inside his body and 'inside' is transitive, then the text does not rule out that he glimpsed Charmides' soul. Socrates has, however, already connected inspecting Charmides' soul with having a conversation with him, and no conversation has yet taken place.

the 'unfathomable look' (*eneblepsen te moi* ... *amēchanon ti*, 155c8–d1) that Charmides shot him in anticipation of hearing from Socrates about the headache remedy. The juxtaposition of these two phrases highlights a more general pattern in the work. Two of the main ways in which the *Charmides* represents human engagement are, firstly, people looking at other people; and, secondly, people conversing with each other.

To take the second first, the dialogue's opening few pages alone feature:

- a conversation between Socrates and Chaerephon (153b4–c6)
- the mention, though not narration, of a series of conversations between Socrates and others (153c9–d1)
- a conversation between Socrates and Critias (154a3–b6)
- another brief exchange between Chaerephon and Socrates upon Charmides' entrance (154d1–5)
- further conversation between Socrates and Critias (154d7–155b8)
- the first conversation between Socrates and Charmides (155e2–157c6)

Interspersed with this conversing is a fair amount of looking:

- Critias looks towards the door and sees Charmides' retinue enter (153d5–154a1).
- Socrates focusses on the boys who in turn gaze at Charmides like a statue (154c6–8).
- Charmides looks at Socrates (155c8–d1).

Since, in the first and third of these latter cases, it is Socrates who reports first-hand, respectively, Critias looking towards the door and Charmides looking at him, Socrates must therefore also be looking at Critias and Charmides in the respective cases, as well as, explicitly, at the boys in the second case. Later on in the dialogue, when the proposed account of temperance as doing one's own things is causing puzzlement, Charmides looks at Critias teasingly (162b11) and Critias looks back at him angrily (162d2–4), with Socrates as first-hand reporter thereby necessarily looking at each.

What is the difference between these two forms of engagement? In the *Charmides* the principal one seems to be that whereas conversation is essentially two-way, looking is not. To approach this point, note that conversation is in turn a very particular subset of speech, its distinctiveness highlighted by consideration of a quite different, one-way form of speech. As pretext for getting Charmides over to talk to Socrates, Critias had instructed his slave as follows:

3.5 Eros, Looking and Talking

[C]all Charmides and tell him that I want to introduce him to a doctor regarding the ailment from which he was telling me lately that he suffers. (155b1–3)

The slave, one assumes, just goes and does what he is told; no reply from him is mentioned.[20] Critias simply resumes his conversation with Socrates, asking the latter: why not claim to know a remedy for the morning headache that Charmides has recently been waking up with (b3–6). Socrates agrees and Charmides soon comes over (b7–9).

Conversation is thus a distinct form of speech in that it is essentially interactive. The way in which looking stands in contrast with conversing in this regard has already, as we have seen, been strikingly conveyed at 154c. Here Socrates, focussing his own attention on Charmides' admirers, reports how not even the youngest 'was looking (*eblepen*) elsewhere, but they were all gazing (*etheōnto*) at him [Charmides] as if he were a statue' (154c7–8).[21] There is no indication that Charmides is looking back at them, as of course a statue could not. So this example in particular brings out the fact that if person x is looking at person y, that does not entail that person y is looking at person x.

If, on the other hand, x is having a conversation with y, then y is having a conversation with x.[22] Now the exchange of looks that we noted above between Charmides and Critias at 162b–d works, one might say, as a kind of visual conversation. But even here, Socrates reasonably surmises (162c6–7) that the purpose of Charmides' look is to get Critias to *talk*, as in fact he does, Critias' angry stare back at Charmides being the prelude to a brief rebuke of Charmides before, at Socrates' bidding, he picks up, in Charmides' place, the reins of conversation with Socrates.

---

[20] As we have seen, another example of one-way speech, at a different compositional level, is the narration by Socrates to his anonymous companion of the events of the *Charmides*.

[21] 'As if a statue' (*hōsper agalma*) is Socrates' choice of language for the way the others beheld Charmides, so it is not a straightforward matter to say just who is doing the near literal objectifying of Charmides here. There is also something ambivalent about the dehumanisation this implies: *agalma* being the standard Greek term for a statue of a god (see Tuozzo (2011), 107 with n. 12), Charmides in this guise is apparently rendered both more and less than human, but in either case unresponsive. Cf. also *Phaedrus* 251a5–7 and 252d6–e1 for *agalma* used more definitively to characterise the beloved as object of worship; and Alcibiades' use of *agalmata* at *Symposium* 222a4 to describe what is to be found in Socrates' words.

[22] One might in this context recall Heraclitus' mockery of those who 'pray to statues (*agalmasi*) as if one were conversing (*leschēneuoito*) with houses' (B5 DK; my thanks to Gábor Betegh for the reference). It is as unreasonable, suggests Heraclitus, to expect responsiveness in the first case as in the second, the point of the witticism being that of course there *would* be responsiveness in the standard case of conversing.

While looking and conversing do therefore mesh in the dialogue, they are also set up to contrast with one another. This combination is nowhere more evident than when Socrates insists that he would rather look at Charmides' soul than his body. The way he puts this, again, is as follows:

> Then why don't we strip this very [part] of him [sc. his soul] and look at (*etheasametha*) that before his [physical] form? For he is certainly, I presume, at his age now willing to have a conversation. (154e5–7)

Socrates here uses the same verb (*theaomai*) to envisage looking at Charmides' soul as he did to describe the onlookers gazing at Charmides like a statue a few lines earlier. The difference of course is that while a literal, visual, looking at Charmides requires no response from the latter (not even a glance back), for Socrates to look at Charmides' soul is said to involve Charmides taking part in conversation. There is, in outline, a parallel process envisaged in the case of both body and soul: the object in question is stripped and thereby exposed to view. But when the object is, as in Socrates' target case, a soul, conversation plays a central role in that process.

Later in the chapter, I shall analyse the working out of this process as applied to a soul (Charmides' soul in particular), and the role of conversation within it, in terms of the joint operation of the art of erotics and the art of soul-medicine.[23] For now, it is not hard to see in principle why looking at Charmides' soul might require Charmides' participating in conversation. While it only takes a functioning pair of eyes to be able to look at Charmides' body, Charmides' soul is not available for such immediate inspection. As we learn once the medical motif is in play, the patient must *offer* (*parechein*) their soul to be charmed (157b3–4, c3–4; cf. 176b6–7).[24]

Indeed, as Socrates goes on to spell out at 158e–159a (a text I examine further below),[25] it is only after Charmides has inspected his own soul and reported what he finds there that Socrates can go on to investigate whether Charmides has successfully identified what he has found. So while this procedure suggests that it is certainly not automatic that one correctly identify the contents of one's own soul – the person to whom one is reporting them may do a better job of that than one has oneself – looking at another's soul requires, nonetheless, that other's cooperation.[26] It is essentially a collaborative enterprise. Hence Socrates' proposal at 158d–e

---

[23] See Sections 3.7 and 3.8. [24] See Laín Entralgo (1970, 123–4). [25] Section 3.8.
[26] See Garver (2018, 476–7).

to work collaboratively (*koinēi*, d8; *meta sou*, e3) with Charmides to investigate whether the latter has temperance.

Looking at another's body might also require collaboration: Charmides has to be willing to strip, for example. But presumably Charmides could be forcibly stripped or, especially in the setting of a palaestra, be naked to start with. It is hard, despite Socrates' initial erotic assertiveness, to see an equivalent way forward in the case of getting to look at a soul. It seems plausible, rather, that Charmides will need to be persuaded to expose his soul by, as a first step, communicating what he thinks is in there. When he reports a belief of his about what is in his soul, he has already, to that extent, begun to expose it. That belief can then in turn be examined, by being connected with other things that Charmides is prepared, collaboratively, to assert or deny, in order to gain a fuller view of what is in his soul.

There is, in short, an active contribution required of Charmides in furtherance of Socrates' attempt to look at his soul. Hence there is a richer, because more interactive, engagement required for looking at his soul than looking at his body. The former kind of engagement, exemplified by conversation,[27] is two-way; the latter is a one-way activity that conceives of the other party as essentially passive – an object even (like a statue) rather than a person.[28] Conversation, by contrast, as I argued above,[29] both reflects and respects the distinctness of persons, since it essentially involves the sharing of perspectives acknowledged by the act of conversation as distinct.

The *Charmides* thus uses the concept of 'looking' to mark a difference between engagement with bodies and with souls. It does so in the 'statue' imagery that Socrates deploys and, as we have seen, in Socrates' very expression of his preference for looking at Charmides' soul rather than his body, which he associates with Charmides partaking in conversation. It therefore seems plausible to understand this preference in terms of the heightened, interactive, form of engagement that examination of a soul affords. Herein we can see a plausible and textually well-founded reason for Socrates' valuing of souls over bodies.

---

[27] One might say that it is possible to discern another's soul through critical reflection on that other's reports rather than direct conversation with them. While perhaps a rather artificial option when the opportunity for conversation with the subject is there, it is, I think, closer to Plato's model for how one should engage with the content of a written text such as the *Charmides*: see further Section 4.3.

[28] By contrast with his passive depiction as a statue, it is Charmides who actually initiates the conversation with Socrates (my thanks here to James Warren) by asking him if he knows the head-cure (155e2–3), though, as Moore (2015, 66) points out, there is a lack of real rapport between the pair until Socrates breaks the ice by making Charmides laugh at 156a3–4.

[29] Sections 2.2 and 3.3.

The theme of the relative value of souls and bodies continues in (and is a prominent feature of) the next phase of Socrates' encounter with Charmides. Recall that Critias had suggested, as a way of luring Charmides into conversation with Socrates, that the latter hold himself out to Charmides as a doctor with knowledge of a remedy for Charmides' morning headache. Socrates accedes to the plan, and Charmides duly comes over. After the resultant pushing and shoving, Charmides sits down between Socrates and Critias (155c4–5), at which point Socrates comments that his former confidence that conversing with Charmides would be easy withered, and he found himself at a loss. We left Socrates aroused and flustered at the sight of Charmides, the contents of the latter's cloak in particular.

What happens next shows how Socrates uses conversation to channel his own erotic desire away from Charmides' body and back to his soul. No longer 'in the place of myself', Socrates' self-possession almost, but not entirely, deserts him. Critias, he reports, tells Charmides that it is he, Socrates, who knows the remedy, and Charmides looks at Socrates 'with those eyes of his' and 'stirred so as to ask' him what the remedy is (155c8–d1). As if fearing he has lost any ability to converse with Charmides, Socrates at least manages to conduct a short conversation with himself, one that consists in telling himself that the lyric poet Cydias is wisest in erotic matters for having warned against becoming the prey of a beautiful young man, like a fawn before a lion (155d4–e1). This inner conversation, reliant on his recollection of another's words, means he is able, when Charmides does ask him if he knows the headache remedy, 'just about' (*mogis pōs*, 155e3) to squeeze out a reply in the affirmative.

Reasonably enough, Charmides then asks him what the remedy (*pharmakon*) is, and Socrates replies that it is a kind of leaf, but that its efficacy is wholly dependent on administering a 'charm' (*epōidē*) to go with it (155e3–8). Charmides asks to take the charm down in writing from Socrates, and the latter makes Charmides laugh by asking him if he will do so whether he persuades Socrates or not (156a1–4). Charmides replies the former, and when asked by Socrates if he has his name right, reveals that he has indeed heard of Socrates, who, he says, has 'no small reputation' among the youth of Charmides' age; in fact Charmides remembers him associating with Critias when Charmides was a boy (156a4–8).

Socrates responds 'you do beautifully' (*kalōs ge su ... poiōn*, 156a9) to remember and says he can now talk more frankly to Charmides about the charm. But a key move has already been made. As we noted earlier,[30]

---

[30] Section 2.2.

3.5 Eros, Looking and Talking

Socrates has deflected Charmides away from talk of writing. Orality prevails; conversation can continue. Socrates next recounts how good doctors say that one should not treat a sick part of the body without treating the whole body, and asks whether Charmides thinks it 'beautifully said' (*kalōs legesthai*, 156c8) and whether he accepts the account. When Charmides says he does 'absolutely' (c9), Socrates relates that he himself bucked up and gradually recovered his confidence (156d1–3). He then relays to Charmides a report he claims to have heard on campaign from a Thracian doctor about the need to treat the soul first before treating the body.

Socrates' journey from quivering wreck to fluent narrator thus occurs in the course of a conversation with Charmides, whose stages are carefully marked in the text.[31] The first stage, concluding in Charmides' showing, admiringly, that he is aware who Socrates is, reassures Socrates that Charmides is unlikely to object if he switches focus from Charmides' body to his soul by further engaging in conversation with him. The second stage – Charmides' assent to Socrates' initial description of holistic treatment – reinforces the first by showing Socrates that Charmides might be open to the extra move, represented by the upcoming Thracian narrative, that the soul be the first focus of treatment. With Charmides' assent that this initial description is of something beautifully said, we also see a hint that Charmides' soul may be amenable to being charmed by the 'beautiful words' (*kaloi logoi*) that the Thracian narrative will deem of primary importance.

It is, then, conversation with Charmides, prompted by Socrates' recollection of the wise words of Cydias, that allows Socrates to shift his own attention from Charmides' body to Charmides' soul.[32] Beauty of soul, unlike bodily beauty, is not immediately manifest and thus has less power to captivate instantly. No wonder that Socrates, pursuer of beauty that he is, was at first bewitched by the sight of that body. His progress from

---

[31] The importance of the role of conversation is unnecessarily occluded if, with Ayalon (2018, 184), we take as ironic Socrates' description of the difficulty that Charmides' appearance caused him.

[32] It seems to me not quite accurate to say, with McPherran (2004, 27), that Socrates recovers his poise 'by recalling the poem of Cydias', something which McPherran claims 'surreptitiously displays' the operation of the kind of poetic charm that he takes Socrates to have in mind. Though recalling Cydias' poem certainly sets Socrates up for recovery, it is through conversation with Charmides that recovery is achieved, as is clear from the fact that Socrates' two explicit markings of his recovery (156a9–b2, d1–3) each occur after a phase of that conversation, whereas in the immediate wake of his recollection of Cydias he does, as we have seen, no more than 'just about' manage a brief reply to Charmides. If it is by a charm that Socrates regains his poise, then it is through conversation that the charm is exercised.

bewitchment by to conversation with Charmides is a reflection of his prioritising of soul over body. But the conversation, less easy but perhaps therefore more significant than Socrates had thought, is itself what enables this prioritisation to be realised. Conversation is, thus far, revealed as the way in which Socrates positions himself to look at Charmides' soul through the very act of engaging with it. What remains is for him to induce Charmides to expose his soul, through further conversation, as potentially (but only potentially) a more compelling source of beauty than his body.

3.6 Temperance and the Turn to Medicine

Socrates moves his attempt at exposure forward via the tale of his encounter with a Thracian doctor that introduces temperance as an explicit theme of the dialogue. Once temperance is thematised, we can ask about Socrates' relation to it and whether, in particular, he is held out as an exemplar of temperance. Evidence includes not just his reaction to the battle but his response to Charmides' bodily beauty. His ability to recover his cool and control his eros does seem impressive,[33] even if one might (as with his response to the battle) find something disconcerting about the level of control displayed. Nonetheless, the radical nature of the Socratic perspective means it is hard not to be provoked by it into thinking about ways of being that we may not have previously considered. We are invited to be neither dismissive nor adulatory, but critical and curious.

In this spirit, and to frame our discussion of the Thracian narrative, let me press a little harder on the question of Socrates' relation to temperance. However we evaluate it, it may at first sight seem natural to describe, as I have done, his behaviour as something like the exercise of self-control or self-restraint. But this description misses something important about the way in which Socrates apparently conceives of his own behaviour. He does not say that he *restrains* himself. In effect, as we have seen, he *reoccupies* his place after experiencing a brief but intense dislocation. The reoccupation consists in a redirection of attention, from Charmides' body to Charmides' soul, through conversation. Socrates' erotic drive is correspondingly not held back but redirected.

The persistence of Socrates' eros – the continuation of his quest to expose Charmides' soul – thus indicates that the relation between his

---

[33] Francalanci (2020, 92) takes it as read that Socrates' response to Charmides is there 'to present Socrates in the full exercise of temperance'.

3.6 Temperance and the Turn to Medicine

behaviour and temperance conceived of as self-control or self-restraint is not a straightforward one, since the restraining of Socrates' eros is not exactly what is described here. That Socrates proceeds by redirecting rather than restraining his erotic drive may suggest, on the other hand, a closer connection between temperance and eros than one might have suspected.

The nature of this connection can be more fully spelled out once we have carried through our analysis of how Socrates' erotic pursuit plays out across the dialogue.[34] However, progress can be made by looking in more detail at the account Socrates gives, his self-possession recovered, of what he (supposedly) heard on campaign, from a Thracian doctor of King Zalmoxis, about the right way to do medicine (156d–157c). Consideration of this tale will provide a basis for understanding the terms on which Socrates continues his erotic pursuit through investigation of whether there is temperance in Charmides' soul.

Socrates leads into the account by asking Charmides, at 156b–c, if he has heard 'the good doctors' say that one cannot treat a part of the body without treating the whole body. Charmides replies 'very much so' and agrees that it is 'beautifully said' (156c7–9), indicating that so far this is meant to capture approvingly a reasonably familiar and local approach to practising medicine.[35] But Socrates moves on to report how the Thracian doctor told him that while the Greek doctors' holism is fine as far as it goes (156d6–7), it does not go far enough. Zalmoxis the Thracian king lays it down that:

> [J]ust as one must not try to treat eyes without [treating the] head, nor head without body, so neither [must one try to treat] body without soul, but this was also the reason why the majority of diseases (*ta polla nosēmata*)[36] elude the doctors among the Greeks, in that they neglect the whole,[37] which one must take care of, since if it is not in beautiful shape it is impossible for the part to fare well. For he said that all things both bad and good for the body and the whole person originate in the soul and flow from there just as from the head to the eyes. (156e1–157a1)

---

[34] See Section 3.12.
[35] On evidence for holism in the Hippocratic tradition, see Tuozzo (2011, 113–14); Moore and Raymond (2019, 46–8).
[36] Not 'many diseases', as Coolidge (1993, 26) renders the phrase at 156e4 (so too Pichanick (2016, 53); West and West (1986, 19)), enabling him to make more than is warranted out of the Thracian apparently allowing some success to the Greek doctors despite their failure to consider the soul.
[37] I tentatively retain here (156e4) Burnet's OCT reading (based in part on Stobaeus) *tou holou ameloien*, against the main MSS reading *ton holon agnooien* ('fail to recognise the whole'). The OCT reading, complains van der Ben (1985, 15 n. 13), 'is highly tautological' given the relative clause (*hou dei tēn epimeleian poieisthai*, 'which one must take care of', 156e5) that immediately follows. But such fullness of style strikes me as highly Platonic and the 'tautology' is surely the point: the Greek doctors neglect that which they should not neglect.

Just how 'the whole' is to be understood here is a matter of controversy.[38] Given the analogy with the head–eye relation, one apparent implication is that the soul itself is to be taken as the relevant whole in Zalmoxian medicine, of which the body is part. This unorthodox metaphysics can, I think, stand as part of an avowedly unorthodox (from a Greek perspective) theory.[39] Perhaps the strangeness can be mitigated if we acknowledge that there is no obvious Greek term for that of which both soul and body are parts.[40] Yet Socrates does supply a phrase, 'the whole person' (*panti tōi anthrōpōi*, 156e7–8), to refer to an entity featuring alongside the body as one whose every good and bad thing flows from the soul. Socrates' descriptions thus seem to muddy the waters about how exactly the body figures in the story. It will turn out, in line with this carelessness, that Socrates' co-option of the Thracian approach envisages care for the body as being of little or no significance.[41]

Greek medicine, according to the Thracian, falls short because all bad and good things for the body and for the whole person flow from the soul (e6–8). Hence one must, as the Greek doctors do not, care for the soul 'first and above all' if the body is to be in beautiful shape (157a1–3).[42] This care consists in certain 'charms' that comprise beautiful words which bring about temperance in souls (157a3–6). Once temperance is there it is easy to procure health for the body (a6–b1). Socrates adds that the Thracian taught him both the bodily remedy and the charms; but enjoined him, under oath, not to apply the remedy until the patient had first provided their soul to be charmed (157b1–4). Charmides is thus set up to receive the Socratic treatment.

Some scholars have doubted that the upcoming examination of Charmides, in the wake of the Thracian narrative, is part of the administration of the charm.[43] For the examination, as we shall see, is to discover *whether* Charmides has temperance, whereas the charm is to be administered to one who does not have it.[44] Certainly, the dialogue's final section

---

[38] For recent discussion see Tuozzo (2011, 119–23); Tsouna (2022, 87–90).
[39] Cf. Levine (2016, 67).   [40] My thanks here to an anonymous reader.   [41] See Section 3.8.
[42] Tuozzo (2011, 125; 332) treats this passage as if it allowed only two readings: either the good condition of the soul brings about physical health (and other goods) or it is a necessary condition for physical health (and other things) to be good. But the most natural reading of the text is simply that the good condition of the soul is by far the most important requirement for physical health (and other goods) to obtain. The metaphor of 'flowing' implies that all (other) good things originate in the soul's being in good condition, but not that the soul is the only determinant of their being good.
[43] See e.g. Szlezák (1985, 143); McPherran (2004).
[44] It at least seems fair to say that any charm that is applied fails to take hold of Charmides in Socrates' examination of him: he does not express enthusiasm for being charmed by Socrates until after the investigation of temperance with Critias. See further Sections 3.7, 3.11 and 5.8.

3.6 Temperance and the Turn to Medicine

has Charmides opine that he is very much in need of the charm (176b2), which may imply that, as far as he is concerned, he has not yet received it. Even so, this does not mean that the examination of Charmides should not be construed as tracking a medical model of some kind. For the investigation of a patient's condition is a natural, even essential, prelude to a decision about whether, and if so what, treatment is necessary.

In his deployment of the 'charm' terminology one may also see a further implication for the status of writing in relation to Socrates' upcoming examination of Charmides. Recall that Socrates had teased Charmides, when the latter proposed to write the charm down, by asking him if he would do so whether he persuaded Socrates or not (156a1–3). It seems that in Socratic hands it is doubtful that the charm is even the sort of thing that can be written down. Socrates varies in his usage between the singular 'charm' and the plural 'charms'. The singular is used at 155e5 (cf. 156b1) when the charm is introduced, as it were innocently by Socrates, and the question of writing it down raised by Charmides, prior to the Thracian narrative. Its first mentions within that narrative, however, are in the plural (157a4 (twice) and 157b1–2), reported by Socrates in indirect speech and in his own name respectively. There is a return to the singular when Socrates purports to quote the Thracian directly (157b4); then back to plural when Socrates, in the wake of the narrative, addresses Charmides at 157c4; and plural again at 158b7–8, with Critias interposing a reference to it in the singular at 157d3.

Once the Thracian narrative unfurls, then, Socrates shows a preference, when not quoting the Thracian directly, for the plural 'charms': an indication that, contrary to Charmides' initial supposition, delivery may consist not in a one-off episode with predetermined content (singular) but a more open-ended process (plural) lacking, as in any conversation, fully determinate content that could be written down in advance. Charmides' own affirmation at the end of the dialogue, that he is free to be charmed by Socrates for as many days as Socrates deems sufficient (176b2–4), shows that, at least by then, he has some inkling of this, despite the reintroduction of the charm in the singular by Socrates at 175e3.

On this basis, we expect Socrates' examination of Charmides to be conducted through conversation, while drawing on a medical model of some kind. Once the Thracian narrative has presented the instilling of temperance in the soul as the purpose of the charm, it thus brings into focus the following question: what is the relation between its medical model for engaging with a soul and the erotic model based on conversation that was Socrates' starting point for engaging with Charmides' soul?

Shedding light on this question ought also to help illuminate the dialogue's view on how temperance and eros are related.

We know that the narrative arises from the plot dreamed up by Critias, in which Socrates is to present himself as a doctor with knowledge of a remedy for headache, in order to get Charmides to come and talk to Socrates. And we know also that this plot is concocted by Critias, and acceded to by Socrates, in response to Socrates' desire to strip and view, through conversation, Charmides' soul, its beauty and goodness having been touted by Critias, who perhaps therefore feels some responsibility to help Socrates fulfil his desire.

Given the way things have been set up, what Socrates subsequently tells Charmides, via the Thracian narrative, about the need to treat the soul prior to treating the body, must be in service of that desire. In short, the medical model is at root a device to serve Socrates' erotic design. So we can refine the new question a little: what is the relation of this model to the erotic model, given that we know that the former is developed in service of the latter?[45]

It is worth noting that the subordination relation between the two models would obtain even if Socrates had been an actual (medical) doctor, approving from his position of medical expertise the Thracian way of practising medicine. If, in that counterfactual scenario, instead of saying 'Socrates, we can get Charmides over if you claim to know a remedy', Critias had said, 'Socrates, we can get Charmides over since you as a doctor know a remedy', then it would *still* be the case that the medical model set out in the Thracian narrative, for all its enhanced scientific credentials (in the counterfactual situation) of approval by an actual doctor, remained in service of the erotic.

That is because the basic logic is the same: Critias would just have thought up a different way, drawing this time on genuine Socratic medical expertise, to enable the fulfilment of Socrates' desire. What we make of Critias' moral standing as one who, in the actual world within the drama, so readily countenances the use of pretence regarding his co-conspirator's status is a further question (no doubt connected to the foreshadowing of the historical Critias' later political misadventures). But it does not change the basic character of the relationship between the medical and the erotic – the former subordinate to the latter – in this context.

---

[45] On the presence of these two models in the *Charmides*, see Moore and Raymond (2019, 45–6). While Moore and Raymond contrast these models with the working of Socratic conversation, on my reading it is these models, suitably repurposed and with the medical subordinated to the erotic, that serve to structure Socrates' conversation in the dialogue.

3.6 Temperance and the Turn to Medicine

What Socrates' actual status does is cast a certain scepticism over the credibility of the Thracian narrative as a piece of medical theory. For who is Socrates, not being a medical doctor, to judge its credentials as a way of doing medicine? It is surely experts in a field who are in a proper position to judge what counts as expertise in that field, something Socrates himself seems later to suggest at 171c4–9.[46] So Socrates has, in this regard, the wrong epistemic relation to the narrative he delivers. At the same time, Socrates' status as a non-doctor makes it unlikely that he has any particular interest in actually treating Charmides' body.

This is not to say that Socrates is necessarily being insincere in his relating of the narrative. We are not forced to decide whether Socrates is improvising a tale of a meeting, rather than reporting it as something that he takes to have actually happened. But the former seems the more likely option given that, in light of the role he has, at Critias' suggestion, committed himself to playing, Socrates needs to say something on the hoof about medicine.[47]

Indeed, Socrates' own praise of body holism as being a practice of 'the good doctors' (156b5) indicates that he himself does not take the Thracian narrative too seriously as a thesis about how to practise medicine. Despite the Thracian doctor saying that the Greek advocacy of body holism is fine as far as it goes (156d6–7), it is hard to see how the attribution of a practice which, in the Thracian view, leads even such holism to miss most diseases, could leave Socrates, if he did consider the Thracian narrative as a genuine contribution to medicine, sanguine about calling the body holists 'the good' doctors. They can be considered good only if one thinks, from the medical point of view, that to cover most diseases this holism needs no radical extension, available elsewhere, beyond the body.

Now even supposing, for the sake of argument, that we are to take Socrates' report, by happy coincidence for his purposes, as in fact relaying a convenient medical narrative he heard from a Thracian doctor about putting the soul first, the epistemic point remains: taken as testimony, rather than storytelling, it would still be testimony about a field – medicine – in

---

[46] Socrates does not explicitly say in that passage that it is only experts in a field who can judge expertise in that field; his train of thought is that experts in a given field cannot judge expertise in a different field (but only their own). But if that is right, then it seems to follow that the non-expert with respect to a field is not in a proper position to judge expertise in that field.
[47] Cf. Coolidge (1993, 28 n. 8). The seemingly gratuitous inclusion by Socrates at 158b7–8 of the fabled healer Abaris the Hyperborean, with whose representatives Socrates makes no claim to have conversed, as one whose charms, together with those of Zalmoxis, Charmides will have no need of should he possess temperance, reinforces this picture; see Murphy (2000, 293).

which Socrates does not have expertise. As a piece of medical theory, therefore, its content as transmitted by a non-expert is not to be taken on trust either by Charmides or by us readers.

The epistemic problem with the narrative, combined with its being delivered in service of Socrates' desire to look at Charmides' soul, as opposed to his body, encourages the idea that what both Charmides and Plato's readers are supposed to take as the purport of the narrative is not a straightforward *medical* thesis at all. The message it intends to convey, albeit in the language of medicine, is not about the best way of treating the body, but about the priority one should give to the soul. As a result, we can refine our question further: we now need to capture the relationship between the kind of engagement with the soul implied by the narrative so understood, and the fulfilment of Socrates' erotic purpose in regard to Charmides' soul.

To delineate this relationship, let us consider the following objection to the idea that the body is not ultimately supposed to be of relevance in Socrates' use of the Thracian narrative: Charmides would surely expect Socrates, given what he has been led to believe, to offer advice about the treatment of his headache. So for the narrative to be efficacious it must be intended, at least in relation to Charmides, to make a point about treating the body.

The objection misses what we already know Charmides knows about Socrates. At 156a6–8 Charmides had told Socrates that the latter has no small reputation among Charmides' contemporaries and that he remembers, even from his boyhood, Socrates associating with Critias. So Charmides has a reasonably solid epistemic relation to Socrates and is therefore not in a position where Socrates could easily deceive him.

To put the point more bluntly: Charmides is well aware that Socrates is not a doctor.[48] No wonder Socrates is so relieved (156a9–b2), having made sure that Charmides has his name right (156a5–6) – that is to say, knows who he is – to hear of Charmides' acquaintance with both his reputation and, as a boy, with him. Charmides will not then be expected to hear the Thracian narrative as an expert valuation of a medical thesis, but as what it is: an attempt to get Charmides to expose his soul.

We have to be a bit careful here, however, particularly with the principle of agnosticism in mind. How clear is it from within the dialogue that Socrates is not a doctor, so that his medical prowess could after all be the source of his reputation (and part of Charmides' boyhood memories)?

---

[48] Cf. Zuckert (2009, 240 n. 47).

3.6 Temperance and the Turn to Medicine

Invoking Socrates' preference for souls over bodies risks question-begging, since the issue is, in relation to the Thracian narrative, precisely what the narrative should be taken to imply in terms of Socrates' interest in the body.

Fortunately, there are various clues within the dialogue to indicate that Socrates is not to be taken as a doctor. Let me pick out two. First is the way Critias talks of Socrates' relation to medicine. Now Critias does not say in so many words that the plan is that Socrates *pretend* to be a doctor (which would obviously mean he was not one). He tells his slave to tell Charmides that he wants to introduce him to a doctor (155b1–2), and then turns to Socrates to ask why not claim (*prospoiēsasthai*) to Charmides that you know a remedy for the latter's headache (b5–6).

The word for 'claim' can mean 'pretend' but it need not. This can be seen from the later, surely non-accidental, example that Socrates gives when illustrating some problems with the idea of temperance as knowledge of knowledge: he speaks at 170e1 of someone 'claiming (*prospoioumenon*) to be a doctor, while not being one'. If *prospoioumai* just meant 'pretend' then 'while not being one' would be redundant. So when Critias encourages Socrates to 'claim' to know a remedy, he is not strictly implying that Socrates lacks the appropriate knowledge. Nonetheless, it seems to me that Critias' wording, even taken this way, allows us to rule out with confidence Socrates' being a doctor. For if he were a doctor, Critias could straightforwardly have encouraged him to engage Charmides' interest by way of his knowledge of the body. There would be no need to talk of *claiming* to know; insofar as he were a doctor, he *would* know.

The second clue comes from Socrates' own mouth. Asked by Socrates to indicate whether he needs the charm, by saying whether or not he has temperance in his soul, Charmides replies that he does not know what to say. So Socrates proposes:

> [W]e should investigate (*skepteon*) jointly whether you do or do not possess the thing I am asking about, so that you are not forced to say what you do not wish to, nor I for my part turn to medicine in an ill-considered way.[49]
> (158d8–e2)

---

[49] *askeptōs epi tēn iatrikēn trepōmai*. The term *askeptōs*, sandwiched between uses of 'investigate' (*skepteon* at 158d8; then *skopein* at e3: Socrates will 'investigate' with Charmides only if the latter would like it), has a punning effect. Socrates implies that one should practise medicine only with proper consideration, a thought that perhaps encompasses the idea both that medicine is itself investigatory and that its potential practitioner needs to examine his own grasp of its methods and techniques.

Now it seems perfectly proper, on good medical grounds, for a doctor not to compel a patient to say what they do not wish to: the doctor, it might be argued, will only get good quality information from the patient about the latter's condition if it is given freely rather than under duress. But a real doctor does not, I think, talk in such circumstances about the danger of an ill-considered 'turning' to medicine. That talk fits someone who is trying their hand or improvising; it would come oddly from one whose actual profession were that of medicine.

So Socrates is not a doctor, and we have no reason to think that Charmides thinks he is. We should not therefore suppose that the Thracian narrative, as a medical thesis, is to be taken at face value. Socrates has a different use for it in mind. Nonetheless, Socrates' talk of his turning to medicine does invite us to consider what exactly he *is* turning his hand to. It seems unlikely that he would consider jumping into Thracian medicine, read literally, without having undergone prior medical training. After all, Thracian doctors are still doctors. True, Socrates tells us that the Thracian taught him the remedy and the charm (157b1–2), but that would seem to fall a long way short of qualifying him as a doctor. As a would-be practitioner of Thracian medicine, particularly one keen to avoid an ill-considered approach, Socrates would need to have a medical professional's knowledge of the body, as well as requisite experience;[50] and that, as we have seen, there is no evidence he possesses.

Even by the narrative's own terms, Socrates does not say that the encounter with the Thracian made him a doctor. The plan he outlines is the more modest one of turning to medicine without making a mess of it. By the same token, however, we need to do something with all these references to medicine. What are they for if not to suggest that an enterprise at least related to medicine is being proposed? The fictionality of the *Charmides* supports this point. It is all very well to acknowledge that in actual oral conversation Socrates might have teasingly spoken of Thracian medicine to pique Charmides' interest, in service of a purpose unconnected to medicine: just some fancy line to pull him in. But since it forms part of a carefully constructed drama, one must, I think, make something more substantial than this of the striking presence of the medical motif.

---

[50] Notwithstanding that, according to the Thracian, procuring of health for the body is 'easy' once there is temperance in the patient's soul (157a6–b1). The Thracian does not say it is automatic. On the historical importance given to training in the ancient Greek conception of the medical practitioner, see Dean-Jones (2003).

3.6 Temperance and the Turn to Medicine

Here, then, is a proposal. Begin with the thought that, on a strict and literal reading, the medicine presented in the Thracian narrative is still medicine: its ultimate aim is to facilitate bodily health (157a1–b1). Thracian medicine is not a different *field* from medicine (or from 'Greek' medicine on Socrates' account of it); it is a distinctive thesis about how that field should be practised to get best results.[51] Contrast this with a distinct field – call it 'soul-medicine' – whose purpose is to treat the soul, as medicine's purpose is to treat the body; and call a practitioner of soul-medicine a 'soul-doctor'.[52]

Now as a matter of historical record Greek medicine did regard the soul as well as the body as being within its ambit.[53] So there is something stipulative in my excluding soul-medicine (as I characterise it) from the scope of medicine proper. However, a substantive distinction underlies the stipulation, namely that between a practice that has the well-being of the body as its internal goal, as seems to be the case with what is described in the Thracian narrative (albeit that there the treatment of the soul becomes essential for achieving that goal), and a practice that has the well-being of the soul as its internal goal, which, I argue, is in fact the practice in which Socrates takes himself to be engaged.

In this sense soul-medicine, since it aims to treat not bodies but souls, is not medicine (nor a branch of medicine) but a relative of medicine.[54] My suggestion is that the prominence of the medical model is there to indicate that Socrates may properly lay claim to a field akin to that of medicine. Insofar as soul-medicine has the well-being of the soul as its specific internal goal, Socrates may be its only practitioner. The less than well-developed state of the field would explain, without our needing to regard him as the Thracian's apprentice, why Socrates talks of his 'turning' to medicine in that tentative way.

It may also explain why Critias is no worse than equivocal in describing Socrates' relation to medicine as something for Socrates to claim rather

---

[51] Hence the Thracian insistence, at the climax of Socrates' report (157b5–7), that the great human mistake is to separate off temperance from health in the attempt to practise medicine. (The phrase *sōphrosunēs te kai hugieias* at b6 has been deleted as a gloss by some scholars but is in the main MSS.)
[52] Cf. Tuozzo (2019, 31), who, however, seems to me mistaken to treat this as meaning that 'Socrates does not approach the boy as a lover'. As I shall argue further below, the latter approach represents Socrates' primary orientation towards Charmides, with his practice of soul-medicine in service of his erotic pursuit.
[53] See e.g. Frede (1987, 227–8); Hankinson (1991, 200–7).
[54] Roochnik (1996, 108) claims that '[b]ecause Socrates *pretends* to be a physician, it is fair to infer that ... he in fact does not have the psychotherapeutic technē' (his emphasis). But even allowing that Socrates merely pretends, the inference only follows if the 'psychotherapeutic technē' is a branch of medicine.

than outright pretend. Soul-medicine is parallel as a field to medicine, but distinct from it – and, as Socrates would presumably hold, given the way he values souls over bodies, more than deserving of its own field. As we shall see below,[55] though it is a distinct field, both the parallelism of soul-medicine, and its debt, to medicine proper is secured by the former's repurposing of some key procedures and techniques of the latter.

3.7 Practical Knowledge

The equivocation on Critias' part may even indicate that this long-time associate of Socrates (as Charmides had revealed) sets Socrates up as a 'doctor' with something like the view of him as soul-doctor in mind. We saw in Section 2.2 that the opening pages of the *Charmides* contain an array of words for, or connected with, knowing, in particular knowing facts (e.g. about battles) and knowing people (e.g. Charmides). But the knowledge-verb that Critias uses (*epistasthai*, 155b6) when he suggests that Socrates set up as a doctor and claim to know a remedy for Charmides' headache is the first occurrence of that particular term in the work. Its substantive correlate *epistēmē* ('knowledge') will be the key term used, in the later discussion of temperance as self-knowledge and knowledge of knowledge, to represent a *branch* or *field* of knowledge.

The term collects the idea of knowledge as something practical: one who has *epistēmē* – in the sense of one who has expertise in a particular field – does not simply know *that* such-and-such is the case, but also *how* to do something (thus we are invited to consider whether temperance itself may be construed as practical in this way),[56] though such knowledge may of course in part be based on knowing that certain things are the case.[57]

One can see the practical aspect brought out explicitly, from a grammatical point of view, the very next time the verb occurs in the dialogue, in Socrates' upcoming description of (what I shall argue is) his suggested application of soul-medicine to the problem of discovering whether or not Charmides has temperance. In the course of that description, Socrates tells Charmides that the latter will be able to report his impression of what

---

[55] Esp. Section 3.8.   [56] Cf. Wellman (1964, 110).

[57] The relation between knowing-how and knowing-that is much discussed in contemporary philosophical literature. A recent collection is Bengson and Moffett (2011). I do not commit the *Charmides* to any overly determinate account of the relation, except to stress that the text's interest in practical fields such as medicine makes it plausible that knowing-how plays a significant conceptual role in the dialogue.

temperance is 'since you know how to speak Greek' (*epeidēper hellēnizein epistasai*, 159a6–7).

This conspicuous example of the 'practical' sense provides a signal that, whether it is medicine or soul-medicine at issue, we are talking about knowledge as practical. The doctor is, as such, a skilled professional who does not just know things (theories, information, and so on) but also, and essentially, knows *how* to do something, namely treat bodies. Soul-medicine, as a branch of knowledge parallel to medicine, will be of the same type, except that its practitioners know how to treat souls. A doctor has knowledge of bodily health, in virtue of which she knows how to heal bodies, while a soul-doctor has knowledge of the good condition of the soul – temperance as it may be – in virtue of which she is able to treat the soul, even if we accept that, in the case of a pioneering soul-doctor such as Socrates, as with any pioneer in a field, his own grasp may be impressive yet rudimentary.

Its typology now sketched, how in more detail does soul-medicine work? Here, as we would expect, the Thracian narrative provides some resources. It works – that is, it treats the soul – by means of certain 'charms' that are beautiful words; from such words, temperance comes about in souls (157a3–6). Now the repeated upcoming descriptions of temperance as beautiful imply that, in making the soul temperate, soul-medicine makes it beautiful. And perhaps, on a like-causes-like principle (one which becomes more explicit later),[58] this is just the result one would expect from the application of beautiful words to a soul.

On the other hand, the formulation does not indicate the speaker of the beautiful words. Presumably, at least in part, they are words of the practitioner. But the text leaves it open that the patient also may contribute to their own treatment. We shall see later, in the case of Charmides, that the process of diagnosis, that is, the ascertainment of whether the patient needs treatment, importantly requires input from the patient. But it is natural and, I think, given our earlier discussion of the role of conversation,[59] correct to suppose that treatment by the soul-doctor also consists not in monologue by the latter but in engagement in conversation between practitioner and patient.

The Thracian narrative also prompts us to ask after the condition of the soul of one who has been successfully treated. Since we are told that temperance is created in the soul 'from' (*ek*, 157a5) beautiful words, we may suppose that temperance in a soul comes about not just as a *result* of

---

[58] See Section 3.9.   [59] Section 3.5.

beautiful words, but is made *out of*, or consists in, beautiful words. This need not imply a static model of the temperate person's condition, whereby one in that condition just possesses, say, a fixed amount of propositional information. Rather, such a person might be temperate in a more dynamic way, in virtue of their having developed, through conversational engagement with the soul-doctor, their own conversational resources.

If we consider how Socratic conversation is presented in the *Charmides*, then it seems likely that such resources will be constituted at least in part by a power of critical and reflective engagement with the kind of fundamental questions that pertain to the soul and that form core elements of discussion as we find it in the dialogue: those that concern, for example, the soul's value and its relation to the body, the nature of the qualities that make it beautiful and good, and so on. And from this, one might hypothesise that temperance itself will be importantly connected to the power to sustain critical focus on such questions.

I shall try, in Section 3.12, to substantiate that hypothesis. But with the framework we have established so far, we can start to present a more determinate picture of the relation between soul-medicine on the one hand and Socrates' erotic pursuit on the other. To do this, we must first reiterate an essential point: the relation between soul-medicine and the erotic will (in the Socratic case) be one of subordination, the former to the latter. That is because, however one interprets the import of the Thracian narrative, it is there, in terms of the dramatic sequence, to serve Socrates' goal of getting to look at a beautiful soul. From this, it is clear in outline how soul-medicine will serve the erotic goal: soul-medicine, if successful, brings a soul to a beautiful condition. And a soul in that condition is just the sort of soul with which Socrates is desirous of engaging.

Now at that point – the achievement of such a condition – the work of soul-medicine is surely done. In terms of demarcation of the field, it is no more part of the work of the soul-doctor to engage with a soul once it is made beautiful than it is the work of a doctor to engage with a body once it is made healthy – let alone for erotic purposes, though the moral connotations of this should not cloud the more basic typological point that when the body (or soul) is healed, the work of the doctor (or soul-doctor) is over.[60] But this then leaves a gap in terms of Socrates' erotic quest: once

---

[60] One might wonder about a role for preventative medicine: but the dialogue's model, as exemplified both by Charmides' headache and by the Thracian narrative, seems to be of medicine as primarily restorative.

3.7 Practical Knowledge

the beautiful soul is there, made so, as it may be, through the art of soul-medicine, how is one, in the service of one's desire for beauty, to get that soul to (continue to) engage? We need a further, different art. So I propose invoking what seems the right art, given the purpose for which it is needed: the art of erotics.

Such an art does seem available, its existence hinted at by Socrates himself. As we saw above, when he is at a loss as to how to converse with Charmides, he recalls the words of Cydias, whom he says he regarded then as 'wisest in erotic matters' (*sophōtaton ta erōtika*, 155d4–5). If the erotic is a field in which one can be wise, then it seems we can legitimately speak of an art of erotics. What is more, it seems likely that, in taking himself to recognise proficiency in such an art, Socrates takes himself to be proficient in it too. And that is because, as we have seen, he considers the ability to distinguish those who have proficiency in a given field to be a mark of practitioners in that field (171c4–9).

Socrates' willingness to acknowledge Cydias' wisdom in erotics suggests, then, that he may be claiming a similar wisdom for himself.[61] One may note by contrast that, for all his complimentary attitude towards them, Socrates does not explicitly attribute either knowledge or wisdom to the Thracian doctors, implying perhaps a relative lack of confidence in his own level of accomplishment in that arena. The fact that mention of wisdom in erotics comes up precisely at a moment of crisis in Socrates' attempt to get Charmides to talk to him further suggests that a principal goal of the erotic art is to gain and maintain access to souls that are or can be made beautiful – for the sake of others than the practitioner perhaps,[62] or, in the case of Socrates in regard to Charmides' soul, for the practitioner himself.

How, then, does the practitioner of the art of erotics achieve this goal? The answer seems to be illustrated right before us: by talking. One might have said, more specifically, by conversing with the object of one's desire. But as we shall see later, in terms of what I take to be Socrates' practice of

---

[61] An anonymous reader wonders whether, in attributing wisdom in erotics to Cydias, Socrates may just 'be half-jokingly pretending to take inspiration from a poet'. Although Cydias' work is unknown outside this passage, the immediate context, with Socrates to all appearances having been genuinely thrown off course by Charmides' bodily beauty (155c5–d4), suggests that his attribution of wisdom in erotics to Cydias is in earnest.

[62] Cf. *Lysis* 204b5–c2, 204e10–205a2. Socrates speaks with apparent authority in that work of what one does who is 'wise in erotics' (*ta erōtika* ... *sophos*, 206a1); and he tells us that he has been giving instruction to Hippothales, who is besotted with Lysis, in how to converse (*dialegesthai*, 210e3) with one's beloved. It is noteworthy, however, that in the *Lysis* Socrates does not single out the soul of one's beloved as object of erotic quest, while in the *Charmides*, in relation to his own quest, that specification is in play.

the art in the *Charmides*, this does not cover everything he does. At any rate, Socrates' momentary loss of ability to engage Charmides in conversation is, as we have seen, overcome initially by means of an internal pep talk drawing on the thoughts of his fellow practitioner Cydias. But then, by conversing with Charmides and, in particular, gaining confidence from the latter's replies that there is some sort of shared outlook between them, he is able to unveil the Thracian narrative. This in turn enables him to work towards the moment when Charmides undertakes officially to reveal the contents of his soul, by attempting to report whether he finds temperance therein.

I shall turn shortly to this development. But let me first take stock of where we are in delineating the relation between the Thracian narrative, with its central medical motif, and Socrates' erotic pursuit. I have argued that one can see this relation in terms of Socrates' deployment of two fields of expertise: erotics and soul-medicine. The goal of the latter is to get a soul into beautiful condition, given a diagnosis from the soul-doctor that the soul in question is deficient in that regard; the goal of the former, insofar as souls are within its purview, is to get access to a soul that is actually or prospectively beautiful.[63] Erotics, then, like soul-medicine, is practical. Clearly, however, the latter is able to serve the former, and not the other way round, since the successful achievement of the latter's goal is to produce the kind of soul (a beautiful one) continuing access to which it is then the task of the former to secure. This structure of subordination in turn maps onto the express purpose of the deployment of the Thracian narrative, as an outcrop of Socrates' plotting with Critias: to engage Charmides in such a way that he will reveal his (putatively beautiful) soul for Socrates to inspect.

Note that the subordination relation does not imply a specific chronological relation in the operation of the two arts. Socrates uses the Thracian narrative as a way to get Charmides to agree to expose his soul, beautiful as it has been touted to be. Thus, in context, the narrative itself is an example of the practice of erotics. However, the exposure does not subsequently provide evidence to Socrates, in the guise now of soul-doctor attempting to diagnose whether temperance is in that soul, that Charmides has a temperate (hence beautiful) soul. For Charmides is unable in discussion to

---

[63] Whatever the precise relation between the two arts, I take it that the positing of a connection, in the context of the Thracian narrative, is further licensed by a background, that the reader is no doubt supposed to have in mind, of connectedness in Greek culture between erotic and medical uses of the 'charm–remedy' combination; see Petre (2007, 53–4). On Hippocratic scepticism about the use of charms in medicine, see Tuozzo (2001, 325 n. 12).

show that what he takes to be in his soul is in fact temperance. Moreover, before the possibility of treatment can properly arise, Charmides withdraws his soul from exposure by deflecting to an account of temperance he heard elsewhere. From that point, Socrates is in the business of further deploying the art of erotics to entice Charmides into exposing his soul once more. The display of intellectual fireworks in the discussion with Critias does produce a Charmides who shows himself more than willing to do that, but there the *Charmides* ends.

What would come next, assuming that Charmides does not yet have a sufficiently temperate (and so beautiful) soul, would be the application of soul-medicine by Socrates to instil temperance. After that, one may need further application of the art of erotics to keep the newly beautiful (in soul) Charmides associating with Socrates. Erotics is the governing art in the *Charmides*, but it can precede the application of soul-medicine, to entice the object of one's desire into exposure of their soul, which, if it proves insufficiently beautiful, will then need treatment from soul-medicine; or it can succeed the application of soul-medicine, to retain one's object of desire once their soul is made beautiful.

What individuates the two arts in question is their distinct goals: exposure of a soul for the purpose of satisfying one's desire for beauty in the case of erotics; instilling temperance in a soul in the case of soul-medicine. In terms of the process by which they achieve those goals, the role of conversation is central to both, but plays a somewhat different role in each. With soul-medicine, the outcome that is achieved is continuous with the process by which it is achieved: conversation led by the soul-doctor, consisting in critical discussion of fundamental questions related to the soul, which stimulates the development of the conversational resources of the patient in regard to the power to sustain critical focus on such questions.[64]

With erotics, the process of getting a (would-be) beautiful soul to reveal itself is in principle broader. Although the conversational element of Socrates' narrative of Greek and then of Thracian medicine is important, since it is Charmides' assent, at 156a6–8 and 156c9, to what precedes each narrative that enables the subsequent narrative to be delivered, Charmides' conversational presence is in fact fairly minimal. The text hereabouts is in the main a Socratic monologue, those preceding portions targeted, as I argued above, largely at Socrates getting himself to refocus on the task of engaging with Charmides' soul.

---

[64] These resources may be internally or externally applied; the internal option (conversation with oneself) is especially relevant if we wish to make room for engaging with a written work.

The same monologic character applies to Socrates' elaborately lavish praise of Charmides' family background (157e–158a) that follows Critias' assurance that Charmides is considered the most temperate of his contemporaries, after Socrates touts the need, in the wake of the Thracian narrative, for Charmides to submit his soul to be charmed. Moreover, although Socrates' later long discussion with Critias about what temperance is does consist in sustained critical conversation, so that this may seem to be an example of the practice of soul-medicine, its objective, as I shall argue, is not the improvement of Critias' soul (though that may be an incidental result) but the enticing back of Charmides to expose his own soul again. Thus the conversation with Critias should also in context be characterised as an example of the practice of erotics, directed at the listening Charmides.

This outline of the relation between soul-medicine and erotics can be corroborated by some later remarks of Socrates, made with particular reference to the art of medicine, about the benefit to practitioners of the art that they practise. At 164a9–b1, in the course of challenging Critias' account of temperance as the doing of good things, Socrates suggests that when a doctor makes someone healthy, the doctor does what is beneficial both for himself and for the one who is healed. A few lines later, at 164b7–9, Socrates further suggests that the doctor may not know when he has healed beneficially and when not, which he generalises and glosses as the possibility of any skilled practitioner (*dēmiourgos*) not knowing when they are going to profit (*onēsesthai*) from the work they have done, and when not.

I do not think we need see a contradiction within these lines, Socrates first stating that the doctor is benefitted from healing the patient and then treating it as an open question, insofar as the doctor does not necessarily know whether the healing will benefit her. Rather, Socrates can, at 164a9–b1, be taken as making the point that no art would be practised were it not beneficial for the practitioner to practise it. The work of the doctor is to make people healthy; but doing that must bring some benefit for the doctor. This is not to say that such benefit simply consists in the healing of the patient. If it did, then since the source of the benefit on this account is internal to the practice of medicine, the doctor, insofar as she (qua doctor) knows when she has healed, would know when she had benefitted. If it does not consist in the healing, the practitioner will not, just in virtue of her healing the patient, know when she is going to benefit, even if there must in principle be a benefit that explains why the practitioner practises.

So the passage invites us to consider what other benefit to the practitioner there might be. Perhaps profit in a very literal sense. The practitioner may benefit from charging a fee that is then paid; one does not always know that it will be paid. Another possible, if somewhat more morally startling, relationship also, however, suggests itself in the cited case of medicine: the doctor might envisage, as the benefit of restoring a patient's body to splendid wholesomeness, that that body can now serve to satisfy her erotic desire.[65] If so, an art of erotics may be needed to persuade the patient to grant the doctor continued access to the patient's body once it has been healed. This, I suggest, in regard to the soul, is what Socrates has in mind in his own case as practitioner of soul-medicine. The art of erotics aims at securing continued access to the patient's soul once it is made beautiful, as it aimed at securing initial access to the patient's soul for inspection and (if needed) treatment with soul-medicine.[66]

3.8 The Treatment of Charmides

I have argued that Socrates, as practitioner of soul-medicine, should be regarded as pursuing an art that is akin to but distinct from the practice of medicine, even in its Thracian form. I would now like to develop this thought a little further, in order to elucidate more precisely how to conceive of the method that Socrates uses to examine Charmides' soul.

When Socrates has performed his encomium of Charmides' ancestral family, we reach an interesting moment of tension. The encomium is, on the face of it, offered as backing for Critias' claim that Charmides is considered the most temperate of his contemporaries (157d6–7). Yet it sits rather uncomfortably with the idea embedded in the Thracian narrative, delivered just previously by Socrates, that to treat the body – in this case Charmides' headache – one first has to treat the soul (157a). If Charmides is (already) so temperate, then despite the headache his soul would not need treatment and the narrative falls away.

---

[65] One may note in this connection that the original Hippocratic oath expressly forbids doctors from exploiting their presence in a patient's house for 'sexual purposes' (*aphrodisiōn ergōn*), an indication that this was a live enough possibility for it to be frowned upon.
[66] It is an interesting question whether, in the standard medical case, there is need of an art external to medicine to secure a patient's submission for treatment: cf. *Gorgias* 456a–b, with rhetoric rather than erotics the salient art. Charmides himself comes over willingly enough on the promise that there is a doctor to deal with his headache. It is to gain access to his soul that the art of erotics is needed.

There are a number of responses one can make to this. Firstly, Socrates' linkage of the qualities of one's soul to those that one's ancestors exhibited may come with a certain degree of scepticism once we take on board that in his own case Socrates seems somewhat neglectful of family in the conventional sense; note again in this regard Socrates' use of the rather dismissive phrase 'and the rest of what is called happiness' (158a1) to speak of the qualities for which poets had praised Charmides' paternal ancestral line.

Secondly, the qualification that Charmides is considered the most temperate of his contemporaries seems compatible, given Charmides' age, with Charmides still needing to develop his temperance further, so that he would need his soul treated. Indeed Socrates will ask whether Charmides is 'sufficiently' (*hikanōs*, 158b6, c3, cf. 158b3) temperate not to need the charm, implying that one might be temperate, but insufficiently so to do without the charm.[67] Thirdly, there is in fact a double qualification: Critias says that Charmides 'is considered' (*dokei*, 157d6) to be much the most temperate of his contemporaries, which does not imply that, even in relation to that peer group, he actually is.

So perhaps Socrates' praise is not that sincere, Charmides' reputation is not that justified, and he needs treatment of his soul after all. That may all be right; but the tension remains. For the fact is that on the Thracian view (156e4–157a3) one needs to treat the soul if any part of the body is to be 'in beautiful condition' (*kalōs echein*, a3); and Socrates says that he swore to the Thracian (157c1) that he would not administer the remedy to anyone, however wealthy, nobly born, or beautiful,[68] before administering the charm.

Yet Critias' mention of Charmides' reputation, and Socrates' subsequent praise of his ancestors, lead quite naturally to the conclusion, spelled out by Socrates at 158b–c, that it is an open question whether Charmides does need the charm; and Socrates invites Charmides to say whether or not he agrees with Critias that he does sufficiently have temperance. That Socrates can contemplate, even if only in principle, the possibility that Charmides is sufficiently temperate not to need the charm, so that the remedy would be administered without it (158b8–c1), implies both a preparedness to breach his oath and a disregard of the Thracian maxim, given Charmides' headache, that the body will not be well without treatment of the soul.

---

[67] Cf. Tsouna (2017, 49).

[68] The idea that Charmides could be beautiful (in body) and yet still need the charm is another hint that the question of whether one is in need of temperance might not after all, for Socrates, be connected with one's bodily condition.

3.8 *The Treatment of Charmides*

This confirms two points: firstly, that Socrates is probably spinning a yarn about an encounter with a Thracian doctor,[69] since one would presumably not be prepared so lightly to breach an oath that had actually been given;[70] but secondly, that the strictly *medical* aspect of the Thracian narrative is not what we are supposed to take away from it. If Charmides' headache does not, for Socrates, necessarily mean that the former lacks temperance, then Socrates may without tension treat as an open question whether Charmides has temperance or not, but just so long as he is uncommitted to the Thracian narrative as a piece of medical theory.

Such lack of commitment on Socrates' part is not to be explained by attributing to him some alternative account of how the condition of the soul affects that of the body. Rather, any bodily effects that temperance (or its absence) may have are neither here nor there for him. Resolving the tension means attributing to Socrates the view that temperance is not to be valued for its contribution (if any) to bodily well-being, but for its making a soul beautiful. His concern, then, is to ascertain the state of Charmides' soul independently of the condition of his body.

This in turn reflects the way in which Socrates, as we saw earlier, values souls over bodies – a scheme of values that, to reiterate, we are to take seriously but not uncritically, given how, for example, lack of concern for the body seems to play out in terms of Socrates' disturbing (as we might think) indifference to what happened at the battle. So although it does not follow that possession of temperance *has* no effects on the body, it reinforces the idea that, whether or not he is himself temperate, what Socrates cares about is temperance's effect on the soul: bodily effects are at most a by-product, not what possession of temperance is for. The causal claims made for temperance do not necessarily track its evaluative status.

This attitude may also explain a seeming looseness on Socrates' part over the precise relationship between the delivery of the charm and of the

---

[69] This of course does not mean that the tale is not supposed to represent some link, however imaginative, with what was thought to be a Zalmoxian, or at least Thracian, outlook – there would be little point otherwise in tying the yarn to this context; cf. Faraone (2010, 151). Redfield (2011, 361) is no doubt right to say that there need not be 'anything reliable' about Socrates' account; but the latter cannot simply be arbitrary. See further Section 5.4 n. 31.

[70] Tuozzo (2011, 125) claims that within the purely medical context there would be no need for the oath, given that the leaf would not work anyway without the charm, and 'once the ... patient understood that, he would have no reason to try to persuade Socrates to proceed straight to the treatment with the leaf'. But given how radical the theory, as a piece of medicine, is presented as being, the Thracian surely has every reason to think it likely that the patient would distrust this element – the need for the charm – and try to be given the leaf directly.

bodily remedy:[71] at 155e6–7 the charm is to be recited at the same time as (*hama kai*) the leaf is applied; at 157b2–4 and c2–5, apparently prior (*prōton*) to the leaf's application.[72] In fact all Socrates strictly says in these latter passages is that the patient is first to *offer* (*parechein*) their soul to be charmed. This is consistent with the charm's actual recital taking place as the remedy is applied; but perhaps more saliently, it throws weight on the availability of the patient's soul as the important thing, whatever the role of the body may be.[73]

I have argued that the tensions arising in the text in the wake of the Thracian narrative can be resolved by reading Socrates as concerned with the well-being of the soul and indifferent to the well-being of the body. His value-scheme is further illustrated by what he says to Charmides immediately after his remarks on Charmides' ancestry:

> With regard to your visible features, my dear son of Glaucon, you seem to me to have yielded to none of your ancestors in any respect. If you are also sufficiently developed in relation both to temperance and to the other qualities (*talla*) that this one [Critias] mentioned, your mother gave birth to you, my dear Charmides, as blessed. (158a7–b4)

Now Critias himself had rather vaguely spoken of Charmides as being, in addition to the most temperate, inferior to no one of his age with respect to 'all the other qualities' (*talla panta*, 157d7). It is Socrates' conjunction that implicitly identifies the qualities at issue more specifically, insofar as they are contrasted with the visible, as qualities of soul.[74] Indeed his formulation strongly suggests that it is these qualities that determine whether Charmides will be blessed. When Socrates expresses his view at the end of the dialogue, he is more specific still: if Charmides has temperance, then he is blessed (175e7–176a1), with nothing else mentioned (despite the allusion to Charmides' figure at 175d7) as contributing, or mattering, to a blessed state.

What, then, to make of Charmides' morning headaches? It has been suggested that these may be hangovers.[75] That would apparently be a case

---

[71] Cf. Coolidge (1993, 25).
[72] Flamigni (2017, 16) conjectures that there are two charms in play: one to heal the soul, the other to make the leaf efficacious. But given that the leaf soon drops out of consideration (see this section below), such a role for a second charm seems moot.
[73] At 158c2, the stated relation between charm and application of remedy is most naturally read in terms of temporal priority but does not have to be: *pro* can mean 'in preference to' as well as 'before'.
[74] While Boys-Stones (2019, 112 n. 9) is right to say that at 154e4 Charmides was not 'said to have an (invisible) beauty of soul', our current passage seems to place the beautiful thing that is temperance firmly in the class of non-visible qualities.
[75] See Hyland (1981, 41).

3.8 The Treatment of Charmides

where getting one's soul in the right shape is a factor in the well-being of one's body:[76] if one were temperate, one would not indulge to the extent of getting hangovers. Though the text does not say that the headache was a hangover, there does seem something immediately plausible about the suggestion. One reason for this is that on its face the Thracian narrative encourages us to *look* for a connection between the possession (or lack) of temperance and one's bodily health (or sickness). So the narrative motivates the imputation to Charmides of something like a hangover.

On the other hand – and here we revisit the earlier tension – Socrates seems to regard it as possible that Charmides, despite his headache, has temperance. This may of course mean that Socrates has a non-standard view of what temperance is, such that its possession is, say, consistent with over-indulgence in drink. But it may compatibly mean, as we saw above in endeavouring to diffuse the tension, that he doesn't think that what matters about temperance is its relation to the body. What it does to the soul is all that counts. So the headache drops quietly out of the picture. It is last mentioned, by Critias, at 157c8, not long before the final mention, by Socrates, of the corresponding bodily remedy (the leaf) at 158c2. Plato, I think, may have expected us to ask whether Charmides' headache was a hangover;[77] but also to notice how little the text seems interested in providing an answer.

With his focus firmly on the soul, then, and fresh from heaping praise on Charmides' ancestors, Socrates tells Charmides that 'If temperance is, as Critias here says, already present to you, and you are sufficiently temperate', then he will have no need of charms (158b5–8). But if he does need them, he must be charmed before the remedy is applied (158c1–2). He then says to Charmides:

> So tell me yourself whether you agree with this one [Critias] and say that you already have a sufficient share of temperance, or are deficient [in it]? (158c2–4)

Leave aside that in speaking of Charmides' temperance Critias did not quite put things like that (157d6–7).[78] Charmides eventually concludes (158d5–6) that he does not know what to reply: something of a problem for the project of getting him to expose what is in his soul. Socrates' artful

---

[76] Ibid., 42.
[77] The Greeks well knew the phenomenon (s.v. *kraipalaō* in LSJ): see, most relevantly, *Symposium* 176d, where Eryximachus the doctor is speaker.
[78] As I shall show, there is quite a pattern in the dialogue of Socrates being careless with the way that others formulate their statements. See e.g. Section 3.9 (Charmides); Sections 3.10 and 4.1 (Critias).

telling of the Thracian tale – an example (I have suggested) of his practice of the erotic art – has engineered a switch in focus from Charmides' body to his soul. But evidently a little more solvent is needed for Charmides to reveal himself.

Not that the explanation Charmides gives in reaching his conclusion is not itself somewhat revealing. He first blushes, leading Socrates to comment on how his bashfulness (*to aischuntēlon autou*, 158c6), so suitable for his age, made him look still more beautiful. Then Charmides says:

> It is not easy right now either to agree to or dissent from the question: for if I deny that I am temperate, it would be odd to put oneself down in such a way, and at the same time show up as wrong Critias here and many others who think, according to Critias' account, that I am temperate; but if on the other hand I affirm that I am temperate, the self-praise will perhaps come across as obnoxious. So I don't have a way of replying to you. (158c7–d6)

One might detect, in Plato's putting this speech into Charmides' mouth, the outline of a critique of a certain sort of aristocratic value-system. How commendable is Charmides' supposedly age-appropriate bashfulness if its effect is to render inexpressible each of the two possible answers to a question about whether he possesses a quality at the heart of Athenian aristocratic values? That there seems, from Charmides' perspective, no safe middle ground to occupy between self-abasement and self-aggrandisement is concerning.[79]

If, moreover, with temperance now an explicit theme, Charmides is a candidate for its exemplification, then his speech shows, insofar as temperance's possession apparently blocks its self-attribution, something problematic about the notion of temperance that he would exemplify. It also anticipates Charmides' difficulties with his later proposal that temperance is the same thing as shame: a proposal that in turn encourages us to reread the present passage with a critical eye and be primed for further critical exploration of the nature of temperance.

From Socrates' point of view, the practical difficulty is that the project to look at Charmides' soul has been temporarily halted. And here we gain insight into just what 'stripping' a soul might involve. Charmides' bashfulness acts as a barrier to his revealing what he takes to be in his soul. Socrates, eager for that soul to be revealed, will need to see if his erotic wiles can remove the barrier. What follows, I argue, is a case of the art of erotics using an aspect of the art of soul-medicine to further its goals.

---

[79] This is consistent with Charmides himself thinking he has done rather well in producing such a non-committal answer; cf. Santas (1973, 107).

3.8 *The Treatment of Charmides*

To find a way out of the impasse, Socrates suggests to Charmides that they investigate together whether the latter possesses temperance and assures Charmides that he does not want to turn to medicine in an ill-considered way or force Charmides to say what he does not want to (158d–e). Charmides says he would very much like (cf. *pantōn malista philon*, 158e4) to investigate with Socrates, and invites him to suggest the best way of doing so. Hence it seems that Socrates' problem at this point is not that he has failed to win Charmides over to the idea of finding out whether temperance is in his soul; what is needed is a procedure of joint investigation to enable the idea to be realised.

Socrates thus looks to proceed in a considered manner; and we have been primed to read the procedure that he will suggest as representing, in some sense, his turn to medicine. He tells Charmides:

> Then it seems to me that the best way of investigating the matter is the following: It is clear that if temperance is present to you, then you are able to have some opinion (*ti doxazein*) about it; for it is presumably necessary that by being in you, if indeed it is in you, it provide some perception (*aisthēsis*), as a result of which you might form a certain opinion (*doxa*) about it, as to what (*hoti*) it is and what sort of thing (*hopoion*) it is. (158e6–159a3)

Since, Socrates adds, Charmides knows how to speak Greek, he could surely then articulate (*eipois*) the content of that thought as it appears to him (159a6–7).[80] Socrates thus goes on to urge Charmides, in order to help them get at whether temperance is in him or not, to say what it is 'according to your own opinion' (*kata tēn sēn doxan*, a10).

Socrates' suggested procedure raises many questions. The most obvious one, perhaps, is about the relation between a subject and the contents of their soul. One possibility is that the subject has special access to what is in her soul (or, as we might say in this context, mind), such that she is in a position to be aware of what is there, as an outside party could not be. Alternatively, it might be a relation peculiar to temperance: the latter is the sort of thing that, if one has it, one is aware of having it. That this seems later agreed upon by Socrates and Critias (164a1–4) perhaps supports the narrower reading. In either case, it seems clear that the subject's access to her mental states, while perhaps privileged, is not infallible. Socrates does not say that the presence of temperance in oneself enables the subject to

---

[80] As we shall see in Section 3.9, the issue of articulating one's thought is less straightforward than Socrates chooses to present it here. For a recent contemporary discussion of the issue see Alshanetsky (2019).

know what temperance is,[81] but to have an opinion about it – an opinion that, as the subsequent exchanges show, is susceptible to challenge; hence indeed the investigation is a joint one.

Now even if a conservative approach inclines us towards the narrower alternative sketched above, namely that the procedure is shaped specifically for a quality such as temperance rather than intended to capture a view about the relation of a subject to her mental content more generally, the question remains: why did Socrates choose this particular procedure as the way to investigate jointly whether Charmides has temperance? It seems somewhat unmotivated, with a lot of detail about the subject's relation to (at least some of) their mental states presented, seemingly from nowhere, as if it were reasonable and obvious.

I propose, as a way of understanding why it is just this way of approaching the question of whether Charmides has temperance that Socrates comes up with, that we follow the medical trail.[82] Recall that the procedure is connected by Socrates at 158d–e with his turning to medicine, supposedly in line with the approach to medicine described in the Thracian narrative. Recall too that Socrates has already modified that narrative to some degree: while the Thracian view seemed to be that, insofar as a patient such as Charmides had a bodily illness, that would mean his soul was in bad shape and needed treating first, for Socrates it is more of an open question. One tests to see whether the subject's soul is in good or bad shape, that is, whether it is or is not temperate, before determining whether treatment (the 'charm') is needed.

This preliminary step, while derogating from the Thracian's strictures, corresponds with a perfectly proper part of procedure in the medical case. For it is evidently good medical practice to perform diagnostic tests to ascertain whether the patient is ill or not (and if so what the illness is) before determining whether treatment is needed. Moreover, I have argued that the way to make sense of the emphasis on medicine in this part of the *Charmides* is to regard Socrates not as practising medicine, insofar as that aims at the well-being of the body, but as practising a sister science, what I have called soul-medicine, which aims at the well-being of the soul.

As he is something of a pioneer in the art of soul-medicine, it is natural, I suggest, for Socrates to draw where applicable on the procedures of its more well-established relative to develop the techniques of the newer art. Once we suppose that this is what Socrates is doing, his choice of

---

[81] Cf. Tarrant (2000, 258).
[82] On medicine as a model for ethics in Plato, and its history, see Torres (2021).

3.8 The Treatment of Charmides

procedure becomes clearer and better motivated. Consider, by way of (fanciful) illustration from the medical realm, the following scenario: let us say that I am suspected of having kidney disease, perhaps because it runs in my family. We may note the emphasis placed, in regard to Charmides himself, on hereditable characteristics of the body as well as the soul (cf. 157e1–158a7).

One way of testing for the presence of the putative disease, especially in the absence of sophisticated diagnostic tools, is to ask the patient whether she is aware of being affected in a certain way. Even with such tools, it may be that the patient's reporting of her being thus affected is the first indication that something needs investigating. It is natural to suppose that, for a range of conditions at least, if I do have something, it will in many instances produce some awareness of it in me; it will feel a certain way or affect me in a way that I can notice. Indeed it seems plausible that, in the era of ancient Greek medicine roughly contemporaneous with the *Charmides*, what were regarded as illnesses were precisely those conditions that afforded some such awareness of their presence: Charmides' headache would of course be an example of this. Such awareness might in turn naturally lead me to form a belief as to what sort of a thing it is that is affecting me, and what it is, which I can report to my doctor, who can then determine whether or not I have the illness in question.

Say, for example, that I have an awareness of my body as feeling hot. So I form a belief as to what sort of thing is affecting me thus – something perhaps that itself has the quality of hotness since it is making my body feel that way. Hence I form the belief as to what sort of thing it is, namely hot, and what it is, namely, let us say, fever. So I report my (fallible) opinion, based on my awareness of how it affects me, that the antecedently suspected kidney disease is a kind of fever. This opinion is then refuted by my doctor who knows that kidney disease is (let us say for the sake of argument) associated with chills not fever. So my condition cannot be kidney disease, even if it is a fever that I have. The doctor, as expert, makes the final determination, but without the initial report there would not be much for the doctor to do.

Before applying this model to the soul, note that it corresponds to some extent with the example of bodily illness that we are given in the *Charmides*, which serves as the occasion for Socrates' turn to medicine: Charmides' headache. To simplify for present purposes a philosophically rather more complex issue, we may say that a headache is not in itself discernible from the outside. It need not, as such, have any visible manifestation; but it is, necessarily, felt from the inside. It is in this sense something to which Charmides, as its subject, has special access. Thus the way Critias says that he found out about it is testimonial: Charmides told him that he had it (155b2–5). The next step, naturally, is to look for a doctor who can determine its underlying cause (e.g. a hangover) and hence its proper treatment, though it must be admitted that Critias' narrative passes over the issue of cause and goes straight for treatment, thereby displaying a not uncharacteristic, though perhaps – given the non-bodily objective in this case – strategic, haste.

One can now adduce evidence that the procedure outlined by Socrates for investigating Charmides' soul has some correlation with at least one major strand of Greek medical theory. In chapter 9 of the Hippocratic *On Ancient Medicine* it is stated, in regard to correct treatment, that for the doctor there is no measure by which one will gain accurate knowledge except 'the awareness of the body' (*tēn aisthēsin tou sōmatos*). Now the interpretation of this latter phrase is debated, but one possible reading of the Greek is that it refers to the patient's perception of their own body. Mark Schiefsky elaborates and endorses this reading as follows:

> The patient is the ultimate authority in reporting his experiences; but even if what he says is accurate, it is at best an imprecise and somewhat unreliable indication of the underlying condition of his body. It is in part because he must rely on the *patient's* report of what he feels in response to treatment that the doctor can attain only limited ἀκρίβεια [accuracy] in treatment.[83]

There is little in Schiefsky's reading of the Hippocratic passage that would not fit Socrates' procedure, as I interpret it. Socrates applies his procedure to diagnosis (of the soul) rather than treatment (of the body). But even this difference reveals a point of analogy. We might have thought that in the medical case, while diagnosis requires the patient's active contribution, treatment is a more passive affair. The Hippocratic text indicates that patients' reports are as integral to treatment as they are to diagnosis.

Socrates also seems less inclined than his Hippocratic counterpart to suppose that investigation might not gain an accurate result, though one should note that at 159a9–10, on one possible rendering of the Greek *topasōmen* (glossed more neutrally as 'get at' above), Socrates asked Charmides to say what he thinks temperance is in order that they might 'guess' or 'conjecture' whether or not it is in him.[84] That would bring the

---

[83] Schiefsky (2005, 199; his emphasis).
[84] Cf. Moore and Raymond (2019, 54–5), who note the use of the term *topazein* in a medical context in Aristophanes *Wasps* 73 (55 n. 62) and offer a critical assessment of Socrates' procedure at this point as quasi-medical (though without mentioning the *On Ancient Medicine* passage).

procedure, epistemically speaking, even closer to the Hippocratic model (as Schiefsky interprets it).

It is of course not necessary to rely on findings within the Hippocratic tradition to interpret Socrates' procedure for examining Charmides' soul in some such way as this. Given how the procedure is previewed by Socrates as his turn to medicine, there is strong independent motivation for seeing it as intended to describe some plausible analogue of existing medical practice. Nonetheless, the availability of what, on one considered interpretation, looks to be a suggestive Hippocratic parallel gives further credence to the reading here proposed.

The medical model can then be applied to illuminate Socrates' approach to investigating what is in Charmides' soul. I leave aside, to return to it shortly, a striking disanalogy with the regular medical case, which is that, as Socrates describes it, what they are exploring in the case of Charmides is whether or not the latter has the equivalent of health (namely, temperance) in his soul, not disease. That apart, reading Socrates' description as an application of a way of doing medicine does, I think, capture much of the detail that he sets down for use in relation to the soul: the report by the patient of their condition, enabled by an awareness that the condition putatively provides to the patient, on the basis of which the patient forms a view as to what, and what sort of thing, the condition is, which they articulate for the soul-doctor, who is then able to test whether or not the report accurately identifies the condition.[85]

To flesh this out further, consider next not Charmides' first account of what he thinks temperance is, which immediately follows Socrates' setting out of the procedure, but his second, namely that it is the same thing as shame (160e3–5). There is good reason to select this for illustration since, as we shall see, it may be the only account Charmides offers that is actually based on his reporting of an awareness of a way he is affected, and will thus represent him as at least trying to adhere to the recommended model. Charmides' first step leading up to his second answer would thus be to notice that he has a feeling of shame or bashfulness, something Socrates was himself earlier able to detect through seeing Charmides blush (158c5–6). Note that this suggests that access to the way a subject is affected in such cases need not be *restricted* to the subject, but is still

---

[85] See also Cooper (2004, 36) on the same *On Ancient Medicine* passage: 'the physician will be the one to ask questions about what the patient is experiencing and to probe the patient's body to help him or her to perceive additional things, in order to generate observations on the basis of which he can then construct his etiological theory – or its application to the given case'. The transferability of this to Socrates' procedure in relation to Charmides' soul again seems striking.

special to the subject: not just (in this example) in that, while blushing may not always be easy to spot from the outside, it seems unavoidable, when it occurs, that one should feel it from the inside; but also, in that the sense of shame that underlies it will be accessible to the subject whether it manifests externally or not.

Before Charmides offers his second answer, Socrates tells him (160d5–e1) to scrutinise himself, focus more, and consider what sort of a person (*hopoion tina*) temperance makes him and what sort of a thing it would be to make him such, and hence what it seems to him to be. Now although, in my view, this is supposed to represent a procedure continuous with, rather than separate from, the one that Socrates set out before Charmides' first answer,[86] it does bring out something distinctive about reporting a quality of soul such as temperance as opposed to a quality of body such as (say) fever: the latter does not make one a certain sort of person, whereas the former does.

Thus Charmides is now asked not simply to say what sort of a thing temperance is through his awareness of its presence in him, but what sort of a person *he* is through its presence, and on that basis what sort of a thing temperance itself would be. The patient of a soul-doctor has to undergo a more direct form of self-examination than does the patient of a regular doctor. Charmides must commit to saying what kind of person temperance makes him, and not merely (as in the case, say, of a bodily disease) what kind of condition it leaves him in. Socrates' exhortation to Charmides before his second answer does not represent an abandonment of the turn to medicine, which would be odd given how prominent the medical motif has been (and will continue to be) in the dialogue, but a further specification of what the turn to soul-medicine implies.

This in turn suggests, in terms of Socrates' initial description of the procedure, that forming a belief on the basis of an awareness of how one is affected may need to be quite a reflective process. Socrates himself remarks that it was only after some 'very manly' self-scrutiny that Charmides this time gave his view about temperance (160e2–3). Charmides' awareness of his sense of shame enables him to report the condition that he is antecedently suspected, or rather reputed, to have – namely, temperance – as making a person bashful (*aischuntēlon*, 160e4). Thus one with temperance is, on this account, bashful. So, in terms of the procedure, the quality of what Charmides possesses is bashfulness, what it is is shame, and

---

[86] Contrast Moore and Raymond (2019, 55), who claim that Socrates 'seems hardly wedded' to that initial procedure and '[s]oon ... abandons the introspective approach altogether'.

Charmides therefore identifies temperance with shame: an identity that Socrates as soul-doctor goes on to show, upon further investigation, fails to hold.

With the basic structure of Socrates' quasi-medical procedure now laid out, we can move to examine in more detail how Socrates tests Charmides' putative reports of his condition. First, however, let me return to the disanalogy in that procedure with its application in the standard medical case, such that Socrates looks to discover whether Charmides has a good, not a bad, condition of soul. The disanalogy is, I think, explained by the fact that we have not one art operating here but two, arranged, as I argued earlier, hierarchically. The art of erotics is in charge, since Socrates' overall aim is to get a look at Charmides' soul in the light of its promise of being beautiful. This means that the point of the exercise for Socrates is to discover whether it is beautiful, and thus apt to satisfy his erotic desire, not whether it is ugly, and so requiring treatment. Of course if it does turn out to need treatment, then that can be applied, with a beautiful soul the result if treatment is successful. But again, the ultimate purpose of the treatment is not to heal Charmides' soul and off he goes, but to have a beautiful soul with which Socrates can engage.

Socrates' suggestion at 158e–159a, preceding Charmides' first answer, of how they should jointly proceed – that Charmides report his opinion about what is in him – is thus itself an example of the erotic art, in that it recommends a particular procedure in order to help discover whether there is beauty in Charmides' soul for Socrates to view. That procedure as described inverts the normal emphasis of medicine – that one is looking for disease, not health – because, insofar as the art of soul-medicine is here serving the art of erotics, its procedures are to be aligned with the goal of that art. The way Socrates subsequently proceeds, in his investigation of whether Charmides does have temperance, is thus an application of the techniques of soul-medicine oriented to, and governed by, the goal of erotics.

3.9 Beauty at Bay

It is time now to turn in more detail to Socrates' carrying out of his investigation with Charmides as to whether or not temperance is in the latter's soul. This will enable us to get a further grip on how Socrates' erotic quest, centred on his co-option of medical procedure, plays out. Socrates reports:

> He [Charmides] at first hesitated and was not very willing to reply. Then, however, he said that temperance seemed to him to be the doing (*prattein*) of everything in an orderly way (*kosmiōs*) and quietly (*hēsuchēi*), both walking in the streets and conversing, and doing (*poiein*) all the other things similarly. 'And it seems to me', he said, 'in short that the thing you ask is a kind of quietness.' (159b1–6)

Charmides, according to Socrates, was at first rather reluctant to reply to the invitation to say what temperance, in his opinion, is. Whether this represents Charmides' general bashfulness, or a more specific lack of commitment to the proposed procedure, despite his earlier enthusiasm for the principle of joint investigation, now that he has heard what it requires him to do, is unclear; but the latter option seems indicated by Charmides' rather equivocal response of 'maybe' (*isōs*, 159a8) to Socrates' breezy suggestion that since Charmides knows how to speak Greek he will be able to report the content of his impression.

Charmides does, nonetheless, then say that he thinks that temperance is doing everything in an orderly and quiet manner, and that in sum temperance would be a kind of quietness (*hēsuchiotēs tis*, 159b5), whereupon Socrates purports to show that this is not what temperance is. For the purposes of my broader interpretation, there are two points of particular relevance in Charmides' first attempt at saying what temperance is and Socrates' response.

To begin with the former, it seems doubtful, as I hinted above, whether the attempt arises from Charmides actually using the recommended procedure. In contrast, at any rate, with what Socrates reports him as doing for his second attempt, for the first we are just told that he was initially reluctant and then gave an answer. There is no mention of his reflecting, in line with the suggested procedure, on how his putatively temperate condition affected him such as to form the basis for his answer.

Moreover, Socrates rather ominously begins his response by noting: 'they do certainly say (*phasi ge toi*) that the quiet are temperate; let us see if they are saying (*legousin*) anything' (159b7–8). Socrates' pointed attribution of the source of Charmides' reply not to the latter's self-examination but to some commonplace about temperance, together with his framing of what is to come as an examination of what (not Charmides but) *they* say, sounds like a rebuke to Charmides.[87] It seems that, rather than having

---

[87] Tuozzo (2011, 136 n. 5) describes such a reading as 'far too subtle'. On the contrary, the juxtaposition of Socrates' initial recommendation that Charmides articulate the impression that his own putative possession of temperance makes on him with the description of what Charmides subsequently comes up with as a stock general characterisation seems rather blunt; cf. Bruell (1977,

3.9 Beauty at Bay

been prepared to look within himself for the presence of temperance and infer its nature from that, Socrates takes Charmides to have grasped at a standard view about the relation between temperance and quietness and broadcast that instead.[88] If so, then Socrates' erotic art has even now not yet succeeded in eliciting from Charmides a view based on what Charmides takes to find in his soul.

The second point concerns Socrates himself. Regardless of the origins of Charmides' first answer, Socrates is to prove, in his response, somewhat cavalier in respect of his interlocutor's words and their meaning: a Socratic fault that will also be illustrated later in the discussion of temperance as doing one's own things. In the case of Charmides' first answer, Socrates' disregard for the nuances of meaning is, I shall argue, so blatant as to make it likely that this is something we are supposed to notice and be critical of – and not just in the narrower context of questioning whether Socrates' refutation succeeds. We are invited also, as interpreters of a text ourselves, to reflect on the project of interpretation, and on the difference in that regard between oral discourse, such as Socrates is depicted carrying on with his interlocutors in the *Charmides*, and written text, such as the *Charmides* itself.

Such reflection is already prompted when Socrates suggests to Charmides, before the latter's first answer, that since Charmides knows how to speak Greek, he can report his impression of what temperance is. Now the verb 'to speak Greek' (*hellēnizein*) can be merely descriptive but can also suggest more normatively 'to speak Greek properly'; and it is in fact striking that the word Charmides uses in his answer for 'quietness' (*hēsuchiotēs*) occurs in only one other place in extant Greek literature of the classical period.[89]

Charmides, it seems, has interpreted Socrates' request, perhaps in keeping with his youthful aristocratic background, as an invitation to show off his Greek language skills. So he comes out with what, we can assume, is

---

153). Given Socrates' pointedness, I am not sure why Tsouna (2022, 124 n. 3) says 'there is no textual evidence' to support the claim that Charmides does not follow the agreed procedure in his first answer.

[88] Cf. McCoy (2005, 141–2), who points out that for someone of a supposedly quiet and orderly nature Charmides seems to cause a lot of disorder around him. The connection between temperance and quietness is, however, also politically freighted, and given the dialogue's resonances of the Peloponnesian war, we are no doubt supposed to pick up on this: in Thucydides we find the connection highlighted in the context of Spartan values in particular, and, interestingly, in view of Socrates' upcoming critique, the term 'quietness' (*hēsuchia*) depicted with positive or negative polarity depending on one's political orientation; see North (1966, 100–4).

[89] See on these points Moore and Raymond (2019, 10–11 nn. 36–7).

a fairly rare word. One suspects that a display of linguistic sophistication was the last thing Socrates wanted from him: he just meant that Charmides, as a Greek speaker, could communicate his opinion about what temperance is. But if so, then this is actually a very odd thing to have said in context. Why not just say to Charmides that once he has formed his opinion he will be able to express it? Charmides does not need to be told that he can speak Greek, or that this is the language that Socrates and the others understand.[90] Yet, I have argued, Socrates is unlikely to have meant the more normatively loaded sense of 'speak Greek'.

The oddness, I think, points to the difference between actual conversation and a written text. Plato's literary art means that Socrates' request, while odd when one thinks about it, does not come over as excessively jarring when it passes one by. On reflection, however, it seems a somewhat gratuitous insertion whose purpose on Plato's part cannot primarily be the enhancement of conversational realism. On the contrary, by noticing the insertion, we notice (are supposed to notice) that the spell is broken and we are reading a piece of well-crafted writing, not eavesdropping on a conversation. But what, then, is the insertion for? To have Socrates talk about 'speaking Greek' where nobody is in fact doing any speaking (we are reminded that this is a written text) is a nice irony on Plato's part, particularly if, as I have suggested, its effect is to make us notice just this. It also, as I suggested earlier, serves as a handy illustration of knowledge as knowing-how. But regarding what Charmides is specifically said here to know how to do, I think there is more to it than this.

If I am right that Socrates, given his not infrequent disdain for linguistic nicety, did not mean to convey that Charmides show how excellently he can speak Greek, then Charmides has misinterpreted him, and has done so (Plato is exquisite here) on the very meaning of a term for speaking a language. Perhaps one should not rule out the possibility that Socrates meant to flatter the young aristocrat on his attainment in Greek, in order to encourage him to articulate an answer. Even so, it would remain a

---

[90] Contrast *Meno* 82b4, where Socrates' asking Meno *whether* Meno's slave speaks Greek has the plain objective of confirming the slave as usable for the role of subject in the demonstration of recollection: I do not think this can be described, with Tsouna (2022, 105), as a comparable case to that of the *Charmides*. An anonymous reader suggests to me that the appearance of redundancy in the case of the *Charmides* passage can be avoided if Socrates' point were taken as follows: given that, by the procedure set out, Charmides will have formed an opinion about what temperance is, 'then only if Charmides were unable to speak Greek (as he actually is not) would it be problematic for him to give an account of what temperance is'. While it is not clear to me that this redescription evades the redundancy, Socrates' formulation may indicate a view on his part that where a belief is formed by a competent speaker of a language, it is straightforwardly expressible by that speaker.

3.9 Beauty at Bay

mistake on Charmides' part to interpret Socrates as requesting by this device mainly a show of linguistic finery.

Yet misinterpretation arises just insofar as interpretation takes place. And interpretation, one might think, is not an optional extra: it is constitutive of any response to a purportedly communicative act. So what Charmides has done, thereby exhibiting in a respectable and necessary sense his comprehension of the Greek language, is interpret Socrates' expression in a charitable way, since it is only when taken in the normative sense that it adds anything substantive and so avoids gratuitousness. This is not to deny that there may also be something self-serving about Charmides' interpretive choice. His initial hesitancy indicates that the prospect of following the soul-doctor's procedure may have intimidated him. He therefore demurs from self-examination, doubling down on the one segment of the procedure that, on his interpretation of it, seems appealing: a display of his sophistication in the Greek language.

Even this small example, then, shows that interpretation makes a difference. In the context of oral conversation, interpretation may have to be quick, perhaps mostly, in the normal course of events, not even conscious, and therefore liable not to be noticed by the interpreter as something they are doing at all. If Socrates could offer the fact that he conducts himself through oral conversation as a pretext for underappreciating the role of interpretation when seemingly wrong-footed by Charmides' construal of 'speak Greek', we as readers of a written text, who are able consciously to reflect on the issues the text raises, have no such pretext. Interpretation is revealed to us, through Charmides' response, as an essential act if we are to treat language (oral or written) as aspiring to communicate at all. At the level of Plato's engagement with his readers, Socrates' apparently gratuitous question to Charmides about language and communication shows that there is no aspect of a carefully written text that is exempt from the need for interpretation.

In outlining a framework for interpreting the discussion of temperance as quietness, I have suggested, firstly, that Charmides may not, for the most part, even have tried to follow the procedure he agreed with Socrates, and to that extent has failed as yet to expose his soul; and, secondly, that Socrates, in using the very term that means 'to speak Greek', may not have reckoned with the niceties of linguistic meaning in quite the way he should have done. Let me add a third point regarding the content of Socrates' response: he begins by securing Charmides' agreement that temperance is one of 'the beautiful things' (*tōn kalōn*, 159c1). The basic structure of his dismantling of the identification of temperance with quietness rests on what therefore seems to have a kind of axiomatic status in the discussion:[91] that temperance is beautiful.

The axiom is restated, in slightly different forms, at 159d8 and d11;[92] then, in the version that a life that is temperate must thereby be beautiful, at 160b8–9; and then back in the original form – temperance is one of the beautiful things – at 160d1–2. These are the first occasions in the dialogue when temperance has been explicitly said to be beautiful, though the idea was hinted at in causal terms during the Thracian narrative in its being said to be brought about from beautiful words.

This foundational status of temperance as beautiful adds a key element in my reading of Socrates' motive, in his interactions with Charmides, as erotic. We have already noted Socrates' desire, prompted by Critias' advertising of Charmides as beautiful and good in soul, to strip that soul to look at it; as well as the centrality, in the Thracian narrative, of temperance as constitutive of a soul's being in beautiful shape. The subsequent attempt to identify whether temperance is in Charmides' soul has now led to the Socratic emphasis on temperance as a beautiful thing. The final piece of connective tissue will be the confirmation, at 167e7–8, of eros as in Socrates' view the proprietary attitude towards what is beautiful.

The emphasis on temperance as beautiful underpins Socrates' refutation of Charmides' first answer. The refutation has two main movements: in the first, Socrates argues that in a range of activities, pertaining to soul as well as body, quickness is more beautiful than quietness (159c–160b). So temperance would not be quietness by that reckoning, since temperance is something beautiful. In the second, he argues that even if one conceded that quiet things were no less beautiful than quick things, temperance would still not be quietness, since temperance has been laid down by them as something beautiful (160b–d).

The mechanism of the first movement seems fairly straightforward. It features an interim, then a more general, conclusion. To begin with the former: having focussed on examples of bodily activities, Socrates concludes:

> Then in respect of the body at any rate it is not quietness but quickness (*tachutēs*) that would be more temperate, since temperance is a beautiful thing. (159d10–11)

---

[91] Cf. *hupetethē* ('has been laid down') at 160d2.
[92] Hē de ge sōphrosunē kalon ti ēn; kalon hē sōphrosunē.

Next, having run through various activities of the soul, he concludes more generally:

> 'Then, Charmides, in all things, both those concerning the soul and those concerning the body, those that pertain to what is quick and sharp appear to us more beautiful than those that pertain to slowness and quietness?'
>
> 'It looks like it,' he said.
>
> 'Then temperance would not be a kind of quietness, nor the temperate life quiet, according to this account at any rate, since it is necessary that if it is temperate it is beautiful.' (160b3–9)

There is a transition across this first movement from a relative claim, that things that are not quiet are more temperate than things that are, because more beautiful, to a non-relative conclusion, that temperance is not quietness since temperance is a beautiful thing. The shift is accounted for if we note that at 159d1–2, having secured Charmides' agreement that certain things are more beautiful when done quickly than quietly, Socrates takes that as equivalent to saying that such things belong in the realm of the beautiful (*tou kalou*) when done quickly, in the realm of the ugly (*tou aischrou*) when done quietly. So if quiet things, in being less beautiful than non-quiet (quick) things, are ugly, then if temperance is beautiful, temperance cannot be a kind of quietness.

The second movement, being concessive – marked by Socrates' statement at 160b9 that 'there are indeed two alternatives' – is less clear-cut, but still governed by the principle that temperance is beautiful. On the first alternative, quick activities have in general turned out to be more beautiful than quiet ones (160b9–c2). On the second, granted that it is indifferent as to which things, those done quickly or those done quietly, are the more beautiful, still, acting quietly would not be temperance any more than acting quickly is, since temperance has been laid down as something beautiful (160c2–d2). Here the thought seems to be that even on this scenario we have been given no reason to accept the identification of temperance with quietness specifically. Since there is as much reason to identify it, qua beautiful, with its opposite, quickness, identifying it with quietness must be on the wrong track.

Now this talk of opposites brings us to what seems to be a flaw in Socrates' argument common to both movements. He takes it upon himself to treat 'quietness' as, in effect, the opposite of 'quickness'. This is confirmed by the fact that in the first movement he glosses 'quietly' as 'slowly' (*bradeōs*: 159c9, e4, e7, e9–10), or as 'with difficulty' (*mogis*: 159d2, 160a9). We are thus encouraged in this first part to treat 'quietly' as evaluatively negative, given that it is contrasted with quick performance in such activities as reading and writing, running and jumping, boxing and wrestling, learning and memorising, and so on. Even in the second movement, the contrast is still with things that are 'quick and strong' (160c2) or 'vigorous and quick' (c3–4), where even in conceding, at least for the sake of argument, that quiet things are no less beautiful than quick things, Socrates seems to imply that the concession is no more than for the sake of argument.

Why does Socrates make the concession at all? There seems no need of it given what the first movement established. That Socrates feels the need even to acknowledge a potential evaluative equivalence between quietness and quickness perhaps indicates an awareness on his part that he has rather blatantly hitherto read Charmides' 'quietness' in the worst possible light. Socrates, like Charmides, can speak Greek. So it cannot be that *hēsuchiotēs* and its cognates *cannot* suggest slowness or even sluggishness.[93] Yet Charmides did after all say that temperance was a *kind* of (*tis*) *hēsuchiotēs*;[94] and his initial association of that concept with doing things in an orderly way (*kosmiōs*, 159b3) equally shows that what he must mean by that is *hēsuchiotēs* as something like, say, 'calmness' rather than 'slowness'.[95]

At its most charitable, perhaps the explanation for Socrates' pejorative reading of *hēsuchiotēs* is that it teaches Charmides to be careful about his words. So, contrary to what I have claimed, Socrates is alive to the nuances of word-meaning and tries to convey its importance to Charmides. But that cannot, I think, be right. Charmides, as we have just seen, has actually been rather careful in indicating what he meant to convey with *hēsuchiotēs*.[96] It is Socrates who carelessly ignores this and just picks a meaning to suit his argument: 'manifestly illegitimately', as one commentator trenchantly but not unfairly puts it.[97]

One might still respond that Socrates is doing here what we must all do: interpret one's interlocutor's words. If he misinterprets them, as perhaps

---

[93] Tsouna (2022, 110) claims that Socrates 'stretches semantic boundaries' in his treatment of the term, though she does not appear to think that this undermines his refutation.
[94] Cf. Kosman (1983, 206); Heitsch (2000, 10).
[95] Tsouna (2022, 114) therefore seems to me uncharitable to Charmides in claiming that the kind of quietness he has in mind 'remains unspecified'.
[96] Moore (2020a, 224–5) therefore seems to me to put the emphasis in the wrong place in drawing attention to Charmides' ability here to encapsulate his answer 'in a word' (*sullēbdēn*, 159b5), though no doubt Moore's claim that this aspect represents Charmides' adaptation to the Socratic manner is a plausible one.
[97] Blyth (2001, 40); see also Santas (1973, 114–15).

Charmides did himself with Socrates' 'speak Greek', then that is just a consequence of the necessity of interpretation. But, again, I do not think that will do. Charmides is shown, when one thinks about it – and even if there is a self-serving element in his choice – interpreting Socrates' words so as to make, from his point of view, the most sense of them. That seems like a sound principle of interpretation, perhaps an essential one if communication is to take place.[98] It being seemingly pointless for Socrates to inform Charmides that he can speak his native language, Charmides reads this instead as a suggestion that he report in a linguistically refined way what he has found. He is, after all, as Critias had informed us, considered – by himself as well as by others – 'very poetic' (155a1).

By contrast, Socrates seems to go out of his way to interpret Charmides' first answer in the most mystifying way possible. How could Charmides have meant something so evaluatively negative, given that he was trying to say what temperance is? The conclusion of the first movement seems, therefore, not to go through. For there is no reason to suppose that there is anything especially negative about, say, doing things calmly. Moreover, even the concessive second movement fails to gain traction. For it is not just, as Socrates seems to suppose there, that one could do no better (and even that generously) than regard calmness as no less positive than quickness, so that one has no more reason to pick out calmness as being temperance than to pick out quickness. Rather, if one takes the contrary of 'calm' to be something like 'agitated' or 'disorderly' then one seems to have better reason to identify the former with temperance than the latter.[99]

Why, then, does Socrates proceed in this way? As I have already indicated, in part because he is genuinely careless about interpretation. He is not as responsible in taking account of distinctions in word-meaning as he might be. But the sheer blatancy with which he ignores such distinctions with regard to *hēsuchiotēs*, given Charmides' careful setting up, should make us wonder whether there is some extra factor in play. I think there is, and that is, as already suggested, the likelihood that Charmides has not even attempted to follow the soul-doctor's procedure

---

[98] This idea has been given prominence in philosophical debate on language by Donald Davidson. See e.g. Davidson (1973, 324); (2004, 35–6).

[99] This is not to say that 'calmness' or 'orderliness' should be identified with temperance, since there are numerous cases one can construct in which performing a certain action in a calm or orderly way (say, drawing up tomorrow's schedule for the torturing of the prisoners) seems more reprehensible than performing that action in an agitated way. Ultimately the attempt to characterise temperance as a style or manner of acting is a category mistake; see Burnyeat (1971, 215–19). Whether Socrates has grasped this point is hard to say, in part precisely because his uncharitable reading of Charmides' proposal keeps discussion of the valence of more charitable readings off the table.

and therefore has made no effort to detect and reveal the contents of his soul. That being the case, and if we interpret, as I have argued we should, Socrates' motive for engaging with Charmides as the desire to look at his soul, then Socrates has every incentive to dismiss Charmides' first answer in order to make room for Charmides to offer another account, based this time on what Charmides takes to be in his soul.

This, it seems to me, makes excellent sense of both Socrates' approach to Charmides' first answer and the transition to his second. For if Socrates had interpreted the first answer with a modicum of charity, then it is hard to see how, without at any rate approaching the matter in quite a different way,[100] even the appearance of refutation could have been delivered. Charmides, after all, had in effect sought to characterise temperance as a kind of calm orderliness; and that crucially seems to have, first, the positive evaluative polarity that would make it apt for the role of temperance, while second, its contrary – agitated disorderliness, say – is not such as to rank equally with it in evaluative terms.

Socrates, I infer, undermines Charmides' first answer in the manner that he does because it was not based on Charmides following the agreed procedure. The answer did not involve Charmides trying to reveal what was in his soul; he reached, instead, for a commonplace about the kind of thing temperance is. And that in turn shows us something about Socrates' own motive in engaging with Charmides. It cannot be aimed primarily at finding out what temperance is, since, faced with an account that seemed to offer, in Charmides' full statement of it, some promise in that direction, Socrates declined to read it in a way conducive to a proper assessment of whether the proposed account was successful. To the extent that the enquiry into what temperance is had become detached from its affording a view of what was in Charmides' soul, Socrates showed little interest in pursuing it sincerely.

The same diagnosis explains the way Socrates frames the transition to Charmides' second answer. He tells Charmides:

> Back again, focus more (*mallon prosechōn ton noun*), look at yourself,[101] and work out what sort of a person (*hopoion tina*) the presence of temperance makes you and what sort of a thing (*poia tis*) temperance would be to render you such, and having reflected on all of this, say well and courageously what it seems to you to be. (160d5–e1)

---

[100] Cf. Socrates' own rather pointed 'on this account at any rate' (*ek ge toutou tou logou*) at 160b8.
[101] The text is uncertain here, though it is clear that Plato wrote some verb with the root *blepō* ('look'). For discussion see Murphy (2007, 220).

3.9 Beauty at Bay

That Socrates reiterates so strongly and in such detail that Charmides needs to offer an account of temperance based on what the latter considers to be the effects of temperance's presence on him suggests less that Charmides simply got it wrong last time (as we have seen, it is not clear that that is even true) than that thus far he has not so much as deployed the procedure by which they had agreed that such an account would be delivered.

That we are supposed to think that Charmides now does actually begin to follow the procedure is then suggested by Socrates' immediate follow-up narration of Charmides' response:

> And he paused and having in very manly fashion undertaken scrutiny in relation to himself, said, 'So it seems to me that temperance makes a person be bashful and a bashful sort (*aischuntēlon*), and that temperance is the same thing as shame (*aidōs*).' (160e2–5)

The detail of this description of how Charmides comes up with his second answer, contrasting with the absence of anything similar preceding his first answer, conveys the idea that it is perhaps only now that Charmides has taken the procedure seriously; and as mentioned, Socrates' own earlier observation of Charmides' bashfulness at 158c6 adds weight to the idea that Charmides actually does here reveal something of what is in his soul.[102]

Alas, what he has revealed turns out not to be the same thing as temperance. Socrates' demolition of the account is swift and brutal,[103] while at the same raising some further questions about Socrates' relation to

---

[102] See Kahn (1996, 188). Critias, it is true, had reported Charmides as being very poetically gifted 'as he seems both to others and to himself' (155a1). The MSS reading *heautōi* ('to himself') is sometimes changed to *emautōi* ('to myself'), but even unmodified this is Critias' presumably contestable view of Charmides' boastful-looking view of himself. In any case I do not think that possession of *aidōs* need to connote modesty about one's gifts, especially where, as here, one's view of oneself is said to chime with that of others. Socrates' citation at *Laches* 201b2–3 of the same Homeric phrase that he is about to use against Charmides' identification of temperance with shame comes in the context of one's being prepared to risk ridicule and sign up as a pupil at an advanced age; so *aidōs* would be more an unwillingness to expose oneself to the reactions of others by ignoring social propriety (and 'shame' a better translation than 'modesty': the original Homeric passage is about being willing to beg). Recall that when Socrates notes Charmides' bashfulness (*to aischuntēlon*) at 158c on the question of whether he has temperance, Charmides reveals that he is worried about the oddness of doing himself *down* (*auton kath'heautou toiauta legein*, 158d2) in denying that he has it, as well as showing up Critias and those others who have said he does have it (cf. 157d), while also being anxious that it will appear 'obnoxious' (*epachthes*, 158d5) if he talks himself up for having it. As we saw (Section 3.8) there is apparently no easy way for him to do the right thing socially in responding to the question. Thus Méron (1979, 108) labels Charmides here 'diplomatic rather than modest'. For a different view of Charmides' behaviour see Benson (2000, 27 n. 36), who takes what he calls Charmides' 'display of modesty' at 158c–d to be insincere.

[103] Whether Charmides should have allowed himself to be so swiftly rebutted is a further issue. For a recent discussion see Raymond (2018).

the act of interpretation.[104] His refutation starts (160e6–7) with a reminder that Charmides has agreed that temperance is a beautiful thing. So again, the beauty of temperance seems to have a kind of axiomatic status in the discussion with Charmides. But this time Socrates goes on to infer that because those who are temperate are good, and that it is not those who are not good that a good thing makes (*apergazetai*), temperance must be a good as well as a beautiful thing (160e9–13).[105]

Socrates then asks Charmides:

> Do you not believe (*pisteueis*) Homer to be speaking beautifully (*kalōs legein*) when he says that "the presence of shame is no good for a man in need"? (161a2–4)

Charmides says that he does and Socrates can then deduce that, if Homer is right, temperance cannot be shame. For temperance, if it makes (*poiei*) anyone to whom it is present good, is a good thing (here we have a causal like-to-like principle made explicit), whereas shame, in being no good for some people (such as the needy), is no more good than bad (161a8–b2).

In contrast to his response to Charmides' first answer, I do not see in Socrates' response to his second any blatant misrepresentation of what Charmides meant. And that is as one would expect if my overall reading is on the mark. Now that Charmides has revealed something – a sense of shame – as present to his soul, it is in Socrates' interest, given that he is ultimately trying to get to look at a beautiful soul, to investigate sincerely (albeit swiftly) whether its presence indicates a beautiful soul or not.

In fact there is evidence that Socrates already has doubts whether temperance can be shame, so that his examination of Charmides is to this extent also a piece of self-examination. When he noted at 158c5–6 that Charmides' blushing made him appear even more beautiful, since his bashfulness was appropriate for his (young) age, that carries the implication that it would not have been appropriate in an adult.[106] If so, then given that temperance is presumably at least as appropriate in an adult as in a younger person, temperance should not be equated with bashfulness, and so, assuming, as Charmides' answer implies, that the two work in roughly the same way, not with shame either.

---

[104] Cairns (1993, 373) not unjustly dubs Socrates' treatment of *aidōs* in this passage 'extremely superficial'. I think we are indeed supposed to notice the superficiality as an example of Socrates' attitude towards interpretation; see further this section below.
[105] The argument looks garbled here and the text may contain a lacuna, but the gist seems clear: if the temperate are good, then by a causal like-to-like principle, temperance must be good to make them so. For defences of the transmitted text see van der Ben (1985, 28–32); Murphy (2014, 1000–2).
[106] Cf. Raymond (2018, 36).

Socrates is, I think, himself of the view that temperance is not to be identified with shame. There is, in contrast to his response to the first answer, no tactical motive to be discerned in this undermining of Charmides' account. That in turn, however, should not obscure a particular oddity in the way that Socrates tackles the second answer, one that is again connected with issues of interpretation. His framing of the question as 'Don't you believe Homer?' – the Greek verb (*pisteuein*) could also be rendered 'trust'[107] – invites Charmides to consider Homer as an epistemic authority, a status presumably based on the cultural authority with which the standing of his poetry endows him.

Now we have already seen evidence, crystallised in Charmides' inability to say at 158c–d whether he thinks he is temperate or not, that prevailing cultural norms are, as a guide to ethical truth, to be viewed with a critical eye. But this does not, and I think cannot be intended to, exempt Socrates himself from our critical scrutiny. It is not just that his reliance on Charmides' predictable deference to Homer smacks of an unearned shortcut to his refutation. It seems also to show something about Socrates' own attitude towards texts (one that, I shall suggest later, contrasts markedly with the attitude of Critias). Socrates plucks a single line – a line that, as it happens, is in its original context freighted with layers of meaning[108] – from a long and complex poem and treats it, peremptorily and without further analysis, in isolation from the rest,[109] as if that were a perfectly adequate procedure for interpreting it.[110]

Nor is this attitude on Socrates' part confined to Homer. In the case of Cydias, whom Socrates seemed to find genuinely helpful, there is a similarly reductive approach: a short extract, quoted with minimal context, and read without any gesture at critical analysis. Now perhaps Socrates' plight at the time, paralysed by the sight of Charmides, precluded a different approach. But when we see the same approach manifested in regard to Homer, in a context where serious analysis is called for and there is nothing preventing its deployment, then we may conclude that Socrates as oral discussant does not seem to have much time or appetite for critical engagement with texts. On the other hand, our ability to respond to the text that depicts this shows us that such engagement *is* possible, its

---

[107] So Moore and Raymond (2019, 14); contra, Tsouna (2022, 133).
[108] See Tuozzo (2011, 164–5); Tsouna (2022, 131). [109] Cf. Halliwell (2000, 99).
[110] One might add that in guilelessly referring to a line spoken by one of Homer's characters (Telemachus) as 'what Homer says', Plato's carefully written character Socrates casually obliterates any distinction between author and character; cf. Benardete (2000, 243).

possibility revealed to us just insofar as we are revealed to ourselves, in mounting such a response, as occupying a critical stance.

No amount of interpretation, one suspects, would have saved Charmides' second answer. And that of course is a disappointment for Socrates, since the evidence so far has not shown Charmides to have a beautiful soul. Still, there has been progress: after not even attempting to reveal his soul in his first answer, Charmides did make such an attempt in his second. Unfortunately for Socrates, what happens next looks like a falling back even from that on Charmides' part. Agreeing that Socrates is right to conclude that temperance is not the same thing as shame, Charmides, without missing a beat, asks Socrates to consider whether an account of temperance is correct that he heard from someone else, namely that temperance is 'doing one's own things' (*to ta heautou prattein*, 161b6).

This move by Charmides threatens to derail Socrates' erotic quest completely. Explicitly this time, Charmides is so far from offering an account of temperance based on a sense of what is in his soul that he resorts to borrowing someone else's account and inviting Socrates to examine that instead. It looks very much as if Charmides, already exposed rather more than he would like by Socratic investigation of what is in his soul, seeks to deflect. At the same time, he indicates, in his twice bidding Socrates to 'examine' (*skepsai*, 161b4; *skopei*, b6) this new account, that he has no objection to, indeed perhaps rather likes the idea of, another's proposal taking the heat of Socratic investigation.

Why Charmides might like that is made clearer from Socrates' response. Teasing Charmides in maybe not so gentle a way, he exclaims (161b8–c1): 'You wretch! You heard this from Critias or another of the wise ones.' If Critias was indeed the source of the account, then the idea of having a proposal attributable to one's esteemed cousin and guardian put through its paces by Socrates no doubt has a certain appeal. Both the identity of the account's source and Charmides' motives are later made clearer still when Charmides, confessing that he cannot say what 'doing one's own things' might be, chuckles, looks at Critias, and says that maybe the one who gave the account does not know what he meant (*enoei*, 162b10) either.[111]

In the wake of Socrates' teasing, Critias intervenes to say that Charmides certainly did not hear the account from him (161c2), in response to which there follows an interesting exchange between Charmides and Socrates:

---

[111] The idea of a subject not knowing what they meant, or were thinking, will be of importance later; see Section 5.1.

3.9 Beauty at Bay

'But Socrates,' said Charmides, 'what difference does it make who I heard it from?'

'None,' I replied, 'for what one should absolutely examine is not who said it but whether what is said is true or not.'

'Now you're speaking correctly,' he said. (161c3–7)

Socrates will go on to examine, and find problematic, this third account. But for now we need to ask why he would say in this context that what matters is whether the proposed account is true rather than who said it. In regard to Charmides' first answer, Socrates was, I have argued, even prepared to dispense for the time being with a genuine attempt to test its truth in favour of ensuring that the account he subsequently got from Charmides was *Charmides'* account, in the sense of its being based on what Charmides took to be present in his soul.

Hence, far from evincing a pious and uncontentious dedication to the goal of truth, Socrates' pronouncement that this is what matters is, in context, puzzling. As we have seen, Socrates' motivation has been the discovery of beauty in Charmides' soul. Beauty will be there if temperance is. So he wants to find out whether temperance is in Charmides' soul. And to do that he needs, firstly, to access what is in Charmides' soul, and secondly, to find out whether it is temperance. Finding out whether a given account of temperance is true is thus an essential but subordinate task for Socrates, rather than something of independent value. Thus far, at any rate, finding out whether an account of temperance is true has been of interest to him just insofar as it enables him to tell whether a quality reported by Charmides as being in his soul is in fact temperance.[112]

What, then, motivates Socrates now to declare that the truth of an account is to be investigated independently of whose account it is? If it is not Charmides' account at issue, in the specific sense of one that will have drawn upon what Charmides perceives to be in his soul, then discovering whether the account is true becomes disconnected from the goal of finding beauty in Charmides' soul. So it seems a striking departure for Socrates to opine at this point that it does not matter whose account it is. What explains the departure is that it has, in effect, been forced upon Socrates. In seeking to deflect the discussion onto another's account, Charmides has made his soul unavailable for scrutiny. Socrates is not for now going to get

---

[112] Notwithstanding Tuozzo's observation, in regard to the question of how 'personal' Socratic method is, that Charmides' beliefs about what temperance is can reasonably have originated elsewhere (Tuozzo 2011, 136–7; 140–1), it is crucial for Socrates' purposes that these beliefs are associated with qualities that Charmides finds within.

any more proposed accounts of temperance emerging from what Charmides finds in his soul.

3.10 Interpreting Critias

If Socrates wants to keep discussion going at all, he will have to fall back to the position that merely discovering the truth is what they are after. And this is corroborated just before Critias agrees to take over discussion from Charmides, when Socrates tells Critias at 162e4–5, putting the objective in a markedly impersonal way, that he would rather examine with him than with Charmides whether 'what has been said (*to lechthen*) is true or not'. The impersonal mode seems to signal that the scaling down of Socrates' ambition to the mere discovery of whether or not a proposal about the nature of temperance is true is a function of Charmides' soul no longer being available for matching with such an account. We see the impersonal emphasis continue during the discussion with Critias, when at 165b7–c1 Socrates says that he investigates 'what is being proposed' (*to protithemenon*) because he himself does not know. So finding out the truth of a proposal is apparently now the enquiry's goal, not getting to look at (what is in) another's soul.

This scaling back prompts the question why Socrates, given his initial motive for enquiry into temperance, does want to keep the discussion going in this way, with Critias in Charmides' place, once Charmides has withdrawn his soul. I return to the question below, though my answer in brief (to repeat) will be that doing so provides a way of ultimately enticing Charmides into exposing his soul once more. Socrates' continued manoeuvrings thus represent an ongoing deployment of the erotic art, whose aim, let us recall, is to get a soul to expose itself for the purpose of satisfying one's desire for beauty. For now, Socrates confides in Charmides that he would be surprised if they could in fact discover how things are with the proposed account of temperance as doing one's own things, since (he says) the account looks like a riddle (*ainigma*, 161c9).

Socrates goes on, as we shall see in more detail below, to spell out why he finds the account puzzling (161d–162a), and then offers some insight into what he means in calling it a riddle (162a–b). He asks Charmides whether he had heard the account from someone stupid. Charmides replies: by no means; the person seemed very wise (*sophos*, 162b3). So, says Socrates, that person was offering the account as a riddle, given that it is difficult to understand what doing one's own things is (162b4–6). We have, then, in effect, a disjunction: if the account was given by a stupid person, then presumably it is just a stupid account; but seeing that it apparently came from a wise person, it is a riddle: obscure or hard to understand.

There is thus a connection suggested here, one that will be further corroborated when Critias later talks of the Delphic inscription as being 'somewhat riddling' (*ainigmatōdesteron*, 164e6), between wisdom and obscurity. The wise produce, in virtue of their wisdom, things that are difficult, at least for those who are not wise, to understand. By implication, and to make sense of the contrast with the foolish, a riddle is not to be taken as false, but as having a truth-value that is difficult to ascertain. This explains why Socrates had begun (161c5–9) by saying that although one must examine whether the account is true or not, he would be surprised if they were able to say how things were with it given that it looks like a riddle.

This view again raises the question of Socrates' attitude towards interpretation. One would not, it might be thought, necessarily expect proposed accounts of temperance to be easy to understand. They might, in other words, need interpreting. It is as if Socrates expects that the *meaning* of any proposed account should in the normal course of events be clear, and the task is simply to discover whether such a proposal, with its clear sense, is true or not. By calling a proposal that does not immediately yield a clear sense a 'riddle' Socrates seems to be elevating it to a plane beyond the comprehension of ordinary mortals, implying that it is to be treated as an outlier in his investigation.

This seems to me problematic in much the same way as Socrates' views on interpretation that we have already examined. It suggests that interpretation, rather than being a constitutive element of communicative discourse, functions as an exception to the supposedly standard case where it is just obvious what things mean. And this seems both false and dangerous, in that failure to put in the work of interpretation can lead investigations astray, as we saw in the case of Socrates' response to Charmides' first account (temperance as a kind of quietness), however deliberate a piece of interpretive sabotage on Socrates' part that may have been.

That Socrates nonetheless does regard interpretation in something like the way I have described is evidenced by the way he fleshes out his original remark that the present account looks like a riddle. He says, at 161d1–2, that in saying that temperance is doing one's own things, the proposer of the account 'was presumably not meaning it in the way in which he expressed his words'.[113] That is, because the meaning was obscure, the

---

[113] *ou dēpou ... hēi ta rhēmata ephthengsato tautēi kai enoei.*

words used could not have been what the proposer really meant. Again, Socrates' expectation seems to be that unless the sense of the words one uses is immediately clear and straightforward, then they were not what the speaker meant; and once again, a role for interpretation is seemingly rendered moot: either the meaning of the speaker's words is immediately apparent, or there is no comprehension of those words to be had. And yet it is arguably in that middle ground between incomprehensibility and obviousness that virtually the whole activity of communication takes place; the ground, surely, on which a complex written text such as the *Charmides* itself must operate.

Given his view, it is no surprise that Socrates makes no real attempt in what follows to interpret the phrase 'doing one's own things' such as to make a maximally comprehensible meaning out of it. This disinclination may in part be a function of the fact that Socrates, as depicted in the work, carries out his business through oral conversation. Perhaps this encourages in him an attitude that, in a sense, there is no call to interpret. Faced with obscurity one can just tell one's interlocutor to try again until they succeed in reporting without obscurity: an option not available to the reader of a written text. If that is how Socrates thinks, it seems to me that he is led astray. As we saw earlier, in the case of Charmides interpreting (appropriately enough) the expression 'speaking Greek', linguistic interpretation is not an optional extra, but a necessity, whether one is listening to spoken words or reading written ones.

In the case of temperance as doing one's own things, rather than attempting to interpret, Socrates doubles down on his claim that it is a riddle and tries to show why the proposal is unintelligible. Still in conversation with Charmides, he gives a series of examples (161d–162a) that purport to demonstrate how it leads to absurdity. Thus, at school, the reading and writing of names other than one's own is evidently not a case of intemperance; and in the practice of the crafts, a city in which the law required that each made their own clothes, shoes and so on, and not those of others, would not thereby be a city run in a temperate way. So, concludes Socrates, we are dealing with a riddle.

When Charmides gives his meaningful glance towards Critias while opining that perhaps the proposer of the account did not know what he meant by it either (162b9–11), Critias is duly roused, with Socrates narrating that he took this as confirmation that Critias was indeed the one from whom Charmides heard the account (162c). Critias indignantly tells Charmides that just because *he* does not know what the proposer meant by 'doing one's own things' does not mean that the proposer does

3.10 Interpreting Critias

not know either (162d4–6). Socrates then invites Critias to take up the account and Critias accepts (162e1–6).

Along the way we get some editorialising from Socrates. He says it was evident that Critias had long been 'spoiling for a fight and looking to impress' (*agōniōn kai philotimōs ... echōn*, 162c1–3) Charmides and the onlookers, and could now hold back no longer. With the example of Chaerephon in mind, we may wish to exercise caution about taking on trust Socrates' description of Critias here. Not so much, perhaps, because it is inaccurate but because, if we are not careful to keep in mind that Socrates' perspective is not necessarily to be taken as authoritative, we may end up assuming that Critias' allegedly competitive motives mean that his way of defending his account is not to be taken seriously; and that, I think, is a mistake.

We can begin to see this if we dwell for a moment on how Socrates characterises Critias' annoyance with Charmides over the latter's failure to understand what 'doing one's own things' means. Socrates says that Critias struck him as being angry with Charmides 'like a poet with an actor (*hupokritēs*) who makes a hash of reciting his poems' (162d2–3). Now this may be more than mere simile. The historical Critias was, among other things, a poet, and doubtless we are supposed to have that in mind. Of more immediate interest, perhaps, is that the situation envisaged within the simile is that of a dramatic recital in which the actor thereby *interprets* the poems he is reciting;[114] the term *hupokritēs* also carries the sense of 'interpreter'.[115] And while Charmides is of course not literally an actor reciting Critias' poems, he has just been engaged in a discussion with Socrates about the apparently enigmatic sense of (what turn out to be) Critias' words.

Thus the simile that Plato has written for Socrates conveys the idea that, for Critias, his formula about temperance as doing one's own things is there to be interpreted (well or badly); and what has happened is that Charmides, insofar as he has not been able to see beyond the absurdities that Socrates contrives to show the formula entails, has misinterpreted it.

The view that Socrates' simile imputes to Critias, that speech requires interpretation and may therefore be misinterpreted, is, I submit, more reasonable than the view Socrates seems to hold himself, that what does not make immediate sense may therefore be dismissed as incomprehensible. We shall see, in Chapter 4, these battle lines over the place of interpretation continue to be drawn as Critias mounts his defence of

---

[114] See also Section 5.7 n. 41.   [115] For the sense, cf. *Timaeus* 72b3.

temperance as doing one's own things. But as we near the point at which Critias takes over from Charmides the discussion of temperance with Socrates, I want to return to the question I raised at the start of this section and follow it through: why does Socrates continue discussing temperance with Critias at all?

To approach this question, let me briefly revisit the one that is logically prior to it, namely why Socrates stops conversing with Charmides. I have argued that this is because Charmides in effect withdraws his soul from exposure. Instead of continuing to look for temperance by revealing what is in his soul, he deflects by inviting Socrates to examine a proposal about temperance that, it turns out, came from Critias and that seems to have nothing in particular to do with what Charmides finds in his own soul.[116] Since Socrates' reason for investigating temperance in the first place was to see if Charmides had it, and would therefore have a beautiful soul with which Socrates could engage, Charmides' refusal to show what is in his soul should have made the investigation of temperance moot. Yet Socrates continues to investigate it with Critias. Why?

If we want to respect the motive that Socrates had given for his interest in finding temperance – namely that he desires to look at a beautiful soul, and temperance makes the soul of one who possesses it beautiful – then we need to explain his willingness to continue discussing what temperance is with Critias in a way that is continuous with that motive. Less convincing, as I argued above,[117] is the hypothesis that Socrates' switch represents a move from the second to the first part of his two-part question: how things are currently going with philosophy. Given that his conversation with the 'philosophical' Charmides already seems to fall under that rubric, it is not clear that taking up the cudgels with Critias is needed on those grounds.[118] Moreover, once we see how Socrates deliberately brings back into conversation, after the long discussion with Critias, a Charmides now more than willing to undergo being charmed by Socrates, it becomes plain that continuing the pursuit of Charmides remained Socrates' goal from afar.

---

[116] Indeed we may note that in calling upon another's account Charmides apparently illustrates failure, in this regard, to do what is one's own; cf. Moore and Raymond (2019, 68).

[117] Section 1.7.

[118] Tuozzo (2011, 127) claims that 'the point of calling Charmides over in the first place was for Socrates to have a philosophical conversation with him'. But that is only part of the story. Conversation is, according to Socrates, the way one gets to look at a soul; but the reason he wants to look at Charmides' soul is that Critias has said that Charmides is beautiful and good in respect of it. So the unavailability of that soul does not make it obvious why Socrates would wish to continue discussion elsewhere.

3.10 Interpreting Critias

We have not yet arrived at that point. For the time being Charmides has shown himself disinclined to expose his soul further. Perhaps, then, we should consider the possibility that Socrates proceeds with Critias in order to find beauty in Critias' soul. If so, that will enable him to carry forward directly the motive that underlay his discussion of temperance with Charmides, except with Critias now as the object of erotic pursuit.

This, however, seems an unlikely explanation. Firstly, Socrates' two-part question at 153d did indeed express an interest in learning who was outstanding in beauty, but that was specifically concerning the young. Secondly, Socrates never says that he, or anyone else, finds Critias beautiful in either body or soul,[119] or indeed that he has any interest in Critias' soul at all. He never, for example, expresses a view about whether Critias himself might possess temperance.[120] As we have already noted, the orientation of the discussion becomes more impersonal in the transition to, and then during, Critias' stretch as main interlocutor. In this connection it is striking, and perhaps not accidental, that the word 'soul' (*psuchē*), while it occurs frequently in the material preceding the main discussion with Critias, is wholly absent in the course of that discussion, even where one might expect it to be found, such as in the review of cognitive and affective capacities at 167c–168a.[121] It only reappears at 175d7, just as Socrates turns once more to address Charmides, with Charmides' soul as the referent.[122]

Now it might be objected that, simply by engaging in discussion with Critias, Socrates is choosing to engage with Critias' soul, and that, moreover, there are at least three occasions when Critias' psychological state seems directly at issue, two of which involve Socrates explicitly commenting on it. On examination, however, these occasions if anything reinforce the idea that engaging with Critias' soul is not Socrates' purpose in continuing the discussion of temperance with Critias.

First, then, as we have seen, at 162c Socrates comments on Critias' competitive desire to impress the onlookers and not be shown up by Charmides' ham-fisted attempts at defending the account of temperance as doing one's own things. Now note that this reaction of Critias' is a response to provocation:[123] in the most immediate context, this had

---

[119] Cf. n. 1 above. Intriguingly, Critias' father is named Callaischrus ('Beautugly'; 153c7, 169b5), suggesting a rather mixed picture for the son to inherit. By contrast, and despite Critias and Charmides being cousins, Socrates emphasises the outstanding beauty for which Charmides' family line is renowned (157e–158a).
[120] Cf. Garver (2018, 486).   [121] Cf. Szlezák (1985, 137–8).
[122] Cf. Dorion (2004, 36); Danzig (2013, 500 n. 31).   [123] Cf. Solère-Queval (1993, 19).

come in the form of Charmides' suggestion that the proposer of the account (namely Critias) may not have known what he meant by it; but in the slightly wider context, it had come in the form of Socrates' claim that the account is like a riddle, together with the latter's insistence on spelling out its supposed absurdity. Socrates himself, that is, along with Charmides, seems intent on provoking Critias into taking up the discussion.

Why, exactly, Socrates wants to continue discussion with Critias is, however, precisely the point at issue. Socrates may well have used psychological engagement to provoke Critias into discussion, but that serves as the means not the motive. Socrates' motive for the provocation therefore remains an open question. Socrates cites Critias' age and experience as the reason why the latter is more likely to know what the account of temperance as doing one's own things means (162e1–2). But our question is why Socrates is now content to take part in an investigation that merely seeks to gain this sort of knowledge. Let us turn, then, to the two examples within that investigation where Critias' psychological state is in play. These will each tell against the thesis that it is engagement with Critias' soul that motivates Socrates here.

At 166c3–6 – the second case of Critias' psychological state coming into view – Critias is not explicitly described by Socrates as getting angry, but evidently does get angry when he accuses Socrates of neglecting the argument and trying to refute him instead. Socrates defends himself (166c7–d4) by telling Critias that, if he does refute him, it is for no other purpose than that for which he would scrutinise himself, to guard against unwittingly thinking he knows something that he does not, and that he examines the argument most of all for his own sake but perhaps also for the sake of his companions. He then asks Critias:

> Or don't you think that it is pretty much a common good for everyone that the nature of each of the things that are becomes clear (*kataphanes*)? (166d4–6)

Critias agrees and is assuaged by Socrates' stated explanation that while there may be a personal dimension to the latter's enquiries, in the sense that an interlocutor's account may well get refuted, the aim of such refutation is to make sure that the enquiry into how things are is not impeded by the mistaken supposition that one already knows the answer. The goal of enquiry is set down here as getting clear about how things are, so in the specific case this will be getting clear about the nature of temperance. Socrates, that is, goes out of his way to deny that the purpose of his enquiry is to expose Critias' soul, whether to see if it is beautiful or for any other reason. Such exposure as takes place serves the purpose of discovering the truth about (in this case) what temperance is.

Now no doubt this is good psychology on Socrates' part. He softens Critias' wrath by explaining how the personal dimension of enquiry merely serves the goal of truth. But that of course is quite compatible with the claim that, as far as his intentions with Critias are concerned, Socrates really does have no further goal beyond the discovery of the truth (if he has even that). As Socrates puts it to Critias (166d9–e2): what matters is not whether Socrates or Critias is refuted, but that Critias focus on how 'the argument itself' (*autos ho logos*) will turn out when it is tested. There is no indication that Socrates' interest is in engaging with Critias' soul as such, whether to expose or improve it. Engagement with his soul is undertaken for the assistance it might provide in getting on with the argument. This is not to say that Socrates' pursuit of enquiry into temperance with Critias might not have some further goal beyond trying to get clear about what temperance is. I argue that indeed it does: to impress Charmides, with a display of argumentative fireworks, into exposing his soul again. But that is a goal that concerns Charmides' soul, not Critias'.

The third example of Critias' psychological state coming to the fore occurs at 169c, where Critias is said to have 'caught' Socrates' aporia about the account of temperance as knowledge of knowledge. According to Socrates, as a result of Critias' constant desire to be thought well of, the latter was embarrassed in front of the onlookers at not being able to explain how the account would work and so muttered something unclear to cover up his being at a loss. Socrates then suggests to Critias that they just assume for now that knowledge of knowledge is possible and proceed to consider a different aspect, its benefit (which they then go on to do), Socrates narrating that he adopted this approach 'in order that the argument go forward' (*hina ho logos proïoi*, 169d2).

Notice that here, unlike in the previous case, the motive of advancing the argument is given as part of Socrates' narrative to his companion, not also as part of what he says to Critias. So here there is no question of its being spun (possibly insincerely) to assuage Critias. The words therefore represent what Socrates took as being his actual immediate motive in the discussion: to move the argument along.

There is a pattern here. As with his anger previously, so with his confusion now, Critias' various psychological states are reduced to little more than impediments to be overcome in the cause of argumentative progress. Critias' aporia is, strikingly, treated by Socrates as an *obstacle* to the argument moving forward.[124] So far from his interest in the aporia being that it represents, say, a development or exposure of Critias' soul,[125] it is, in this context, for Socrates simply something to be pushed past so that the argument may proceed. I conclude that Socrates' motive for continuing the discussion of temperance with Critias is not the opportunity it affords him to see Critias' soul, even if he gets to glimpse his soul in the course of that discussion.

3.11 Eros as Unifier

A different reason for the continuation, also consistent with Socrates' express motive for investigating temperance, is that he hopes thereby to get to look at something beautiful: not now a soul that has (or may come to have) temperance, but temperance itself. This is consistent in that Socrates' reason for wanting to look at Charmides' soul was the promise that it was beautiful. It turned out that its being beautiful (if it is) will obtain if it is temperate. Since temperance is indeed presented, frequently and importantly during Socrates' discussions with Charmides about what temperance is, as something beautiful, then it seems that Socrates' quest for beauty could be satisfied by his coming to see temperance itself. Investigating what temperance is with Critias, then, will be a way of pursuing the beautiful thing that temperance is.

Because it *is* consistent with Socrates' express motive, I would not wish to rule out of court this explanation of why Socrates continues with Critias. Indeed, to the extent that Critias is better equipped to help discover what temperance is – as Socrates implies, in drawing him in, at 162e1–2 – discussion with him should increase the chances of getting that beautiful object in view. Nonetheless there seems reason to doubt that coming to behold the beauty of temperance itself is Socrates' principal motive for continuing with Critias.

One reason for doubt is precisely that the beauty of temperance itself, though frequently cited during the discussion with Charmides, is only

---

[124] In his searching study of the role of aporia in the *Charmides*, Politis (2008, 9–10) acknowledges that Critias' aporia here represents a 'failure' of the investigation thus far but not, I think, the stronger point that it is presented by Socrates as actually inhibiting further investigation because of the shame it induces in Critias (169c6–d2). Politis (2007, 236) points out that (by contrast) when Socrates describes himself as being in aporia at 167b that initiates a new phase of enquiry. On the contrasting modes of Socratic and Critian aporia, see also Levine (2016, 255).

[125] On what Critias' aporia might represent in a more positive vein, independently of Socrates' treatment of it, see Section 4.9.

mentioned once during the discussion with Critias, namely at 175a11, not long before Charmides is brought back into the discussion. A second reason is that while eros is said to take what is beautiful as its object at 167e7–8, and temperance itself is, as we have seen, said to be beautiful, the only entity in the work that is explicitly represented as an object of eros is a concrete individual, namely Charmides at 154c2 (cf. a5, c4). Thirdly, the horizontal structure of the *Charmides* suggests that looking upon the beauty of temperance is not in itself Socrates' ultimate aim. For if it were, he would not return to Charmides and draw him back into discussion, with Charmides eventually agreeing to be 'charmed' by Socrates for as long as Socrates deems adequate (176b2–4). Given that Critias is presented as a more adept discussant than Charmides, if getting temperance in view was (or had become) the principal aim, then discussion should have continued with Critias; but it does not. It seems to me, then, that while we should take the dialogue as encouraging us to reflect on the idea of an abstract object as object of erotic pursuit, it does not present such pursuit as Socrates' ultimate goal in his turning to discussion with Critias.

Here, instead, is a reading that seeks to account for the unity of the dialogue along its horizontal dimension by keeping Charmides at its centre throughout. Socrates wants to get to view Charmides' soul in prospect of discerning beauty, insofar as that soul possesses temperance, therein. Charmides briefly exposes his soul, in his second account of temperance, then withdraws it in the face of Socrates' withering examination, calling instead on an account he had heard Critias give. Socrates, his erotic pursuit at least temporarily thwarted, then abandons Charmides and defaults to discussion of the truth of various accounts of temperance offered by Critias. But this manoeuvre represents a regrouping of Socrates' erotic forces, not a defeat. For, by dazzling Charmides with a display of intellectual fireworks, on the very same topic, in his discussion with Critias, he plans to make Charmides realise just what he has been missing in his refusal to engage. Enthralled by Socrates' virtuosity, and piqued by exclusion, Charmides in the end duly shows keenness to re-engage. In getting Charmides back ready to expose his soul, the art of erotics has made progress.

Let me defend this reading of the narrative by considering an objection to it. I used above, in relation to the switch of interlocutor from Charmides to Critias, the language of 'abandonment' advisedly, to indicate the strong erotic undercurrent that, I have argued, characterises Socrates' dealings with Charmides. But (the objection may run) it is not Socrates who abandons Charmides; if anything, it is the other way round. It is

Charmides, after all, who provokes Critias into conversation by implying at 162b that even he, as hinted-at proposer of the idea that temperance is doing one's own things, might not know what he means by it. We are, as it were, egged on in this interpretation at 162c6–d1 when Socrates claims mischievously that Charmides, wishing not to uphold the burden of discourse, was trying to provoke Critias into shouldering it. Thus, we conclude, it is Charmides who lobbies, successfully, for himself to bow out of the discussion and for Critias to take up the task of defending the proposal.

Now it is true that at this point Charmides may be as eager to relieve himself of the dialectical pressure as Socrates is to move on from him as interlocutor. Charmides has been stung by the brusqueness of the refutation of the idea of (his) sense of shame being the same thing as temperance, while Socrates has been set back by Charmides' consequent withdrawal of his soul and deflection to Critias' account. That both may have connived at it, however, is no reason to deny that Socrates is instigator of the separation. Consider: when Charmides' proposal that temperance is the same thing as shame has been refuted, Charmides immediately turns to the suggestion that he says he heard from someone else, that temperance is doing one's own things, and asks Socrates if he thinks the proposer is correct on this (161b4–7).

Instead of directly giving a view, Socrates picks up the first part of Charmides' remark and tells him that he must have heard the suggestion 'from Critias or another of the wise ones' (161b8–c1). In response to this, Critias, perhaps not so eager himself at this stage to be subject to Socratic questioning – we are still prior to Charmides' mishandling (as Critias sees it) of the suggestion – hastily denies that he was Charmides' source (c2). When Charmides then asks Socrates what difference it makes from whom he heard it (c3–4), Socrates, as we saw, says none: what matters is whether it is true or not (c5–6).

While this reply meets with Charmides' approval ('now you're got it right', c7), it is evidently Socrates who has originally tried to prompt Critias into joining the conversation.[126] Since Socrates will tell us at 162c4–6 that he suspected all along that Charmides heard the suggestion from Critias, he is clearly hoping, when he first mentions Critias as possible source, that the latter will pick up discussion of it with him. And that is because his hope of seeing beauty in Charmides' soul has been frustrated, with Charmides indicating, by the turn to what he heard from

[126] So Tuozzo (2011, 138).

Critias, that for now he is either unable or unwilling to suggest further qualities of his own that might represent temperance.

Only in the light of this does Socrates opine that what matters is not who originated the proposal that temperance is doing one's own things but whether it is true. As long as the revealing of Charmides' soul was in train, everything turned on the various proposals for temperance being *his* proposals, insofar as it was supposed to be articulations of his impressions of what was in his soul that provided the material for Socrates to test whether he had temperance (and so beauty) therein. It is not until Charmides has given up even trying to report such impressions that Socrates states that one should merely examine whether or not a proposal about temperance is true, not whose it is.

There is, plausibly, an additional reason for Socrates putting things this way. It gives cover for Critias to take on the role of discussing the new account of temperance without having to risk the exposure of being explicitly identified as its proposer. If so, that would provide further confirmation that Socrates is paving the way for Critias to replace Charmides. What is more, Charmides himself gives no indication that he wants to stop acting as Socrates' interlocutor. He happily continues in that role as Socrates presses the account of temperance as doing one's own things to absurdity. So although Charmides' comment, that the proposer of the account may not have known what he meant by it, may be the final straw for Critias, Socrates is clear that Critias has 'long' (*palai*, 162c1) been itching for the fray as a result of Charmides' failure to put up any resistance to Socrates' efforts to undermine the account.

Two conclusions, then, seem indicated. Firstly, that Socrates in fact does most of the work in provoking Critias into intervening; but secondly, that Charmides wants to have his cake and eat it too. He is happy to (continue to) act as interlocutor in a Socratic investigation so long as it is not his ideas that are being investigated and his soul thereby exposed. Notice, then, the brusqueness with which Socrates disallows this state of affairs. Straight after Critias informs Charmides that just because the latter doesn't know what the proposer of temperance as doing one's own things meant, that does not mean the proposer doesn't know, Socrates tells Critias:

> [I]t is no surprise that this one [Charmides] is ignorant (*agnoein*) at his age, whereas I suppose it is likely that you, on account of your time of life and concern, do know. So if you accept that temperance is what this one says and take over the account, I would find it far more agreeable to examine with you whether what has been said is true or not. (162d7–e5)

It is not clear that this is how Charmides had envisaged the taking down of Critias panning out. Thanks, I suggest, to Socrates' mastery of erotics, it rather looks as if the tables have been turned and Charmides, so lauded earlier for his philosophical and moral qualities, is now made to look rather foolish. His humbling has a twofold element: firstly, the golden boy is dismissed as predictably ignorant, given his age, about what temperance is; then, to add insult to injury, Socrates tells Critias that he would therefore find it 'far more agreeable' (*polu hēdion*, 162e4) to examine the truth of the proposed account of temperance with him (sc. than with Charmides). All this of course in Charmides' hearing. The outcome – Critias duly agreeing to take over – may be what Charmides was angling for; but the putdown from Socrates is harsh.

Here we can see how the switch to (mere) discovery of truth as the goal of enquiry works dramatically for Socrates. The idea that investigating the truth of the proposal in its own right is what matters was rolled out by Socrates in response to Charmides asking what difference it makes who the source of the proposal was. That response seemed to suit Charmides – who wanted to deflect the investigation away from his own soul – more than it did Socrates, given his aim of seeking for beauty in Charmides' soul. But in lauding Critias as far more suitable than Charmides for the task of investigating the truth, Socrates makes the best of a bad hand.

Socrates, I submit, rather deftly humbles Charmides for having withdrawn his soul from discussion. He pivots to Critias without a word to Charmides, his complimentary remark to Critias at 162e4 indicating that he is apparently glad to cut Charmides loose. That Charmides has, as we shall see when he is eventually brought back by Socrates into the conversation, stayed to listen seems to be his choosing. Socrates expresses no preference for him to remain.

Given, however, the unlikelihood of Charmides absconding while his guardian is in conversation with Socrates, the latter may in fact have seen an opportunity here, as I have argued, to show a captive Charmides just what he is missing when another takes his place: what, specifically, he is missing when a free-standing enquiry into the truth about temperance, of the sort that Charmides had seemed to favour, takes place without his (direct) participation.

This, it seems to me, shows Socrates' practice of the art of erotics at its most cunning. One might, after all, wonder why it is continuation precisely of an enquiry into what temperance is that Socrates provokes, rather than initiation of some other form of conversation with Critias.[127]

---

[127] My thanks to Verity Harte and Vasilis Politis for pressing this question.

3.11 Eros as Unifier

The answer, on my reading, is that the humbling of Charmides works in part by his hearing Socrates inform Critias that, on the very topic they have been discussing, the latter is likely to be by far the better interlocutor. The sting of rejection would not have been so sharp had the switch of interlocutor brought with it a change of subject, and thereby avoided a straight comparison of the relative prowess of Charmides and his guardian.

We can at this point venture to put a name to this aspect of Socrates' deployment of the art of erotics. His behaviour bears a resemblance to the disreputable practice known (I am told) in contemporary parlance as 'negging', in which an object of one's affections is deliberately undermined in order to make them more pliable.[128] Charmides is humbled by the brutal clarity with which Socrates expresses his preference to continue the conversation about temperance with Critias instead of with him. The rejection, combined with the bravura display subsequently put on, principally for Charmides' benefit, with Critias, makes Charmides gratifyingly keen to re-engage when Socrates eventually grants him the opportunity. That Socrates does choose to bring Charmides back into the discussion when he does underlines the sincerity of his aim throughout as being the securing of Charmides' soul for inspection.

I hope this offers one plausible way to read the unity of the *Charmides* across its horizontal dimension, analysed in terms of Socrates' motives for engaging with his interlocutors in the way that he does. Having placed the discussion with Critias within that context, it will soon be time to examine the discussion itself in more detail. Before doing so, however, we need to address a further point that threatens to call this account of the dialogue's unity into question: a point that goes to the heart of the issue of how eros, temperance and beauty are related.

---

[128] For external evidence that Socrates might endorse such a practice, see *Lysis* 206a–c, 210e, a dialogue that bears some dramatic resemblance to the *Charmides*, though there seem to me two key differences in this regard between the texts. Firstly, while the humbling of Lysis is achieved through Socrates' conversation with Lysis, that of Charmides is achieved in part through withdrawal by Socrates from conversation with Charmides. Secondly, Socrates' deployment of erotics in the *Lysis* is for the benefit of Hippothales; in the *Charmides*, it is for the benefit of himself. An anonymous reader objects that this 'fails to point out the single most important difference. In the *Lysis* Socrates very explicitly promises to teach Hippothales a lesson in how one should talk to one's beloved (206c), and after doing so he is equally explicit that this is what he has just achieved (210e).' If that is a difference, it is accounted for by the second of the differences already noted, since it would be dramatically odd for Socrates to announce that he was going to show *himself* how to treat a beloved. In any event, as I have argued in the main text above, the putdown of Charmides is pretty explicit.

3.12 Temperance as a Form of Attention

When Malcolm Schofield looked to encapsulate what is distinctive about the Platonic, as opposed to the Ciceronian, form of philosophical dialogue, he selected among the notable features of the Platonic variety 'the erotic complexities of the gymnasium and the symposium, and even more the nagging of Socratic dialectic'.[129] The *Charmides* was, if we may add the palaestra to the tally of erotically suggestive locations, no doubt one of the Platonic dialogues that Schofield had in mind.

This coupling, however, raises a puzzle, though not one taken up (since his own main business is with Cicero) by Schofield himself: what is the relation between 'the erotic complexities' on the one hand and 'the nagging of Socratic dialectic' on the other? In the *Charmides* we have, after all, what seem to be two starkly different sections: one, filled with erotic tension, in which Charmides himself is the main focus; the other, a dense and sophisticated discussion with Critias – Socratic dialectic has scarcely been more 'nagging' – but which to all appearances is wholly unerotic in character.[130]

We have already discussed how this phenomenon leads some scholars to treat the *Charmides* as not really getting started until the discussion with Critias begins. Even within the first section, however, the eroticism and the 'nagging' of Socratic enquiry into what temperance is sit side by side. I have offered an account of how these various pieces fit together by claiming that Socrates' pursuit of beauty underlies them. In his urging the switch of attention from Charmides' beautiful body to his soul, we have seen that Socrates explicates coming to look at Charmides' would-be beautiful soul in terms of having a conversation with him, the subsequent investigation with Charmides into what temperance is then being carried out in order to ascertain whether temperance, and so beauty, is present in his soul. So it is the pursuit of beauty that underlies and unifies the erotic and the dialectical elements.

---

[129] Schofield (2008, 63).

[130] Tuozzo (2011, 104) claims that 'the erotic dimension of the opening scene [of the *Charmides*] should be taken to have very little direct effect on our understanding of the subsequent philosophical investigation', but that is to state, rather than resolve, a version of our puzzle. While Rutherford (1995, 91) may be right to say that in comparison to some Platonic works the *Charmides* is of 'lighter and more amicable tone', I confess to bafflement at Garver's (2018, 472) assertion that it is 'so amiable that it lacks the erotic or contentious affects found in most of the dialogues'. By contrast with these present-day scholars, Marsilio Ficino both noticed and took seriously the erotic elements of the *Charmides*, but argued that they should be read allegorically, citing for comparison the Song of Solomon; see Arthos (1959, 272).

Yet, it might be argued, this attempt to find unity merely shifts the burden to a different level, where we now face what one may call the problem of the unity of beauty (*kalon*) itself. What I have claimed unifies the transition from the initial erotic interest in Charmides' body to the investigation into temperance is that both of these are beautiful objects and so offer, across the transition, a sense that the same thing, namely beauty, sustains this development in a cogent way, with Charmides' soul a potential bearer of beauty insofar as it should turn out to possess temperance. But in what sense can the quality of a concrete object such as Charmides' body really be the same as, or even sufficiently similar to, that of an abstract object such as temperance, in a way that would offer a substantial rather than merely verbal continuity between the two in respect of their being beautiful?

I do not claim a complete answer to this question. Attaining one would require a broad investigation of the concept of *kalon* that it is not within the remit of this book to undertake. Nonetheless, progress can be made towards an answer even if we confine our consideration of the problem to the *Charmides* itself. In doing so, we can not only begin to vindicate the conceptual unity of *kalon* but also shed light on the way in which the dialogue asks us to think about the nature of temperance.

To flesh out the problem, let me turn to a forceful articulation of it, in relation to the *Charmides*, by Alexander Nehamas.[131] Nehamas wonders if the application of *kalon* in the contexts both of bodily beauty and of temperance is so broad as to make it hard to forge any real link between them. In particular, he questions the way the term is used 'to pay a compliment both to a boy who provokes an excess of sexual desire and to the virtue that produces the restraint of considered judgment'.[132] He suggests that this reflects a 'contrast between the sexual magnetism of Charmides' beauty and its effect on Socrates, which are crucial to the dialogue's opening scene, and the nobility of temperance, on which the philosophical discussion depends, [that] is extraordinarily stark'.[133] Nehamas sees this starkness as undermining the supposedly 'seamless transition' envisaged in the text 'from excitement to repose, from passion to moderation', the use of *kalon* for both qualities perhaps serving, according to Nehamas, as an attempt (presumably unsatisfactory) 'to emphasize the continuity between Socrates' dialectic and the rest of his behavior'.[134]

Despite his use of 'beauty' to describe *kalon* as applied to Charmides' physical charms and 'nobility' when it attaches to temperance, Nehamas's

---

[131] Nehamas (2007).   [132] Ibid., 101.   [133] Ibid., 100.   [134] Ibid., 100–1.

worry is not, I think, primarily about terminology, and if it were, it would be misguided. It is, after all, perfectly proper in English to apply the same term –'beautiful' – both to what is physically attractive and to what is morally admirable ('you have a beautiful body'; 'that was a beautiful thing you did').[135] What concerns Nehamas, rather, is the unity of the *concept* of *kalon*: for him, its equal application both to what arouses excitement and to what produces restraint 'seems to depend on little more than a pun'.[136]

Nehamas raises a serious challenge, even aside from its Platonic overtones of puzzlement about the same thing apparently being the cause of opposites. Can we say anything in defence of the unity of *kalon* as deployed in the *Charmides*, and to that extent sustain a defence of the unity of the dialogue as a whole?[137] I think that a key to defusing Nehamas's puzzle lies in questioning whether temperance is especially connected in the *Charmides* with restraint. A definitive answer would require analysis of the various accounts of temperance attempted in the dialogue, and an assessment of how we are to respond to them. I have not so far undertaken anything so comprehensive, though once we have examined the discussion with Critias in more detail I will have some suggestions to make, salient to the present question, about how temperance is to be conceived.[138]

Equally, however, regarding the stretch of text that chiefly interests Nehamas, which is the repeated dubbing of temperance as *kalon* during the enquiry with Charmides (especially during the latter's first answer), I see nothing that compels us to view it as holding that temperance entails restraint. Charmides' proposals that temperance is, respectively, quietness and shame may suggest such a view;[139] but even if we leave aside the rebuttal of those proposals (fairly or not) by Socrates, neither represents an

---

[135] Cf. Taylor's description, in relation to the *Charmides* itself, of 'the beautiful characteristic called by the Greeks *sophrosyne*' (1949, 47).
[136] Nehamas (2007, 101).
[137] Citing 160a10, Nehamas (2007, 101) makes (but does not develop in relation to the *Charmides*) the suggestion that praiseworthiness might be intended as a common feature of all that is *kalon*. However, as Nehamas himself notes, one might doubt whether (physical) beauty is worthy of praise (the reference at 160a is specifically to intellectual qualities, a8–9). Moreover, praiseworthiness does not seem especially apt to elicit eros, making it harder to see why what is *kalon* should take eros as its proprietary response. On the status of *kalon* in Plato and its relation to eros, see also Barney 2010 (which, however, does not discuss the *Charmides*).
[138] See esp. Chapter 5.
[139] Cf. Brouwer and Polansky (2004, 236). I do not therefore think it quite right to say, with Witte (1970, 39) – see also North (1966, 158) – that Plato here disregards such a conception of temperance. 'Doing one's own things' may also imply a notion of restraint, but that is compromised when Socrates persuades Critias that what the latter really means by the phrase is the doing of good things (163d–e).

3.12 Temperance as a Form of Attention

outright commitment to that relation. Indeed, it seems barely an exaggeration to speak, with Kosman, of the 'striking *absence* from the *Charmides* . . . [of] the question of *self-control*'.[140]

So it may, instead, be Socrates' own behaviour that suggests to Nehamas the connection between temperance and restraint. Yet here too we have a notable, but also explicable, absence of such a connection. Certainly, it seems tempting to regard Socrates' success in moving past the initial effect on him of Charmides' physical beauty as an example of restraint indicative of temperance. Yet, as I argued above,[141] it seems that Socrates does not achieve recovery by restraining himself but, on the contrary, by *doing* something – namely, conversing with Charmides. His choice of Cydias' verses to describe his plight, and provide the initial impetus to recovery, implies, far from a situation needing to be overcome by restraint, a state of paralysis (fawn before lion) from which one must actively wrench oneself free.[142]

As we have seen, Nehamas speaks, in the context of Socratic dialectic, of temperance as 'the virtue that produces the restraint of considered judgment'. But, as with temperance itself, I see no evidence that Socratic philosophical discussion, however much it may involve considered judgement enabled by temperance, is connected in the text specifically with restraint, other than on one occasion as a kind of background condition (see below on 165c). I suggest instead that the key requirement envisaged in the *Charmides* for such discussion to proceed well is not restraint but *focus*.

Consider in this regard Socrates' injunction to Charmides at 160d5–6 to 'focus more' (*mallon prosechōn ton noun*) on discovering what temperance might be, and compare his encouragement of Critias to 'focus on the argument itself' (*autōi prosechōn ton noun tōi logōi*) at 166e1–2. Compare

---

[140] Kosman (2014, 236; his emphases). See also Notomi (2003, 248–9); Dorion (2004, 39); Rademaker (2005, 5); Sedley (2010, 71).
[141] Section 3.5.
[142] Cf. Tuozzo (2011, 109); Herrmann (2013, 285). Schmid (1998), while referring (misleadingly in my view) to Socrates' 'self-control' and 'self-restraint' in this context (8, 91) – see also Santas (1973, 106); Sue (2006, 48 n. 11) – seems to me more on point in describing Socrates' recovery 'as achieved through the process of dialectical engagement' with Charmides (9); cf. also Gonzalez (1998, 42). Reece (1998, 71) rightly rejects as implausible ways of reading the Cydias quote – an example is Vlastos (1987, 91 with n. 40) – that place Socrates in the role of lion and Charmides his prey, though as Hazebroucq (1997, 106) notes, there seems to be something deliberately paradoxical about the inverted casting of the 'old lion' Socrates and the 'tender youth' Charmides as victim and predator respectively, which might prefigure a role reversal at the end of the dialogue; cf. Morgan (2021, 160–1) and see further Section 5.8. The effect is spoiled if we label, with Brennan (2006, 294), Socrates' self-characterisation as 'dishonest'.

likewise how Charmides, before finally averring that temperance is the same thing as shame, 'pauses and undertakes scrutiny in relation to himself' (*epischōn kai ... pros heauton diaskepsamenos*) at 160e2–3; and how Socrates, at 165c2, bids Critias to 'wait while I examine' (*episches heōs an skepsōmai*) Critias' idea that temperance is knowing oneself, the examining confirmed by the further exchange at c3–4. Here we can see Critias, who had offered at 165b3–4 to give an account of this idea, being asked by Socrates to hold back in order to give time for Socrates to consider the proposal himself. While restraint on the part of the interlocutor, Critias, is thus sought to enable Socrates to form a considered judgement, it does not feature as something displayed by the one making the judgement. Rather the pause – the restraint, if you will – is requested from the interlocutor to allow the other party to give proper attention to the question.

If this is how the right attitude of participants to the discussion is characterised, recall in turn how the assembled company's reaction to Charmides' appearance is highlighted at 154c6–8: they are said to focus on him, even the youngest looking nowhere else but at his beauteous form (while Socrates, with his rather different set of priorities, focusses on them: *tois paisi proseschon ton noun*, c6). I suggest, then, that one way to think about what unites things that are *kalon* in the *Charmides* is that they are such as to elicit one's focus:[143] just how much will depend on how one values the particular category of *kalon* thing that is before one (as well as, no doubt, on how *kalon* it is). Apart from having the textual support I have cited, this reading has the further advantage of illuminating the connection between erotic desire and, as its proprietary object, what is *kalon*, since it seems natural to represent eros in terms of attention to its object of a particularly intense kind. And such attention seems equally apt where something *kalon* is in prospect (as, it is hoped, in the case of Charmides' soul) as where it is present. This means in turn that eros is (depicted as) more than just a causal response to the presence of beauty, but as an agential response with beauty as its intentional object.

We can, then, begin to offer a unified account of how *kalon* functions in the text by giving due weight to the consistency of response that the text presents, in terms of focussed attention, as directed towards what is

---

[143] As Verity Harte points out to me, one can also direct a fascinated gaze at what one finds horrible. On the other hand, it seems true and significant that what is horrible also tends to be unbearable to observe. One should perhaps then say that a significant difference between the case of beauty and its contrary is that the former is such as to elicit one's *continuous* focus: the temporal factor is again important here (cf. Section 2.3). With what is horrible, one eventually has to look away.

kalon.[144] The intrinsic nature of beauty, such that it is apt to elicit such attention, I consider further in Chapter 5.[145] But what the account outlined already brings with it is a way of considering temperance not just as a proper object of attention insofar as it is something beautiful, but also as something that has, as a core element of its own, the power of exhibiting not restraint but attention of a certain kind. The notion of attention connects in turn with ideas of perspective and of looking that, as we have seen, feature prominently in the dialogue's conceptual economy.

There are two examples of Socrates' behaviour whose status as cases of temperance we seem particularly encouraged to reflect on, and which this reading of temperance can help illuminate: his attitude towards the battle, and his coping with the effects on him of Charmides' physical beauty. As I have been at pains to emphasise, it is unlikely that these cases are to be read as straightforward manifestations of an incontestable exemplar of temperance. Nonetheless, it seems equally unreasonable to deny, given how central a theme of the dialogue temperance turns out to be, that the cases are there to offer the opportunity for reflection on what temperance might be. If so, then restraint, I have argued, is not the right way to characterise what is fundamentally going on.

Socrates' detachment from the horrors of battle is not some freestanding exercise of self-control. It is, instead, more plausibly explained in terms of the power of his attachment to other things, and in particular his ability to focus on matters that (we soon learn) are of special interest to him: philosophy, beauty, and wisdom among them. Another way to put this is that a detachment that may seem, in itself, not just unhuman but inhuman, gains in normative power if viewed as the subsidiary complement of a passionate attachment elsewhere.

A similar explanation fits the second case. Socrates' otherwise merely unnerving ability to break away from the pull of Charmides' physical beauty is afforded by his attachment to the soul and its own potential for exhibiting beauty.[146] If this brings the powers of temperance and of eros rather more in alignment than one might have expected, that may be

---

[144] The concept of attention (one that is of considerable interest in contemporary philosophy and psychology; see e.g. Mole, Smithies and Wu 2011) needs more analysis than I can give it here. In terms of my reading, the informal idea is that one can focus one's power of attention (as Socrates is shown to do) across objects that differ widely in metaphysical status.

[145] See esp. Sections 5.2 and 5.3. On beauty in the *Phaedrus* as what catches our attention (I would rather say: what is apt to catch our attention), see Lear (2019, 45–8).

[146] One is reminded of Iris Murdoch's remark: 'Deliberately falling out of love is not a jump of the will, it is the acquiring of new objects of attention and thus of new energies as a result of refocusing' (Murdoch 1970, 56).

just what is needed to account for qualities so memorably, if still contestably, united in the depiction of Socrates. Assuming indeed that we find this Socrates to be a convincing personality (however singular), then in Plato's depiction of him we gain independent support for the analysis of those qualities suggested here.

We have, at any rate, sketched an outline of temperance as something possessing a cognitive dimension – represented by the power of attention – together with a metaphysical underpinning: the non-corporeal as object of attention. I shall use this as a basis on which to build, in Chapter 5, a more elaborate picture of what temperance might be, in terms of the resources for considering the question that the *Charmides* offers. To do this, we need first to examine the lengthy enquiry into temperance that Socrates now conducts with Critias, and to which I turn in the next chapter.

3.13 Conclusion

In Chapter 2, I defended the unity of the *Charmides* with reference to that layer of its vertical structure that pertains to Plato's relationship with his readers. In this chapter I have argued for its unity at the level of Socrates' interaction with his interlocutors, by defending the thesis that we are to read Socrates as engaged in an erotic quest to which his investigation of the nature of temperance is subordinated. As we turn now to the centrepiece of that investigation – Socrates' discussion with Critias – we will have the opportunity to consider whether its overtly aporetic character allows us nonetheless to discern a positive thesis about the nature of temperance.

In inviting his readers, as preparation for the discussion with Critias, to occupy what I have dubbed the stance of enquiry, Plato thereby encourages us to emulate Socrates, not by assuming that he is intellectually (or morally) flawless, but by being ready to undertake careful scrutiny of his critique of Critias' various proposals about what temperance is. What starts to emerge more clearly from such scrutiny is that there is dialogue between the vertical levels of the *Charmides*. Socrates, as we have noted, is depicted as conducting his business principally through the medium of oral conversation, whereas Plato is author of a written text. Rather than simply yielding first place to oral conversation as the gold standard for the conduct of critical enquiry, Plato, I shall argue, offers material for a defence of his own chosen medium. In this regard, as we shall see in what follows, the question of the nature and role of interpretation, and therefore of our role as readers, remains prominent.

CHAPTER 4

Interpreting Temperance

Towards the end of the previous chapter (Section 3.11), we left Critias agreeing to take over from Charmides the defence of the account of temperance as doing one's own things. In this chapter I shall examine the greater part of the lengthy and complex discussion that ensues between Socrates and Critias on the nature of temperance. Whether with deliberate mischievousness or not, Socrates tells Critias that the latter is 'doing beautifully' (*kalōs ... poiōn*, 162e7) in taking on the discussion,[1] thereby picking out a term, *poiein* ('make' or 'do'), that is about to feature centrally in the discussion of whether 'doing one's own things' can be defended as an account of what temperance is.

Critias will soon give up his defence of that account, eventually to settle on the claim that temperance is knowing oneself, a proposal that he in turn explicates as temperance being knowledge of itself, that is, knowledge of knowledge. Both the very possibility and the purported benefit of knowledge of knowledge then come under intense scrutiny from Socrates. In analysing his critique, we will again need to examine closely how the text invites us as readers to adopt our own critical stance towards the discussion. I shall argue that, in various ways, the text presents itself as needing to be interpreted, and that in adopting this stance towards it, and understanding ourselves as doing so, we are encouraged to leave room for temperance, so construed, to be both possible and beneficial. Beginning with Socrates' critique, and then Critias' defence, of temperance as doing one's own things, I shall try to show in developing my reading how questions about interpretation help drive the discussion.

---

[1] Cf. 156a9 where Socrates uses the same phrase to acknowledge Charmides' statement that he remembers Socrates from his boyhood.

4.1 A Merely Verbal Disagreement?

To take forward his critique, Socrates secures Critias' agreement that craftsmen 'make' (*poiein*) others' things as well as their own, and in reply to Socrates' follow-up question whether they are temperate in not making only their own things, Critias asks why not (162e8–163a5). Socrates then purports to explain: Critias had claimed that temperance is doing (*prattein*) one's own things, so he should consider whether he can then say that there is no reason why those who make (*prattein*) others' things should not be temperate (163a6–9).

Now if *prattein* and *poiein* are interchangeable,[2] then it looks as if Socrates has indeed put his finger on a problem. Critias claims the following:

(1) Temperance is *prattein* one's own things.
(2) In *poiein* others' things one can display temperance.[3]

If *prattein* is substitutable for *poiein*, as Socrates has evidently taken it to be, then we get:

(1) Temperance is *prattein* one's own things.
(2*) In *prattein* others' things one can display temperance.

(1) and (2*), while not formally inconsistent, do suggest that the account of temperance as *prattein* one's own things has not captured the character of temperance by Critias' own lights, insofar as he takes it as possible that *prattein* others' things also displays temperance.

This only goes through, however, if *prattein* is substitutable for *poiein*; and that is something that Critias makes haste to deny (163a10–b3). He grounds his denial by an appeal to the epic poet Hesiod, in which he offers an interpretation of a phrase from Hesiod's *Works and Days*: 'work is no reproach' (*ergon d'ouden oneidos*, 311). Now in the Athens of the day Hesiod was second only to Homer as a canonical literary figure. So we are

---

[2] Charmides had treated them so in setting out his first answer (*prattein*, 159b3; *poiein*, 159b5).
[3] This modal reading I take to be the import of Critias' statement 'what prevents it?' (*ti kōluei*, 163a5; glossed above as 'why not') in response to Socrates asking him whether those who do not *poiein* only their own things are temperate; see Tsouna (2022, 148). Brennan (2012, 242) takes 163a5 as Critias' assent that such people *are* temperate, on the basis of which he then argues (245) that Critias ends up, his distinction between *poiein* and *prattein* notwithstanding, committed to the contradictory thesis that 'they are both acting temperately and not acting temperately'. Contradiction is avoided if we take Critias' 'what prevents it?' as meaning no more than that *poiein* others' things does not rule out one who does this being temperate, which is consistent with one who does this in fact not being temperate.

4.1 A Merely Verbal Disagreement?

no doubt supposed to compare Socrates' earlier use of a quotation from Homer to refute Charmides' second answer with Critias' use here of Hesiod to defend the third.

Both manoeuvres are evidently based on the cultural authority of these poets, from which epistemic authority is inferred. In the case of Hesiod, this bestowal of epistemic authority is explicit in Critias' assumption that Hesiod is one of those who are 'wise' (*phronimos*, 163c7). So if one can show that support for what one says is to be found in Homer or Hesiod, then that gives what one says extra epistemic weight. This paradigm, however, is put to very different use by Socrates and Critias respectively. Socrates, as we saw, seems to exploit Charmides' uncritical acceptance of Homeric authority to bulldoze a quick admission that, since 'shame is no good for a man in need', temperance, which is a good thing, cannot be the same thing as shame. I suggested that the approach towards interpretation displayed there by Socrates was questionable: taking a single line and reading its meaning incuriously and in isolation from any context.

Now in one way Critias displays the same approach, or an even more discreditable variant thereof, since he does not cite even a whole line of Hesiod.[4] But in other respects his stance is different, in relation to principles of interpretation, from that of Socrates. To arrive at the idea that the quotation shows that *poiein* is not the same as *prattein*, Critias does a lot of inferential exegesis based on what he takes to be the precise sense of Hesiod's term 'work' (*ergon*), which in turn rests on certain normative assumptions that Critias takes to be operative in Hesiod (which may of course be projections of Critias' own).[5]

Thus, Critias says, if by 'work' Hesiod had meant such lowly activities as cobbling, pickle-selling or prostitution, he would never have said that these were no reproach (163b5–8).[6] Rather, Critias continues:

> He [Hesiod] too, I believe, thought making (*poiēsis*) a different thing from doing (*praxis*) and working (*ergasia*) and that sometimes what is made (*poiēma*) turns out to be a reproach, whenever it fails to turn out with beauty, whereas no work (*ergon*) is ever a reproach. For things that are made (*poioumena*) both beautifully and beneficially he was calling "works", and such makings both workings and doings. One ought at any rate to say that he considered such things alone as also belonging to one (*oikeia*), while

---

[4] The continuation of the line is: *aergiē de t'oneidos* ('but lack of work is a reproach').
[5] Since Critias says that he 'learned' (*emathon*, 163b4) the relevant distinctions from Hesiod, one should probably allow that he takes himself genuinely to have discovered them there.
[6] Dover (1989, 108) notes the oligarchic outlook implied by Critias' willingness to bracket a trade such as cobbling with prostitution.

harmful things all belong to another. Hence one should think that both Hesiod and anyone else wise (*phronimos*) calls this person, the one who does their own things, temperate. (163b9–c8)

Critias seems here to avoid a type of mistake that played a major role in the failure of Charmides' first two accounts (notwithstanding Socrates' highly uncharitable reading of the first account). He defends a normative construal of *prattein* such that his account of temperance as 'doing (*prattein*) one's own things' respects the positive evaluative polarity of temperance. At the same time he shows that, if he is right, Socrates could not legitimately treat *poiein* and *prattein* as interchangeable, as the latter had done in seeking to show that Critias offered a problematic account.

In particular, one cannot treat (2) and (2*) above as equivalent by replacing *poiein* in (2) with *prattein* in (2*), since even if every case of *prattein* is a case of *poiein*, the converse, on Critias' construal, does not apply. The cases in which one can display temperance in relation to others' things can therefore be cases of *poiein* without being cases of *prattein*: one can *poiein* others' things without this meaning that one thereby *prattein* other's things. If so, then (2) can be true without (2*) being true, so it is illegitimate to substitute the latter for the former. Critias, it seems to me, shows considerable mettle here and marks himself out as a more formidable interlocutor for Socrates than Charmides was.

He also demonstrates a more subtle and complex attitude towards interpretation than Socrates does, and this, I think, has two main components. Firstly, Critias reads Hesiod in such a way as to make him, from Critias' point of view, maximally intelligible: an (admirable) approach that we also saw Charmides exemplify in relation to Socrates' comment on Charmides' knowledge of the Greek language.[7] Hesiod, reckons Critias, could not reasonably, at least by Critias' lights, have meant that any old examples of work, such as the lowly ones that Critias lists, were unworthy of reproach. So Hesiod must have had in mind by 'work' only examples that have, by those lights, a positive connotation. Secondly, Critias is alive to the significance of nuances in word-meaning, where Socrates, as I argued above in relation to his treatment of Charmides' first answer, is prepared to ride roughshod over them. Thus Critias claims that one can

---

[7] See Section 3.9. It thus seems excessively one-sided of Kirk (2016, 317) to opine, in relation to the *Charmides*, that 'those who need the kind of communicative intervention that Socrates offers are at the same time those whose communicative practices act as obstacles preventing them from benefiting from his interventions'.

distinguish, on the one hand, *prattein* and *ergazesthai* as terms with a positive connotation whereas *poiein*, on the other hand, is evaluatively neutral.⁸

Now I am not denying that, in respect of both components of his interpretive approach, Critias proceeds in a rather far-fetched and over-elaborate way.⁹ But it is important to separate Critias' application of his principles of interpretation from the underlying principles themselves that his treatment of Hesiod embodies. These, it seems to me, have much to commend them. Their presence in Critias' toolkit at any rate contrasts sharply with Socrates' seeming neglect of (or opposition to) such principles. Nor need it be denied that one could read, in their concrete manifestations, Socrates' interpretation of Homer and Critias' of Hesiod as forming a critique, on Plato's part, of certain approaches to the interpretation of texts. Certainly, both characters in the end seem to use such interpretation as little more than a vehicle for advancing their own agendas.

Indeed, it may be that we are at least supposed to draw some negative moral about the interpretation of *poetry*, since that is the genre at issue in these two cases.¹⁰ But criticism of a genre's lack of susceptibility to reasonable interpretation (if that is what Plato intends) is not the same as a blanket critique of the viability of the interpretation of texts. Such a critique cannot, I think, be Plato's aim here. The *Charmides*, after all, is itself a written text, a complex and subtle one at that. To read it as warning us off textual interpretation in an unqualified way would be self-defeating, since discerning such a warning would already, and necessarily, be an act of interpretation on our part.

Put more prosaically, it seems unlikely that Plato as author of a written text would wish to deter his readers from interpreting that text. It is more probable, then, that he uses the contrasting approaches of Socrates and Critias to stimulate us, as interpreters, to think critically about what we are doing in interpreting a text and how we should be doing it.¹¹ In this it may be expected that neither Critias (the real-life poet) nor Socrates has a fully satisfactory take on interpretation. But given the historical Critias' status as author, Plato may have set up his fictionalised counterpart to offer a weightier contribution on the theme.

---

⁸ It is worth noting in this regard that the historical Critias seems to have had considerable interest in word-meaning; cf. B53–73 DK.
⁹ See, however, Joosse (2018) for a defence of Critias as interpreter of Hesiod.
¹⁰ On poetic interpretation in the *Protagoras* see Brittain (2017), with references.
¹¹ Cf. Joosse (2018, 590).

The contrast between Critias and Socrates on this issue is vividly on display in Socrates' response to Critias' Hesiodic defence of temperance as doing one's own things:

> Critias, I pretty much understood your account as soon as you began, that you were calling both things that belong to one and one's own things "good", and the makings (*poiēseis*) of good things "doings" (*praxeis*). (163d1–3)

Socrates proceeds to declare that he has heard the sophist Prodicus 'make thousands of distinctions among terms' (d3–4), a way of putting things that hardly conveys respect for the niceties of word-meaning,[12] before continuing:

> 'But I allow you to place each term wherever you wish; only make clear (*dēlou*) what it is to which you are applying whatever term you use. So now start again and mark temperance off more clearly (*saphesteron*): do you agree that the doing (*praxis*) or making (*poiēsis*), or however you want to name it, of good things, is what you say temperance is?'
>
> 'I do,' he said. (163d5–e3)

Voula Tsouna claims that Socrates merely denies here that 'verbal distinctions *alone* can settle the philosophical problem' (my emphasis),[13] which would imply Socratic recognition of some role for such distinctions. But in permitting Critias to apply terms wherever he wishes so long as he 'only' (*monon*, 163d6) makes clear that to which the terms are applied, Socrates apparently advocates that all weight be placed on the relation between terms and things, rather than between terms. No philosophical role for the drawing of verbal distinctions such as that between *poiein* and *prattein* is granted.

Neither, however, except to a very limited degree, is Socrates' move an indication of his 'willingness to accept his interlocutor's terminology, provided they explain what they mean thereby'.[14] Socrates has *denied* that Critias' distinction between *poiein* and *prattein* is meaningful. His concession, such as it is, is that it makes no odds which of these terms, so recently and carefully distinguished from one another by Critias, are used in the account of temperance.

---

[12] Corey (2008, 4) mistranslates d4 (*Prodikou muria tina akēkoa peri onomatōn diairountos*) as Socrates saying that he has '"heard Prodicus myriad times making distinctions about words"', and uses this rendition as part of a case that Socrates was actually a pupil of Prodicus. But what Socrates says rather less respectfully is that he has heard Prodicus make myriad distinctions.

[13] Tsouna (2022, 153). [14] I quote here an anonymous reader.

4.1 A Merely Verbal Disagreement?

One may therefore note the seemingly sharp demarcation implied by Socrates' remarks at 163d–e between the words that one uses, on the one hand, and the clear conveyance of meaning, on the other. It may come as a surprise, especially to those who have tried their hand at the business of writing, to learn that transmission of meaning is something that one achieves, or ought to achieve, more or less independently of the precise terms one deploys, one's words serving as placeholders for an underlying meaning that one then stipulates. Socrates' stance, influenced as it may be by his having his interlocutor available to him in live oral discussion, seems to amount to the rejection of a constructive role for interpretation, whereby one tries to make sense of the particular words selected by the speaker in their context (even) where these do not yield up immediate clarity.

Hence Socrates makes no attempt to construe the phrase 'doing one's own things' such that it would have nuances of meaning distinct from the apparently less obscure 'doing good things'. Rather, he proceeds to declare that by the former Critias meant, and by implication would have done better to have said, the latter. For Socrates, it seems that the call to interpret signals a bug in the communicative system rather than an essential feature of it. Meaning is not to be patiently teased out from a speaker's formulation as given; rather, an impression of unclarity is a sign that the formulation itself is misconceived.

If that is right, then evidently Critias' dwelling on the nuances of word-meaning is beside the point. One simply picks a word and (clearly and unambiguously!) lays down what one means by it. And yet, it might be argued, Critias had proceeded in a perfectly principled way. Socrates' complaint, we may recall, was that the terms used by the proponent of temperance as doing one's own things did not express their proponent's meaning (161d1–2). Rather than disavowing those terms, Critias painstakingly tried to show that they did, by distinguishing *prattein* as having an evaluatively positive sense, with *poiein* evaluatively neutral, that sense then governing the way we read 'one's own'. That is not the same as treating 'one's own' as expressible without loss in this context by 'good'. Socrates' invocation of Prodicus, and his lofty granting to Critias of freedom to use whichever terms he wishes, looks, as a response to this, like mere bluster.

Socrates' elevation of clarity to something like a supreme communicative virtue finds echo in contemporary philosophical thought. One detects it, and its ancestry, in Timothy Williamson's claim that 'Obscurity is the oracle's self-defense. To be precise is to make it as easy as possible for others to prove one wrong. That is what requires courage.'[15] But it is striking that, in a defence of the importance of precision, Williamson appears here to conflate obscurity with imprecision.[16] The former is neither the same as, nor inevitably brings in its train, the latter. Evidence for this is apparent in the case at hand. 'Doing good things' may be a clearer formulation of what Critias was trying to say than 'doing one's own things'. It hardly follows that it is a more precise one. If Socrates himself equates (or conflates) clarity with precision, then Williamson is in good company in upholding what might be called the Socratic prejudice.

4.2 A Question of Status

Critias at any rate has been pushed into saying that what he really meant is that temperance is the doing of good things. Since it is not evident that this retains the sense of the original formula of doing one's own things, it is perhaps as well that the new account has a fairly short shelf-life. We are indeed, I suggest, meant to feel that something has been lost as a result of a Socratic approach that, in the interests of alleged clarity, discounts nuanced interpretation of one formula in favour of straight substitution by another. Critias is nonetheless anxious to show, at least at first, that he cannot now be faulted for clarity, responding to Socrates' plea that he start again and mark things off more clearly (163d7) by reiterating the new account with the declaration 'I mark it out clearly (*saphōs*) for you that temperance is the doing of good things' (163e10–11).

This is part of a pattern of Critias' confidently stating an account of temperance, only to go on swiftly to withdraw it. I shall return to this pattern in the next section; but the key to Critias' imminent withdrawal of the new account is, in this instance, Socrates' securing of his agreement that those who are temperate are not unaware that they are (164a2–4). In a passage we examined earlier (164a–b),[17] Socrates gains Critias' assent that sometimes it is possible for a craftsperson such as a doctor to have exercised their craft beneficially without realising that they have. Socrates continues:

> 'And yet, in having acted beneficially, they acted, by your account, temperately. Or were you not speaking thus?'
>
> 'I was.'

---

[15] Williamson (2007, 289). On Critias and the Delphic inscription, see Section 4.3.
[16] The conflation is tempting enough to reappear in Williamson (2018, 88). [17] See Section 3.7.

> 'So, it seems, sometimes, in having acted beneficially, one acts temperately and is temperate, but is unaware of oneself (*agnoei heauton*) as being temperate.' (164c1–6)

This Critias accepts as an intolerable conclusion and goes on, by way, interestingly, of a further piece of interpretation of a written text (which I shall consider in the next section), to alter his account once again, this time proposing that temperance is, in fact, knowing oneself. In rejecting the conclusion that one can act temperately without being aware that one is so doing, Critias takes himself to have to reject the idea that temperance is the doing of good things. For evidently one can do good things, or act beneficially, without being aware that one is so acting; but Critias does not accept that one can be temperate without being aware that one is temperate.

Why does Critias find this unacceptable? The previous reference to a connection between being temperate and being aware that one is came when Socrates suggested to Charmides at 159a1–2 that if temperance is in one then it must provide some awareness (*aisthēsis*) of its presence. So on the face of it, there is agreement between Critias and Socrates that one who is temperate must be aware that they are. But it is not clear that they are agreeing to the same thing. Socrates, I argued above,[18] models his suggestion by analogy with medicine in relation to the idea that a medical condition will produce some awareness of itself to the patient. Of course, one of the things that may have attracted Socrates to this model was an independent belief that one cannot be temperate without being aware that one is. But why one should hold that belief receives no further explanation on Socrates' part.

Since Critias gets into trouble with the omission of the self-awareness requirement once the spotlight is on his account of temperance as the doing of good things, it seems reasonable to go back one stage and see if his previous account can accommodate it. This may in turn shed light on why he might feel committed to the requirement. In the course of defending that previous account – that temperance is doing one's own things – against the charge of absurdity, Critias turned, as we saw, to Hesiod. From the scorn he heaps on the kinds of lowly work that evidently would not qualify, by his lights, as doing one's own things, it seems that for Critias the notion is intimately connected with ideas of status. So 'doing one's own things' might be construed by him as doing things worthy of

[18] Section 3.8.

one's status,[19] namely (in his case) that of an Athenian gentleman: a sense, we may note, both different from and more precise than the simple doing of good things.

On this construal, it seems plausible that being temperate would involve awareness of one's status and of that status as imposing certain constraints on oneself.[20] One is aware of one's position, and of the constraints that go with it; one manifests temperance in not stepping outside them.[21] This does reflect an aspect of the classical Greek notion of temperance;[22] and if something like this is behind Critias' swift agreement that one who is temperate must be aware that they are, then we have a reasonable explanation of why he is so ready to agree. It makes little sense, after all, to talk of a temperate person as one who does what is appropriate to their status and does not stray outside those boundaries, unless one takes such a person to be aware of their status and of the boundaries that go with it that must not be transgressed on pain of having forfeited one's claim to that status. Certainly, that will be so on a conception whereby the agent's acting so as to express their status is an essential part of the ethical outlook that this notion of temperance purports to capture.

Notice that this still treats self-knowledge of a certain kind as a necessary condition of temperance, not as what temperance consists in.[23] One needs to know who one is – what one's status is – in order to be able to act such as to keep faith with that status without straying. To be sure, this idea of temperance does deliver an intelligible sense of knowing, or being aware of, oneself: if one takes one's social status to define one (as Critias may do, even if Socrates does not), then in identifying the status one has with who one is, knowledge of one's status will, quite reasonably, be knowledge of oneself.[24] Moreover, temperance on this conception will also display a connection with an element that I have suggested the dialogue may be interested in as a core feature of temperance, namely focus or attention.[25] For if temperance is a matter of adhering to the boundaries imposed by

---

[19] It may be that for Critias questions of status do not even arise in the case of those who do the kinds of work he scorns.
[20] See Annas (1985, 121–5).   [21] Cf. Ebert (1974, 58).
[22] See, with particular reference to Aeschylean and Sophoclean tragedy, North (1966, 32–68).
[23] Cf. Tuckey (1951, 25–6).
[24] This may help explain why, as Kosman (2014, 228–9) observes, Critias is prepared to switch from agreement that one who is temperate could never be unaware of oneself as temperate (164c7) to the unqualified (or, as Kosman cautiously puts it, 'less qualified') claim that one who is temperate could never be unaware of oneself (164d2–3).
[25] For a distant contemporary echo that analyses modesty as a virtue of attention see Bommarito (2013).

one's status, then one will need to be focussed continuously on what one is saying and doing, monitoring oneself lest one commit a breach of those boundaries (Charmides' albeit problematic response at 158c–d seems a good example of this).[26]

Doing only what is appropriate to one's status, then, plausibly involves, as a necessary condition, the kind of self-knowledge suggested above. Hence Critias says that he would rather give up anything he had said before than concede that a person who is ignorant of himself (*agnoounta auton heauton*) could ever be temperate (164c7–d3). Critias is thus eager to put on the table a new account of temperance that does not have the flaw, attaching to temperance construed as the doing of good things, of being independent of the notion of self-knowledge. He may, however, himself overstep the boundaries of his previous account of temperance as doing one's own things in now claiming, in a characteristically rapid transition, not just that knowing oneself (*to gignōskein heauton*) is a necessary condition of temperance, but that it 'pretty much' *is* temperance (164d3–4).[27] Before seeing how this new account of temperance as knowing oneself changes the landscape of the enquiry into temperance, let us consider how Critias offers further support for it.

4.3 Reading the Mind of God

As we have just seen, Critias begins by saying that it could not be the case that one is temperate without being aware that one is. It is worth laying out how emphatically he states his readiness, as a result, to drop his previous position:

> But this, Socrates, could never happen, but if you think that anything of necessity has this consequence on the basis of what has previously been agreed by me, I would give up any of those [statements], and would not be ashamed to say that I spoke incorrectly, rather than ever concede that a person could be temperate who does not know themselves. (164c7–d3)

We may wonder here at how Critias can switch so rapidly and wholeheartedly from the confident declaration that temperance is the doing of good things to the horrified disavowal of the same. This rather dizzying

---

[26] In addition to failure to attend to oneself, MM McCabe suggests to me that there may be room here for a contrary vice, such as excessive self-attention.

[27] It may be significant that when Socrates asked Critias at 163d7 to mark off or 'define' temperance more clearly (than doing one's own things), the term Socrates uses (*horisai*) is etymologically connected to the Greek *horos* ('boundary'), Critias going on to proclaim at e11 that he now does mark out or define (*diorizomai*) it clearly.

approach is further brought out if we compare his 'I mark it out clearly (*saphōs*) for you that temperance is the doing of good things' at 163e10–11, with his subsequently reiterated willingness at 165a8–b1, in the wake of his appeal to Delphi, to 'give up for you all the previous [statements]', followed by his declaration at 165b2–3 that 'nothing of what we [he and Socrates] said was clear (*saphes*)'.

From clear pronouncement to nothing (it seems) having been clear is quite a shift. No doubt the shift says something about Critias' own (intemperate?) personality. But it also raises the issue, which I shall pursue below,[28] and which will be relevant to the dialogue's exploration of self-knowledge, about whether Critias can even be said to believe, in the light of his willingness to drop one and pick up another at short notice, any of the accounts that he offers of what temperance is, and whether we are thus invited to consider that norms may apply that have to be met if one is to count as holding a belief at all.

Critias at any rate does signal what appears to be a particular attachment to his latest proposal about temperance, that it is knowing oneself, since he goes on to tell Socrates that he is willing to 'give an account' (*didonai logon*, 165b3) of the proposal if Socrates does not agree with it. But leading up to that pledge, Critias offers a remarkable piece of support for the idea that temperance is knowing oneself, in the form of an appeal to the famous phrase 'Know thyself' (*Gnōthi sauton*, 164e7) inscribed at the entrance to the temple of Apollo at Delphi.

Now, if we have read Plato's *Apology*, we will no doubt think of Socrates' own indirect encounter with Delphi reported there, in which he undertakes to interpret the negative answer given by the Oracle in response to Chaerephon's question whether anyone is wiser than Socrates. In line with the principle of agnosticism, I shall avoid reading the apparatus of the *Apology* into the *Charmides*. However, we may note one key contrast, and then one similarity, relevant to the present discussion, in particular as regards the issue of interpretation.

In the *Apology*, Socrates only attempts 'very reluctantly' (*mogis panu*, 21b8), after a 'long period of puzzlement' (*polun men chronon ēporoun*, 21b7) about its 'riddling' (*ainittetai*, b4) response, to figure out what the Oracle means. In the *Charmides*, by contrast, when Critias takes up the task of interpreting the 'somewhat riddling' (*ainigmatōdesteron*, 164e6) Delphic inscription, he does so with evident zest.

---

[28] See Section 5.1.

On the other hand, a salient point of similarity between the two works lies in Socrates' tendency to base his enquiries on a rather lax approach to what his interlocutors say. Thus, to the examples from the *Charmides* that we have already noted, most recently Socrates' treatment of Critias' account of temperance as doing one's own things, one might add, in reference to the *Apology*, Socrates' way with what Chaerephon tells him that the Oracle replied, namely that 'no one is wiser [than Socrates]' (*Apology* 21a7).

Socrates proceeds to wonder what the Oracle could have meant in stating that 'I am wisest' (*eme sophōtaton einai*, 21b5–6). Now the Oracle, notoriously and designedly cryptic that it is, demands interpretation. Still, it is notable that, as with Critias' 'doing one's own things', Socrates does not bear with the Oracle's pronouncement as reported to him, but, in this case instantly, reformulates it. The two expressions are, however, not equivalent. Being wisest implies being one than whom no one is wiser; but the converse does not hold: in Greek as in English, the formulation 'no-one is φ-er than x' can, but need not, imply 'x is φ-est'.[29] If Socrates and his fellow Athenians were all equally wise, one would not describe Socrates as 'wisest'.

Note, then, that Socrates' reformulation does not solve a puzzle, it creates one, given that he has no idea why the Oracle should have called him (as it did not exactly) 'wisest'. This then becomes the target of his investigation. It is a nice irony on Plato's part thereby to represent the impetus for Socrates' critical enquiries as resting on a piece of loose reformulation by the latter; a habit that seems alive and well in the *Charmides*.[30]

When it comes to Critias' approach to the Delphic inscription, the gist, according to Critias, is that it is a somewhat riddling way of saying 'Be temperate', so that, as he puts it, '"Know thyself" and "Be temperate" are the same' (164e7–165a1). Critias' procedure once more consists in an interpretation of a text: a piece of writing (cf. *gramma*, 164d5; *grammata*, 165a1), namely the inscription, in which we see, again, how different his attitude towards interpretation is from that of Socrates. Whereas Socrates, in relation to 'doing one's own things', regarded obscurity as a sign that the chosen words were a failure to express what the author meant, so that all one could do was try to demonstrate this, for Critias obscurity is an invitation to interpret the words in question on the assumption that sense

---

[29] Cf. Stokes (1997, 116).
[30] For a further case of this Socratic practice in regard to Critias' statements, see Section 5.7.

can be made of them – above all, perhaps, in the Delphic case, where obscurity is a reflection of the divine source, so that there should be no question that the god has, at any rate unwittingly, failed to express what he meant; it is just that one needs to do some interpretive work to figure the meaning out.[31]

Now things are complicated here by the fact that the inscription 'Know thyself' is taken by Critias, reasonably enough, not to be the direct word of god but an attempt by the writer of the inscription in effect to read the mind of god. Critias puts it thus:

> In fact, it seems to me that this is why the inscription was put up, as precisely a greeting by the god to those entering, instead of "Cheers", on the grounds that this is not the correct form of greeting, namely "Cheers", nor should one use this to exhort one another, but rather "Be temperate". This is how the god addresses those who enter the temple, in a manner different from humans, as the one who put up the inscription had in mind, so it seems to me: and [the god] is saying to anyone who enters nothing other than "Be temperate", he [the inscriber] affirms. But, like a prophet, [the god] indeed says it in a somewhat riddling way: for "Know thyself" and "Be temperate" are the same, according to the inscription and to me. (164d6–165a1)

Even leaving aside the reader's interpretation of what Plato is up to (which I shall pick up in a moment), we are presented here with a double layer of interpretation. Critias interprets the author of the inscription in such a way that the author is seen, by Critias' lights of course, to interpret the purport of god in a maximally intelligible way relative to the context. So 'Know thyself' is inscribed instead of a standard greeting, given the reasonable view that god does things differently from humans, and, since the god at Delphi is riddling, 'Know thyself' must have been intended by its author to require interpreting. Since Critias himself now affirms that temperance is knowing oneself, he takes the meaning of the inscription, intended by the author to represent the mind of god, as 'Be temperate'.

The final piece of the jigsaw is Critias' no doubt self-promoting speculation that the inscription's form has been *mis*interpreted by those who added later inscriptions as pieces of advice (*sumboulas*, 165a6). 'Know thyself', he insists, must be read as intended by the author to be a greeting; and here there may be meant no more than that what one expects to

---

[31] A contrast with the *Apology* again seems telling; there Socrates does not tackle, through interpretation, a puzzling statement from the Oracle. He *constructs* such a statement by reformulation and takes that as the target for investigation.

receive when one enters a house, whether of god or of human, is a greeting not a piece of advice.[32] So, in terms of form as well as content, Critias seeks to maximise the intelligibility of the inscription relative to its context. In contrast with Socrates' earlier attitude towards a supposedly obscure pronouncement ('doing one's own things') as an account of temperance, Critias gives no sign that he takes his reading of 'Know thyself' as 'Be temperate' to *invalidate*, rather than explain, the use of the original expression. Critias' reading thus represents a genuine act of interpretation whose substance, as before, may be somewhat overheated, but which still embodies a sound and important interpretive principle.

In the end, in terms of our interest as readers in interpretation, Plato surely does not mean to commend Critias' particular co-option of such a principle for the latter's interpretation of the Delphic inscription – except presumably to warn us, as in the case of Critias' treatment of Hesiod, against the misuse to which it may be put. But there is every reason to think that, as the author of a complex and layered written work himself, Plato's aim is to bring his readers to reflect on both the perils and the principles of interpreting difficult pieces of writing, foremost among them the very work of his that we are reading.

If so, then we may note a certain parallelism between the structure of Critias' interpretation of the Delphic inscription and what is involved in interpreting the *Charmides*. Critias' interpretation is, as we have observed, two layers deep. He interprets a phrase written by an intermediary, not by god; but the inscription is treated by Critias as representing an attempt to capture the purport of god. So we get at god's meaning not directly, but through the words of the intermediary (the author of the inscription). God's meaning, if we are to fathom it at all, must be worked out via the interpretation of an intermediary's words.

When we approach the *Charmides*, we are confronted with a similar task: we have to read what a variety of characters say in order to figure out the purport of Plato the author who, like the god, says nothing explicitly in his own name, but whose characters' words are all we have to go on to figure out his meaning. The triadic relation between Critias, the inscriber's Delphic phrase and the Delphic god parallels to this extent the relation between the reader of the *Charmides*, the words of its characters, and Plato.

It will be noticed that the place of the Delphic god in the first triad is occupied by Plato in the second. I do not myself think that Plato intends to bestow upon himself, via this parallel, divine status, any more than

---

[32] See for other possibilities Tuozzo (2001, 347); Notomi (2003, 253); Moore (2015, 60–71).

I think he identifies himself straightforwardly with the 'great man' of 169a1–2.[33] But Plato is the author of a written work whose meaning can be accessed only through words spoken by his characters, one of whom is shown interpreting the written words of an inscriber who mediates between the interpreter and god.

It therefore strikes me as plausible that Plato means to compare himself with the Delphic god in at least the following respect: like the god, Plato is hidden. He does not speak explicitly in his own name. The vertical structure of the *Charmides* makes it impossible simply to read off Plato's meaning from what his characters say. The written work, that is, needs to be interpreted to find Plato's meaning, just as the Delphic author's phrase needs to be interpreted, as Critias is shown doing, to find the god's meaning. Interpretation is needed, in either case, not, or not just, because the words in question are cryptic or ambiguous (though they may be) but because they are not identifiable as the unmediated words of their ultimate source: god in the one case, Plato in the other.

Critias' miniature piece of interpretation thus serves to illustrate the necessity of interpretation in relation to the *Charmides* itself. And that in turn is encouragement for the reader to occupy the stance of enquiry and engage critically with the work, since the vertical structure entails that there is no direct or automatic route from what Plato's characters say to what Plato means. In this regard it seems to me that the very flamboyance of Critias' way of going about interpretation, with the Delphic inscription as well as the line of Hesiod, is there to make it conspicuous that he is interpreting. We cannot help but notice what he does as an act of interpretation, and can thus come to see how interpretation is also necessary for us, in trying to figure out what Plato means in the dialogue as a whole.

To be sure, that very extravagance also serves to illustrate the perils of interpretation. We might care to take a slightly more disciplined (dare one say temperate) approach in our own interpretive efforts. But the perils of interpretation would not be of interest if the necessity of interpretation were not a given. So here we have another example of how the way in which Critias goes about his business should not prevent us from reading him as intended to convey a serious authorial point: if we want to figure out Plato's meaning at all, we must take some interpretive risk, given that he lies out of view, mediated by his characters' words. And that is no accidental bug, but a reason why the *Charmides* has its vertical layering in

---

[33] See Section 1.3.

the first place. The structure prompts us to be interpreters, who thereby critically engage with the work.

4.4 Knowing What One Believes

Let us, then, in critical mode, begin to investigate the discussion of Critias' proposal that temperance is knowing oneself. To start with, a brief reminder of how we got here. Critias agreed wholeheartedly with Socrates that one who is temperate could not lack self-knowledge (164c7–d3) and added (d3–4) that he 'pretty much' (*schedon ti*) affirms that temperance is this very thing, knowing oneself (*to gignōskein heauton*). Thus Critias moves from the claim that self-knowledge is a necessary condition of temperance to the claim that it actually is temperance. The 'pretty much' seems in turn to indicate a certain carelessness about the move, as if going on to identify self-knowledge with temperance was something one might as well do once one has asserted that the former is a necessary condition for the latter.[34]

Yet these are of course very different claims. As I argued in Section 4.2, the motivation for Critias to regard self-knowledge as even a necessary condition for temperance is likely to be his previous claim that temperance is doing one's own things, where one construes this as doing only those things proper to one's status, such that one would need to be aware of that status, as constituting who one is, in order not to transgress its boundaries. This kind of self-awareness or self-knowledge does not, in this case, seem to be the same thing as what temperance is. Rather, it is needed in order for one to be temperate, i.e. to act only within the boundaries given by one's status.

Critias' willingness to move from necessary condition to identification, treating the first as a green light for the second, indicates a certain lack of self-knowledge on his part: a lack of awareness of what his own claims amount to. This is in keeping with a propensity that we have already noted: his moving rapidly, and with apparent unconcern for the proposals left in his wake, from one account of temperance to another. Though capable of acknowledging, perhaps even at times prematurely, when he is wrong, that doesn't seem to induce any sense that the next try won't be

---

[34] More charitably, one might read the 'pretty much' as a cautious qualification of full-throated identity (cf. Tsouna 2022, 160); if so, then Critias has thrown caution to the winds by the end of his appeal to Delphi, where he is prepared to dispense with everything that has gone before to defend an account of temperance as knowing oneself (165a8–b4).

right, or that in some fundamental way he is ignorant on the subject. Yet in switching around in this breathless fashion,[35] can Critias be said, first-order ignorance aside, even to know what he believes about temperance? Can he be said, regarding the nature of temperance at least, to really believe anything? These questions will be important as we come to consider how temperance as self-knowledge might be construed.

Is this already unfair to Critias? As we have seen, he does, when it comes to interpretation, undertake painstaking, even if (as it may be) misapplied, scrutiny of others' words in order to support his proposals. That may seem to sit ill with an assessment of him as exhibiting a kind of giddy groundlessness in making those proposals. I think in fact that there is a fascinating split here in Critias' approach, which is not to be wished away by pointing out how far-fetched his interpretations tend to be.

What the split amounts to is this: on matters such as the nature of temperance, Critias generally believes that p (where p is some proposition), to the extent that he does believe it, because someone else whom he takes to have, or be backed by, authority, can be shown to speak in favour of p. All his analytical efforts go into showing whether the authority in question supports p. It is as if, for Critias, the principal source for one's holding that p is precisely that an authority can be found to support it. Thus he tells us that he 'learned' (*emathon*, 163b4) from Hesiod how temperance is doing one's own things; and he 'concurs' (*sumpheromai*, 164d5) with the inscriber at Delphi on the idea that temperance is knowing oneself.

This chimes well with the idea that for Critias the self is essentially a social entity: one's social status is who one is. If so, then it is natural that one should regard one's beliefs as derived from their being favoured by those who are deemed figures of authority within one's society. Hence, in coming to affirm p oneself, one does not scrutinise p directly; one scrutinises whether a given authority figure holds that p. To this extent, the 'social authority' model of the self has an important cognitive dimension in regard to its conception of self-knowledge, in that it suggests a distinct source for discovering what one thinks, namely what one takes appropriate figures of authority within one's society to think.

We can also now see Charmides in turn as occupying an intriguing middle ground with respect to his own attempts to say what temperance is. His first answer seemed very much in line with the social authority model, even if it was a more general tradition rather than a specific individual that he drew on as a basis for saying that temperance was a kind of quietness.

---

[35] 'une véritable girouette' (Dorion 2004, 46).

4.4 Knowing What One Believes

His second answer seemed drawn from inspection of his own soul but his follow-up evinced a distaste for actually having his soul subjected to scrutiny, since his third answer deflected to Critias. Now as older cousin and guardian the latter certainly occupies a position of social authority in relation to Charmides. But one might argue that at this point Charmides demonstrates the worst of both worlds: deferential to Critias' proposal (temperance is doing one's own things) not in a spirit of healthy curiosity, but only insofar as he seemed to relish the idea of Socrates picking it apart; hence apparently motivated by a combination of youthful malice towards his cousin and the desire to avoid subjection of any further proposals of his own to scrutiny.

If Critias himself is interested more in figuring out support from authority to ground his proposals than in subjecting them to independent scrutiny, one can see, if we return to the proposal that temperance is self-knowledge, a sharp difference emerge between Socrates and Critias in this regard. As we noted earlier, Critias offers to give Socrates an account of his proposal that temperance is self-knowledge, if Socrates does not agree that it is (165b3–4). Socrates responds as follows:

> But Critias, you are treating me as if I claim to know (*eidenai*) the things that I ask and will agree with you should I so wish (*ean dē boulōmai*). However, that is not the case; I investigate with you what is proposed on a given occasion (*aei to protithemenon*) because I myself do not know. Hence it is once I have examined [the matter] that I am willing (*ethelō*) to say whether I agree or not. But wait while I examine. (165b5–c2)

In expressing a future willingness to say whether or not he agrees with Critias, Socrates does not say, as he might easily be read as saying, that he is unwilling to agree with Critias until he has examined the matter. Rather, in stating that Critias treats him as if he claims to have knowledge and thus will agree 'should I so wish', Socrates implies that it is not yet in his gift to agree with Critias before the examination has taken place. His suggestion is that, in view of his lack of knowledge, he will not be in a position to say whether he agrees with Critias until he has reflected on the question for which his agreement is sought. He needs to *work out* whether he agrees with Critias that temperance is knowing oneself, and one does this by reflecting on whether temperance is knowing oneself.

Where Critias, then, had seemed ready to affirm all manner of things, in quick succession and not always compatibly with one another, pausing only to interpret, to his own satisfaction, the word of an authority as being in agreement with him, Socrates, who conversely (and, I have argued, ill-advisedly) disdains the business of interpreting others, relies on independent reflection to discover whether he agrees that temperance is self-knowledge.

Given that such reflection is needed in order for him not just to know that something is the case, but even to be in a position to agree that something is the case, this begins to suggest on Socrates' part a distinct model of self-knowledge: one in which one is not in a position to know what one believes, for example about the nature of temperance, such that one can say whether one agrees that a certain proposition about its nature is true or not, in advance of critical reflection on that proposition. Such reflection is, on this view, necessary to so much as figure out what one believes in the first place. Whether one believes p will thus in part be constituted by the process by which one comes to believe p.

If, on the other hand, having a belief is just a matter of what one finds oneself affirming, then knowing what one believes will, as it were, be automatic. One simply refers to what one has affirmed. Or, if one's having a belief is a matter of what appropriate authorities believe, one perhaps refers to what *they* say in order to know what one believes oneself. But, as I have already suggested, one may doubt in Critias' case whether it is right to speak of him as having beliefs at all. If so, then we have motivation for what one might call a reflective model of self-knowledge,[36] such that coming to know whether I believe that p is a matter of having gone through a process of reflection as to whether p.[37] On the social authority model attributable to Critias, by contrast, one discovers what (if anything) one believes by ascertaining what is held by some figure of authority.[38]

4.5 Knowledge and Method

I shall develop such considerations further as we move forward with the dialogue's discussion of temperance as self-knowledge.[39] Whatever Critias'

---

[36] Cf. McCabe (2007a, 16–18).

[37] For a penetrating contemporary study of such a model of self-knowledge see Moran (2001); cf. Evans (1982, 225) and in a Platonic context, with particular reference to the *Theaetetus*, Burnyeat (1977, 11–12).

[38] The question arises (my thanks to Bill Brewer and M. M. McCabe for pressing it) whether the reflective model itself encompasses a social dimension: Socrates, after all, investigates the various proposals in company with others. One way of approaching the issue in regard to the *Charmides* is to consider again the distinction between written and oral. Reflective engagement with the text of the *Charmides* is not social in the way that Socrates' encounters with his interlocutors are. Plato's cultural standing may, on the other hand, mean that one finds oneself approaching the *Charmides* as a work of authority; part of the argument of this book is that the dialogue is written so as to discourage the reading of it in a deferential or uncritical spirit.

[39] See esp. Section 5.1.

4.5 Knowledge and Method

own motivation for his interest in self-knowledge – I have suggested it may arise from the idea of temperance as doing one's own things – he does not explicitly connect his claim that temperance is self-knowledge with any of his previous proposals. Thus detached, and identified full-strength with temperance, the question of what knowing oneself is stands as an open one. The first move that Socrates makes to fill the gap, after (with Critias' leave) considering the matter, is therefore important. He says at 165c4–6 that if temperance is knowing (*gignōskein*) something, then it would be knowledge of some kind (*epistēmē tis*), and of something (*tinos*). Critias agrees, specifying, in regard to the latter point, 'of oneself' (*heautou ge*, 165c7).

In thus placing *epistēmē* centre-stage as the operative knowledge-term in the discussion of temperance as self-knowledge, Socrates invites consideration of self-knowledge as a branch or field of knowledge. In so doing, he also suggests a treatment of it as a form of practical knowledge or skill – knowledge of *how* to do something. This is evident from the first of the illustrative examples he gives. Medicine, he says, is knowledge of what is healthy (165c8). Now although Socrates, in line with his point that any branch of knowledge is 'of something', has thus gone on to state what medicine is knowledge of, it is clear that medicine, in being 'of' health, is at the same time knowledge of how to bring health about.

Socrates indicates this by connecting medicine as knowledge of what is healthy with the idea that it will thereby be in some way useful (*chrēsimē*) and bring something about (165c10–11): what it brings about (*apergazetai*) is 'the no small benefit' of health (165d1–2).[40] One might then suggest, given the earlier prominence of medicine in the dialogue, that this particular choice as first example is not accidental. The second example, house-building, which also involves production, is less resonant, given the way that medicine has already been thematised. Let us follow through on what the medical example may imply. If medicine, as knowledge of health, is the art of realising health, then along the same lines, temperance as knowledge of oneself should be the art of realising oneself. I shall argue in due course that a view of temperance as the power of self-realisation is indeed suggested by various features of the discussion.

---

[40] Balaban (2008, 667) seems unjustified in claiming that Plato rejects a conception of knowledge such that, in addition to having health as its object, medicine also concerns itself with the question of knowing how to heal.

Socrates' turn to medicine back at 158e2 I interpreted as referring to his practice of the art of (what I called) soul-medicine, while the Thracian narrative held that temperance arises in the soul as a result of the soul's being treated. If so, then soul-medicine would be the art of creating temperance in souls that are deficient in it, as medicine is the art of creating health in bodies that are deficient in it. If, moreover, it is right that the power of self-realisation of a certain sort can be inferred as a candidate for explicating what temperance as self-knowledge might be, then we can place this also in relation to the practice of soul-medicine: the soul-doctor will, in successfully exercising that art, create in the patient the power to realise herself.

I shall argue these points in greater detail as we proceed. For now, we should note that, whatever positive account might be constructed from the idea of knowledge of oneself as a branch of knowledge belonging to the same broad genus as medicine or house-building, the idea of treating it in this way clearly makes Critias uncomfortable. It was, after all, Socrates, in the wake of Critias' proposal that temperance is knowing oneself, who introduced the idea that temperance would thus be a kind of *epistēmē* (165c4–5). When Socrates then asks (165d8–e2) what beautiful product does temperance, as knowledge of oneself, produce as medicine produces health and house-building houses, Critias replies as follows:

> But Socrates, you are not seeking in the correct way (*ouk orthōs zēteis*). For this is not of a nature (*ou pephuken*) that is like the other branches of knowledge (*tais allais epistēmais*), nor to be sure are the others like one another. But you are conducting your search as if they are alike. For tell me, what is the product (*ergon*) of the art (*technē*) of calculation or of geometry that is of such a kind as a house is of [the art of] house-building or a cloak of weaving or many other such products of many arts that one might be able to show? Are you also, then, able to show me such a product of these [arts]? But you will not be able to. (165e3–166a2)

What is interesting about Critias' response is that it is one of method not of substance. The charge is that Socrates conducts his enquiry incorrectly; specifically, that he over-generalises. Socrates has taken a number of favoured examples of branches of knowledge that have a certain feature and demanded to be shown that any given example of a branch of knowledge – knowledge of oneself, in this case – has that feature. But, as Critias attempts to show, not every agreed case of a branch of knowledge has that feature, so Socrates' request was unreasonable.

In saying that Critias' response is not one of substance, I seek to draw attention to a peculiar feature of it. The response denies that knowledge of oneself belongs in that favoured class, yet Critias has given no reason for this denial.[41] Perhaps it strikes him as obvious that knowledge of oneself is not going to be of the same type as, say, knowledge of health, but that does not mean he is right to think that. That Critias himself does not give grounds for excluding knowledge of oneself from the favoured class may be an indication that we are supposed to reflect rather more than he does on whether it should be excluded.

Socrates at any rate concedes Critias' point of method: he has overgeneralised. The concession indeed is not surprising – and not simply because Critias does seem to be right here. Socrates himself had indicated in making his generalisation that it was only a subclass of branches of knowledge that do have products. After speaking of medicine and house-building, he says at 165d6 that his point about production applies to 'the other crafts' (*tōn allōn technōn*) too. In not using *epistēmē* here but a different term – *technē*: 'craft' or 'skill' – Socrates seems to imply, wittingly (if he is using the term as more than a stylistic variant) or unwittingly (if he is not),[42] that the point only applies to that subclass of branches of knowledge that are the productive arts.

Nonetheless, Socrates insists, there is a feature of all branches of knowledge that knowledge of oneself would have to possess, namely that each has a subject-matter different from itself (166a3–5). He points out, picking up one of Critias' earlier counterexamples, that the subject-matter of the art of calculation is the odd and the even, and these are different from calculation itself (a5–10). After giving the further example of the art of weighing whose subject-matter, the heavy and light, is distinct from the art of weighing, Socrates asks Critias to say what the subject-matter is of temperance, as a branch of knowledge, that is distinct from temperance itself (166b1–6).

Critias responds with what looks like a sharpened version of his previous objection. There he pointed out that Socrates had, in looking for similarity between branches of knowledge, over-generalised about their each possessing some product. Now he tells Socrates:

> You have in enquiring reached the very point by which temperance differs from all the [other] branches of knowledge. But you seek a particular similarity of it with the others. But that is not so; rather all the other

---

[41] Cf. Ahbel-Rappe (2018, 35).
[42] In his response Critias refers both to calculation and to geometry as cases of *technē* (165e6), so he at any rate construes the latter term broadly. On the relation between *epistēmē* and *technē* in Plato see Hulme (2022).

branches of knowledge are of something else, while it alone is knowledge both of the other branches of knowledge[43] and itself of itself (*autē heautēs*). (166b7–c3)

Critias' response looks sharper than before because, whereas the purport of his earlier objection was that it is a mistake to think that a feature of some branches of knowledge (e.g. that they have a product) will occur in all branches of knowledge, this version implies not just that there is no reason to expect similarity of features across all branches, but also that one should expect to reach a point where each branch *does* have a feature different from the rest; and we have now reached it, as specified, in the case of temperance.

Now it is possible that Critias' point is a narrower one, that it is part of the uniqueness of knowledge of oneself that it lack the feature of a subject-matter distinct from itself, rather than the broader thesis that each branch of knowledge will have some feature by which it is distinct from the others.[44] He does indeed say at 166b9 that Socrates is seeking some similarity of it to the others. Nonetheless it is likely that Critias has the broader point in mind. That is because even in the earlier version of his objection, Critias is in fact explicit that his point is not specific to temperance but to branches of knowledge in general. He said, as we saw, that it is not in the nature of the case that temperance is similar to the other branches of knowledge, nor those others to one another (165e3–5). So it seems that when Critias brings forward the second version of the objection, he intends to make a general point of principle: each branch of knowledge will have some feature that distinguishes it from every other.

The principle seems close to unimpeachable: if there are distinct branches of knowledge, then presumably each must have some feature that makes it distinct from the others. As in previous cases, we ought to

---

[43] The awkward (in English) plural 'knowledges' is a more literal rendition of the Greek *epistēmai* than 'branches of knowledge' as translated in the text, and makes it easier to see why Critias takes knowledge of the other branches of knowledge and knowledge of knowledge to go together as subject-matter not distinct from knowledge, the 'knowledges' being, as such, forms or species of knowledge.

[44] As Duncombe (2020, 38) points out, Critias' statement of temperance as the only (*monē*, 166c2; e5) branch of knowledge that has itself and the other branches of knowledge as object does not, as worded, rule out its also having, like other branches of knowledge, an object (that is not some sort of knowledge) distinct from itself, and so is not formally equivalent to Socrates' construal of it at 167b11–c1 as having no such distinct object (*ouk allou tinos estin*). However, Critias' statement is in response to Socrates' asking him to say which object temperance has that is distinct (*heteron*, 166b6) from itself. Critias' insistence that temperance alone has itself as object would not serve as a response to that question unless understood as denying that it has an object distinct from itself, at least in the sense that the other branches do.

distinguish the basic soundness of the principles that Critias upholds from his sometimes maladroit application of them. Note in this regard that the principle says nothing about what it is that will make a given member of the class distinct from each other member. So the particular individuating feature that Critias imputes to knowledge of oneself as a branch of knowledge, namely that it lacks a subject-matter distinct from itself, was not entailed by the application of the principle. There could be other features that individuate branches of knowledge from one another – for example, that each branch of knowledge has a subject-matter that is distinct from that of every other branch. Whether this is in fact true is a further question, but it is certainly suggested by the examples that Critias and Socrates have exchanged, where each given case of a branch of knowledge had a cited subject-matter distinct from that of each of the others.[45]

Indeed, as even with the narrower subclass of productive arts, so too with temperance as a member of the wider class of branches of knowledge, there seems nothing to compel Critias to treat temperance, as knowledge of oneself, as distinct, in the particular way that he claims, from the other branches. Just as it seemed too quick of him to deny that temperance as knowledge of oneself will have a product, so here his implied view, that knowledge of oneself does not have a subject-matter distinct from it, does not appear to receive justification. It is at any rate not obvious that 'oneself' is not (or could not be) a subject-matter distinct from knowledge of oneself.

4.6 The Socratic Turn

Why, then, does Critias, in a characteristically flamboyant way, assert that temperance, as knowledge of oneself, is knowledge of itself and of the other branches of knowledge? One clue might lie in the accusation with which he follows that assertion:

> And you [Socrates] are far from unaware of these matters (*tauta se pollou dei lelēthenai*), but in fact I believe that you are doing what you just denied that you do: you are trying to refute me, neglecting what it is that the account is about. (166c3–6)

---

[45] Geometry, however, does not have a subject-matter explicitly attributed to it, which at least leaves open the possibility that it may share subject-matter with another branch (e.g. calculation).

Now it is not completely clear from this what Socrates is supposed to be far from unaware of. But given that the accusation does immediately follow Critias' claim that temperance is the only branch of knowledge that has itself and the other branches as its subject-matter, it seems that Critias assumes that Socrates himself will be well aware of this way of looking at temperance. Why might Critias think this? An indication is given in the defence that Socrates immediately offers against the accusation:

> What a thing you're doing to suppose that, however much I may refute you, I do so for any other reason than that I would scrutinise myself as to what I say, namely for fear that I might unawares (*lathô*) ever think that I know (*eidenai*) something when I do not know it. (166c7–d2)

Here Socrates expresses a fear of overstepping not social boundaries but cognitive ones through thinking that his knowledge extends further than it in fact does. His way of avoiding this is to scrutinise proposals (whether his own or others') to ensure that he does not mistakenly regard the affirmation of them as representing knowledge on the matter in question.

Such scrutiny will, in turn, help ensure that, rather than think that one has knowledge when one does not, one will only take oneself to have knowledge in those cases when one does in fact have it. Socrates' own procedure as he describes it, then, seems to be measured by its achievement of self-knowledge in the sense of the ability to distinguish what one knows from what one does not. Given that aim, and its connection (as Socrates sees it) with a certain sort of focussed enquiry, it does not seem overly speculative to suggest, in the light of Critias' accusation, that Socrates has, in the course of his association with Critias, raised the idea of temperance as knowing oneself,[46] with a particular cognitive conception of the self in mind: who I am as a function of my epistemic, not my social, status.

On such a conception, the subject-matter of temperance will plausibly be, or at least include, knowledge, insofar as the temperate person must be able to identify what does and does not count as knowledge in order to tell whether or not they have it. It will then follow that in order to have knowledge of oneself one must have knowledge of knowledge. So if temperance is knowledge of oneself, it will mean that one who has temperance has knowledge of knowledge. Given Critias' tendency, as noted earlier, to equate something's being necessary for temperance with

---

[46] Cf. Rappe (1995, 9). One might see here an echo of the move that produced, in Charmides' case, an account of temperance that originated with Critias.

4.6 The Socratic Turn

something's being temperance, he identifies, on what he takes to be Socrates' authority, temperance as knowledge of knowledge.

If that is so, then we may have an answer not just to the question why Critias should suppose that Socrates is 'far from unaware' of this way of conceiving of temperance, but why Critias chooses to advocate that conception himself. It will be on similar grounds to those that he looked to in his adoption of other proposals of his about what temperance is, namely that some figure of authority has favoured it. Appropriately enough, given that we seem now to be dealing in a notion of the self as specifically epistemic, the authority that Socrates represents for Critias is not cultural – he is neither a canonical poet nor, as far as we are told (and in contrast to Critias and Charmides), of noble family – but intellectual: Socrates has a certain authority with Critias because his piercing intellect means his ideas demand to be taken seriously.

Of course, taking an idea seriously is not the same as advocating it uncritically. So Critias' habit of grounding his own affirmations by reference to support from an authority figure may have caused him to miss the point here, or at least to have directed his ire at Socrates unfairly. For what Socrates says in response is precisely that, in order not to think mistakenly that he knows, his own ideas are as much up for scrutiny by him as those of others. Critias has misunderstood Socrates if he takes it that adopting an idea of Socrates' exempts that idea from criticism by Socrates. That may be why, once Socrates has reminded Critias of his procedure, the latter is fairly quickly assuaged. Socrates assures him, as we have seen,[47] that the scrutiny is in service of the 'common good' of getting clear about how things are, and he bids Critias focus on how the argument will turn out when tested (166d4–e2). Critias allows that what Socrates has said is 'reasonable' (*metria*, 166e3), and we are ready to see how the testing proceeds.

Socrates' first move is to secure Critias' agreement that if temperance is knowledge of knowledge, then it will also be knowledge of lack of knowledge (*anepistēmosunē*, 166e7–8). Presumably this is on the grounds that if one knows the 'positive' member of a pair of contraries one knows the 'negative' member: if I know what health is, I will also know what lack of health (sickness) is.[48] But the move also shores up a connection with Socrates' own procedure. He has just said that he would scrutinise his own

---

[47] Section 3.10.
[48] Note how the dialogue elsewhere describes objects of the same branch of knowledge in terms of a 'positive' and 'negative' pair: health and sickness (171a8–9), good and bad (174b10, c3, d5–6); cf. Dorion (2004, 137 n. 140).

proposals so as not to think he knows something that he does not. It follows from this that he would need to be able to tell knowledge from ignorance. Without this ability, it is hard to see how he could avoid thinking he knows something that he does not. Of course, it may well be that the test for whether a claim counts as knowledge or ignorance just is whether it survives rational scrutiny. This would explain why Socrates cites scrutiny of a claim as what will prevent him from mistaking lack of knowledge for knowledge. But that no less entails that one with knowledge of knowledge will also have knowledge of lack of knowledge.

Socrates then turns to what seems to be, in the light of what he will go on to mark out as one of two key points that need investigating about the proposal that temperance is knowledge of knowledge (and of lack of knowledge), groundwork for an account of temperance's unique benefit. If one grants the proposal:

> Then only the temperate person will both know (*gnōsetai*) himself and will be able both to examine what he in fact knows (*eidōs*) and does not know, and in regard to others likewise will have the power (*dunatos estai*) to assess what someone knows when they think they do, and what in turn someone merely thinks that they know but does not know; and none of the others [will have this power]. And this indeed is being temperate and temperance, and knowing oneself: to know both what one knows and what one does not know (*ha te oiden kai ha mē oiden*). (167a1–7)

Since the Greek verbs at the end of the quotation have no explicit subject (in English the subject is supplied by 'one'), this seems to indicate, given Socrates' previous explication, that self-knowledge is conceived here as giving its possessor the power to know what anyone, oneself or others, knows and does not know.

One should note that Socrates treats temperance on this account as indeed implying the power to do something,[49] namely to examine oneself and others with respect to whether one knows or merely thinks that one does. Thus it is clear that we are still holding to the idea of a given branch of knowledge as involving knowledge-how. Nonetheless it is this account – temperance as knowing what one does and does not know – that now itself requires scrutiny.[50] Socrates sets two specific tests: what the account describes needs to be, firstly, possible and, secondly, beneficial (167b1–4). In regard to

---

[49] Cf. Tuozzo (2011, 206).
[50] While Tsouna (2017, 55; cf. 2022, 26) is right to point out that Socrates refrains from using *epistasthai* in this passage, opting for other verbs of 'knowing' instead (*gignōskein, eidenai*), I am not sure this is sufficient to indicate, as she claims, that Socrates means to offer thereby an alternative conception of self-knowledge to one, with *epistasthai* as the dominant term, promulgated by Critias.

possibility, what Socrates will in fact focus on is temperance as knowledge of knowledge, while the construal that he has taken to be implied by this, namely temperance as knowing what one does and does not know, will serve as the focus of the enquiry into benefit.

Socrates does not say that if the account passes these two tests, it would thereby be certified as a correct account of temperance, or whether it would merely be a necessary rather than sufficient condition for its being correct that it pass the tests. He names no other tests that he thinks suitable, so it seems fair to say that, as far as he is concerned, the account's passing the tests would at least go a substantial way towards its validation. Both tests seem reasonable: if a proposal for what temperance is turns out to be of something impossible, then on the assumption – one the dialogue seems to take as read – that temperance is not an impossibility, the proposal should be rejected. Similarly, a proposal that does not reveal temperance as of benefit might be regarded as failing to capture an essential feature of temperance as something good.

4.7 Socrates' Challenge I

Socrates says that he is puzzled (*aporō*, 167b7) about these issues, and the immediate cause of his puzzlement seems to be the question of possibility. For he goes on to produce a series of examples – let us call this 'Socrates' challenge' – featuring powers other than knowledge, that purports to show that a model analogous in form to knowledge of itself and of the other branches of knowledge, and of lack of knowledge, is inapplicable to these powers. In the end this results in Critias being puzzled too (169c). Socrates then suggests, as a way forward, that they concede for the sake of argument that knowledge of knowledge *is* possible and turn to the question of whether it would in fact follow, from this account, that one knows what one knows and does not know (169d). Although Socrates mentions that he does not go so far as to conclude decisively from the examples that temperance is impossible if construed as knowledge of knowledge

---

Tsouna concedes that '*epistasthai* and *gignōskein* can be used interchangeably in certain Platonic contexts' (2017, 55). In effect they are so used in *this* context. It is Critias who uses *gignōskein* in his first official formulation of temperance as knowing oneself at 164d3–4 and 165b3–4, albeit prompted by Socrates' use of the term at 164b7 and c1; and Socrates, as acknowledged in Tsouna (2001, 46), who then infers at 165c4–5 that if temperance is *gignōskein* something it would be some sort of *epistēmē*. Socrates then continues to use the latter term at 165c8, c10–11, d4, d7–8 and e1, Critias only eventually picking it up explicitly at 165e4. This, I think, makes it hard to discern a genuine terminological division of labour that would underpin an allocation, in the way that Tsouna construes it, of alternative conceptions of self-knowledge to Socrates and to Critias.

(169a8–b1), their role is evidently to target that account and put its possibility in doubt.

Now 'knowledge of knowledge' is only part of a longer account of temperance as knowing oneself that also includes, under the same branch, knowledge of the other knowledges and of lack of knowledge (167b11–c2). However, it is the first element of the account, what one might call its explicitly reflexive or self-directed aspect, that is of most concern, with its underlying idea that knowledge can be of itself rather than of something distinct from itself. Socrates does not say what the implications are for the other parts of the account, such that they are taken together in his challenge;[51] but it may be that he supposes that if knowledge of knowledge turns out to be impossible, then so too will those other elements. For, one might think, one has knowledge of lack of knowledge just to the extent that one has knowledge of knowledge (one counts as knowing the absence of x by knowing at least the necessary conditions for the presence of x); and that knowledge of other branches of knowledge, insofar as the latter are to be regarded as forms or species of knowledge, requires knowledge of knowledge too. Thus, calling into doubt the possibility of knowledge of knowledge threatens to place the whole account in doubt.

That Socrates' challenge does concern the question of possibility is confirmed by consideration of its two respective main sections, 167c–168a and 168b–169a. To turn to the first: at 167c4–6 Socrates suggests that the present account of temperance is a 'strange' (*atopon*) undertaking given that in other cases than knowledge this same structure will, he supposes, strike Critias as impossible (*adunaton*). Let us illustrate this with the first of these other cases that Socrates reviews, that of sight (*opsis*).[52] He asks Critias:

> 'Consider whether there seems to you to be some sight, which is not sight of those things that the other sights are of, but is sight of itself and of the other sights, and of lack of sights likewise, and which, being sight, sees no colour, but [sees] itself and the other sights. Does there seem to you to be such [a sight]?'
>
> 'Not to me by Zeus.' (167c8–d3)

Socrates then gives a list of other such cases in similar form (167d–168a), all of which, broadly speaking, are drawn from among the powers or

---

[51] It is, however, worth noting that the 'lack of' part of the account drops out of the analogies given in the challenge after the first two examples (sight and hearing).

[52] Sight's first place here sits naturally with the predominance of the 'looking' terminology in the dialogue that we have previously examined.

capacities of the soul (though, as we remarked earlier, not named as such).⁵³ In order, these are: hearing, the senses in general, then appetite, wish, eros, fear, and belief (*doxa*). At the end of this section Socrates reiterates that it is a strange thing, given the putative lack of application of self-directedness in these other cases, if it does apply in the case of knowledge, though they should not yet insist that it does not apply, but examine further whether it does (168a10–11).

Now there seem to be two distinct issues one might raise about this first section, respectively of substance and of method. In terms of substance: how problematic, for the idea of self-directedness, are the cases other than knowledge, considered in their own right, that Socrates describes? And in terms of method, to what extent is it legitimate to infer, on the basis that one did accept self-directedness to be problematic in this range of cases, that it is problematic in a further sort of case, such as knowledge?

Let me approach the question of substance by way of a further question: does the challenge as to whether a thing can have itself as its own object concern the various *powers* that the soul may possess (e.g. the power to see or hear) or does it concern individual *acts* that express a given power (e.g. token acts of seeing)? In terms of fit with Critias' original account, one can ask whether that account was about knowledge as a power, or about token acts of knowing. The answer seems to be the former: his reference to 'the other knowledges' that temperance would be knowledge of, as well as itself, is surely to various powers, understood as various branches of knowledge that one might be expert in, such as medicine, rather than individual expressions of such knowledge, such as a token healing of a patient. So in the case of knowledge at least, the question seems to be: is there a branch of knowledge that takes itself and the other branches of knowledge as its object? Socrates claims that this sort of relation is puzzling in other cases of cognition such as sight.

Now Socrates' language does not by itself determine whether 'sight' refers in his exposition to the power to see or to an act of seeing. At 167c8 he speaks of 'some sight' (*opsis tis*) as candidate for self-directedness, as he had referred to 'some single knowledge' (*mia tis epistēmē*) in the analogous case at 167b11, these formulations being linguistically compatible with either reading, though suggestive of the power reading in the knowledge

---

⁵³ It may be that Socrates is simply noncommittal about these all being powers specifically of the soul. On the other hand, the grounds for grouping just these together as the initial comparators for knowledge are less clear if they are not held to be such powers. On various intellectual qualities and forms of cognition as belonging to the soul, deployed as part of Socrates' refutation of Charmides' first answer, see 159e–160b.

case. We might think that with regard to sight, however, it does not quite work to read the reference to 'other sights' as being (analogously to knowledge) about powers of sight, since it is unclear what this plurality of powers would be.[54] In the case of knowledge, we *have* the various powers (medicine, house-building and so on) given to us to flesh out what the referent of 'knowledges' in the plural is.

With sight, the plural seems more naturally to refer to particular token instances, or acts, of seeing.[55] But if that is right, then there do seem to be acts of seeing that take acts of seeing as their object. We need look for illustration no further than the *Charmides* itself:[56] at 154c6–8 Socrates (as we saw) says he focussed on the boys, noticing that none looked (*eblepen*) elsewhere but gazed (*etheōnto*) at Charmides as if he were a statue. Now Socrates does not say precisely that he saw the boys seeing. He uses a different vocabulary. But the situation depicted certainly seems to amount to a case of a seeing of a seeing.

For another example, consider 155c8–d1, where Socrates reports that Charmides 'gave him an irresistible look (*eneblepsen*) with his eyes'. Socrates is presumably able to glean this because he is looking at Charmides as the latter looks at him. So here too we have a case of a seeing of a seeing. A third example is slightly different but linguistically even closer to home: in summarising his challenge at 168e, straight after returning to sight as a problem case, Socrates asks Critias 'do you see' (*horais*, e3) that such cases are problematic, where seeing is itself given, in regard to what Critias is asked to display, a cognitive richness that belies the rather relentless schematism of Socrates' earlier presentation, in which seeing is grouped with other sense-faculties and differentiated from knowing and believing.[57] Socrates' question indicates that, in its richer guise, seeing can indeed be directed at seeing.

It seems, then, that we can find cases within the dialogue that show certain acts that express a power of the soul to be self-directed. But we have to be careful here. We are talking, in Socrates' formulation at 167c8–d2, about the possibility of some sight that sees itself and the other sights, and

---

[54] Here, nonetheless, is a pair of possibilities: the different kinds of visual systems of different animal species (compare fawn and lion); the different sorts of ways humans can exercise the power of sight (compare the onlookers' awestruck gaze, 154c8; Charmides' mischievous glance, 162b11).

[55] Cf. Tsouna (2022, 204).   [56] See Moore (2015, 93).

[57] Cf. for similarly rich uses 167c4, 172a7 (both seeing); 156c5 (perceiving). On the cognitive richness of perception in the *Charmides* see McCabe (2007a); Levine (2016, 247; 251). In regard to belief, note that at 168a3–5 Critias, in denying that there is belief that has belief as its object, to all appearances expresses a belief that has belief as its object, namely the belief that belief does not take belief as its object; cf. Schmidt (1985, 57).

there is a more and less stringent way of construing 'itself' on this reading in a phrase such as 'some sight that sees itself'. On the less stringent construal, we take this to mean simply that there can be a seeing whose object is a seeing. This seems to fit cases like that of Socrates' seeing the boys seeing Charmides, but also has a problem associated with it: it is not clear on this construal what differentiates seeing that sees itself from seeing that sees other seeings. If the phrase just means a seeing that takes some seeing as its object, such that that can already include as object any act of seeing, this leaves unclear what is added by the mention of 'other seeings'. So let us turn to the more stringent construal, whereby the phrase would imply that a given act of seeing has that very (token) act as its object. And that, I take it, is more puzzling. This is not to say that such cases are impossible, but it would mean that the examples from the text of the *Charmides* no longer count, on the stringent reading, as cases of some sight seeing itself.

To see how one nonetheless might make sense of this even on the more stringent reading, one may turn to the place where Socrates, having made puzzles of sight that sees itself and then hearing that hears itself, goes on to generalise to 'all the perceptions' generally and asks, in respect of them, whether Critias thinks there is 'some perception (*aisthēsis*) of perceptions and of itself' (167d7–8). One might respond: it certainly seems that I can perceive that I am seeing. One might further say that it is in virtue of the operation of my visual capacities that I am able to perceive this. It also seems possible to say that, rather than posit a separate act of seeing to see my first-order seeing (of, say, this blue jug), it is in virtue of that very first-order act of seeing that I am able to perceive my seeing (of the jug).[58]

The example becomes more complicated if one notes that Socrates' generalisation from sight and hearing to 'all the perceptions' seems most naturally construed as talking about powers, or modalities, of perception. Having selected sight and hearing as examples, Socrates will now be extending the argument in similar fashion to the other perceptual powers: smell, touch and taste. If that is right, then the discussion of perception seems now to hew more closely to the target case of knowledge. We might even want to say that the generalisation leaves open the possibility of positing a power of perception – perhaps a kind of 'inner sense' – by

---

[58] One might call this (anachronistically and without of course wishing to beg any interpretive questions) the 'Aristotelian' reading. See Aristotle, *De anima* 3.2, 425b12–17. On the relation between *DA* 3.2 and the *Charmides* see Caston (2002, 772–3; 778–9), Sorabji (2006, 202–3; 207–8), McCabe (2007b).

which we perceive our (other) sense modalities. If so, that would then leave room, in a way that is no longer anomalous, for a power of knowledge that takes the various (other) powers or branches of knowledge as its object. If we then read 'perception of itself' on the less stringent construal, this further type of perception would have perception as its object, in that the various first-order modalities would be what it perceived.

I shall not attempt to chase down all the twists and turns to which such reflections may lead. We have already gone somewhat beyond the above-noted rather bare schematism with which Socrates presents his examples. In view of this, and to return to the first of our two main questions about this section, namely how problematic for the idea of self-directedness are the (non-knowledge) examples that Socrates gives, it seems fair to point out that his own setting out of them in that schematic way (leaving aside whatever further investigations one might thereby be prompted to undertake) does not itself involve his offering any specific reason why we should find these cases problematic or worse.

It is perhaps worth recalling, then, that all Socrates actually said at 167c5–6, in introducing the examples, was that he thinks that they will strike *Critias* as impossible.[59] And Critias duly rejects the application to each of these cases of the structure in question.[60] Yet despite this, he is ready at the end of this section to (re)affirm (*phamen gar*, 168a9) that the structure *is* applicable to the case of knowledge. And that then throws weight on the second of our questions, about the soundness of Socrates' method in using these cases to throw doubt on the case of knowledge.

Critias does not seem terribly fazed. This is brought out, as we just saw, by the fact that he apparently concedes that the structure of self-directedness cannot be applied in those other cases, while still prepared to affirm its application in the case of knowledge. He does indeed say at 168b1, in response to Socrates' saying at 168a10–11 that they should not rule out its applicability to knowledge but examine the question further, that Socrates is right about this, though it is not clear if his agreement extends to Socrates' immediately preceding remark (a10) that it is strange if it does apply in the case of knowledge. Critias looks to be not wholly convinced that Socrates' method is sound even with regard to its throwing doubt on, let alone ruling out, the applicability of the structure to the case of knowledge.

---

[59] *doxei soi, hōs egōimai, adunaton einai*. Pace Tsouna (2022, 225), the Greek does not mean 'will strike you [Critias] as impossible, as it does me [Socrates]'. Socrates is expressing his belief about what Critias will think about the matter, not saying what he thinks about it.
[60] See his responses at 167d3, d6, d10, e3, e6, e9, 168a2, a5.

In this, of course, Critias would be consistently upholding his earlier doubt about Socrates' tendency to (over)generalise. There, the fact that, in general, a branch of knowledge has a subject-matter distinct from itself did not persuade Critias that there cannot be some branch of knowledge that does not have a subject-matter distinct from itself. So too in this case he seems unpersuaded, thus far, that the inapplicability of a certain structure to other capacities of the soul casts doubt on its applicability to knowledge. If so, then he may be sceptical about the idea that one can infer, from a certain set of species of a genus having (or lacking) a given feature, that a given other species has (or lacks) that feature. And, as in the previous case, here too, I think, it is hard to object in a principled way to such scepticism.

4.8 Socrates' Challenge II

The first section of Socrates' challenge, then, does not appear to offer good reason for supposing that Critias' most recent account of temperance risks turning temperance into something impossible. It does not show, as a matter of substance, where the impossibility would lie or, as a matter of method, why we should infer impossibility in the case of knowledge even if we accept it, as Critias seems to, in the other cases. So the burden falls on the second section, clearly marked as a new phase by Socrates' 'Well, then' (*Phere dē*) at 168b2.[61] Here, interestingly, he expands the range of cases well beyond capacities of soul to cover relations more generally. So he moves from the relation 'knowledge of' something (*tinos epistēmē*, 168b2) to the relation 'greater than' something (*tinos meizon*, b6) and points out that the relatum in the latter case will be 'something smaller' (*elattonos tinos*, b8).

Socrates can now issue a fresh challenge. As he puts it:

> If we were to find something greater, that is greater than the greater things and than itself, but greater than none of the things than which the other greater things are greater, then I presume that the following would certainly apply to it, if it were greater than itself, also to be smaller than itself. (168b10–c2)

So too, in the case of the relation 'double', whose relatum is 'half': if there is some double that is double the other doubles and itself, then it will also be half of itself (168c4–7).

---

[61] Cf. Ebert (1974, 69).

After running swiftly through some more cases of quantitative relations, with similar consequences, Socrates turns back to perception, having generalised to point out that whatever exercises its own power (*dunamis*) with respect to itself will also have that quality (*ousia*) which characterises its relatum: so just as a double (of itself) will also be a half (of itself), so too a hearing that was of itself would possess sound, and a sight that was of itself would possess colour, the relata of hearing and sight being sound and colour respectively (168c9–e1).

It is only at this point that Socrates returns to the issue of impossibility and says that in some of the cases they have been through, namely the quantitative ones, it appears 'altogether impossible' for a power to be directed at itself; Critias agrees (168e3–8). In other cases, Socrates continues – the perceptual ones, and some others that he appends (motion and heat) – the idea of self-directedness might at least 'stretch credulity' (*apistian an paraschoi*) in the eyes of some though not perhaps others (168e9–169a1). So a 'great man' will be needed to determine whether no thing is such as to have its power directed at itself, or whether some things are such, others not, and if so whether knowledge is in the former category (169a1–7). Socrates then says 'I do not trust myself' (*ou pisteuō emautōi*, 169a7) to be adequate to determine such questions, wherein he uses an example of cognition directed at oneself in the very act of wondering whether such cognition, in the case of knowledge, is possible as currently construed.[62]

In a nutshell, Socrates has shown that certain relations among those belonging in the quantitative category cannot be self-directed, since that would result in a contradiction: something's being both bigger and smaller than itself, or double and half itself, and so on. But this section of his challenge seems to show little else. Note that even in the quantitative category there are cases friendlier to the idea of self-directedness that Socrates could have chosen: for example, 'equal to',[63] where it is unproblematic, indeed a necessary truth, that a certain quantity is equal to itself. Other such unproblematic relations, outside the strictly quantitative, include being 'like' or 'the same as'. One wonders whether Socrates'

---

[62] Cf. Moore (2015, 92). One might read Socrates' statement as meaning (1) that he distrusts himself, which would overtly express a self-directed cognitive attitude, or (2) that he simply refrains from trusting himself, which may seem rather more in line with the questioning of self-directedness that has preceded it. Even under (2) however, cognitive self-assessment on Socrates' part is implied to explain his withholding of trust in himself.

[63] See Halper (2000, 311).

4.8 Socrates' Challenge II

statement at 170a2 that 'I always end up being the same (*homoios*)' is a Platonic hint at this.[64]

It is in any event noteworthy that, in terms of method, the clearly impossible cases are obtained by looking into a class of powers more remote from the case of knowledge than those (the ones pertaining to the soul) that were deployed in the first section. If we were sceptical then about what could be inferred about one species in a genus from what was the case with others, then we are likely to be more sceptical still, now that the genus has been considerably broadened to include relations in general rather than just those from the sphere of the soul's operations.

Even in the case of that latter sphere, if one recoils from the idea that, say, a power of sight would have to be something coloured if that power were directed at itself, then the conclusion that a power of knowledge would have to have the quality of a regular object of knowledge were that power directed at itself seems less paradoxical. Why should not a power of knowledge be, in that way, knowable? The apparent difference from the perceptual case seems to offer independent evidence for a weakness in Socrates' method of casting doubt on the application of a structure to one case by showing that structure to be impossible or doubtful when applied to other cases.

Yet this is not itself quite enough to rule the method out. The issue of scope continues to be pertinent. Certainly, it seems implausible that conclusions one draws about, say, the structure of the relation 'greater than' should have anything much to tell us about the structure of the relation 'knowledge of'. Yet the less remote the cases in question are from one another, the more credible the method seems: it may be reasonable to doubt, for example, whether hearing could be related to itself were it shown that sight could not be. On the other hand, what counts as the right kind of class comparison to use seems itself a difficult question, not unconnected with the difficulty of being able to show determinately whether the method itself is sound.

There may indeed be a more general difficulty about confirming or undermining a method of argument. To do so one needs to employ some form of argument oneself, and then it seems as if one will have to assess the method underlying that form of argument with presumably a further form, and a regress beckons. While a problem of this sort is not formally presented in the *Charmides*, Socrates' uncertainty about how to spell out

---

[64] It may thus not quite be true, as von Kutschera (2000, 41) claims, that Socrates is 'silent' on the relation of identity.

precisely what the application of his method has shown does perhaps indicate some recognition of the issue. The fuzziness of the outcome reflects a problem about validating the method that generated it.

4.9 The Role of Aporia

If so, then it is intriguing that Socrates' whole challenge to the possibility of temperance on the present account is framed by puzzlement (aporia): firstly, on Socrates' own part, since the challenge is introduced as the explanation of why he is puzzled (167b7–8); and subsequently, on the part of Critias, though this does not ostensibly arise until after the second section of the challenge. Socrates tops it off by inviting Critias (169b–c) to show that temperance as knowledge of knowledge is not just possible but also beneficial. At this point, as Socrates picturesquely tells it, the sight of Socrates' own puzzlement is said to have set off puzzlement in Critias, as the sight of someone yawning sets off yawning in others (169c3–6).

Whatever the merits of Socrates' method of argument, the setting out of his challenge seems, according to Socrates, to have in fact finally induced puzzlement in Critias about the account of temperance as knowledge of knowledge. And the fact that Socrates' laying out of his challenge to the account's tenability succeeds, as a matter of psychology, in generating puzzlement, suggests that when it comes to the idea of the soundness of a method, the normative has here yielded to the psychological. That the method works psychologically – that, in this case, Critias takes the account of temperance to be less secure as a result of contemplating Socrates' challenge – invites the question whether this is the only test there is ultimately of a method's soundness.[65]

Now clearly the application of the method need not affect everyone psychologically in the same way; and here context might be important. Thus, working one's way in a more leisurely manner through Socrates' challenge as a piece of written text might produce more doubt about its effectiveness than being confronted with it, as Critias is within the drama, in live discussion. Since the *Charmides* is a written text, Plato may himself have supposed that we as readers are in a position to draw a different conclusion from the use of Socrates' method than Critias does. But that only helps bring out a further contrast: as well as that between normative

---

[65] It might certainly be claimed that a method's soundness is distinct from, and independent of, its practical psychological effects. But that such a distinction can be drawn in a principled way itself requires defence.

4.9 The Role of Aporia

and psychological, and written and oral, we also have the contrast between personal and impersonal.

Whether one finds something puzzling is a matter of individual response, a point already suggested in Socrates' remark at 167c5–6 that *you* (Critias) will find self-directedness impossible in the cases other than knowledge. Critias' explication of knowledge of oneself as knowledge of knowledge moved the emphasis of the account from the concrete ('oneself') to the abstract ('knowledge'), and in so doing also moved it from the personal to the impersonal. The role of aporia in challenging the account, however, reminds us of the ineliminability of the personal, and might in turn begin to induce puzzlement in (some of) us readers about the relation, somewhat in the background during Socrates' challenge, but one that Plato is about to make us attend to again, between knowledge of oneself and knowledge of knowledge.

There is, however, a further dimension to aporia as personal: it is self-conscious. After rounding off his challenge, and noting that Critias seemed to have caught aporia from him, Socrates narrates that Critias, due to his continual desire for esteem:

> [F]elt shame (*ēischuneto*) before the onlookers and, unwilling to concede that he was unable to make the determinations that I had summoned him to make, covered over (*epikaluptōn*) his aporia by muttering something indistinct (*ouden saphes*). (169c7–d1)

We do well to remember here that Socrates has form in declaring, fairly or otherwise, Critias guilty of unclarity; as ever, it is through Socrates' perspective that our view of Critias is channelled. But whether or not we find Socrates' report reliable is no bar to the passage revealing something distinctive to us about the nature of aporia.

Critias is said to cover over his aporia. If that is what he does, he has evidently made a poor fist of it given that Socrates, if his diagnosis of what is going on is correct, has discerned the aporia that Critias moves to conceal. But Critias, in turn, would not be in a position to try to cover up that which he was unaware of experiencing. Aporia is thus self-conscious, and it seems that Critias' aporia, manifested in his (self-conscious) inability to tackle Socrates' challenge, has precisely revealed to him his own lack of knowledge. So while the challenge was aimed at undermining the credibility of the idea of self-knowledge as knowledge of knowledge, from which the impossibility of knowledge of lack of knowledge was supposed to flow (cf. 169b5–8), the dramatic frame suggests, in counterpoint, that awareness of one's lack of knowledge is both possible and real.

Now there are two distinct elements to the self-consciousness of Critias' response here: his aporia, brought on by his confrontation with Socrates' challenge; and his shame, brought on by the exposure of his aporia in front of others. One should, I think, as always in this work, take with a pinch of salt Socrates' characterisations, from within his own perspective, of his interlocutors' reactions. His description of Critias' sensitivity to the esteem of others and resultant shame reads rather like a put-down, and one suspects that in Socrates' mouth it was meant to be. But I think there is something more positive to be extracted from Critias' shame. It seems to show, again in a way that has the psychological underpinning the normative, that the intellectual realm *matters* to him.

It is easy to look at his response and say that it was only because it showed him up in front of the onlookers that he minded not knowing, and that therefore he does not value the realm of the intellect in the right sort of way. That, I think, firstly, underplays the significance of the aporia itself: one does not feel the self-consciousness of puzzlement on a matter about which one does not care. But secondly, the fact that an intellectual failing was the cause of his feeling shown up in front of the others means that, for this feeling of shame to be intelligible, Critias must at least take it that he has fallen short of a standard that it is considered one ought to meet. And if Critias, characteristically, derives his norms from his social environment, then that standard will, all the more, be *his* standard. Critias' shame indicates that he is revealed to himself as falling short of a public criterion that he also makes his own.[66]

Plato, I think, uses this scene to demonstrate that, whether or not it is possible to prove from the outside that the intellectual realm is something one should care about, one finds oneself caring about it from the inside by being made to see one's own reactions to engagement with it. In isolation, the fact of Critias' puzzlement is positive. It shows (him) that he cares about that by which he is puzzled. Critias' shame, however, has a downside: it causes him, at least temporarily, to withdraw from the enquiry – a rather vivid demonstration, perhaps, of the Homeric dictum about shame that Socrates drew on in refuting Charmides' second answer. But here it seems pertinent to note once more the difference between oral debate, as Plato depicts it, and the written text that he composes. We as readers have no onlookers, and so none of the deterrent effects of shame, to concern

---

[66] I do not attempt to cover here all the complexities of the relation between an agent's shame and their social environment. For recent discussion see O'Brien (2020) and, with reference to Charmides in the *Charmides*, Raymond (2018, 34–5).

4.9 The Role of Aporia

ourselves with. If puzzlement is induced in us, then we are free to let it stimulate, rather than cow, our critical engagement.

One way in which we might do this is, as we have seen, to question the soundness of the method that Socrates uses to mount his challenge against the possibility of temperance construed as knowledge of knowledge. The pattern of Critias' responses to the first section of Socrates' challenge suggests, I have argued, that Critias is at any rate willing at that point to accept that knowledge could be an anomalous power of the soul in admitting self-directedness. Even Critias, however, takes Socrates' point that this is something that needs further examination (168a11–b1), which brings us to the second section of the challenge and Critias' eventual aporia.

We are invited, then, even if we are sceptical about what exactly the accumulation of examples by Socrates of other powers of the soul can show as being applicable to the case of knowledge, to seek to explain what it might be about knowledge that allows it to behave anomalously, in being able (if it is) to be directed at itself. What we are thus encouraged to do, in responding to Socrates' puzzlement, is to try to bring out what is distinctive about knowledge. And to do this, one needs to presuppose that one can have an explanatory grasp of what knowledge is.

So the act of seeking to understand knowledge that the text encourages us to undertake serves to undercut the idea that knowledge of knowledge is not to be had. For in problematising the reflexive relation in the case of knowledge, Socrates paves the way for an investigation into the nature of knowledge, and *that* investigation he thinks is difficult (requiring a 'great man') but shows no sign of thinking cannot be brought to fruition. His call to investigate the case of knowledge would indeed be close to unintelligible without the assumption that knowledge of knowledge is possible.

What is shown, then, by Socrates' performance of his problematisation of knowledge of knowledge – that we need to investigate more – stands in opposition to the calling into question of the possibility of knowledge of knowledge expressed in that problematisation. It is plausible that the understanding of knowledge (as of anything else) progresses through an act of enquiry into what its (purportedly) distinctive characteristics are; and this is what the text bids us do here, in regard to whether knowledge is applicable to itself. If we readers take up the challenge of furthering that enquiry (which Socrates himself lays to one side),[67] we do not thereby

---

[67] Socrates says at 169d4–5 that they will investigate later (*authis*) whether or not knowledge of knowledge is possible, though this is not something that happens within the remainder of the *Charmides*: a signal perhaps that we are to take up that enquiry.

acquire knowledge of knowledge, but we do find ourselves performatively affirming that it can be acquired. As with the relation between Critias' aporia and the idea of knowledge of lack of knowledge, so too here, the text's framing of the argument stands in tension with the argument itself: a structure that neither proves nor disproves the point at issue but offers us stimulus to engage critically with it.

4.10 Knowing That and Knowing What

In order, as he says, for the argument to move forward (169d2), Socrates now turns from examining the possibility of temperance, on Critias' account of it as knowledge of knowledge, to examining what he had identified as the second key issue, its benefit on this account. Since the discussion to come is perhaps the most dialectically complex of the whole dialogue, let me first recall its initial setup and then briefly preview the general contours of the argument. At 167a Socrates had spelled out, with Critias' assent, that if temperance is knowledge of itself and of the other branches of knowledge and of lack of knowledge, then the temperate person will know herself and be able to assess what she herself and others know and do not know. It is this formulation – temperance as knowing what one knows and does not know – that Socrates then says will have to be examined for its possibility and its benefit (167a9–b4).

When it came to investigating the question of possibility, Socrates, as we saw, in fact focussed on the formulation of temperance as knowledge of knowledge and of the other branches of knowledge and of lack of knowledge. This in turn implies that the other formulation – knowing what one knows and does not know – is taken to be of particular salience for assessing benefit. At any rate, when Socrates suggests, in the wake of Critias' aporia, that they concede for now that knowledge of knowledge is possible, his first move in the next phase of the discussion is to query (169d–e) whether it is legitimate to infer from a person's possessing knowledge of knowledge that they are able to know what one does and does not know.

Socrates then argues at 170a–171c that someone with knowledge of knowledge will, rather than knowing *what* one does and does not know, merely know *that* one knows (or does not know) something or other. From there, he suggests at 171d–172c that there would indeed be great benefit in being able to know what one knows and does not know, but rather less in knowing merely that one knows or does not know.

At this point, Socrates intensifies his doubt about benefit by arguing, at 172c–173e, that even if they grant the inference to knowing what one does and does not know, such knowledge would not, contrary to what they had previously agreed, be of great benefit. Rather, it is knowledge of what is good and bad, not knowledge of what one knows and does not know, that would fulfil the role of producing benefit (173e–174d). If so, then temperance as knowledge of knowledge, since it lacks the job of producing benefit, will not be of benefit (174d–175a).

So much for an outline of how the argument about benefit proceeds. Let us now look more closely at its initial stages. Socrates queries at 169d5–8 whether, even if one grants that knowledge of knowledge is possible, one is thereby able to know what one does and does not know. Critias argues in reply (169d9–e5) that someone who possesses knowledge that knows itself (*hautēn*) will thereby be one who knows *themself* (*heauton*). Socrates replies that he was not questioning the validity of that inference, but of the inference from having knowledge of knowledge to knowing what one does and does not know (169e6–8). It is this latter inference that Socrates then goes on to challenge in more detail.

This exchange throws interesting light on the status of the account of temperance as knowledge of knowledge. Recall that the account was unfurled by Critias under pressure from Socrates to show that temperance construed as knowledge of oneself had a subject-matter distinct from knowledge. Critias' reply in effect defied the pressure by asserting that temperance is knowledge of knowledge and, as I argued above, in doing so probably drew on a conception that Socrates himself had put forth at some prior point in their association.

Regardless of that latter hypothesis, we can see Socrates himself a little earlier in the dialogue simultaneously draw both the inference he accepts and the one he now rejects. After having Critias confirm that, if temperance is knowledge of knowledge, then it would be knowledge of lack of knowledge as well, he goes on to say, as we have seen:

> Then (*ara*) the temperate person alone *both* will know himself *and* will be able both to examine what he in fact knows and does not know and likewise will have the power to assess others … (167a1–3)

The initial 'both … and' (*te … kai*) at 167a1, that I have emphasised above, takes the inference from knowledge of knowledge and lack of knowledge to knowledge of oneself, and distinguishes it from the more expansive inference from knowledge of knowledge and lack of knowledge to knowledge of what one does and does not know. It also makes clearer the relation envisaged here between temperance as knowledge of knowledge and temperance as knowledge of oneself. Evidently the former account is seen by Socrates as underpinning the latter, since he here proposes (and never questions the inference) that it follows from having knowledge of knowledge (and of lack of knowledge) that one has knowledge of oneself. If knowledge of knowledge is shown to be impossible, that does not of course show that knowledge of oneself is impossible; but it does leave one needing to find other support for the claim that it is possible.

Now it is a mechanism for inferring knowledge of oneself from knowledge of knowledge that Critias goes on to spell out, using what looks remarkably like a version of the method that Socrates himself had deployed in calling into doubt the possibility of knowledge of knowledge. Critias, that is, appeals to a feature common to a set of examples and then generalises from that to the case at hand. He says:

> If one has knowledge that knows itself, then one would be such as the thing is that one has. Just as whoever has speed is speedy, and whoever has beauty is beautiful, and whoever has knowledge knows, so whoever has knowledge of itself will then presumably know himself. (169d9–e5)

I shall not rehearse here, since this was discussed in the earlier context, what one might say about the soundness of such a method. But it would indeed be a shrewd dialectical move on Critias' part if he is applying Socrates' method in an effort to persuade Socrates of a conclusion: in this case, that one who has knowledge of knowledge will have self-knowledge. The problem for Critias is that, as we have noted, this is not the inference that Socrates questions. The latter's critical gaze is about to fall instead on the validity of inferring that someone who has knowledge of knowledge knows what one does and does not know.

Even if Socrates does not do so, we may care to query the validity of the first inference as explicated by Critias. One way to do this would be to assess the case of knowledge by working through other cases of powers of the soul, following roughly the procedure that Socrates used earlier in attempting to undermine the possibility of knowledge of knowledge. If we do this, then it seems that it does not, as a structural matter, follow from one's having knowledge of itself that one has knowledge of oneself. Take the case of fear, and let us say that I have fear of fear itself. It surely does not follow from this that I am afraid of myself. Similarly with love (construing eros this way for present purposes): let us say that I love love itself. It does not follow from this (though one suspects here a certain correlation) that I love myself. Formally, then, it does not follow from my having knowledge of knowledge that I know myself.

That does not of course mean that, if one added in some extra assumptions, self-knowledge would not then follow from knowledge of knowledge. One key assumption would appear to be that one's self consists in the things one knows and does not know. If so, then at least in having knowledge of knowledge and of lack of knowledge, I would not need knowledge of any other powers of the soul in order to be able to know myself. But the assumption does not seem by itself sufficient to license inferring knowledge of oneself from knowledge of knowledge. There remains what one might call the question of access. To know myself I presumably need not just to know what knowledge is but to be able to determine what it is that I have that counts as knowledge (or lack of knowledge).

Consider again the analogy with medicine. To be a doctor it is not enough just to know what health and sickness is; one needs also to know whether this patient is healthy or sick. And to do that, one needs to know how to examine the patient. So, in the case of knowing myself, I need to know how to examine myself to determine what I have that is knowledge or lack of knowledge. For it is not a given that one has access to this. As Socrates said at 166d1–2, he would need to scrutinise his own pronouncements to discover whether he has knowledge or merely thinks that he does. Thus the practice of the kind of critical scrutiny that Socrates undertakes is also a requirement for the attainment of self-knowledge on this construal. Once again, the conception of knowledge as knowing how is relevant to interpreting temperance as a kind of knowledge.

That Plato bothers to write a scene in which Critias elaborately spells out an inference that Socrates then says he does not question should in turn put us on alert. We are surely supposed to examine the inference rather more than Socrates does. If we do, we are likely to question at least the assumption, however much it may be needed to make the inference work, that one's self consists in what one does and does not know. But notice what happens when we do that. We take it upon ourselves to examine whether it is true or not to regard the self in this way. And that is presumably because we want to know whether things are that way or not. In responding to the provocation by the text, we thus identify ourselves with the search for knowledge, an identification that self-reflection can reveal to us. While the fact of our response does not itself answer the question of who we are (e.g. knowers), that we responded in this way already constitutes evidence, available to ourselves, that is relevant to any answer we may give.

When it comes to the inference that Socrates now does question, from having knowledge of knowledge and of lack of knowledge to knowing what one does and does not know (169e6–8), notwithstanding Critias' claim that the two are the same thing (170a1), there is an important preliminary point to be made. When Socrates said at 166d1 that he would scrutinise his own pronouncements, he was not talking idly. It was Socrates who, as we have seen, originally suggested that someone who has knowledge of knowledge and of lack of knowledge will know what one does and does not know.[68] His questioning of that inference is therefore (also) a piece of self-scrutiny. Let us see how he pursues it.

To do so, it will first be helpful to clarify what sense of 'knowing what one knows and does not know' is at stake in the upcoming argument. To judge by the examples he uses, Socrates' focus, in relation to what one does and does not know, will be on fields of expertise that one may have (or lack) knowledge of, in the sense of being an expert (or not) in the given field – say, medicine. So in arguing against the idea that knowledge of knowledge means knowing what one does and does not know, Socrates seeks to rule out, among other things, the idea that having knowledge of knowledge means knowing the very things that experts in these various fields know. If that idea stood, knowledge of knowledge would bestow expertise in those fields. But that clearly cannot be the case: to put it a bit anachronistically, an epistemologist does not acquire the expertise of (say) a doctor just by being an epistemologist.

Even allowing for the anachronism, one might suppose that that conclusion hardly needs arguing for, whatever Critias himself might have intended by the idea of a branch of knowledge that knows the other branches of knowledge. To explain why Socrates puts so much effort into arguing against the inference, then, we need to assume that he is also, and primarily, arguing for something that looks more contentious, namely, that one who has knowledge of knowledge, such as to be in a position to know whether or not someone has expertise in some field or other, does not thereby know even so much as *which* field of expertise the putative expert has (or lacks) knowledge of.

One may, roughly, map the less and the more contentious alternative here onto the grammatical distinction between, respectively, relative and interrogative senses of 'knowing what one knows/does not know'. In the first, relative, sense, to say that I know what *x* knows is to say that I know

---

[68] 167a1–7. Socrates concludes by asking Critias whether the inference represents 'what you mean' (a7) but its content is entirely his own spelling out.

the very things that *x* knows; so if *x* knows Pythagoras' theorem, then so do I. In the second, interrogative, sense, to say that I know what *x* knows is merely to say that I know which are the things *x* knows; so if *x* knows Pythagoras' theorem, then I know that *x* knows that. The more contentious of our alternatives thus asserts that one who has only knowledge of knowledge fails not just to know the things that *x* knows (e.g. the content of the science of medicine) but which are the things *x* knows (e.g. that *x* knows the science of medicine).

This is more contentious because it seems that one can readily identify which field of expertise is at stake in a claim about whether someone has expert knowledge, without one's possessing that expertise oneself – and surely Critias at least meant this by his inclusion of 'the other branches of knowledge' within temperance's purview. If, for example, someone makes various claims about ways to treat diseases, then I surely know that it is the field of medicine in relation to which the claimant's expertise is to be assessed. In this sense, it seems as if knowledge of knowledge, applied to this case, will indeed tell me, not just that it is some expertise (assuming it at least does this) but that it is medical expertise that the claimant has or lacks.

Socrates begs to differ. His attack on the inference can be divided into two main sections. At 170a6–e3 he argues that knowledge of knowledge will enable one to determine that someone (oneself or others, 170b9–10) does or does not have some knowledge, but not what the knowledge is of. Then at 170e3–171c3 he reinforces that conclusion by spelling out what one *would* have to do to determine the latter and showing that without being an expert in the relevant field (e.g. a doctor, in the case of health and sickness), as opposed to one who merely possesses knowledge of knowledge, it could not be done.

The argument of the first section turns on the idea that knowledge, which is what temperance is said to be knowledge of, is not the same as a specific branch, such as knowledge and lack of knowledge of health or knowledge and lack of knowledge of justice (170a10–b1). These latter two are medicine and politics respectively, while the former is, as Socrates puts it, 'nothing other than knowledge' (170b3–4). Given this, it is a peculiarity that Socrates speaks at a10–b1 of knowledge and *lack* of knowledge of health and justice.[69] Clearly medicine does not involve lack of knowledge of health, and equally politics, qua branch of knowledge, does not involve lack of knowledge of justice. Socrates presumably over-anticipates here the

---

[69] Cf. Ketchum (1991, 88).

point he will make at 170d, that one who simply has knowledge of knowledge will not be able to tell who does and does not know health, or justice, specifically.[70]

For now, he can claim that unless one has, say, knowledge of health or of justice in addition to knowledge of knowledge, one would only be able to know *that* someone has some knowledge; but *what* they know, in the sense of what their specific area of expertise is, cannot be determined by knowledge of knowledge alone: the field of health is known through the art of medicine, that of harmonics through the art of music, and so on (170b6–c11). Hence, Socrates concludes, temperance would not mean knowing what one knows and does not know, but only that one knows and does not know (170d1–3).[71] So one with temperance (on this conception) will not be able to test whether someone else claiming to have some particular knowledge (*ti epistasthai*) actually does have it or not; temperance will only be able to determine that they have some knowledge or other (*tina epistēmēn*), not what it is of (170d5–9).

4.11 The Case of Medicine

Socrates now turns explicitly to the case of someone claiming to be a doctor (*ton prospoioumenon iatron einai*, 170e1), which must be there in part to put us in mind of Socrates' own role in the dialogue as one who claimed to know a remedy for Charmides' headache (155b5–6). I shall return to the significance of this reminder shortly. With the example, Socrates pivots to the second main section of his attack on the inference from knowledge of knowledge to knowledge of what one knows and does not know. Thus he draws the further conclusion that temperance will not be able to distinguish the one claiming to be a doctor, but who is not, from the one who genuinely is; and although he adds that this will apply to the matter of distinguishing any expert from non-expert (170e2–3), when he moves to spell out (with 'let us consider from the following' at e3) what being able to do this would involve, the example of medicine is the one used throughout.

To distinguish, then, the real doctor from the quack, one will not, says Socrates (170e4–171a1), converse with the person in question about

---

[70] Socrates may, compatibly, be using 'knowledge and lack of knowledge of *x*' loosely to stand for 'knowledge of *x* and of lack of *x*': medicine as knowledge of health and disease, and so on.
[71] Socrates is, however, careful not to commit himself to saying that the doctor does know what he knows, as Leigh (2020, 268) claims.

4.11 *The Case of Medicine*

medicine; that is because the doctor only knows about health and sickness, not about knowledge, whereas medicine is in fact knowledge, so that, he concludes, 'the medical expert does not know about medicine' (170e12). This somewhat paradoxical way of putting things is, I think, intended to bring out the fact that the knowledge given by medical expertise is of health and sickness, not of knowledge. So one does not, to determine whether a putative doctor is a genuine one, talk to that person about medicine just to the extent that one does not talk to them about knowledge, given that medicine is a branch of knowledge. Knowledge, after all, is not the field of expertise represented by medicine; health and sickness is (171a8–9).

Thus one who wishes to examine the credentials of a putative practitioner of the art of medicine will examine matters 'within the field, not outside it', that is, in the present case, matters of health and sickness (171a11–b5). This in turn means that one will assess those credentials by considering whether what is said and done in regard to such matters is said truly and done correctly (171b7–9). But to be able to do that requires that one possess medical expertise oneself; that, however, is possessed by the doctor, not by the person who is temperate (171b11–c2). So, concludes Socrates, if temperance is only knowledge of knowledge and of lack of knowledge, it will not be able to distinguish the genuine doctor from the fake, or any other expert from non-expert – except, he adds, as is the case with all practitioners, in one's own field (171c4–9).

Socrates, then, has sought to deny that simply having knowledge of knowledge and of lack of knowledge puts one in a position to know what someone knows and does not know, for example, health and sickness. We are no doubt supposed to subject this conclusion to critical scrutiny, and in fact the text itself suggests this. At 170e6 Socrates spoke of 'conversing' (*dialegesthai*) with the would-be doctor, the term he had used earlier, at 154e–155a, to describe his own procedure, with particular reference to the uncovering of Charmides' soul. Here, by implication, it is his own soul that is up for scrutiny, and this on two grounds. Firstly, as I have already suggested, since Socrates was the one who originally drew the inference from knowledge of knowledge to knowing what one does and does not know, the scrutiny that he has been undertaking of that inference is in fact a piece of self-scrutiny.

Secondly, however, is the motif of examining the person claiming to be a doctor. What Socrates has described is the procedure for examining such a person. But the choice of example, given that earlier he conspired to make such claims about himself, implicitly places Socrates in the role of examinee. Since he could of course also occupy the role of examiner, here too we would have a case of Socratic self-examination. Yet the way he actually envisages the examination of the would-be doctor is chiefly as one person examining another: the temperate person or anyone else testing the would-be doctor (170e4–5, cf. 171a3–4, b4–5).

We have, then, the figure of the would-be doctor placed before us, unmistakably signalling Socrates' own claim in that regard, together with the idea that someone other than the would-be doctor is to examine that person. Who might that be? I submit that this is a Platonic cue for us as readers to subject what Socrates says to critical examination, not just here but throughout the dialogue, since Socrates' claim is never formally withdrawn. There is, however, under the particular rubric that Socrates' argument is concerned with, a snag. How can we, who are not (except in some coincidental cases) medical doctors, be qualified to undertake such an examination? If Socrates' argument is right, then we cannot do this. All we can do is examine whether or not Socrates has some knowledge, not whether or not it is medical knowledge that he possesses.

I shall not pursue this line of thought for its own sake. Perhaps we are indeed in no position to know, despite my own speculations on the matter, which field of knowledge Socrates is (or is not) expert in. It is, for reasons I will outline below, not so obvious, without our possessing expertise of the relevant sort (medical expertise in this case), that we can know what the area is in which some putative expert has or lacks knowledge. It might, on the other hand, seem that we can know this without such expertise. That we can do so, one might suppose, may already be shown by appropriate scrutiny of Socrates' claim that a temperate person will know that someone has some sort of knowledge but not what that knowledge is of (e.g. health and sickness).

Let us say, for the sake of argument, that we are at least in a position to discover whether or not a putative expert has some knowledge or other. We examine the expert and conclude, say, that they do have some. What is the problem about then generating the conclusion that they are expert in, as it may be, health and sickness? On Socrates' account, if we are to try to ascertain which expertise they possess, we will have to talk to them about some determinate field, such as health and sickness (171a–b). But it is hard to see how even determining whether someone has *some* expertise or other will not have involved talking about matters within one or other specific field of expertise – for example, health and sickness. Even though we will not, as knowers of knowledge, be experts in that field, we are surely able to conclude, on this scenario, that they are expert in (say) health and sickness.

4.11 *The Case of Medicine*

Such might be the objection to Socrates' argument that mere determination of someone's possessing some knowledge or other does not mean determination of what their (field of) knowledge is. But the objection is in turn misguided. We are led astray here by the idea that, in order to establish which relevant field of knowledge it is when one is talking to a putative expert, one does not need to be an expert in that field: one can recognise, for example, that one's interlocutor is talking about the field of health and sickness without being a doctor oneself.[72] Yet Socrates' own performance as would-be doctor, which the argument seems designed to put us in mind of, provides resources to help rebut the idea.

Recall that, after relating the Thracian narrative, Socrates tells Charmides that if the latter has temperance in addition to other qualities then he is blessed (158b2–4); but if he lacks temperance, he will need to be charmed before the headache remedy can be given (158c1–2). So Socrates at this point is open-minded about whether Charmides has temperance. Yet not long before that, at the climax of the narrative, Socrates told us that he had sworn not to administer the remedy in any circumstances without the charm (157b7–c6). On the face of it, this endorses the narrative's idea that bodily illness is a sign that one does not have temperance. For all good and bad things for the body flow from the soul (156e6–8), such that bodily well-being will require that one's soul first be treated, which is to say instilled with temperance (157a1–b1).

Charmides' headache should mean, by the terms of the narrative that Socrates appeared to endorse, that Charmides lacks temperance. So Socrates seems to hold both that Charmides must lack temperance, given his headache, and that he may have temperance, given what is said at 158b–c. And that is an inconsistent pair. We have, then, scrutinised the pretender, as 170e bade us do, and found inconsistency. On the not unreasonable assumption that consistency is necessary for knowledge, we have managed to learn that Socrates lacks knowledge.

---

[72] Morris (1989, 56–8) bases his conclusion that the text itself suggests this idea on the claim that, in its respective use of the verbs *gignōskein* and *epistasthai* in Socrates' argument, it trades on a distinction in knowing between 'recognising' a certain field of knowledge and 'understanding' it. However, at no point in the argument from 170a to 171c is the verb *epistasthai* used to characterise the cognitive stance of the temperate person towards the would-be expert, whereas *gignōskein* is used extensively but not exclusively in that role, in regard both to knowing what and knowing that. So it is not clear whether it is intended to contrast with *epistasthai* in the relevant way. The closest the text comes to using *epistasthai* in a similar role is at 170b7–8 where one is said to *gignōskein* only knowledge inasmuch as one 'has *epistēmē* only of this', which implies a model whereby *gignōskein* is achieved on the basis of *epistasthai*. Whether we are then supposed to consider ways to attain *gignōskein* independently of *epistasthai* is not obvious.

Lacks knowledge of what though? Of medicine? Well, that assumes that the Thracian narrative is about medicine. It certainly purported to have been delivered to Socrates by a Thracian doctor with a radical view about medicine – enough, perhaps, to make us question whether it is medicine that the narrative is really about. And, as I argued earlier, since we can be independently confident that Socrates is not a doctor, it is unclear whether he himself has any standing to determine the narrative's subject-matter. I also argued that the narrative is *not* ultimately intended to be about medicine, but, as I read it, about the related (but much less developed) field of soul-medicine, the practice of which Socrates thereby undertakes. Even if one disputes that, it seems reasonable to conclude that the narrative is written in such a way as to make us query what its subject-matter really is.

It is in part because of this opacity over subject-matter that Socrates ends up making the inconsistent claims that he does about Charmides' possession of temperance: Charmides may have temperance (where Socrates' approach is not controlled by the relation between soul and body presented in the Thracian narrative); Charmides does not have temperance (where it is). Note, then, that the inconsistency is clear even though it is not clear, or even determinate, what the subject-matter is in relation to which the inconsistency arises.

To be sure, the specific inconsistency concerns temperance. But the question is whether identification of inconsistency (and hence lack of knowledge) means that one thereby knows what field it is in relation to which the inconsistency arises. I have argued that one is not in such a position here: one does not know whether the sample of discourse at hand pertains to the field of medicine or not. And this in turn offers support for Socrates' argument that knowing that someone has or lacks knowledge of some field does not mean knowing what field it is of which they have or lack knowledge.

Now since this example is about inconsistency, and hence lack of knowledge, one would need to do more work to show that identifying the possession of knowledge does not in itself mean knowing what area the knowledge is in. But if one regards a field of knowledge, as such, as constituted by relations between propositions rather than by what those propositions are about (on which see further Section 4.13), then there seems no obstacle in principle to one's identifying the possession of knowledge without knowing to which field the knowledge pertains. If so, then it seems that knowing that someone possesses knowledge in some or other field does not thereby mean knowing what field of knowledge it is that they know.

We have, as the text encouraged us to, undertaken scrutiny of Socrates' position concerning what one may and, in particular, may not infer from the possession of knowledge of knowledge; and we have found that it withstands it. With both the scrutiny and the findings prompted by elements from earlier in the dialogue flagged up subsequently in the course of Socrates' arguing out of his sceptical position on the inference from knowledge of knowledge to knowing what one knows and does not know, it seems possible now to adduce other, somewhat more distant, examples that tend to support his sceptical conclusion.

Say, then, that I am faced with a purported expert and ask her what the tools of her trade are. She replies that the main one is a 'flinge', which I have heard of but about which I know nothing. She adds that the flinge can only be used at an acute angle. Later on, she makes statements that entail that a flinge can sometimes be used at an obtuse angle. I reasonably conclude that she is confused, and so lacks knowledge of her supposed field of expertise. I have learned that she lacks knowledge without knowing which area it is in relation to which she lacks it. To the extent that I am able to identify lack of knowledge without identifying the field to which it pertains, it seems that knowledge of knowledge does not by itself deliver knowledge of what one knows and does not know.

4.12 Knowledge, Benefit and Utopia

If so, then we may accept the coherence of Socrates' conclusion that one who only possesses knowledge of knowledge will, in virtue of that, be able to determine that someone does or does not know something, but not what it is that they do or do not know. Socrates next turns to the consequences of this conclusion. The account of temperance as knowledge of knowledge has failed to show in what way temperance is, as it must be, of benefit. Socrates elaborates this in an interesting way, by contrasting the benefits that would have accrued if knowledge of knowledge had put one in a position to know what one does and does not know (171d–172a) with the supposedly more meagre benefits of just possessing knowledge of knowledge (172b–c).

We should therefore note that Socrates does at least apparently see some benefit to knowledge of knowledge even without the inference to knowing what one does and does not know.[73] To this extent, the text seems to leave

---

[73] I see no reason to regard, with Adamietz (1969, 50), the representation of benefits in this passage as ironic.

room for us not to discard altogether the idea of temperance as knowledge of knowledge. Let us, however, consider next the benefits that Socrates thinks we forego now that the inference has been shown to fail.

It would, he suggests, have been 'massively beneficial' (*megalōsti ... ōphelimon*, 171d5–6) to be temperate if temperance had meant knowing what oneself and others do and do not know:

> For both we ourselves who possess temperance, and all the others who were ruled by us,[74] would have lived life through without error, since we ourselves would not have tried to do things which we did not know, but would have found those who do know and handed [those things] over to them; nor would we have entrusted the others whom we ruled to do anything other than what in doing they would do correctly – and this would have been, what they had knowledge of; and so indeed a household administered by temperance would be beautifully administered, as would a city so governed, as well as everything else that temperance ruled. For with error eliminated, and correctness leading the way, in every action (*pasēi praxei*) those in this situation necessarily do beautifully and well, and those who do well are happy. (171d6–172a3)

The intuitive idea here is fairly clear, and will be spelled out further, though in more critical vein, by Socrates himself later: if the only doctors practising are genuine (i.e. knowledgeable) doctors, the only builders genuine builders, and so on, then everything will be done correctly – since, presumably, knowledge is incompatible with error[75] – and everyone living under such a regime will therefore do well and be happy. This ideal picture, however, even before we come to Socrates' own later criticism of it, looks problematic. In particular, it seems to involve accepting two large and by no means secure assumptions to make it work.

The first is that, in order for temperance to be of benefit, those who are temperate get to be in charge. Recall how the attitude of the characters towards Homer and Hesiod suggested a phenomenon whereby epistemic authority was derived (rightly or wrongly) from cultural authority. Socrates' vision of the benefits of temperance requires a certain inversion of that order: political or, more generally, administrative authority based

---

[74] I accept, with Burnet's OCT, Heindorf's deletion of *kai* ('and') at 171d7, retention of which would have the text read 'both we ourselves and those who have temperance and all those others who are ruled by us', mysteriously leaving those who are doing the ruling in a separate category from those who have temperance.

[75] One should perhaps rather say: incompatible with non-deliberate error. An assumption that any skilled practitioner will (or will be made to) direct their knowledge towards realising the internal goal of their craft may be a further element of the utopian vision.

on epistemic authority. Socrates makes no proposal about how this would come about, and there seem both practical and theoretical difficulties.

On the practical side, there is the question of how the temperate people win power:[76] do they run for office, take over by force, get appointed by a grateful populace? What if their social status is different from that of those who usually rule, whether in city or household? On the theoretical side, there is the question of how the temperate people are *recognised* as such. If, as Socrates had indicated at 171c, a practitioner can only be properly judged by a fellow practitioner, then it is unclear how the temperate people are to be identified by those outside that group such that at least in principle they might be considered by the non-temperate as candidates for ruling well.

The second assumption needed for Socrates' utopian picture to work is that every field of knowledge be represented by an appropriate number of genuine experts in the given field. There is a suspicion of fallacy in the way Socrates sets up his picture here. The temperate person, he says, will ensure that every action is done knowledgeably, from which he concludes that we will all do well and be happy. But there is a big difference between everything *that is done* being done knowledgeably, and *everything* being done knowledgeably. The first is all that seems licensed by the operation of temperance as knowing what one knows and does not know; but the second is needed for the utopian picture to obtain. To see this, consider a situation in which there were no, or insufficient, genuine doctors in a population. Socrates talks blithely, at 171d8–e2, of finding others, in areas where they themselves lack knowledge, who have knowledge, and allotting work in those areas to the knowledgeable folk. But that already helps itself to the assumption that there will be sufficient knowledgeable people in those areas.

Perhaps, at least, the temperate person will be able to identify the specific areas where sufficiency does not obtain, but it is unclear what would happen next. Presumably try to train, say, some doctors: but why suppose we have the right number of even potentially good doctors? And who is to do the training, particularly if there is a lack of doctors to start with? It would be a rather hollow boast for a ruler to proclaim that medical treatment was suspended because it had been established that nobody claiming to be a doctor knew what they were doing. To be sure, everything

---

[76] This may not be a problem for Critias if he makes the additional assumptions that he and those like him are the temperate ones and that they tend to be the ones in power. But the first of these assumptions seems at least questionable.

that is done would be done knowledgeably on this model; but that hardly seems like a recipe for utopia.

We might at this point ask why Socrates has chosen to conceive of the benefits of temperance in this way at all. One reason might be because of his interlocutor Critias (and perhaps too the listening Charmides). It is striking that when setting out these benefits Socrates puts things in a pointedly personal way, centring on a use of the first-person plural pronoun. He starts by appearing to use the pronoun relatively innocently, speaking of how beneficial it would have been for 'us' (*hēmin*, 171d6) to be temperate on this view, where the 'us' can in isolation be construed as meaning people in general. But in spelling this out, he then explains at 171d7–8 that those benefitted would be 'both we ourselves who have temperance and all those others who were ruled by us (*huph' hēmōn*)'. Suddenly then, not so innocently, it is 'us' in *contrast* to everyone else that is meant.[77] Socrates apparently dangles a vision of himself and Critias being at the helm. This starkly personal locution is thrown further into relief by the contrastingly abstract way in which Socrates goes on to speak of temperance ruling at 171e7.

It seems plausible, then, that part of the reason why Socrates offers this conception of benefit in this personal way is dialectical: it appeals to the political ambition of Critias and is thus more likely to secure his agreement. This would be the great point of temperance: 'we' get to be in charge! The thought is strengthened if we note that, right next to the supposedly innocent 'us' of 171d6 for whom temperance would be beneficial, Socrates adds parenthetically of the upcoming vision that it captures what 'we say' (*phamen*), the first-person plural implying that his account of the benefits is one he expects to be endorsed by his interlocutor. Critias indeed goes on to give strong endorsement – 'very much so' – at 172a6.

Yet it is no straightforward matter to regard Socrates' vision here as entirely political, and not just because the vision seems so hard to achieve even on its own terms. The abstract way, noted above, in which Socrates also chooses to speak of *temperance* ruling goes hand in hand with his application of that rule to city, household and 'everything else' (*allo pan*) that temperance might oversee (171e5–7). That is why, I think, we would more accurately dub Socrates' vision as administrative rather than (specifically) political.[78] Indeed if we recall the almost casual way that politics was

---

[77] On Plato's use of the 'wandering we', see further McCabe (2017, Lecture 2); (2021, 119–21).
[78] Sprague (1992, 89 n. 67) calls Socrates' reference to government of a city at 171e6–7 'the real point'. Yet it seems to me that Socrates goes out of his way at e5–7 not to describe his point as

characterised as being about what is *just* at 170b1–3, there may be a hint that the successful practice of politics is a matter for the just rather than the temperate person.[79] If so, it will be unsurprising if temperance turns out not to be a particular fit with politics at all.

In this regard, the abstract character of temperance as ruling intensifies the utopian character of the vision, but also hints at a certain kind of connection that seems almost to have been buried under the grand scheme. For if we consider how the 'everything else' that temperance might rule could be filled out, one candidate is surely 'oneself'. It is salutary to recall at this point that the account of temperance as knowledge of knowledge, from which the inference to knowing what one does and does not know, together with its accompanying benefits, was (it turned out illicitly) made, has the function of underpinning the account of temperance as knowledge of oneself.[80] And we may feel that Socrates' vision of utopia has strayed rather far from this latter account in two distinct but connected ways.

Firstly, the vision seems to require, for its realisation, so much that is beyond oneself. In its political aspect at any rate, the vision depends, in ways sketched above, on a great deal that is not in the temperate individual's control, in relation both to the obtaining of power and to the achievement of that total administration by knowledge that justifies the power. Secondly, it is not simply that the vision requires so much that is independent of oneself; it is not clear, either, how it is in any significant sense *about* oneself any more. It seemed to move with dizzying speed, again at least in its political guise, onto a territory of universal administered happiness far removed, on the face of it, from an idea of self-concern that an account of temperance as knowledge of oneself might be thought to suggest.

If that is right, and if we see the text as in principle leaving open a place for oneself to be ruled by temperance, then we might start to think, if we lack the political ambitions of a Critias, that for the most part the vaunted benefits we have lost may glitter rather more brightly than their underlying

---

applying either specifically or paradigmatically to the city. Note that in the later reprise of the utopian vision, Socrates speaks quite generally of 'the human race' (173c7) as beneficiary of temperance.

[79] It is of course true, to take a familiar analogy, that medicine is knowledge of what is healthy, yet the medical practitioner does not need to be healthy to do the job well. But the issue regarding politics is not whether the practitioner of politics may lack the positive quality that politics is about (i.e. justice), but why, given that (the text says) politics is about justice, we should suppose a positive quality other than justice to be the relevant one for its practitioner to possess.

[80] See Section 4.10.

substance merits. So when Socrates now turns to describe the supposedly lesser benefits that obtain for knowledge of knowledge when divorced from the illicit inference, benefits which seem more focussed on oneself, we may be motivated to take these a little more seriously than the surface disappointment about the failure of the inference – 'you see', Socrates informs Critias, 'that knowledge of this sort [of what one knows and does not know] has turned out nowhere to exist' (172a7–8) – would indicate.

4.13 Benefit without Utopia

Let us, then, take a look at these benefits, suggested by Socrates as belonging to temperance as knowledge of knowledge and of lack of knowledge. They boil down to two (my numbering):

> [W]ill the one who possesses this [1] learn whatever else one learns more easily and have everything appear to one more perspicuously inasmuch as one discerns the knowledge (*tēn epistēmēn*) over and above each individual thing that one may learn; and [2] then examine others more effectively (*kallion*) about whatever things one also learns oneself, while those who examine without this will do so in a more weak and feeble way? (172b3–8)

Having posited the benefits, Socrates ramps up the disappointment again by immediately asking Critias whether, if these are the fruits of temperance, 'we are looking to something greater and seeking temperance as something greater than it in fact is' (172c1–2). Critias, interestingly, is guarded in replying 'Maybe so' (172c3). One wonders whether this is in part because at least the second of the supposedly more meagre benefits promises some kind of roundabout restoration of utopia. Socrates may have shown that knowledge of knowledge, and to that extent temperance, will not itself enable one to determine who has, say, medical expertise, unless one possesses such expertise oneself. But a solution is at hand in the addition of the other things one may learn:[81] one acquires some medical knowledge (that is, knowledge of health and sickness), to complement one's knowledge of knowledge, and one is ready to go out and distinguish with particular effectiveness the knowledgeable doctors from the quacks.

The restoration of utopia is, however, I think, limited. It runs out just at the point where the subject is no longer in control of the outcome: one may question putative doctors as much as one likes, but there is not much one can do if one discovers that there are no genuine ones to be had, one's

---

[81] I do not think, contra Dyson (1974, 110–11), that this is inconsistent with the idea that knowledge of knowledge can itself only discern whether someone has some knowledge or other.

own presumably not limitless capacity to train others itself dependent on there being those with the potential to be trained. It may be just as well, then, that the first of the benefits that Socrates sets forth seems to pull in the opposite direction: rather than tempt us back to the Elysian fields of knowing what one knows and does not know, it offers further support for the coherence of the idea of knowledge of knowledge as, simply, knowing that one knows or does not know.

In the course of setting out this first benefit, Socrates places 'the knowledge' as something over and above the individual items one may learn. This implies that it is in virtue of discerning some kind of *structure* to these items that one possesses knowledge of knowledge.[82] That idea then has at least two significant corollaries. Firstly, it draws a tight connection between what it takes to be a knower of knowledge and the kind of thing that can be known. If discerning structure is a necessary condition for being such a knower, then that seems to place branches or fields of knowledge, which, as we have seen, comprise the dominant model in this section of the dialogue for what things that are known look like, in close correspondence with the conception of being such a knower as requiring the discerning of structure.

That is because, to constitute a branch of knowledge at all, the individual items that comprise it must hang together in a systematic way. They must, at least, form a consistent and coherent whole.[83] To have knowledge of a branch of knowledge as such, one must in turn therefore grasp those individual items as a consistent and coherent whole. If a learner understands this as a requirement, then it is plausible to suppose that such understanding will produce a certain sensitivity to the existence of the structures in question and, therefore, in line with what Socrates says, a heightened ability to discern them.

If that analysis is right, then our second corollary is in view. The analysis suggests that the knowledge of knowledge would at least include – as underpinning the power to discern consistency and coherence – possession of (something like) the rules of logic,[84] themselves organised as a coherent and consistent whole. The exercise of the power of knowledge of

---

[82] See here Morris (1989, 50).
[83] No doubt even this is a somewhat idealised picture, but it does, I think, get something important right about what we expect a branch of knowledge to be, though the fact that even for a specific branch of knowledge this seems like an idealisation will have implications for the possibility of achieving a completely structured self (as discussed in Chapter 5) and therefore for the ongoing centrality of the process of critical scrutiny by which that achievement would be won.
[84] Cf. Martens (1973, 73; 78); Liske (1988, 177); Carone (1998, 270 n. 5; 283).

knowledge would then entail the application of these rules in such a way as to be able to determine, for example, whether a given proposition that the speaker (oneself or another) asserted were consistent (or not) with other propositions that the speaker is prepared to assert. But given the idea of knowledge thus being related to a *system* of propositions, not a proposition in isolation, then in exercising the power of knowledge of knowledge one would be in the business of discerning, in virtue of one's command of the rules of logic, the relations among the whole set of propositions that a speaker is prepared to assert. The speaker would not be counted as having knowledge unless the propositions in question were mutually consistent.

'The whole set' has, one might think, rather indeterminate scope. Does it mean the whole set of propositions asserted by a speaker within a particular field or fields (and how does one determine what counts as a 'whole' here?), or all the propositions that a speaker is, quite generally, prepared to assert? I shall return to the question of scope in Chapter 5,[85] but for now we can specify how the reading given provides the further support to which I alluded above for the idea that we can make sense of the power of knowledge of knowledge without the questionable inference that knowledge of knowledge means knowing what one knows and does not know, rather than merely that one does or does not know something or other. For discerning whether logically hygienic relations obtain between propositions does not require one to form a view about the objects that the propositions are about (we saw this in the case of the 'flinge'). Knowledge of knowledge is, on this view, directed at internal relations between propositions, not relations between propositions and the world.

Now Socrates evidently holds that truth is a requirement for knowledge, since the testing of a practitioner for knowledge of their relevant field, say health, involved investigating whether their statements about health were true (171b). So how can the possessor of knowledge of knowledge even so much as judge, as Socrates had also claimed (170b–d), that a practitioner has *some* knowledge, let alone knowledge of a particular field, if they are only able to determine the internal structure of the propositions asserted by the practitioner?

I take it that Socrates must assume that possession of a suitably organised body of consistent propositions all of which were false is not a realistic possibility,[86] so that in such conditions consistency entails truth.

---

[85] See esp. Section 5.5.
[86] Note that Socrates had in fact proposed at 170b8–9 that one who only knows knowledge would 'probably' (*eikotōs*) know that one has some knowledge, which seems to leave it open that additional assumptions might be needed for (even) that consequence to obtain.

As 171b implies, this does not commit him to the view that consistency is all there is to truth: the investigation by a practitioner of whether a putative fellow practitioner is speaking truly remains a meaningful independent exercise that presumably consists not in investigating the logical relations between the statements that the examinee utters, but (as one might say) the relation between those statements and reality. By the same token, however, discerning the structure of a set of propositions, with structure distinguishing a body of knowledge from a collection of piecemeal truths, remains the province of the knower of knowledge.

With this support in place, we are now in a position to consider further what the benefit of knowledge of knowledge as the discerning of structure might amount to. We already have some elements at hand, among them that, conceived as knowledge of knowledge, temperance will itself have the status of a branch of knowledge and, given the force of the comparison with medicine, a branch of knowledge which, like medicine, involves the power – the knowing how – to bring something into being. As important, we need to construe the benefit of knowledge of knowledge in a way that makes perspicuous its status as underpinning the account of temperance as knowledge of oneself. That is, we need to find a way to explain how what it is that knowledge of knowledge brings into being is related to oneself.

If medicine, as knowledge of health, involves not just knowing what health is (or requires) but the power to bring health about, then knowledge of knowledge should by analogy involve not just knowing what knowledge is but the power to bring knowledge about. Moreover, both instances of 'knowledge' in 'knowledge of knowledge' should be modelled as cases of a branch or field of knowledge, or as something analogous to that.

This is clear in the case of the first 'knowledge' in 'knowledge of knowledge',[87] as we can see from the long-form version of the account of temperance at issue. When Critias responds to Socrates, at 165e3–4, by saying that temperance, as knowledge of oneself, is not like 'the other knowledges' (*tais allais epistēmais*), then, since Socrates has just given a pair of examples of branches of knowledge, it follows that knowledge of oneself is also being classified as a branch of knowledge. When, after the listing of more branches of knowledge by Socrates, Critias again rebukes him, at 166b9–c1, for treating temperance like 'the other [knowledges]' (*tais allais*) and adds that temperance is different by being 'knowledge of the other knowledges and of itself' (166c2–3), it likewise follows that temperance as knowledge of knowledge is treated as a branch of knowledge, albeit an anomalous one.

---

[87] Cf. LaBarge (1997, 56).

It is clear too that the second 'knowledge' in 'knowledge of knowledge' will have a form akin to that of a branch or field of knowledge. When Socrates probes the validity of the inference from knowledge of knowledge to knowledge of what one does and does not know, arguing instead that all one can legitimately infer is that one does or does not know something or other, the examples given of what the person with knowledge of knowledge investigates are branches or fields of knowledge: in particular, as we have seen, medicine.

Now of course Socrates concludes that the person with knowledge of knowledge will not know, from such investigation, that the subject of the investigation has (say) medical knowledge, just that they have some knowledge. But the fact that it is indeed a (putative) practitioner of a branch of knowledge who is investigated strongly suggests that what temperance, as knowledge of knowledge, takes as its object will be something that has the structure of a branch of knowledge. Indeed, in the course of his argument, at 170c6 (cf. 174d4–5), Socrates speaks of temperance not as 'knowledge of knowledge' but as 'knowledge of knowledges' (*epistēmōn epistēmē*), the plural long established as referring to branches of knowledge. This indicates that a given object of the knowledge of the temperate person (who has knowledge of knowledge) will have the form of a branch of knowledge.

The form in question is, or includes, a systematic body of consistent propositions. And, as we have seen, the passage about the (lesser) benefits of temperance as knowledge of knowledge also implies that to know 'the knowledge' is to grasp a set of propositions as forming a consistent whole. If that is right, then temperance as knowledge of knowledge, insofar as this conception serves to underpin the account of temperance as knowledge of oneself, ought to be something like the following: the power to create something that comprises a set of mutually consistent propositions, where what is created thereby is oneself. I shall call this conception, for short, temperance as self-realisation.[88] Its more detailed investigation will be the main task of the following chapter.

---

[88] Compare here Moore's (2015, 100) construal of self-knowledge in the *Charmides* as what he calls 'aspirational self-constitution'. Moore suggests that 'Self-knowledge is this kind of "knowledge in addition", a knowledge that allows one to act on one's knowledge' (98). But although the reference to 'knowledge in addition' indicates a connection with Moore's preceding discussion (96) of Socrates' claims for the benefit of knowledge of knowledge at 172b, Moore's reading depends on an acceptance of the inference from knowledge of knowledge to knowledge of what one does and does not know which that passage rests on denying.

4.14 Conclusion

In this chapter, I have argued that despite its overt problematisation of temperance as knowledge of knowledge, the *Charmides* leaves space for a reading of temperance, so construed, as not just possible but even (in ways to be further elaborated) beneficial. In making this case, I have tried to show how the carving out of that space is in part a function of the way in which the text encourages us as readers to adopt a critical stance towards it, and in particular to see ourselves as responding to a written work that needs interpretation and tells us that it does.

The invitation to interpret is in turn a product of how the text's two principal vertical levels – that of Socrates' engagement with his interlocutor (oral) and that of Plato's engagement with his reader (written) – are themselves in dialogue with one another. Critias' reaching for the interpretation of written texts draws the reader's reflection up to the written medium in which Socrates' conversation with him is embedded, and means that that medium, and with it the question of how to read a written text, becomes a participant in the conversation, rather than merely a transparent device through which to view it. The exposition and defence of a positive account of temperance – temperance as self-realisation – mounted in the next chapter I take to be the continuation of an interpretive response elicited by this dynamic relation between the vertical levels of the text.

CHAPTER 5

The Art of Self-Realisation

At the end of the previous chapter, I sketched an account of what I called temperance as self-realisation or, more precisely, temperance as the power to realise oneself. Elaboration of this account, which in bare outline may sound a little mystical, is the principal aim of the present chapter. I shall examine what the exercise of this power consists in and why it may, as it must to count as temperance at all, be of benefit.

I begin by further motivating the account via a brief preview of the next (and close to last) main segment of Socrates' discussion with Critias, in which Socrates returns to the utopian vision of temperance as knowing what one does and does not know and argues that it would not in fact generate benefit in the way they had thought. The knowledge that brings benefit is knowledge of good and bad; hence, Socrates concludes, temperance as 'the knowledge of knowledges at any rate and of lack of knowledges' (*epistēmōn ge kai anepistēmosunōn hē epistēmē*, 174d4–5; a locution I return to shortly) would be something other than beneficial (d6–7): an unacceptable conclusion, given the intuition, voiced by Socrates at 169b4–5 (cf. 175e6–7), that temperance is something beneficial and good.

Socrates' argument, even if for now we leave aside its detail, has an interesting place in the economy of the dialogue as a whole. He returns, for the purpose of burial rather than praise, to a utopia based on the idea of knowing what one knows and does not know: a set-up Socrates had already argued was not licensed by the conception of temperance as knowledge of knowledge and of lack of knowledge. Why, then, bother to argue that the vision does not deliver the benefit we thought it did, if Socrates had already ruled out the inference that allowed the vision in the first place? The effect of doing this is, I think, to make it even clearer that working with the idea of knowing what one does and does not know is a non-starter. Grant, as Socrates does for the sake of argument at 172c8–d1, the inference to knowing what one knows and does not know, and we still fail to show how temperance is of benefit on that conception.

Note, then, that at 174d4–5 Socrates does not highlight this failure as accruing to temperance characterised as knowledge of knowledge and of lack of knowledge; he speaks, as we saw, of knowledge of knowledges and of lack of knowledges. The pointedly plural formulation (highlighted by the *ge*, 'at any rate', at 174d4) indicates a focus on knowledge of a range of branches of knowledge (and, in the case of charlatans, lacks of such knowledge).[1] That is, we are encouraged to see benefit as ruled out on the conception according to which one knows what fields would-be practitioners do and do not know. Examples can be drawn from the list that Socrates provides, as part of his critique, at 174c5–7: medicine (first again), cobblery, weaving, navigation, generalship.

This focus, reinforced by Critias' own use of 'knowledges' (plural) at 174d9 in response, will then govern the return of the singular formulation at 174e6–7, whence Socrates argues that if temperance is knowledge only of knowledge and of lack of knowledge, then it cannot be claimed as producer of benefit, and therefore as beneficial (175a). Given that the salient conception of knowledge of knowledge and of lack of knowledge, in relation to which the hope of benefit has now been dashed, was, as highlighted by the plurals, that according to which one knows what one does and does not know, it seems left open that the more austere conception of temperance as knowledge of knowledge, entailing merely knowledge that one does or does not know something, may yet, in some sense, be of benefit.[2] And that is as it should be, since 172b–c argues, as we have seen, that there *are* benefits accruing on this conception.

Moreover, although Socrates suggests at 172b–c that the benefits discernible thereby are underwhelming in relation to what had been hoped for from temperance, the suggestion is not wholeheartedly endorsed by Critias (c3). It seems, then, given that the text, as I argued earlier, did not

---

[1] Given this, it seems desirable to be able to pick out a substantive range of 'lacks of knowledge' in such a way that they correspond to respective branches of knowledge. One might adduce 'quackery' as the lack of knowledge corresponding to medicine. A more concrete modern example might be homeopathy, though for concrete Socratic examples of pseudo-sciences one would have to look outside the *Charmides* (cf. *Gorgias* 464b–466a).

[2] Tuozzo (2011, 282–4) rightly argues that we should not take Socrates' talk at 174e6–7 of temperance as knowledge only of knowledge and lack of knowledge and of no other thing as referring to this austere conception. However, I take issue with his claim (2011, 279) that 174d 'shows that what Socrates characterized as the meager benefits of the reduced knowledge of knowledge were, after all, also illusory'. It seems to me that the specific deployment of the plurals at d4–5 in the denial of benefit tells against this reading, as also against Tsouna's view that the distinction between knowledge (singular) and knowledges (plural) in the discussion of benefit 'is not philosophically significant' (2022, 244).

rule out the *possibility* of knowledge of knowledge,[3] that we are free to investigate whether this more austere conception can in fact carry the weight of delivering benefit in a way worthy of temperance.

5.1 Knowing What One Thinks

Based, therefore, on what 172b–c has to say about the benefits of knowledge of knowledge, and on the principle that any interpretation of such benefits must be true to the role of knowledge of knowledge as support for the account of temperance as knowledge of oneself, it is time to flesh out the view of temperance that I have dubbed temperance as self-realisation. One key element of the view will be the idea, to be gleaned from various remarks that Socrates makes, that I find out what I think is the case (or not the case) by a process of critical examination. To discover, for example, whether I think that the one who does good things and not bad ones acts temperately, I must critically assess whether or not it is true that the one who does good things and not bad ones acts temperately.

The example is derived from 163e, where, in response to Socrates' asking if it is not the case that the one who does good things and not bad ones acts temperately (e4), we have the following exchange between Critias and Socrates:

'Don't you think that it is so?'

'Hold on; let us not yet (*mē pō*) examine what I think (*to emoi dokoun*), but what you are now saying.' (163e5–7)

The crucial phrase in Socrates' reply is 'not yet'. Socrates does not refuse as a matter of principle to give his opinion and only test those of others. If, on the other hand, he already has an opinion to express, then why not express it? Opting for concealment seems both unmotivated and unfair. The 'yet' indicates, rather, that Socrates does not at this point regard himself as being in a position to say what he thinks, in advance of examining the proposition about which he is being asked to give his view. Indeed, it seems quite natural for Socrates to have to examine a sophisticated proposition such as 'temperance is the doing of good things' before he can say whether he agrees with it.[4]

---

[3] Hence I am unable to concur with Hyland (2019, 56) that a lesson of the dialogue is that 'self-knowledge *understood as an epistēmē* would be neither possible nor desirable' (his emphasis).

[4] Note, however, that in principle the point has wider application: in order to figure out, for example, whether I believe that it is now raining, I may at least need to *check* whether it is now raining. Socrates does not himself indicate just which kinds of propositions he takes to fall within its scope.

5.1 Knowing What One Thinks

This is not an isolated example. At 165b3–4, in a passage we have already considered,[5] Critias tells Socrates that he is ready to give an account (i.e. a defence) of his proposal that temperance is knowing oneself 'if you don't agree' that it is, to which Socrates replies:

> 'But Critias, you are treating me as if I claim to know the things that I ask and will agree (*homologēsontos*) with you should I so wish (*ean dē boulōmai*). However, that is not the case; I investigate with you what is proposed on a given occasion (*aei to protithemenon*) because I myself do not know. Hence it is once I have examined [the matter] that I am willing (*ethelō*) to say whether I agree or not.' (165b5–c2)

As in the previous case, so here, it is not standoffishness on Socrates' part that is responsible for his declining to say whether he agrees with the proposition in question. The point he seems to be making, rather, is that Critias assumes it is in Socrates' gift whether he agrees, whereas in fact Socrates is not in a position to agree with a proposition until he has examined whether or not that proposition is true. Only such examination results in willingness to say whether he agrees, because before that he would not have been able to say whether he agrees. His being able to tell what he thinks is not something he can do as he pleases, 'should I so wish'; it results from careful consideration of the matter at hand.

Socrates explains his inability to agree on demand in terms of his lack of knowledge of the matter; and he claims that, once having investigated, he is willing to say whether or not he agrees. By implication, he takes himself to be in a position to tell whether he thinks the proposition in question true or not only once he knows whether it is true or not. Presumably, then, the investigation that puts him in a position to tell whether he thinks the proposition true, so that he can agree (or not) that it is true, is also the one that results in his knowing whether it is true.

These passages thus seem to envisage the view, encompassing a demanding notion of belief, that there may be no gap, in principle, between being in a position to know what one thinks in relation to some matter and possessing knowledge on the matter in question. The process by which one comes to know what one thinks is the very process, that of critical examination of propositions, by which one comes to have knowledge of the truth or falsity of those propositions.

It follows, from this view of what it takes to know what one thinks, that one's access to what one thinks is indeed not available on demand, and

---

[5] Section 4.4.

that I may mistakenly take myself not just to know, but even to think, that something is the case when I do not. Now clearly Socrates holds that one can take oneself to know something when one does not know it, as is evident from 166d1–2, where he tells Critias that he would scrutinise himself 'as to what I say (*ti legō*)' for fear of unwittingly thinking he knows something that he does not. But it seems that also on the table is the idea that one can take oneself to think something is the case (or not the case) when one does not. After all, Socrates does not here speak of scrutinising what he thinks or believes, but what he *says*; and he goes on to talk about examining the *logos* (d3) – that is, what has been said, here about temperance. It may, then, be that merely asserting something to be the case is not sufficient for it to be true that one thinks it is the case, and that merely referring to what one asserts will not necessarily tell one what one thinks.

This idea is also suggested in the dialogue by means of Critias' rapidly changing series of assertions about what temperance is. He is portrayed as willing to throw out, in quick succession, a series of different, sometimes inconsistent, declarations:

- 'I very much agree (*sunchōrō*)' that temperance is doing one's own things (162e6; note how readily Critias, unlike Socrates, seems to be able to say he agrees).
- 'I clearly distinguish' temperance for you as the doing of good things (163e10–11).
- 'I pretty much affirm (*phēmi*)' that temperance is knowing oneself (164d3–4).
- 'I say (*legō*)' that temperance is knowledge of itself and of the other knowledges (166e5–6).

Evidently Critias can hardly be said to *know* what temperance is given the haste with which he takes up and discards his proposals. But, as I suggested earlier,[6] it is not even so clear that this is someone who has *beliefs* about what temperance is, so flimsy do his commitments to some of the things he says that it is prove to be. One may at any rate conclude that, from his performance, Critias does not really know *what* he thinks about the matter of what temperance is; and so one might reasonably deduce that he does not have beliefs in this regard about temperance at all.[7]

Recall, then, Charmides' provoking of Critias:

---

[6] Section 4.4.
[7] For a similar point, with regard to Gorgias and his assertions about rhetoric in Plato's *Gorgias*, see Doyle (2010).

> 'But perhaps nothing prevents even the one who says it [that temperance is doing one's own things] from not knowing at all what he was thinking (*mēden eidenai hoti enoei*).' (162b9–10)

And Critias' angry riposte:

> 'So do you suppose, Charmides, just because you don't know what on earth the one who said that temperance is doing one's own things was thinking, that he doesn't know either?' (162d4–6)

What the exchange envisages on both sides is that one can fail to know what one thinks. Critias' disagreement is not over the possibility that one might not know what one thinks; he just takes offence at the idea that *he* might not know what he thinks in this case. And while we do not have, at the level of the drama, a theoretical exchange here about self-knowledge, there is nothing to prevent us from supposing that Plato, via this exchange, conducts a conversation with his readers that puts into play the idea that one does not necessarily, or automatically, know what one thinks.

Now the proposal from Critias that is at issue, that temperance is doing one's own things, requires interpretation; and I have already argued that the task of interpretation should be seen as an essential part of any communicative exchange, and that Socrates is mistaken if he sees no middle ground between proposals being so clear that they need no interpretation (just, where applicable, refutation) and so obscure that no intelligible meaning can be attached to them. All this is compatible with Critias in fact not knowing what he thinks in the case at hand. If we set aside for the moment the coyness over whether he was the source of the proposal, Critias at any rate goes on to confirm his agreement, at 162e6, that temperance is doing one's own things. In view of his rapid cycle of affirmations and withdrawals about what temperance is, I have suggested that his asserting that temperance is such-and-such does not necessarily amount to his thinking or believing that it is such-and-such.

That may, however, leave the fact of his making these assertions look rather mysterious. What, after all, can it mean for one to make an assertion that p if this does not amount to one's believing that p? One explanation may derive from a phenomenon found quite prominently within the *Charmides*, namely one's asserting something because one has heard someone else say it. I have already discussed some textual evidence that Critias takes himself to be borrowing from Socrates both in proposing that temperance is knowledge of knowledge and in treating the proposal as connected with an account of temperance as self-knowledge.[8]

---

[8] See Section 4.6.

Consider also the three answers as to what temperance is given by Charmides. For the first, that temperance is a kind of quietness, Charmides only answers after initial reluctance (159b1–2) but does at least present himself as expressing his opinion in giving his answer (cf. *dokoi*, 159b2; *moi dokei*, b5). Socrates, however, having pointedly invited Charmides to answer 'according to your own opinion' (*kata tēn sēn doxan*, 159a10), goes on in the wake of Charmides' answer to indicate his suspicion, by his use of the phrase 'they say' (*phasi*, 159b7) the quiet are temperate, followed by the injunction that he and Charmides see 'if they are saying anything' (*ei ti legousin*, b8), that Charmides – perhaps because of the pressure to come up with something – has simply reached for a view that he has heard. That he is prone to do this is of course revealed in the context of his third answer when he unabashedly states that he is putting forth what he heard someone else say. If Socrates thus sets up his examination of Charmides' first answer as addressing what 'they' (not Charmides!) say, then it seems that he does not consider Charmides to have yet given his own opinion at all.

Now the first answer was supposed to be an expression of Charmides' belief about what temperance is, based on the awareness provided by its presence in him. Since it is probable that Charmides did not follow this procedure for his answer,[9] one may recall that before Charmides' second answer Socrates insisted that Charmides reflect on what sort of a person the presence of temperance makes him and what temperance would have to be like to make him so, and only 'after having reckoned all this up' (*panta tauta sullogisamenos*, 160d8) say what he thinks temperance is.

It seems likely, then, that in his first answer Charmides is not counted by Socrates as having actually done what the latter asked him to do and express his own belief, in that the answer asserted something that Charmides had heard others say without having thought it through himself. Socrates' contrasting insistence on careful reckoning prior to Charmides' second answer may therefore indicate that for Socrates it is not simply that such careful examination is one route to forming a belief, or even that it is the way one ideally ought to form a belief, but that it is a requirement for a belief to be formed at all. If so, then on this view one can know what one believes only if one has undertaken such a process of examination.

The idea of making an assertion that does not amount to a belief is brought out also, in a slightly different way, in the transition from

---

[9] See Section 3.9.

Charmides to Critias as main interlocutor for the discussion about what temperance is; and here we return to the account of temperance as doing one's own things. As we have noted, there is great play over the identity of the person from whom Charmides heard the account. While it is made clear by implication that this was Critias, no one explicitly acknowledges this. Socrates' motive for not doing so is no doubt to enable Critias to take over the account without losing face. So he compliments Critias on his suitability to defend the account based on his age and interest, and says that he would gladly investigate whether what has been said is true or not 'if you agree (*sunchōreis*) that temperance is what this individual here says it is and take over the account' (162e2–3). Critias, as we saw, says that he 'very much' agrees and takes over (e6).

No wonder, one might say, that Critias is so keen on taking on the account: he is the source of it. But we need to distinguish between the dramatic use – saving Critias' face – to which the text puts the idea of taking over what someone else says, and the idea itself. Critias' eagerness to take over the account confirms him, from the dramatic point of view, as its source. Charmides, on the other hand, who had, in fact, taken over the account from Critias, seems less committed to it than the latter is. Beneath the drama, then, the core idea seems to be a distinction between taking on a proposal that someone else makes and the proposal being one's own.

Socrates, as we have seen,[10] narrates to his anonymous companion at 162d2–3 a simile to describe Critias' attitude to Charmides taking on the proposal, one that centres on the difference between an actor reciting (badly – *kakōs* – in the case at hand) someone else's poems, and the poems being one's own. Now notice that this is embedded in a discussion of what 'doing one's own things' (*to ta heautou prattein*) means; the connection between this and 'one's own poems' (*ta heautou poiēmata*, 162d3) is even closer when one takes into account that the root of *poiēmata* is the verb *poiein*, to 'make' – one may thus render the phrase more literally 'one's own makings' – whose interchangeability with *prattein* Socrates will insist on in his upcoming discussion with Critias.

The transition from Charmides to Critias, then, invites us to consider what it means for something to be 'one's own' in the context of a contrast with merely accepting a proposal that someone else has made.[11] The contrast does not, I think, imply, that we are doomed never to be able to make something we have taken over from someone else our own. After all, the distinction in the simile is not between poet and actor as such, but

---

[10] Section 3.10.   [11] Cf. Moore and Raymond (2019, 68).

between poet and bad actor who does not really seem to understand the lines they are reciting. It is only if we take over a proposal without thinking it through ourselves that it remains resolutely another's; Critias himself will argue that in general things done badly are not one's own but another's (163c3–6). I suggest, then, that one makes a proposal one's own by critically examining it, as Socrates says he would like to do with the proposal that temperance is doing one's own things (162e4–5). Only if it survives such scrutiny does the proposal then become one's own and not another's. It becomes at this point something one believes, not merely something that, like an actor reciting their lines, one says.

I have argued that one can draw from the *Charmides* a conception of belief such that one discovers what one believes only by critical examination of proposals that are made by oneself or by others. One makes a proposal one's own, such that it then rises to the status of something one believes, just if it survives a process of critical scrutiny in which one engages. If that is right, then coming to know what one believes, through subjecting proposals to that scrutiny, is at the same time coming to *have* the beliefs in question. And if one's self consists in what one thinks or believes (a hypothesis I return to shortly), then in this process of critical scrutiny one creates, or realises, oneself.

In English, 'realise' may bear (what one might call) both an epistemological and a metaphysical sense, captured respectively in a sentence such as the following: 'I realised [i.e. was aware] that my dreams would never be realised [i.e. brought about].' In this regard, the use of the term 'self-realisation' in my reading of temperance in the *Charmides* purports to capture something distinctive about the model of temperance so construed, namely that its metaphysical and epistemological aspects are continuous. On this model, one discovers what one believes by coming to have the beliefs in question. That is, insofar as one's self consists in what one believes, one realises oneself epistemologically – becomes aware of what one believes – by realising oneself metaphysically, in coming to have those beliefs by a process of critical scrutiny of propositions.

Is this a model of knowing oneself that is therefore confined to the stage of belief-acquisition? It might be argued that once I have acquired a belief that *p* by this method, such that I thereby know that I have that belief, I am subsequently able to know that I have it simply by noting that it is there in my head. I suspect that for Socrates the distinction between belief-acquisition and standing belief is an artificial one. He states, as we have seen, that what he says is up for scrutiny lest he think it represents knowledge when it does not (166c8–d2). Evidently one cannot scrutinise simultaneously everything one affirms. But by the same token, any position that one has arrived at is in principle open at any time to further challenge: we shall, in Section 5.3, see this concretely illustrated in the *Charmides*. If so, then the model applies not simply to the acquisition of a belief but to the maintenance of a belief already acquired. The difference will be not that once it is acquired the belief is simply there for inspection, but that given the rigorous process by which it will have been acquired on this model, its identity as a belief may be less susceptible to (if never wholly immune from) further challenge.

Now the account of temperance as knowing oneself seemed to treat one's self as comprising what one knows and does not know,[12] rather than simply what one thinks or believes. But if the analysis in this section is correct, then as I suggested above, there may not on this view be such a consequential difference between what one knows and what one believes. If one does not come genuinely to believe a proposition unless it has survived critical scrutiny, then one is arguably already, if this is achieved, in a cognitive relation to that proposition not substantially different from knowledge, given the rigorous investigation of the proposition's truth that one has conducted for it to so much as count as a belief.

It is striking in this regard that, when Socrates, in his examination of the possibility of reflexive relations at 167c–168a, lists the proprietary objects of the various powers of the soul, 'belief' (*doxa*) is the only one whose object is not specifically named.[13] While, to take a few examples, the object of sight is described as colour, that of eros what is beautiful, that of fear what is dreadful, and that of knowledge a piece of learning (*mathēma*, 168a7), the objects of belief are given simply as 'those things of which (*hōn*)' there are beliefs (168a3–4). 'Belief' immediately precedes the target case of knowledge (*epistēmē*, 168a6), and one wonders if one reason for its not getting a named proprietary object is that it is regarded as merely borrowing its object from, and in that sense sharing it with, knowledge.[14] If so, then the text seems to encourage us to assimilate belief with knowledge in terms of what the operation of the respective powers results in.

---

[12] See Sections 4.6 and 4.10.   [13] Cf. Clark (2018, 778).

[14] Sedley (2004, 178 n. 39) claims about this passage that 'the object of *doxa*, referred to but not specified, is undoubtedly assumed by Socrates to be something other than a *mathēma*', but he offers no grounds for this assertion. Moss (2021, 56) also struggles to make the passage come out as saying that *doxa* and *epistēmē* each has its own proprietary object. To observe that 'the fact that all the other members of the list have proprietary objects suggests that these [*doxa* and *epistēmē*] do too' rather begs the question as to why *doxa* alone is characterised in purely formal terms: the more so in an argument where similarity and difference between powers is part of the point at issue.

Support for this idea can be found if we return once again to Socrates' account of the residual benefits of temperance as knowledge of knowledge, where it is notable that 'the *epistēmē* one discerns is regarded as *additional* to (*pros*) each individual thing one learns (*manthanēi*, 172b5). This suggests, if anything, that we should now see the contrast as being between a grasp that takes an individual piece of learning (a *mathēma*) as its object and a grasp that counts as possession of *epistēmē*. At the very least, then, it seems as if there is room here for a cognitive grasp – belief – that can take an individual piece of learning as its object, so that any distinction between knowledge and belief is not to be found there, but at a higher level, whereby the grasp constituted by *epistēmē* proper requires a discernment of the structure that obtains between such individual pieces of learning.

5.2 The Structured Self

One realises oneself, on this view, by coming to know what it is that one believes. The process by which one does so is by critical scrutiny of propositions. Since, I have argued, one does not, on this account, so much as have a belief until one has subjected the things one is prepared to assert to such scrutiny,[15] then the process by which one comes to know what one believes is the very process by which one comes to have those beliefs. This means that whether one holds a belief is in part a function of the process by which one comes to hold it. And that in turn, as we have seen, might suggest that there is not such a sharp distinction to be drawn between knowing what one knows and knowing what one believes, given the nature of the process by which one comes to know what one believes. This may offer a way to understand why it is (simply) knowledge of knowledge that is invoked to underpin the conception of temperance as knowledge of oneself.

Now it may further be objected at this point that knowledge of oneself is explicated as knowledge of knowledge and *lack* of knowledge. If so, wouldn't one's self consist in what one does not know as well as what one knows? I think one must concede at least this: in critically scrutinising the things one is prepared to assert, one will discover which of them do not, as well as do, count as knowledge. Along the way one will no doubt discover thereby things that one mistakenly thought one knew, the identification of

---

[15] Hence, perhaps, the idea at *Theaetetus* 189e–190a (cf. *Sophist* 263e–264a; *Philebus* 38b–e) that *doxa* is the result of internal dialogue; on this account, a carefully worked out epistemological position rather than a tendentiously 'intellectualist' one.

5.2 The Structured Self

which Socrates presents at 166d1–2 as the reason why he would undertake scrutiny of proposals that he (not just others) may make. Indeed, I have argued that his scrutiny of the proposal that temperance is knowledge of knowledge, the very one that Critias has just put forth there, could count as an example of this sort of self-examination, since Critias has probably taken the idea of knowledge of knowledge as at least required for temperance from Socrates. Presumably, proposals that do not survive one's scrutiny will not be retained (or in the relevant cases make their debut) as things one is prepared to assert, let alone as things one believes, so they will not feature as elements of what one knows when one knows oneself. What, then, to make of the apparent equation of oneself with one's knowledge *and* lack of knowledge?

It should be noted that the dialogue is in fact rather guarded in making that equation. When Critias first introduces the relevant proposal, it is of the form: temperance is knowledge of the other knowledges and of itself (166c2–3); lack of knowledge does not (yet) appear. It is Socrates who makes the extension to lack of knowledge at 166e7–8 and, given Critias' ready agreement (*panu ge*, e9), that seems to be on the general grounds that if one knows the positive element of a pair of contraries one will thereby know the negative, rather than a specific statement about what it means to know oneself. Indeed, when Socrates further spells out, at 167a1–7, the (doomed) inference to knowing what one does and does not know, it seems clear, as we have seen,[16] that this is chiefly in anticipation of the purported benefits of knowledge of knowledge and of lack of knowledge, rather than a focus on the connection with knowledge of oneself. Moreover, when Critias, at 169d9–e5, explicates the link back to knowledge of oneself, expressly uncontested by Socrates, it is purely knowledge of itself (*gnōsin autēn hautēs*, e4), that is, knowledge of knowledge, that does the work, Socrates then going on to critique the further inference from *that* to knowing what one does and does not know.

Thus far, then, one may retain the equation of one's self with, specifically, the things that one knows, such that realising oneself would consist in acquiring knowledge through a process of critical scrutiny of propositions, including, but not restricted to, those propositions one is already prepared to assert. By this process of knowledge acquisition, one comes at the same time to know which propositions are the ones that one knows, and hence to know oneself. But this account still, I think, misses

---

[16] Sections 4.6 and 4.10.

something about the dialogue's view of what marks out knowledge of knowledge as underpinning knowledge of oneself.

I have argued that one can glean, from Socrates' remarks at 172b–c about the ('lesser') benefits of knowledge of knowledge, the view that what it is that one knows is a structured whole comprising mutually consistent propositions.[17] Knowing on this view would therefore require grasping those propositions as a mutually consistent set. If that is so, then strictly speaking what one knows is not individual propositions, but the structured set as such. That in turn reopens space for distinguishing between knowledge and belief. Individual propositions may be objects of belief, even (as they would be through having survived critical scrutiny) well-grounded belief, but not objects of knowledge.

This too, however, needs qualification. For one important element in the process of scrutiny is testing whether the proposition in question is consistent with other propositions one is prepared to assert. The first two answers that Charmides gives about what temperance is both seem to fall at this hurdle. Temperance is agreed to be a thing that is both beautiful and good, with the first answer unable to account for temperance as something beautiful, the second for temperance as something good. So, in the former case, the proposition that temperance is a kind of quietness is argued to be inconsistent with the propositions that temperance is a beautiful thing and that quietness can be ugly. In the latter case, the proposition that temperance is the same thing as shame is seen to be inconsistent with the propositions that temperance is a good thing and that shame can be not good. Or take Critias' proposal that being temperate is doing good things. Critias withdraws it when he acknowledges that the temperate person must know that they are temperate, whereas a person who does good things need not know that they are doing good things.

If one reason for a proposition to fail to survive scrutiny is its inconsistency with other propositions that one is prepared to assert, then a proposition that survives scrutiny will already thereby be part of a mutually consistent subset of the propositions that one is prepared to assert. That in itself does not yet of course establish a mutual consistency across the whole set of propositions that one is prepared to assert. But it does mean that the cognitive difference between grasp of an individual proposition and of a whole set may be one of degree rather than kind. Essentially the same criterion operates for testing whether one proposition is well-grounded as for testing whether a whole set is, since, even in the individual case,

---

[17] See Sections 4.13 and 5.1.

surviving scrutiny will establish some subset of mutually consistent propositions. The difference is that one has not fully realised oneself – that is to say, not established oneself as, strictly, an object of knowledge – unless one has tested whether those propositions are consistent with all others that one is prepared to assert.

With this in mind, let me now recapitulate the model of temperance that I have suggested Plato's text, despite its aporetic outcome at the level of the conversation between Socrates and his interlocutors, invites us to consider. The model works to flesh out what temperance as knowledge of knowledge would be, in such a way as to illuminate its role in underpinning the account of temperance as knowledge of oneself. Temperance, then, as I read it, will be the power, involving but not exhausted by knowledge of what knowledge is (a core requirement of what knowledge is on this account being a set of mutually consistent propositions grasped as such), to realise oneself by means of critical scrutiny of propositions across, at least, the range of those that one is prepared to assert.

A realised self is thus a structured self,[18] comprising the set of propositions that one is (or has come to be) prepared to assert, inasmuch as one is prepared to assert them through their having passed scrutiny as mutually consistent. In being a structured entity of this sort, such a self will have the correct form to qualify as an object of knowledge by the terms implied in Socrates' account of the residual benefits of knowledge of knowledge at 172b1–8. To exercise competently the power that is temperance will thus require a grasp of logical relations, and I take it that such a grasp forms a major theoretical constituent of the branch of knowledge that is knowledge of knowledge.

Temperance will thus itself be a branch of knowledge that, as such, consists in a coherently structured set of propositions. Moreover, temperance, as the power to realise oneself, is the power to bring about a structured set of propositions that consists quite generally in the propositions, among those that one is prepared to assert, that survive (and because they survive) critical scrutiny. If that is right, we can see how on this view temperance will, as Socrates insists, be a beautiful thing, and a temperate person will, insofar as she is temperate, have a beautiful soul. For it is plausible that a structured entity whose elements fit together coherently is something beautiful. While we get no explicit theorising in the *Charmides* about the nature of beauty, the text invites us, to the extent that

---

[18] I borrow the phrase from Gill (2006).

temperance is consistently presented as possessing the attribute of beauty, to make good on that attribution.

Indeed, insofar as the discernment of how the parts of a complex structure fit together demands one's focussed attention, this account of beauty offers an explanation of why what is beautiful is, as I have argued the *Charmides* plausibly suggests, such as to elicit one's attention.[19] And since temperance, being itself a beautiful thing, has the power to bring about what is beautiful (namely, a structured self), it is natural to conclude that its being beautiful is a cause of beauty in that which it brings about. If so, then in this causal role temperance will represent a source of value that entitles it to be called good.[20] Recall in this connection that it was by reference to its causal powers that the goodness of temperance was first asserted, in the course of Socrates' refutation of Charmides' second answer (160e9–13, 161a8–9).[21]

5.3 Temperance and Self-Care

Building on this picture of its nature and evaluative status, let me now explore how the dialogue offers a way to elaborate more concretely on the benefit of temperance so construed. Though not argued for explicitly, the idea of a relation between, on the one hand, caring for oneself and, on the other, adopting a stance of critical examination towards propositions is expressed by Socrates; and it seems appropriate that he does this when about to cast doubt on whether the benefits he had taken to accrue from temperance when treated as knowledge of what one does and does not know – the benefits ascribed to what I have called the 'administrative' model – really amount to anything.

At 172c5–6 Socrates says that 'certain strange things' (*atop' atta*) appear to him regarding the supposed benefit of temperance construed in this way. He reiterates at 172e4–5 that when he 'focusses' (*apoblepsas*; note again the motif of attention) on the matter, these strange ideas 'appear before' (*prophainesthai*) him, making him fear that they have not been

---

[19] See Section 3.12. I venture to add that possession of such a structure is one source of the pull that the *Charmides* itself exerts on its readers. See further Section 5.9.
[20] Given that the formal features of knowledge constitute its beauty, Tuozzo (2011, 326) sets up what seems to me a false dichotomy in contrasting a reading of knowledge of knowledge whereby it constitutes what he calls 'a value-free understanding of the logico-dialectical features that characterize any *epistēmē*' with a 'more expansive reading' of knowledge of knowledge as 'an understanding of knowledge as a truly good thing – that is, an understanding of how individual knowledges can be used to produce true benefit'.
[21] See Section 3.9.

5.3 Temperance and Self-Care

correctly inquiring into whether temperance brings us good. It seems that once the ideas have appeared Socrates cannot simply dismiss them. He explains:

> I suppose that I am talking nonsense; nonetheless it is necessary to examine (*skopein*) what at any rate appears before one (*to ge prophainomenon*) and not let it randomly go if, at any rate, one cares even a little for oneself (*ei tis ge hautou kai smikron kēdetai*). (173a3–5)

These striking words link self-care with the examination, as opposed to the dismissal, of propositions that appear before one. They also recall, in the words I have underlined, Critias' phrasing of the idea of temperance as knowledge 'of oneself' (*heautou ge*) at 165c7. The text thus invites us to consider a connection between knowing oneself, enquiry, and self-care – and moreover, given what Socrates is problematising here, a connection that might reveal a benefit to knowledge of oneself that does not depend on the administrative model. I have already argued that in Socrates' view we do not know what we think simply by inspecting our minds and finding it there; we come to know it by testing propositions against others that we are prepared to assert. In so doing we work out what it is that we think, with the resultant well-grounded beliefs partly constituted by the process by which we have arrived at them.

If the self is viewed as cognitive – that is, as consisting in what (at its most general) one thinks – then this process of critical enquiry is part of the process of realising oneself. Merely letting propositions that appear before one randomly disperse without chasing them down is, on this view, a failure in the most basic sense to care for oneself. For it is a failure to establish, by comparing such propositions with others that one is prepared to assert, what it is that one thinks. In neglecting this, one leaves oneself empty before the parade of appearances. I may be a subject of those appearances, as the one who experiences them: they do, after all, appear 'before' me. But I am, thus far, only a minimal subject – a bare self. The appearances have content; but since I have not made them my own through critical scrutiny, I do not.[22]

---

[22] In Woolf (2008) I proposed that the extraordinary thing about the Platonic Socrates is that, in regarding all his beliefs as subject to critical scrutiny, he manages to live without a self, since he cannot from that stance be committed to anything. I would now place more emphasis on the idea that adoption of this stance is necessary if one is to come to have the well-grounded commitments that would comprise one's substantial self. The need for a distinction between appearances (what he calls 'impressions') and commitments is well noted in Moore (2015, 32 n. 87); see also Kamtekar (2017, 37–8). Yet the distinction must remain blurry, since the commitments one may have, or take

In the case at hand, Socrates introduces the strange appearances as challenging the soundness of what he and Critias had previously been prepared to assert:

> What we were saying just now, that temperance, if it were that sort of thing, would be a great good if in charge of administration of both household and city, we do not, Critias, seem to me to have agreed beautifully (*kalōs hōmologēkenai*). (172d3–5)

Socrates then spells out (172d7–10) that the agreement he has in mind is that temperance would bestow great benefit if it were knowledge of what one does and does not know and had authority, on that basis, to ensure that tasks were done only by those with knowledge. In the face of Critias' incredulity that that agreement was unsound (172e3), Socrates goes on to explain, as we have seen, that if one cares for oneself even a little one must nonetheless examine such appearances.

He does so by propounding a lengthy objection (173a–174d) to the idea that temperance construed in this way bestows benefit, whose setting out, he explains, alluding to Penelope's dream in the *Odyssey*, has the purpose of determining whether the appearances, 'my own dream' (*to emon onar*), have come through the gates of horn or of ivory (173a7–8) – that is, whether they are true or false.[23] Socrates' procedure here, and his connecting of it with self-care, corroborates the idea that to care for oneself is to discover what it is that one thinks. His talk of dreams, and of strange appearances, suggests a weak cognitive relation at this point between himself as subject and the content of those appearances. Socrates does not yet quite either accept or reject them; he inclines to the former but suspects he is talking nonsense. By implication, that cognitive relation will be made more determinate through examination of the appearances as to their truth or falsity.

My suggestion, then, is that Socrates in the *Charmides* is represented by Plato as modelling in a certain way – imperfectly so, I shall argue in Sections 5.4 and 5.5 – the process of self-realisation. The latter entails, on the conception I have been drawing out, the discovery of what it is that one thinks. At its broadest, in making this discovery one realises oneself – brings oneself into being – as a structured self, and thereby a self that is beautiful. The process of self-realisation, insofar as it is constituted by the critical examination of propositions, is thus the process of realising oneself

---

oneself to have, are in turn open to challenge by fresh appearances: self-realisation is, by its nature, a continuous process. See further Section 5.5.

[23] More on the dream and the objection in Section 5.7.

5.3 *Temperance and Self-Care* 225

as possessing a coherent – hence beautiful – structure. For a self to become substantial is therefore, necessarily, for it to become beautiful. The benefit, or goodness – namely, establishing what it is one thinks – proprietary to the art of self-realisation is thus non-contingently connected with the beauty of its product.

Now Socrates is about to argue that even if we were to concede that knowledge of knowledge could be construed as knowing what one does and does not know, it is still hard to discern wherein its benefit lies. We shall turn to that argument in Section 5.7. But that of course was a concession he didn't think we were entitled to make; all one can strictly say is that, in having knowledge of knowledge, we would know *that* we know and do not know something, not what we know (say, health and sickness); and with the former option Socrates sees the benefit as being, supposedly, rather less.

If, on the other hand, we think of the benefit of temperance as being connected with self-realisation, then what is central on this model is that one's self (regarded as cognitive) consist in certain well-grounded beliefs, items of knowledge (if we allow individual items this appellation), and so on, that, as such, hang together with one another. What I thereby know, which, now in terms of Socrates' contrast between knowing-that and knowing-what, means what specific branch of knowledge these items fall under, is not directly relevant to the question of whether, and to what extent, self-realisation has been achieved. So we can allow Socrates to retain the specific sense of his thought that, in itself, knowledge of knowledge delivers knowledge only *that* we know certain things, rather than what it is we know, and still keep intact the benefit that, on this view, would accrue. I may, on this model, know which are the propositions I know, without thereby knowing what field of knowledge it is to which any such propositions relate.

At this point it is worth restating that the picture I have argued for, of temperance as the art of self-realisation, is not presented explicitly in the text. Nor do I intend it to represent some 'hidden' meaning beneath the (mostly) aporetic surface. There is, if my general interpretive approach is correct, nothing 'beneath' the conversations and events that the work depicts; its surface is its substance. Rather, my reading is a product of critical scrutiny of the statements and arguments of a text that, I have argued, is written so as to invite a critical response. Such engagement aligns with the way that the text is composed, its vertical structure and formal separation of Plato from his characters encouraging a critical stance towards the first-order events and conversations depicted. Moreover, in having to work out any such interpretation for ourselves, we are liable to end up doing the very thing that self-realisation, on this construal, consists in, namely discovering what we ourselves think: in this case about the question of how to conceive of temperance as knowledge of knowledge.

If we *are* doing that, then we are revealed to ourselves as valuing self-realisation just because we have found ourselves responding in an enquiring fashion to the question at hand. And lest this sound like special pleading for a speculative interpretation, the text does, I think, at least at one point, encourage us quite strongly in the direction of the reading I have been advocating. When Critias proposes that temperance is knowledge of oneself, and Socrates replies by demanding that it must be shown to have a structure similar to a branch of knowledge such as medicine or building, Critias, as we have seen, tells Socrates that not all branches of knowledge are like the ones that Socrates has mentioned (165e3–166a2).

Yet it was open to Critias to take a quite different route in response.[24] He could have said, consistently with Socrates' demand: knowledge of oneself is knowledge of how to bring oneself about, just as knowledge of health is knowledge of how to bring health about. By setting up this route as an option and having Critias ostentatiously decline to take it,[25] the text allows us to notice it and to exercise our critical faculties in tracing it out for ourselves. In being moved to discover what we think about this possibility, we find ourselves both exemplifying and finding value in the process of self-realisation.

5.4 Socrates and Self-Realisation

The critical examination of propositions, integral to temperance as self-realisation as I have interpreted it, is evidently a core part of Socrates' own procedure as he both describes and practises it in the dialogue. And whether or not one accepts my interpretation of how temperance is conceived, it is hard to doubt that we are supposed to ask whether, and if so to what extent, Socrates himself is shown as temperate in the dialogue. His response to the battle, and to the effects on him of Charmides' bodily beauty, though in some ways, I have suggested, offering a false trail in this

---

[24] Cf. Pichanick (2005, 258).
[25] Coolidge (1995, 216) claims that Critias does regard knowledge of oneself as a form of knowing how, specifically knowing how to satisfy a particular sort of need. But if that were so, one would not expect Critias to insist that knowledge of oneself is not like branches of knowledge (such as medicine) that know how to satisfy needs.

regard, do invite questions about Socrates' relation to temperance once we become aware that temperance is a major theme of the work.

If I am right that the way the dialogue is constructed prompts us to regard Socrates with a critical eye, it would be unwise to assume automatically that he is presented as an exemplar of temperance therein. Rather than attempt a definitive answer to the question of whether Socrates is depicted as temperate in the *Charmides*, I aim now to pull together some textual threads that indicate ways in which one might approach the question. The first concerns a point I have already urged in the context of Nehamas's puzzle about the unity of the *Charmides*. If we *are* to see Socrates as exhibiting temperance, then it would be tempting but wrong (the false trail I mentioned above) to see this as constituted by his manifesting restraint or self-control. Instead, the uncanniness of his attitude towards both the battle and Charmides' body is, I contend, the complement of the power of attention that he displays in relation to the non-bodily.

Temperance on this view is about committing, not restraining, oneself. It is Socrates' focus on the non-bodily, whose basis I argued for in Chapter 3,[26] that enables him to pursue his relentless scrutiny, be that of Charmides' soul or Critias' proposals. If that is right, then this characteristic of Socrates is certainly compatible with the dialogue's view of temperance as I have interpreted it, since both the focus and the scrutiny is part of what is required to achieve self-realisation. Equally, however, this is only part of the story. In order for temperance as knowledge of knowledge to be competently practised, it requires, I have argued, a grasp of the rules of logic and a sensitivity to logical relations. If Socrates does display such a grasp, he does so, I think, imperfectly.[27] To cite just one example already mentioned, he seems to conflate, in the course of setting out his utopian vision, 'doing everything knowledgeably that is done' with 'doing everything knowledgeably'.

It is, it seems to me, unfeasible to try to determine in general whether, when Socrates does argue fallaciously (assuming that can be reliably identified), he is portrayed knowingly by Plato as doing so or not. My own sense is that even if Plato is not himself infallible in matters of logic (it would be extraordinary if he were), the Socrates we find in the *Charmides*,

---

[26] See esp. Section 3.5.
[27] In critique of Schirlitz (1897), Tuckey (1951, 71) cautions, on the grounds of anachronism, against speaking of logic in this context, 'since the *Charmides* was written before anything that could be called "logic" was in existence'. That, however, seems true only in the sense that logic was not yet a developed branch of knowledge, which is consistent with the idea that, in conceiving of temperance as knowledge of knowledge, the dialogue *models* such a branch of knowledge that (even) Socrates only begins to fill out.

while on the whole surpassing Critias (let alone Charmides) in logical acumen, is also someone whom ulterior motive (for one thing) at times causes to be careless in argumentation. The way he treats Charmides' first answer is, I take it, an example of this.[28]

If Socrates is an imperfect logician, this fits readily enough with the idea found in the dialogue, particularly in relation to Charmides' condition, that one's possession of temperance may come in degrees, where the question is not whether one completely has it or lacks it but whether it is possessed to a sufficient degree.[29] How should one assess this idea? I wonder if seeing temperance (understood as knowledge of knowledge) as, in the way I have suggested, a branch of knowledge with the same basic structure as, say, medicine, may help.

What would it mean, then, to speak of a perfect doctor? Socrates spoke at 156b5 of doctors who practise body holism as good. If the Thracian narrative is to be taken literally, however, these doctors would be making large and systematic errors – as according to the Thracian they do (156e3–4). I argued that this provides one piece of evidence that we are not supposed to take the narrative at face value. Let Socrates retain his high opinion of the body holists.[30] That does not imply that good doctors do not sometimes make mistakes. What the Thracian scenario seems to exclude is the territory on which for the most part good practice of medicine, like that of similar fields, must actually operate: somewhere between gross error and faultlessness. The perfect doctor implied by the Thracian narrative seems more like a reductio of the idea than serious support for it. That Zalmoxian medicine should at any rate be taken to be an art outside the human realm is indicated by Socrates' reporting that the Thracian doctors are said to make people immortal (156d5–6), presumably the logical conclusion of perfect medical practice, Zalmoxis himself being described by Socrates' Thracian correspondent as a god (156d8).[31]

---

[28] See Section 3.9.   [29] See e.g. 157d1–7, 158b2–3, c3–4; cf. 176a4, b3–4.

[30] Smith (2021, 146) creates more of a puzzle than is warranted in characterising Socrates' report of the Thracian's disparaging remarks about Greek doctors as something that 'Socrates observes' in his own name. Smith's more general thesis, that expertise is regarded by Socrates as coming in degrees, is well taken.

[31] Our main pre-Platonic evidence for Zalmoxis (Herodotus 4.94–6) tells a colourful tale about the latter's supposed rise to divinity in which he promises immortality to his followers (the Thracian tribe of the Getae) but is not said to have any particular connection with medicine. One may in any event wonder whether, in his turn to (soul-) medicine, Socrates does not 'correct' the Zalmoxian doctors by showing, in characteristic Socratic fashion, that they have not thought through their own position: if immortality is the aim, one does not bring it about by using the soul to create perfect bodily health; one does so by attending to the soul in its own right.

5.4 Socrates and Self-Realisation

A similar moral, except now applied to temperance itself, follows for Socrates' utopian vision of knowing what one does and does not know. It seems to me significant that *this* is the option we are given in the dialogue if we want to consider temperance as something that can be perfectly realised. It is a vision that Socrates himself ultimately disowns when he argues that it is not temperance but knowledge of good and bad that would achieve the utopian benefit. But even before that, the thin and schematic character of the vision, with its gap between the temperate person's powers and what those powers are required to achieve, gives the game away. Relatedly, I have argued, we are given a vision from which the individual subject of temperance disappears in a blur of total administration. If this is the view on which the possibility of a perfect exercise of temperance depends, then so much the worse (we might think) for that possibility.

I offer these considerations, contestable though they may be, in the hope that they provide a framework, from within the dialogue's own resources, for assessing the relation of the character Socrates to temperance that does not depend on prejudgement (perhaps derived to some extent from other parts of the Platonic corpus) about that figure's moral standing. Nor perhaps is there a chance of debate being anything other than sterile if it is based on one's own visceral reaction to the character. I have, instead, tried to encourage the view that the dramatic structure of the *Charmides* leaves room for the critical distancing of Plato from Socrates, so that an assumption that we are, for example, presented with a moral hero in Socrates need not be false, but requires defence rather than passage by default.

If so, then in regard to his exemplification (or otherwise) of temperance, my suggestion has been that we look at how temperance is modelled in the dialogue, in order to see whether its structure lends itself to the idea of perfect exemplification; and I have argued that, if temperance is modelled after the structure of a practical field of knowledge, such as medicine, we should not find intelligible the idea of perfection in its practitioners. If there is a default, then, it is that Socrates is presented as falling somewhat short of flawless exemplification in regard to temperance, not because of his manifest (to the eyes of this reader at least) oddities of character but because of what the practice of any branch of knowledge of that kind entails.

There is something more that we can take from the Thracian narrative to suggest that we are not to regard Socrates as an ideal exemplification of temperance. Whether we think the instilling of temperance is, as in the view of our Thracian correspondent, within the purview of medicine or (as

I have argued) should be interpreted as having, for Socrates, a goal distinct from medicine, brought about by a distinct practice that I labelled 'soul-medicine', the narrative makes it clear, with its reference at 156e to all the diseases that elude Greek doctors because of their neglect of the soul, that treatment of the soul does not, in any systematic way, currently happen outside the (possibly mythical) realm of Zalmoxis. In Greece, at any rate, Socrates is therefore something of a pioneer – at soul-medicine, and so presumably also at the practice of temperance as the power of self-realisation, to the extent that possession of temperance is a result of the operation of soul-medicine.[32]

Socrates may thus be a paradigm in at least the following sense: Thracian genius aside, and with the instilling of temperance, by implication, largely absent from Greece, he is a pioneer in what he does. But that in turn suggests that, like all pioneers, he will make mistakes, take wrong turns, and perhaps generally be functioning at a relatively primitive level by comparison with the practice of more developed fields such as medicine itself.[33]

His very status as a pioneer, then, hugely impressive though it may be, should caution us against the thought that he gets everything (or even most things) right. His own self-presentation, after all, is of one who does not (even) know what temperance is, despite apparently possessing a charm by which to administer it. And this suggests that, as much in soul-medicine as in its bodily counterpart, discovering what constitutes the right outcome of a practice and discovering the right process for achieving that outcome are not independent of one another. Getting the nature of temperance right and developing the process by which one instils it are intertwined. This should, again, encourage us as readers to scrutinise Socrates' practice with a critical eye, the more so given that the practice has critical scrutiny at its heart.

5.5 The Life of Temperance

There is a further feature of the practice of temperance as the power of self-realisation that might suggest a reason for regarding it as necessarily

---

[32] See Section 3.7. If one can be healthy without the intervention of doctors, then perhaps one can be temperate without the intervention of soul-medicine. But the flipside of the myth of the perfect doctor is the myth of the perfect subject whose state of health could never benefit from intervention (which might include self-intervention). So too, on this model, for temperance and soul-medicine.

[33] Note too that Socrates is aged around forty at the dialogue's dramatic date, which leaves him three decades of life to develop the procedure. Contrast the *Apology*, in which he is able to summarise what he does as a relatively systematic method, whatever its precise relation to the procedure in the *Charmides* may be.

imperfect: the practice is, by its nature, ongoing. One can never be said to have scrutinised for their mutual consistency all the propositions that one is prepared to assert. This is not just because one might not have got around to scrutinising all such propositions, or that one might have done so imperfectly, though both those scenarios are of course inevitable in any real human situation. It is because one can never even in principle draw a line around such propositions and say that now one has the complete set. New challenges can always arise, from others or from oneself, that introduce propositions that one may (come to) be prepared to assert but which need to be critically examined in relation to other propositions one is prepared to assert.

If so, then the process of self-examination, and thus self-realisation, has no determinate end.[34] Its scope being in principle limitless, it is, thus, essentially a lifelong activity. This feature is, I think, brought out by the way that the later parts of the discussion with Critias are structured. As we have seen, even after Socrates argues that one cannot infer knowledge of what one does and does not know, with its accompanying benefits, from knowledge of knowledge and of lack of knowledge, he turns to critique the idea that these *were* benefits, a move one might think moot insofar as the benefits had already been said to be illegitimately inferred. But as we noted, the 'strange things' that appear before Socrates' mind cannot be ignored if he cares even a little for himself.

The new 'appearances' sit uneasily with the earlier endorsement of the benefits, and so must be investigated. Indeed, Socrates will re-emphasise more generally, at 175b–c, the points they had conceded for the sake of argument 'that do not follow' (*ou sumbainonta*, 175b5), highlighting a new one he had not explicitly brought up before – the alleged impossibility of knowing in some way what one does not know at all (c3–8). What might seem like a rather gratuitous piling on at this stage, with so much already having been questioned, helps underline, through the ostentatiousness of the Socratic case, the open-ended nature of self-examination.

There is, then, no fixed point at which, on this view, one can say: now my deliberations are over. Self-realisation is continuous. Far from this being an inbuilt flaw in the conception of how temperance is to be practised, it offers support for an essential element in that conception to which Socrates draws attention on several occasions: the value of temperance lies in part in its ability to characterise a whole life.

---

[34] Cf. McCabe (2007a, 18). Stern (1999, 410–12) offers some salutary reflections on how this aspect bears upon the utopian vision.

The idea first occurs at 160b where Socrates tells Charmides, in respect of the latter's first answer, that temperance could not be quietness nor could 'the temperate life' (*ho sōphrōn bios*, b8; cf. 160c7) be quiet. Formally, Socrates could have conducted his refutation by just talking about temperance and not mentioning the idea of a temperate life at all. The fact that he does so evidently means it has independent significance for him. Indeed, though Charmides' own proposal was put in terms of what temperance is, Socrates, as we saw earlier, immediately talks about those who are temperate (159b8), as if to lay stress on the idea that we are interested in temperance as something that can characterise human lives and serve as a basis for living one's life. In so doing, he implicitly acknowledges that Charmides' first answer may have got something important right, since in setting it out Charmides spoke of temperance as 'doing everything (*panta*) in an orderly and quiet way' (159b3), thus apparently picturing temperance as something capable of suffusing a whole life.

As with Charmides' first answer, so too the utopian vision, despite its being questionable in other ways, connects tightly with this aspect of temperance. Socrates says that, had the vision obtained, both those who have temperance and those ruled by them 'would have lived their life through' (*an ton bion diezōmen*, 171d7) free from error. It is perhaps significant, and in line with what I argued was part of the flawed character of the vision, that those who, by implication, do not have temperance apparently get the same lifelong benefit as those who do. It certainly seems as if something has gone askew, in terms of the motivation to possess temperance, when its benefit turns out to accrue equally to all even with only one segment of the beneficiaries possessing it. But the flaw here is not in the idea that temperance is a possession fit to shape a whole life.

The skewed picture is, in any event, corrected, and the linkage of temperance with oneself implicitly reaffirmed, in Socrates' words to Charmides when the latter is summoned back into conversation towards the end of the dialogue: 'I think temperance is a great good, and if you have it, you are blessed' (175e6–176a1). You (*se*, second person singular) are blessed; no mention here of benefit to non-possessors, or any others at all.[35] Viewed in this light, Socrates is no less sure that, despite the investigation overtly failing to show what the benefit is, temperance will

---

[35] Of course, Charmides has been the one on whom the question of possession of temperance has been most explicitly focused, so perhaps it is no surprise that Socrates singles him out here. Nonetheless, Socrates' description seems emphatically personal in relation to a young man whose future promise has been so closely connected, via the exploits of his ancestors, to the civic realm.

benefit Charmides 'if present in your life' (*en tōi biōi parousa*, 175e2). Temperance, then, is significant in that it is transformative of the person who possesses it: it makes them blessed. But that is not because, in making its possessor blessed, it delivers to them some end-state, sufficient unto itself, whose relation to the rest of their life is then moot (or mysterious). On my construal, the practice of temperance is itself a form of life whose continuous exercise is its essence. This, I think, makes good sense of the way temperance is regarded in the dialogue as closely tied to the concept of a life.

That concept perhaps nonetheless needs enriching so as to imply not merely a continuous stretch of (eventually punctuated) existence, arguably as such still too austere to serve as bearer of blessedness, but one constitutively connected, in addition, with structure and direction. In this sense, temperance as self-realisation will befit a life not merely in its aptness for continuous exercise, but in its orientation towards improvement. Relevant here, again, is the idea suggested in the text of temperance as an attribute possessed not all-or-nothing but susceptible of development,[36] together with the picture of Socrates as a practitioner who, qua pioneer, is learning his trade and (therefore) making mistakes. This suggests a direction of travel for one's practice, as that of a subject able to grow in self-realisation over the course of a life in the exercise of the practice in question.

5.6 Temperance and Discipline

So much for how, on my reading, temperance as self-realisation is modelled in the dialogue. Before turning, in a little more detail, to the final portion of Socrates' main discussion with Critias, I want to say something about how the model might line up with traditional conceptions of temperance in Plato's day. There is, however, a snag in trying to do so. Temperance itself seems, on the available evidence, to have been characterised in a bewilderingly wide variety of ways.[37] One piece of evidence is of course the *Charmides* itself, which in its own variegated set of proposals both reflects and expands the menu of choices.[38] If Critias' dizzying frequency of proposal indicates, as I have suggested, that he does not know

---

[36] See 157d5–6, 158b6, c3–4, 175e1, 176a4–5; cf. n. 29 above.
[37] On the 'polysemy' of the Greek term see Rademaker (2005). Burnyeat (1971, 216) calls the term 'untranslatable, because the phenomena it grouped together for Greek culture do not form a whole to our outlook'.
[38] See Rademaker (2005, 3–7).

what he thinks about temperance, that is perhaps a dramatic reflection of a culture largely in the same boat about one of its principal ethical notions.

The dialogue does nonetheless reserve a particular place for the idea of temperance as knowledge of oneself. That is not just because, despite the problematising that the underpinning idea of temperance as knowledge of knowledge undergoes, temperance as knowledge of oneself is left essentially unscathed (albeit in part because its supporting conception bears the brunt of the attack); indeed it goes curiously unmentioned in Socrates' final litany of the inadequacies of the investigation at 175a–d. It survives, also, because of the Delphic backing it receives in Critias' account. Now such backing has all the ambivalence one would expect of its source: divine validation, if Critias is right, on the one hand; the necessity for interpretation of an obscure pronouncement on the other. I have argued, however, that one thing the *Charmides* insists upon is the necessity of interpretation. My reading of temperance as self-realisation is the product of interpretive work. But this insistence, if not the interpretation itself, does, I think, come with the dialogue's warrant.

If so, then it may be possible, indirectly, to approach the question of the relation of the idea of self-realisation to a classical Greek conception of temperance. In the introduction to their recent translation of the *Charmides*, Moore and Raymond make a thoughtful defence of their choice to translate *sōphrosunē* as 'discipline'.[39] My own selection in these pages of 'temperance' to translate the term is very much by default. Still the most common rendition in English, its somewhat archaic flavour has the merit of not suggesting anything too determinate for its rather Protean original.

Nonetheless, Moore and Raymond make a case that 'discipline' does the best job of capturing key features of the Greek term, both in the *Charmides* itself and in the wider cultural context. If that is right, then the account of temperance as self-realisation that I have offered resonates with the notion of discipline in at least one significant respect. Self-realisation requires, as we have seen, continuous scrutiny of the propositions one is prepared to assert. There is thus, at the heart of the practice, a need for focussed attention that is plausibly understood as a form of discipline. We saw earlier how this idea of attention features quite explicitly in the way Socrates describes what is required for the proper conduct of investigation into proposals about temperance. Thus far, then, temperance as self-realisation does collect what is, arguably, a core idea in the classical concept of *sōphrosunē*.

---

[39] Moore and Raymond (2019, xxxiv–xxxvii).

5.6 Temperance and Discipline

This also, however, brings out what I think is a weakness in rendering *sōphrosunē* as 'discipline' for these purposes. The latter term seems to fall short of the normative weight that the Greek term demands. It is hard, for example, to square the sense of 'discipline' with Critias' proposal that *sōphrosunē* is the doing of good things. Now of course that proposal is itself shown to be deficient, insofar as it misses out on the reflexive element that Socrates and Critias agree must obtain. But there is no indication in this that the doing of good things is regarded as irrelevant to, rather than falling short of, the concept of *sōphrosunē*. By contrast, it seems to me that 'doing good things' could not seriously be offered as even a candidate account for what discipline is. There is simply a lack of fit between the two, generated in part by the relatively lowly normative rank occupied by the concept of discipline.

Now Moore and Raymond are aware of the problematic nature of discipline in this context, even claiming it, in the light of Greek debates about the normative status of *sōphrosunē*, as a point in favour of their choice. They diagnose the problem with discipline in terms of its tendency to sound 'rather more a matter of external conformity than of aspirational internal comportment'.[40] But I do not think this gets to the nub of the issue. One can consider discipline as being as much a matter of internal comportment as one likes; that still does not rid it of its modest normative status.

What explains this status, it seems to me, is that we think of discipline as borrowing its normative colour from the ends it is put to serve. If someone has, for example, the discipline to starve themselves to death, we do not necessarily regard such discipline as praiseworthy, just to the extent that we do not approve of the goal for which it was enlisted. Discipline in the service of, say, the winning of an Olympic medal might elicit a rather different evaluative response. And this, I think, indicates in turn that discipline, construed as a kind of focussed attention, occupies the right sort of place, important but limited, in the reading of *sōphrosunē* that I propose.

The focus that Socrates demands for the scrutiny of propositions helps that scrutiny to proceed in as precise and sustained a manner as possible, thereby serving the cause of realising oneself, which, if (but only if) taken as something worth achieving, will lend a commensurately positive glow to the discipline that helps bring it about. The case is no different in principle from, say, the art of medicine as the power to heal. The discipline

[40] Moore and Raymond (2019, xxxvii).

connected with its practice is admirable just to the extent that the aim of the practice is something good. If discipline, even as a kind of internal comportment, still has this derivative normative character, then it cannot match what the *Charmides* regards – insists on – as the unqualifiedly positive polarity of *sōphrosunē*.

If the dialogue's view in this latter respect represents at least one significant strand in the traditional conception, against which debate about its status was mounted, then temperance (let us resume calling it) as the power of self-realisation will bear the kind of relation to discipline that, normatively speaking, one would expect: endowment of the latter with an evaluative status contingent on the goodness of the power's internal goal.

5.7 The Good of Self-Realisation

Is, then, self-realisation a good thing? The question brings us back to Socrates' final assault, with regard to benefit, on the idea of temperance as knowledge of knowledge. After recalling, by way of preface at 173a7–8, Penelope's dream in *Odyssey* 19,[41] Socrates goes on to argue that even if the idea were allowed to imply knowledge of what one does and does not know, the benefits earlier envisaged as arising from that will turn out to be illusory.

First, Socrates recapitulates what they had thought those benefits were in terms of the utopian vision. The recapitulation does not speak, as the original vision did, of 'we who have temperance' ruling, but simply of temperance ruling 'us' (173a8–9) and, if anything, more starkly reveals the problems already inherent in that vision. With the ability in place to detect non-experts who hold themselves out as experts, Socrates asks:

> [W]ould it not follow for us that we would be more healthy in our bodies than currently, and kept safe when in danger at sea and at war, and our tools and clothing and every piece of footwear and all our possessions would have been made expertly (*technikōs*) for us, and many other things besides, because of our using genuine practitioners (*dēmiourgois*)? (173b4–c2)

---

[41] See Sections 2.1 and 5.3. For readings of the reference to the dream in this context, see Witte (1970, 133); Lampert (2010, 216–17; 224), and on its epistemic status Burnyeat (1970, 104). In regard to what I have argued is Socrates' rather cool attitude towards the idea of interpretation, it is noteworthy that in the Homeric original Penelope bids her interlocutor (Odysseus disguised as a beggar) to hear and *interpret* (*hupokrinai*, *Odyssey* 19.535) her dream; Socrates merely tells Critias to 'hear' his dream, whether it has come through horn or ivory. The Platonic text has us, as interpreters, notice what word is missing in Socrates' reprise. The term 'interpret' is also the verb form of the noun (*hupokritēs*) that Socrates used at 162d3 to capture the role of Charmides as (mis) interpreter of Critias; see Section 3.10.

5.7 The Good of Self-Realisation

To the extent that this is a comparative claim (cf. *mallon*, b5) – things would be better than now – it is plausible, since presumably removing the non-experts from the pool of those claiming to be experts would leave no one, in the case of medicine, at the receiving end of bad medical treatment, or in the case of (say) cobblery, of badly made shoes. But it does not follow from temperance, as Socrates puts it, 'forbidding lack of expertise (*anepistēmosunē*) from interfering as a collaborator with us' that 'the human race would act and live knowledgeably' (173c7–d3), at least in the sense that Socrates requires. As before, that simply helps itself, if the vision is to be even prima facie appealing, to the assumption that after the removal of non-experts we will be left with experts of sufficient range and quantity to cover the human race's needs.

In any event, even granting the assumption at full strength, Socrates' fear is now that, contrary to what had previously been agreed, acting knowledgeably would not mean doing well and being happy (173d3–5). Interestingly, Critias is allowed some pushback here (not for the only time in this section), asking Socrates what other way of achieving the goal of doing well would there be if one scorned acting knowledgeably (d6–7). This, however, only facilitates the making of Socrates' point. He asks what form of knowledgeable action is it exactly that would achieve that goal (d8–9). Various mundane crafts such as shoemaking and woodworking are rejected by Critias – perhaps he finds them easy to reject because they are mundane – which enables Socrates to say that it is not, then, the one living knowledgeably in general who is happy, but the one who exercises certain specific forms of knowledge (173d9–e10).

Socrates thence suggests to Critias that even if, to the knowledge of the future possessed by the expert seer, we were to add knowledge of past and present, we would still need to know which areas of such knowledge would make its possessor happy (173e10–174a11). Not all alike, agrees Critias when prompted by Socrates, certainly not knowledge of checkers or of calculation, more so knowledge of health, he says, but most of all knowledge of good and bad (174a11–b10).

Socrates then takes this response and claims that knowledge of good and bad 'is the one that alone' (*mias ousēs tautēs monon*) makes one do well and be happy (174b12–c3). He argues that without this branch of knowledge medicine would still make us healthy, shoemaking make us shod, and so on, but 'that each of these comes about well and beneficially will have abandoned us if this [knowledge of good and bad] is absent' (174c3–d1). Since this, whose job it is to benefit us, rather than knowledge of knowledges and of lack of knowledges, is beneficial, temperance would be something other than the latter (174d3–7).[42]

Here Critias gets his second moment of pushback:

> But why would this not be of benefit? For grant that temperance is as much as you like knowledge of the knowledges, and oversees the other knowledges too; presumably, in ruling over this knowledge concerning the good, it would benefit us. (174d8–e2)

Socrates insists in response that, just as medicine rather than temperance produces health, and each form of expertise (*technē*) has its proprietary job or 'product' (*ergon*), so too it would not be temperance as knowledge of knowledge and of lack of knowledge that produces benefit, but the form of expertise whose proprietary job it is, namely, knowledge of good and bad (174e3–175a4). If temperance is thus not a producer of benefit, it will not on this showing be beneficial (175a6–7).

Let us begin our analysis of Socrates' critique with the second pushback by Critias. Whatever ulterior motive the latter may have, in terms perhaps of his own political ambitions, for a reluctance to see the administrative model of temperance undermined, his actual point seems a good one:[43] temperance would presumably need to oversee knowledge of good and bad as much as it would the other branches of knowledge in order to prevent non-experts in the field from operating. Someone allowed to decide what is good and bad without genuine knowledge of those things would presumably be even more of a public danger than someone allowed to treat patients without knowledge of health and sickness.

That in turn surely suggests that temperance on this model would still be of benefit. After all, it was already clear, before knowledge of good and bad was introduced, that temperance in its oversight role did not *supplant* medicine and the other branches of knowledge. Its role, and therefore the benefit it offered, was the detection of inexpert practitioners in the various fields so they did not get to practise in those fields. From that point of view its benefit remains the same: ensuring that the only practitioners who practise in a given field are experts. And that seems as necessary, if not more so, in relation to purported experts in what is good and bad as it does in relation to their counterparts in the realm of health and sickness and the other branches of knowledge.

---

[42] The text here is murky, but the gist seems clear: if temperance is knowledge of knowledges and lack of knowledges, then it cannot at the same time be beneficial, since benefit is the job (*ergon*) of knowledge of good and bad.

[43] Cf. von Kutschera (2000, 46).

5.7 The Good of Self-Realisation

This, I think, points to an important limitation in Socrates' argument. While it might be right to say that temperance would not itself be a *producer* of benefit on this account – benefit is indeed not its 'product' (*ergon*) – it would remain an *enabler* of benefit, insofar as it prevents the operation of those who, through lack of expertise, would do harm, thus leaving the field clear for the experts alone to operate. This in turn indicates a further potential problem with the argument. It does not in fact show that nothing but knowledge of good and bad *would* produce benefit. Socrates is actually quite careful here. In speaking of temperance as not being a 'producer' (*dēmiourgos*, 175a7) of benefit, he personifies temperance by attaching to it a term that standardly describes a skilled practitioner, that is, a person who in virtue of their expertise is able to produce reliably good outcomes.

This is important because of course it is perfectly possible for someone to produce benefit without being a skilled practitioner in the relevant field. A quack might happen to give a patient the right drug, for example. So Socrates may be making the narrower point that it is the systematic and reliable production of benefit that temperance lacks, insofar as that job is the sole province of the branch of knowledge concerned with good and bad. This in turn, I think, explains Socrates' linkage of the knowledgeable life, albeit subsequently restricted to knowledge of good and bad, with doing well and being happy. His point is not that nothing other than knowledge of good and bad can bring about benefit. It is, rather, that only knowledge of good and bad can produce the systematic and reliable benefit in which the happy life plausibly consists.

What, then, is the relation between knowledge of good and bad and other branches of knowledge such as medicine? It is all very well for Socrates to claim (174e3–175a4) that each field of expertise has its own proprietary product (*ergon*), so that, health being the product of medicine (and not of knowledge of knowledge and lack of knowledge), benefit in turn was allotted to the knowledge of good and bad (and not to the knowledge of knowledge and lack of knowledge). But surely the other branches too produce benefit in a systematic and reliable way? Medicine, for example, produces the benefit of health in that way (cf. 165c10–d2). Indeed, it seems perfectly possible, on Socrates' own conception, to regard knowledge of good and bad as a genus, with branches of knowledge of specific good and bad things (health and sickness, for example) ranged under it, including, as it may be, knowledge of knowledge and of lack of knowledge.

Here, I think, it is noteworthy that Socrates ends up apparently oversimplifying Critias' rather careful replies – betraying a lack of nuance similar to what he had displayed in some of his previous glosses of Critias' statements – on the subject of what it is that makes us do well and be happy. Let us lay out the key steps in this part of the conversation:

- Socrates asks Critias at 174a10–11 whether all branches of knowledge 'alike' (*homoiōs*) make us happy.
- When Critias replies no, Socrates asks which one does so 'most of all' (*malista*, 174b1), offering a number of examples.
- Not knowledge of checkers-playing or calculation, says Critias; knowledge of health 'more so' (*mallon*, 174b8) he says.
- Finally, to Socrates' reiteration of which one does so most of all (*malista*, 174b9), Critias replies: knowledge of good and bad (b10).

Critias' sequence of responses indicates that for him there is a hierarchy of branches of knowledge that contribute to happiness, not necessarily just one. Yet Socrates then states, in mock-accusatory tone,[44] that Critias had all along been 'concealing' (*apokruptomenos*, 174b11–12) – note the familiar imputation of obscurity to Critias – the fact that knowledge of good and bad is 'the only one' (*mias ousēs tautēs monon*, 174c2) that makes us do well and be happy. Concealing it so much, one might retort, that even now Critias has committed himself to no such restrictive an answer.[45] Indeed the implication of what he has said is that medicine makes some contribution to happiness,[46] more than, say, knowledge of how to play checkers (which makes none) but less than knowledge of good and bad.[47]

---

[44] He calls Critias a 'wretch' (as he had done Charmides at 161b8) and charges Critias with dragging him back round in a circle, presumably because of the return of the theme of good and bad; the doing of good things, and not bad ones, was Critias' first attempt unambiguously in his own name to state what temperance is (163e8–11). With knowledge of good and bad, one can ensure that only good things are done.

[45] Cf. Ebert (1974, 80–1). Schofield (2006, 148) is mistaken to say that the view that only knowledge of good and bad can make us happy is something that Critias 'volunteers'. It is Socrates who introduces the idea and gratuitously attributes it to Critias.

[46] Cf. Reshotko (2006, 170), though Reshotko seems to attribute this position to Socrates as well as to Critias. I do not see how one can, with Tuozzo (2001, 338), read Critias' stated view that knowledge of health makes us happy 'more' than does e.g. knowledge of checkers, as amounting to the claim that health is a mere 'analogy' of the human good.

[47] It is therefore odd that Tsouna (2022, 266) calls the idea that different branches of knowledge might contribute to happiness in different degrees 'conspicuous by its absence' in the passage . Critias' response strongly suggests the idea, which is then ignored by Socrates. Tsouna (2022, 265 n. 79) also claims that Socrates' use of *malista* is not intended to mark a difference of degree view but to indicate that one branch of knowledge 'is essentially responsible' for happiness while others may bear on it 'in some contingent way'. No such distinction is drawn in the text; and its flow from

5.7 *The Good of Self-Realisation*

The position of Critias seems quite reasonable. On this view the relation between knowledge of good and bad and (say) medicine might be something like the following: medicine produces, in a reliable and systematic way, health, something which we take to be a major benefit. But we cannot of course *know* that health (or anything else) is such a benefit without knowledge of what is good and bad. Notice that this view is quite compatible with medicine earning its place in Critias' hierarchy by in fact *being* a systematic and reliable producer of benefit of a certain kind (namely, health). It is just that without knowledge of good and bad we cannot know this. So the latter branch of knowledge would make the greatest contribution to happiness in allowing us reliably to identify, across the board, good and bad things respectively.

In this light, let us consider how Socrates defends his more restrictive claim that knowledge of good and bad is the sole producer of happiness. As we have seen, he tells Critias that without such knowledge medicine would no less make us healthy, cobbling no less make us shod, and so on, 'but that each of these things turns out well and beneficially will have abandoned us if this [knowledge of good and bad] is absent' (174c9–d1).

It is hard to know what exactly to make of this statement. But one thing that can be said with relative confidence is that it seems to conclude more than it is entitled to. If things turning out well 'abandoning us' means that, without knowledge of good and bad, things would not in fact turn out well for us, that seems false. Just because, for example, we do not know that health is a benefit does not mean that it is not a benefit or that medicine does not systematically and reliably produce it. If, on the other hand – what seems linguistically less likely – 'abandoning us' just means we will not have epistemic access to whether things turn out well, that seems true but has no tendency to show that things will not in fact turn out well.

Less clear is the matter of what Socrates' precise target is here. The talk of things 'turning out' (*gignesthai*) well and beneficially suggests that Socrates may not be expressing scepticism about the general tendency of a practice such as medicine to produce benefit, insofar as it produces its proprietary product (e.g. health).[48] Rather, his may be a question about

---

homoiōs through *mallon* to *malista* means that, whatever Socrates' intention, the degrees view is in plain sight.

[48] Compare here Tuzzo (2011, 317), who reads health (and other products of the regular practical fields of knowledge) in the *Charmides* as what he calls a 'local good' such that its goodness is 'relative to certain discrete aspects of human being'; so health is a good 'simply insofar as it [human being] is a living body', which Tuozzo contrasts with 'That which is good for the human being as a whole'. It seems to me, however, not to follow from health being a good for me insofar as I have a body, that it

how we are to tell whether producing health is of benefit in specific circumstances (whether, in that sense, it 'turns out' well), for example if one heals a cruel tyrant (or future tyrant) or, more parochially, if the recovered patient is unable to pay their fee.[49]

This reading, as well as being quite natural linguistically, is a better fit for the division of labour envisaged in the administrative context. It would not have the experts in good and bad threatening, as part of their role, an enquiry into whether medicine or cobblery were generally beneficial. Rather, it would have these experts make something more akin to political or administrative decisions, including decisions about who should and should not be recipients of the resources of (say) medical treatment given particular circumstances, where this does not question, but assumes, that medical treatment is, in general, a good thing. It is in this sense that knowledge of good and bad would be the producer of benefit: by administering (say) the practice of medicine so as to maximise, given relevant circumstances, its production of beneficial outcomes.

If that is right, then Socrates' argument leaves the basic status of the various individual branches of knowledge as producers of goods intact. Yet he evidently sees his argument as further undermining the administrative conception of temperance. Even if it is as hard as ever to determine with certainty whether the flaws in the argument are overlooked by Socrates, Plato, or both, it does seem to me that the switch, within a few lines, from knowledge of good and bad 'most of all' making us happy, in the exchange with Critias, to its being the 'only' kind of knowledge to make us happy, in Socrates' conclusion, is so blatant that the author must have expected us to notice and to conclude, I think correctly, that the invocation of knowledge of good and bad does nothing extra to subvert the role of temperance as knowledge of knowledge within the utopian vision. Knowledge of good and bad is one more branch for temperance to supervise. The latter offers benefit, just to the extent that it ever did, by weeding out charlatans in the various fields, including now this additional field. If the utopian vision,

---

is not good for me as a whole. That is, I think, to conflate the notion of the obtaining of a good for me being dependent on a certain part of me existing (my body in the case of physical health) and that good, when it obtains, being good only for that part of me.

[49] I would not regard health on this reading as a 'conditional' good in the sense proposed for the *Charmides* by Tuozzo (in addition to his notion of a 'local' good; see previous note), such that health would only be 'truly beneficial' (2011, 317) – by which Tuozzo seems to mean 'beneficial' – if correctly used. Health, rather, might be called a 'default' good: in general, it brings benefit, though in particular cases it may not do. Separate is the question of how significant (or otherwise) such benefits are conceived to be.

5.7 The Good of Self-Realisation

and the place of temperance within it, is flawed (as I have argued is certainly the case), it carries its flaws over from its earlier appearance.

Socrates is keen – keener, I think, than his present argument justifies – to divorce temperance from its administrative role. Why might that be? One reason, I suggest, is that the administration at issue is predominantly concerned with the bodily and material realm.[50] While the first appearance of the utopian vision at 171d–172a was so abstract as to be devoid of mention of any specific branches of knowledge that temperance would rule, the second at 173a–d has them, or their practitioners, in abundance: navigator, doctor, general (173b1–3); the skilled production of utensils, clothing, footwear (b7–c1); and then the rather harder to classify art of the seer (c3–7). However content Critias may be to allocate knowledge of health an important place in his hierarchy of happiness, this is a vision in which care for our souls as opposed to our material well-being seems conspicuously lacking.[51] Yet Socrates, as we have seen, values souls considerably more than he values bodies.

Whether Socrates sees care for the soul as something that can be scaled up to the political or administrative level is an interesting question but one to which the *Charmides* neither provides nor, I think, suggests an answer.[52] Rather, I have argued, the dialogue points towards consideration of a conception of temperance as (what I have called) self-realisation, at the centre of which, insofar as it is the seat of cognition, lies the soul.[53] One thing that the second appearance of the utopian vision, with its emphasis on the bodily, does, then, is throw into relief the contrast between soul and body and encourage us to seek a way of explicating temperance that would have the soul as its main object. Temperance as self-realisation fits the bill, but – to return to our original question – is it something beneficial?

What the discussion of knowledge of good and bad has shown is that there is no reason to suppose in general that the other various branches of productive knowledge are not still systematic and reliable providers of benefit. If, however, my reading of the role of knowledge of good and bad is correct, then in one important respect knowledge of good and bad is not relevant for temperance as self-realisation. That is because one of the roles of such knowledge is the determination of whether the practice of a particular branch of knowledge will produce benefit in the specific

---

[50] Cf. Dorion (2004, 148–9 n. 194).   [51] Cf. Schofield (2006, 149).
[52] See, however, Adams (2020) for some interesting reflections on the political implications of Socrates' dream.
[53] For a reading of temperance as knowledge of good and bad applied to the care of the agent's own soul, see Clark (2018).

circumstances that obtain. It rests on the idea, plausible enough, that there may be some circumstances in which, say, medical treatment will not produce benefit.

Temperance, by contrast, as Socrates insists, is something good in the specific sense that there cannot be circumstances in which it is bad; recall how the (Homeric) idea that shame could be bad for one ('in need') scuppered Charmides' proposal that temperance is the same thing as shame. This leaves, I think, the following situation in relation to temperance, and here knowledge of good and bad becomes pertinent again: such benefits as one may invoke – for example, on the conception of temperance as self-realisation, being in a position to know what one thinks – must inevitably still be counted as provisional in the absence of knowledge of good and bad.

That is why Socrates, who of course claims no knowledge of good and bad, says simply that he 'intuits' (*manteuomai*) that temperance is something beneficial and good at 169b4–5; and that he 'thinks' (*oiomai*) that it is a great good, that makes its possessor blessed, at 175e6–176a1 when Charmides is brought back into the discussion. Lacking knowledge of good and bad, one cannot pronounce with certainty that temperance is, in Socrates' demanding sense, something good; let alone, if one supposes that it is, that a particular construal of it has captured its goodness.

That, it seems to me, in the context of the *Charmides*, is as it should be. Provisional status implies the need for further investigation. In the absence of knowledge of good and bad, the same applies in principle to the status of any purported good, such as medicine. But if Socrates is right about how great a good temperance is, there seems a special urgency about confirming (or disconfirming) *its* status, as opposed to that of bodily goods such as health.

If we too share the intuition that temperance is something good in this way, then in investigating whether, for example, temperance as self-realisation meets that standard, we attempt to solidify its credentials in this regard as a correct account of what temperance is. But those credentials must wait on a determination of whether temperance is something good; and that determination is ultimately delivered by knowledge of good and bad. This is not to say that the investigation of what goodness is proceeds in splendid isolation. The exploration of what things are good, and why, itself provides material for an informed view of what goodness is. That view then influences what things we consider as good. In this reflective process propositions must, as ever, stand before the tribunal of scrutiny together.

Is self-realisation something good? If, like the strange ideas that appear before Socrates, we are sufficiently intrigued not to let the question fall by the wayside, then in trying to figure out what we think about the question, we seem to affirm the value of self-realisation just insofar as we become aware of ourselves as motivated to undertake that very thing – scrutiny of propositions – in which the process of self-realisation consists. It is, I have argued, a refrain of the *Charmides*, and a product of the way it is written, that it leads its readers into the occupation of a stance of critical enquiry. Rather than seek to promote that stance by arguing directly for its value, the dialogue aspires to show us to ourselves as valuers of such enquiry by having us see ourselves drawn to undertake it.

5.8 The Return of Eros

With the administrative conception of temperance dealt, as Socrates sees it, a further blow, and the enquiry having overtly failed to produce a satisfactory account of temperance, it is time for Socrates to bring Charmides back into the discussion, addressing him at 175d, for the first time since 162b, and lamenting the prospect of the latter being most temperate, yet temperance being of no benefit, together with the resultant worthlessness of the Thracian charm (175d6–e5). But Socrates swiftly rallies to the view that instead he is just a feeble enquirer and that temperance is in fact a great good, and that if Charmides has it he is blessed (175e5–176a1). He bids Charmides see (once again) if he has it and has no need of the charm, and if he does have it, to regard Socrates as talking nonsense and being incapable of conducting an enquiry; and to regard himself as happy in proportion to his being temperate (176a1–5).

Charmides exclaims that he cannot know if he has temperance when even Socrates and Critias are unable to discover what it is, adding that he doesn't really believe Socrates and considers himself very much in need of the charm, willing in fact to be charmed by Socrates for as many days as the latter deems sufficient (176a6–b4). Critias, drolly punning on the key term, tells Charmides that submitting himself to be charmed by Socrates and not deserting him will be evidence that 'you are sound' (*sōphroneis*, 176b6). Charmides says that it would be wrong of him to disobey orders issued by his guardian; and when Socrates, as if out of earshot for this exchange despite reporting it,[54] asks what the two have been plotting, Charmides replies that the plot is hatched, and then, in response to

[54] Cf. Morgan (2021, 162).

Socrates' mock-plaintive plea, that he will force Socrates to comply with what Critias commands without so much as a hearing (176b9–c8). When Socrates then comments that no one can resist Charmides when he uses force, Charmides advises him not to resist, and Socrates says he will not (176d1–5).

With this remarkable vignette of Plato's dramatic art, the dialogue closes, poised beautifully if uneasily between the flirtatiousness of the surface exchange and the grim foreboding with which, as we saw earlier,[55] its language – with the talk of plot, force and command – predicts the brutal regime of the Thirty, still twenty-five years or so in the future in relation to the dialogue's dramatic date. These two aspects, the flirtatiousness and the foreboding, perhaps need some separating out, though we shall see in the end that they are to some extent intertwined.[56]

The return to Charmides offers a kind of instant relaxation of the pressure built up by the intense enquiry that Socrates had just carried out with Critias. With Charmides reintroduced, there is a sense of panning out, a revealing thereby that Socrates' interest in Charmides has not abated and a suspicion that the discussion with Critias, far from being free-standing once underway, was aimed from afar at having an effect on Charmides. That effect is, I think, clear: Charmides, so eager before to avoid Socratic scrutiny that he refused to continue examining his own soul and deflected to Critias' proposal about temperance instead, is now keen to re-engage with Socrates and be charmed by him indefinitely.

A gratifying result for Socrates. He dropped Charmides in favour of Critias, not (I have argued) in order to move on from Charmides, but to show him what he was missing by his refusal to put his soul on the line. Having impressed him with the intellectual fireworks on display in his discussion with Critias – Socrates' powers now shown to Charmides as concrete reality rather than reputational hearsay (cf. 156a6–7) – Socrates has Charmides where he wants him, ready to expose his soul to Socrates' charms for as long as Socrates wishes.[57] This, it seems to me, is a triumph of the art of erotics as practised by Socrates. His combination of brusque

---

[55] Section 2.5.
[56] Certainly, one cannot rule out that there is sexual as well as political violence hinted at in Charmides' closing remarks; cf. Schofield (2000, 190–1). Note, however, that these would be at different levels: the sexual internal to the erotic drama, the political a future historical reality known only to Plato and his readers; cf. Section 2.5.
[57] One might see a certain symmetry here. At 155a4 Socrates urged Critias to call Charmides over and 'display' (*epideixas*) the young man to him; in return, Socrates has put on quite the display for Charmides.

5.8 The Return of Eros

abandonment of Charmides, long virtuoso display with Critias, and only then re-engagement, has manipulated Charmides into falling for him.

If that is on point, then a passage in Plato's *Symposium*, perhaps the only one in another Platonic work that incontrovertibly suggests a reference to the *Charmides*, offers corroboration. In the course of his encomium of Socrates Alcibiades says the following:

> He [Socrates] has done this not only to me, but also to Charmides the son of Glaucon and Euthydemus the son of Diocles and very many others; this man presents himself to them deceptively as lover (*erastēs*) but turns out, rather, as himself beloved instead of lover. (*Symposium* 222b1–4)

It is hard to resist the thought that Alcibiades' reference to Charmides is to be read as a Platonic allusion to the *Charmides*.[58] And what Alcibiades describes Socrates doing to Charmides is rather like what, on my reading, he does do to Charmides in the eponymous dialogue. Starting by presenting himself as a lover of Charmides, he has Charmides end up falling for him as purveyor of beautiful words.[59]

As always with Plato, however, assessing such an allusion is not a straightforward matter. Indeed, if I read the horizontal structure of the *Charmides* correctly, Alcibiades' summary of Socrates' machinations is not quite accurate. Socrates desired and still desires Charmides alright.[60] It is by placing Charmides in thrall to him that Socrates has increased the chances of getting at a beautiful soul to satisfy his erotic desire. One should, contra Alcibiades, read Socrates and Charmides as lovers and beloveds alike.

If so, then we have a ready explanation for Alcibiades' 'inaccuracy'. Alcibiades himself of course is not referring to Plato's *Charmides*. But Plato, through the medium of Alcibiades' words, almost certainly is. And with his characteristic dramatic care, Plato has those words come out in line with the personality of their speaker. Not untypically of his speech as besotted lover in the *Symposium*, Alcibiades here paints a portrait of Socrates that is insightful if somewhat overwrought. In particular, Alcibiades' experience of Socrates' apparent indifference to his physical charms (*Symposium* 217a–219d) has no doubt created in that excitable

---

[58] Cf. McAvoy (1996, 90 n. 61); Reece (1998, 72).
[59] On the erotic table-turning see Lewis (1982–3, 161); Halperin (1986, 69 with n. 23); Edmonds (2000, 281–2); Scott (2000, 4–7); McPherran (2004, 24); Petre (2007, 50); Morgan (2021, 162–3).
[60] So Morgan (2021, 163).

character's mind the idea that Socrates is simply intent on inverting the lover–beloved relation. If my reading of the *Charmides* is right, Socrates is a little more complex than that.

One thing that does seem to have become clearer between Charmides' leaving and his rejoining the conversation is that finding beauty in Charmides' soul will be a matter of making his soul beautiful rather than having a beautiful soul already there to behold. Socrates having deployed the art of erotics to render Charmides willing once more to expose his soul, the motif of delivering the charm indicates that to all intents and purposes Charmides is no longer taken (including by himself) as possessing temperance to an adequate degree. Socrates' task, then, is to practise the art of soul-medicine in such a way as to instil temperance in Charmides' soul, making it beautiful thereby.

As I have interpreted it, instilling temperance in a subject is a matter of developing the subject's power of self-realisation, that is to say, the power to critically examine propositions so as to determine what it is that one thinks. Once Charmides has been helped to develop that power through conversation with Socrates, he will be in a position to take the lead himself and exercise the power in a more autonomous way, without the need of a Socrates. It is, after all, as a rule, a poor doctor who never weans his patients from dependence on treatment.

What this no doubt means is that the process of developing Charmides' powers of self-realisation will consist in Socrates engaging him in critical discussion of the sort we have seen displayed at an advanced level with Critias. That suggests in turn that there will be significant continuity, in terms both of process and content, between the practice of soul-medicine and the exercise of temperance. This, I think, is exactly what one should expect. After all, the practice of soul-medicine, insofar as it instils temperance, is essentially the development of the subject's powers of self-realisation. If the process of self-realisation consists in the critical examination of propositions, then it is natural that preparation of the subject for the autonomous practice of that process would consist to a large extent in engaging the subject in that process until their powers are sufficiently developed to be exercised autonomously.

It is evident that, for the subject in training, the process may be an arduous one. In that regard it retains its affinity with medical treatment. But there is a crucial difference. In the medical case the arduousness may be entirely passive, the treatment consisting in things that are done to one. That one's body may – perhaps must if the treatment is to be successful – actively respond in various ways to the treatment does not itself,

5.8 The Return of Eros

interestingly, incline us to say any the less in such a scenario that one is having things done to one rather than actively responding.[61]

In the case of the soul it is different. If soul-medicine is to work, then in his conversations with Socrates, Charmides will have to follow intently, and engage in wholeheartedly, the scrutiny of propositions. Without such active participation, it is hard to see how he can develop his own powers of scrutiny appropriately. And here one must register some doubt not so much about how willing Charmides is to make the effort but about whether he has any conception of what the treatment requires from him in the first place.

To approach this point, let us look more closely at Charmides' response to Socrates' invitation to him to see if he has temperance and does not need the charm. Charmides declares:

> But by Zeus, Socrates, I for my part (*egōge*) do not know if I have it or not. For how would I know, when even the two of you are unable to discover what on earth it is, or so you say. (176a6–b1)

Charmides' addition of the fateful words 'or so you say (*hōs phēis su*)', the second-person singular 'you' contrasting with the plural form of 'you (*humeis*) are unable' earlier in the sentence, shows that the remark is addressed specifically to Socrates. Socrates had indeed labelled himself a poor enquirer; and while one may bridle at this label (though Socrates is, as we have seen, by no means a flawless enquirer), it is quite another thing to suppose, as Charmides appears to, that Socrates really does have up his sleeve knowledge of what temperance is that he has chosen not to reveal. It is as if Charmides regards Socrates' aporetic discussion with Critias as *just* a display and no more.

I think we can make sense of Charmides' stance if we recall the erotic context and consider how Charmides' speech continues. It contains, within the space of a few lines, multiple occurrences of 'I' and 'you' (second-person singular) and cognates, as Charmides declares his need to be charmed by Socrates:

> But I (*egō*) do not really believe you (*soi*); and myself (*emauton*), Socrates, I consider very much in need of the charm, and for my part at least (*to g'emon*) nothing stands in the way of being charmed by you (*sou*) until you (*su*) say it is enough. (176b1–4)

---

[61] There are implications here for how we should conceive of the relation between the body and the self, though note also the active role for the patient undergoing treatment apparently envisaged in the Hippocratic corpus; see Section 3.8.

Charmides' language, in its lavish use of these pronouns, bespeaks a youth who regards himself and Socrates as, just for the moment, the only two people in the world,[62] with Critias pointedly if temporarily out of the picture. Tsouna cannot, I think, therefore be right to say that Charmides 'endeavours to associate with Socrates chiefly because he anticipates his guardian's wishes ... it is doubtful that he values Socrates' company and conversation in its own right' (Tsouna 2022, 294). Though his subsequent pledge of obedience to Critias is no doubt supposed to strike the reader as disquieting, the intensity of the you-and-me language that Charmides directs at Socrates, and its exclusionary force in regard to Critias, is not explicable merely as the product of a desire to please the latter.

Charmides is a willing player of the game. He knows that he is being seduced by Socrates via the display that the latter has put on with Critias, and as the sequel highlights, he is not at all unhappy about that. Whether Charmides thinks that only someone who did know what temperance was could mount such a display, given that temperance is its subject-matter, is a further question. It may, at any rate, be natural for the recipient of a seduction ritual to assume that the relationship itself will not consist in variations of that ritual on continuous loop. In this, Charmides is in danger of being gravely mistaken. He will, as his core treatment, have to participate, for as long as Socrates deems fit, in something akin to the process that Socrates had taken pains to represent to him in his discussion with Critias.

This suggests a potentially yawning gap between what Charmides expects, even as he embraces the prospect of ongoing Socratic attention, and what in all likelihood he is going to get.[63] If he thinks that Socrates really does know what temperance is, then he may regard the delivery of the charm as consisting in his being taught something by someone who already knows. This, he may not unreasonably expect, might be a process of a rather gentler and less demanding type than the one he has just witnessed (and even the one that he earlier participated in). Given that gap in expectation, it would be no surprise if Charmides' enthusiasm for engaging with Socrates does not survive, and that consequently, as in any relationship where expectations are thwarted, a certain frustration and disillusionment ensue.

---

[62] Socrates had himself addressed Charmides in similar me-and-you vein in his immediately preceding speech (*egōge soi ... eme ... seauton*, 176a2–4).

[63] Sufficient, I think, to render dubitable the claim made by Wolfsdorf (2008, 218) that Charmides here 'demonstrates a genuinely philosophical attitude'.

5.8 The Return of Eros

That of course is speculation. What we know historically is that Charmides met his fate as a servant of the regime of the Thirty, one of whose principal leaders was Critias. Charmides' stance of staunch obedience to his cousin's orders (cf. 176b9–c8) apparently carries through, at least in this regard, to the end. I argued above that were Charmides to prove unequal to the task of treatment, that would be no great blow to Socrates.[64] His interest in Charmides extends only insofar as the latter offers the prospect of having, or coming to have, a beautiful soul. If he fails to have or to develop one, or if (for example) death in battle removes him, and it, from the scene, Socrates can move on to other targets.

If, on the other hand, the treatment does succeed, then Socrates must expect that Charmides will still want to engage with him – as Socrates engages with others – even when he is capable of autonomous practice. For one key feature of my interpretation has been that the fundamental way that Socrates relates to Charmides is not as (soul-)doctor to patient but as subject of erotic desire to object of such desire; making Charmides desire him is a way of securing Charmides' continued availability. In Socrates' engagement with Charmides, soul-medicine is subordinate to the art of erotics.

The point of the enterprise is that Charmides, in contrast to the situation in which he were simply occupying the role of patient, not desert Socrates when treatment is finished (cf. 176b7–8). For it is then that Socrates will have brought into being the beautiful soul, engagement with which was, for him, the treatment's objective. Not, to be sure, a perfectly beautiful soul, since self-realisation is a lifelong process (Section 5.5). The question, after all, was whether Charmides is *sufficiently* temperate (158b–c); and even at the end Socrates speaks in comparative terms: the more temperate Charmides is, the happier (176a4–5). That, intuitively, does not prevent one becoming beautiful in soul any less than the recipient of medical treatment becomes healthy in body. Perfection is not the yardstick. No bad thing if Socrates had been able to say to Charmides: you become more beautiful every day (cf. 176b3–4). It is, then, as I suggested above, not that Charmides is Socrates' only option; but losing him just when he comes to develop a beautiful soul would be a wasted effort nonetheless. The art of erotics will need to be watchful during, and beyond, Charmides' treatment.

---

[64] See Section 2.5. I cannot, however, quite concur with Tsouna's (2022, 297) view that the close of the dialogue shows a Socrates who seems 'indifferent to the prospect of keeping Charmides close to him and enchanting him with *logoi*'. Socrates need not have brought Charmides back into the conversation at all, nor reintroduced the question of whether or not he needs the charm; that he does both does not sound like indifference.

5.9 Plato versus Socrates

It is here, I think, that one can see a substantial contrast between Socrates' engagement with Charmides and Plato's engagement with his reader. Plato's aim, I have argued, is to stimulate us readers into occupying a stance of critical enquiry, in which we too find ourselves scrutinising propositions in order to determine what it is that we think. Once his written words have achieved that aim, we can and should exercise our power of scrutiny autonomously. Plato does not see his relationship with his readers as an erotic one in the way that Socrates, as I set out above and in Chapter 3, sees his relationship with Charmides. If Socrates is to some extent invested in Charmides not straying, Plato has no stake in our cleaving to the *Charmides* once it has, to the extent that it can, enabled us to practise as autonomous thinkers.

In that sense Plato, I suspect, wishes to represent himself as more purely the soul-doctor than Socrates, despite the fact that Plato must practise his art remotely. And this in turn serves to reflect the core difference between Plato and his character Socrates: Plato is formally absent from his readership, utilising the medium of the written word, while Socrates conducts himself through direct oral engagement with his interlocutors. If my argument in this book has been correct, the *Charmides* should be seen, in the effects it purports to induce in us and in the techniques it uses to achieve those effects, as a written work committed to vindicating its own medium as a stimulus for critical reflection.

This may, finally, mean that, when it comes to his readers' relationship with his written work, the erotic dimension is not intended by Plato to be altogether absent. The *Charmides* is, I have argued, a work that possesses a complex but coherent structure. If so, then it will itself rank as something beautiful that, as such, demands our focussed attention. The text encourages us in the right way to direct our attention if it does have that status, namely, to engage in critical discussion with it. We are to use the work for doing philosophy with, rather than objectify it as a beautiful representation of philosophy done. In that critical engagement, as I have tried to emphasise, we show ourselves participating in the process of self-realisation and acknowledging the value of doing so.

CHAPTER 6

Conclusion
The *Charmides* as a Written Work

In the preceding chapters I have tried to discharge, in regard to the *Charmides*, what I take to be the basic obligation of any interpreter: the offering of a coherent and well-supported reading of the text. Regardless of how successfully, in the present case, this has been achieved, with a work as rich and intricate as the *Charmides* there are many interpretations, and many kinds of interpretation, capable of fitting the bill. That being so, it seemed important to place my reading within a framework that governed the interpretive choices in a transparent and intelligible way. In this concluding chapter I would like briefly to revisit that framework and in so doing offer some final thoughts on the status of the *Charmides* as a written work.

The framework I adopted consists of two main, related, elements, as set out in Chapter 1. The first is a pair of interpretive principles: the principle of agnosticism and the principle of separation. Agnosticism – the idea that we attempt to read the *Charmides*, and in particular the character of Socrates, as independently as possible from what we (think we) know about what goes on in other works of Plato – had, to simplify a little, a ground-clearing role. In order to take Socrates as we find him in the *Charmides*, it seemed prudent to start by avoiding the importation of assumptions that might cause us to prejudge the figure depicted in that work. Separation – the idea that one should not by default identify the aims and methods of Plato the author with those of Socrates his character (or with any other character) – had a more positive orientation. It encouraged us to look carefully at Socrates' aims and methods in their own right, without need to take these as either shared or endorsed by Plato in his writing of the work.

The second element of my interpretive framework is the identification of two dimensions, which I termed respectively horizontal and vertical, along which to delineate the structure of the work. I hope it is fairly clear how these two dimensions are reflected in the two interpretive principles, and how some interpretive dividends may result from the application of the principles in this context. With agnosticism in place, we are free to look in an unmediated way, when considering the horizontal dimension of the *Charmides*, at how Socrates' motives are presented therein. His fundamental motive in the work is, I have argued, an erotic one, manifested in particular as the pursuit of beauty in Charmides' soul. This construal provides the resources for an account, at one level, of the unity of the dialogue. As outlined in Section 1.8, at the level of Socrates' engagement with his interlocutors we can see the sequential flow from the Charmides section through the Critias section to the final section as the playing out of Socrates' erotic quest.

By the principle of separation, such a motive on Socrates' part may, however, be different from Plato's purposes in constructing the dialogue in that way. To understand those purposes, we had to tackle the question of what, at the level of Plato's engagement with his readers, the Charmides section is really doing. If, as some scholars have thought, the main business of the work does not get going until as late as some way into the Critias section, then we have a rather puzzling and lopsided structure to contend with. The earlier material may well function as a preamble to the later, but how exactly does it do so? I addressed this issue in Chapter 2 by arguing that there are a number of features of the material of the Charmides section that function, both thematically and in mode of composition, to induce the reader into occupying what I called the stance of enquiry; that is, an attitude of critical scrutiny towards what is said that prepares us to engage with the complex material found in the discussion with Critias. Indeed, I tried to show that a principal aim of Plato in constructing the *Charmides* as he does is to prompt us to occupy that stance, and to see ourselves as doing so. Only having made a case for this reading of Plato's objectives did I turn to a more detailed account, in Chapter 3, of Socrates' own motives and their place in the overall unity of the dialogue.

By attending to its vertical structure, I thus hope to have shown that one can offer a unified account of the work both at the level of Plato's engagement with his readers and at the level of Socrates' engagement with his interlocutors. In themselves these are separate accounts, imputing a purpose to Plato in engaging with his readers that is not the same as that of Socrates in engaging with his interlocutors. This is not something that need cause consternation. One thing I have tried to emphasise is that it follows from the principle of separation that one should not necessarily expect Plato's purposes as author to coincide with Socrates' purposes as leading character. Indeed, given the basic fact that Plato conducts his business by composing a written work and Socrates conducts his, within the drama, by oral conversation, there is no reason to think that the purposes of the two should coincide.

Nonetheless, it seems to fair to ask, in terms of the work's overall unity, what connection there is between these two levels. And here I have tried to make the case, particularly in Chapter 4, that there is dialogue between the levels that revolves precisely around the differences in communicative medium that Plato and Socrates respectively employ. For those who suppose that Plato is an uncomplicated advocate of how Socrates operates, there is an immediate tension. If oral conversation is how things should be done, then what is Plato doing devoting his energies to writing such an intricately crafted written work? Surely, on this view, his time would be better spent being faithful to Socrates' chosen medium rather than forging a path as an author.

My proposal is that Plato does not, in writing the *Charmides*, show himself to be an uncritical admirer of the Socratic approach. As illustrated in Chapters 3 and 4, there is evidence, especially if one examines the role of Critias, whose historical counterpart was a noted author and who has a penchant within the dialogue for quoting and interpreting written texts, that Plato is engaged in a complex discussion about the nature of interpretation, one in which Socrates' own attitude, in that regard, is found wanting. Indeed, I have suggested that at key moments Socrates is shown as disdainful towards the business of interpretation, and that we are supposed to notice this and reflect critically on it. Critias, by contrast, has a habit of earnest but florid over-interpretation; but one does not evade the necessity of interpretation by neglecting, in the Socratic manner, to engage seriously in it.

Plato, it seems to me, between his respective depictions in this fashion of Socrates and of Critias, attempts to carve out a space for the written word (and work) to function as a stimulus for critical reflection. The Socratic approach, remarkable though it is, does not have all the best tunes when it comes to the conduct of enquiry; perhaps it even has some shortcomings. A written work may, in its content and construction, offer richer prospects than oral dialogue for interpretive engagement and the progress of enquiry. The *Charmides*, I have argued, in both form and content, suggests this view of itself and urges us to do the proper business of interpretation by engaging critically with it.

My own interpretive engagement with the dialogue's central enquiry into the nature of temperance was set out in Chapter 5, via a reading of temperance as (what I called) the art of self-realisation. I shall not revisit the detail of that reading here; it will be for others to judge its merits. What I would like to emphasise, in closing, is that my reading is meant as an example of a *critical* response to the dialogue. Socrates mounts an intensive assault on the various proposals put forth about what temperance is. I do not myself see what he does here as an example of 'positive elenchus',[1] insofar as this means that we are supposed to move towards some truer grasp possessed by Socrates of what temperance is.[2] Rather, it is Plato who constructs the work in such a way as to encourage us to adopt a critical stance towards what Socrates says. A more positive account than anything Socrates is made to deliver represents a critical response to his arguments, not an exercise in closing in on a more enlightened Socratic state.

Readers must now be left to formulate, as I hope they will, their own critical responses to what I have written. Whether favourable or not, I like to imagine I am at least doing right by Plato in inviting them.

---

[1] I borrow the phrase from the subtitle of Tuozzo (2011).

[2] Tuozzo (2011, 49) describes this conception, which he takes to apply to the *Charmides*, as 'an attempt on the questioner's part to move the interlocutor to greater insight into the truth ... [t]his requires that the questioner himself know the truth towards which he is guiding the interlocutor – or at least that he should have progressed farther toward it than his interlocutor has'; Plato's purpose is in turn 'to show how the process of elenchus can, in Socrates' hands, bring his interlocutors some distance toward the truth, and to provide materials for the philosophical reader to go some distance further in that direction'.

References

Adamietz, J. (1969). 'Zur Erklärung des Hauptteils von Platons *Charmides* (164a–175d)', *Hermes* 97, 37–57.
Adams, D. (2020). 'Refutation, Democracy and Epistemocracy in Plato's *Charmides*', *Méthexis* 32, 26–44.
Ahbel-Rappe, S. (2018). *Socratic Ignorance and Platonic Knowledge in the Dialogues of Plato*. Albany: State University of New York Press.
Alshanetsky, E. (2019). *Articulating a Thought*. Oxford: Oxford University Press.
Altman, W. (2010). '*Laches* before *Charmides*: Fictive Chronology and Platonic Pedagogy', *Plato Journal* 10, 1–28.
Ambury, J. and German, A. (eds.) (2019). *Knowledge and Ignorance of Self in Platonic Philosophy*. Cambridge: Cambridge University Press.
Annas, J. (1985). 'Self-Knowledge in Early Plato', in D. O'Meara (ed.), *Platonic Investigations*. Washington DC: The Catholic University of America Press, 111–38.
Arthos, J. (1959). 'Milton, Ficino and the *Charmides*', *Studies in the Renaissance* 6, 261–74.
Ayalon, N. (2018). '"Exactly as you see me" (*Charmides* 153b8): The Function of Narration in Plato's *Charmides*', *Journal of Ancient Philosophy* 12, 179–91.
Balaban, O. (2008). 'Le rejet de la connaissance de la connaissance, la thèse centrale du *Charmide* de Platon', *Revue philosophique de Louvain* 106, 663–93.
Barker, A. (1995). 'Problems in the *Charmides*', *Prudentia* 27, 18–33.
Barney, R. (2010). 'Notes on Plato on the *Kalon* and the Good', *Classical Philology* 105, 363–77.
Benardete, S. (2000). 'On Interpreting Plato's *Charmides*', in *The Argument of the Action: Essays on Greek Poetry and Philosophy*. Chicago: University of Chicago Press, 231–56.
Bengson, J. and Moffett, M. (2011). *Knowing How: Essays on Knowledge, Mind, and Action*. Oxford: Oxford University Press.
Benson, H. (2000). *Socratic Wisdom: The Model of Knowledge in Plato's Early Dialogues*. New York: Oxford University Press.
  (2003). 'A Note on Socratic Self-Knowledge in the *Charmides*', *Ancient Philosophy* 23, 31–47.

Beversluis, J. (2000). *Cross-Examining Socrates: A Defense of the Interlocutors in Plato's Early Dialogues.* Cambridge: Cambridge University Press.

Bloch, G. (1973). *Platons Charmides: Die Erscheinung des Seins im Gespräch.* PhD dissertation, Tübingen.

Blondell, R. (2002). *The Play of Character in Plato's Dialogues.* Cambridge: Cambridge University Press.

Blyth, D. (2001), 'Tyrannical Power in Plato's *Charmides*', in D. Baltzly, D. Blyth and H. Tarrant (eds.), *Power and Pleasure, Virtues and Vices.* Auckland: Prudentia suppl., 35–53.

Bommarito, N. (2013). 'Modesty as a Virtue of Attention', *Philosophical Review* 122, 93–117.

Bowery, A.-M. (2007). 'Know Thyself: Socrates as Storyteller', in G. Scott (ed.), 82–110.

Boys-Stones, G. (2019). 'Order and Orderliness: The Myth of "Inner Beauty" in Plato', in P. Horky (ed.), *Cosmos in the Ancient World.* Cambridge: Cambridge University Press, 108–21.

Brann, E. (2004). 'The Tyrant's Temperance: *Charmides*', in *The Music of the Republic: Essays on Socrates' Conversations and Plato's Writings.* Philadelphia: Paul Dry Books, 66–87.

Brennan, T. (2006). 'Socrates and Epictetus', in S. Ahbel-Rappe and R. Kamtekar (eds.), *A Companion to Socrates.* Oxford: Blackwell, 285–97.

(2012). 'The Implicit Refutation of Critias', *Phronesis* 57, 240–50.

Brisson, L. (2021). 'The Prologue of the *Charmides*', in Kaklamanou, Pavlou and Tsakmakis (eds.), 63–9.

Brittain, C. (2017). '*Deinos* (Wicked Good) at Interpretation (*Protagoras* 334–48)', in V. Harte and R. Woolf (eds.), *Re-reading Ancient Philosophy: Old Chestnuts and Sacred Cows.* Cambridge: Cambridge University Press, 32–59.

Brouwer, M. and Polansky, R. (2004) 'The Logic of Socratic Inquiry: Illustrated by Plato's *Charmides*', in V. Karasmanis (ed.), *Socrates: 2400 Years since His Death.* Athens: European Cultural Centre of Delphi, 233–45.

Brown, L. (2018). 'Rethinking Agreement in Plato', in D. Brink, S. Sauvé Meyer and C. Shields (eds.), *Virtue, Happiness, Knowledge: Themes from the Work of Gail Fine and Terence Irwin.* Oxford: Oxford University Press, 18–31.

Bruell, C. (1977). 'Socratic Politics and Self-Knowledge: An Interpretation of Plato's *Charmides*', *Interpretation* 6, 141–203.

Burger, R. (2013). 'Socrates' Odyssean Return: On Plato's *Charmides*', in C. Dustin and D. Schaeffer (eds.), *Socratic Philosophy and its Others.* Plymouth: Lexington Books, 217–35.

Burnyeat, M. F. (1970). 'The Material and Sources of Plato's Dream', *Phronesis* 15, 101–22.

(1971). 'Virtues in Action', in G. Vlastos (ed.), *The Philosophy of Socrates: A Collection of Critical Essays.* London: Macmillan, 209–34, reprinted in Burnyeat (2012), 205–23.

(1977). 'Socratic Midwifery, Platonic Inspiration', *Bulletin of the Institute of Classical Studies* 24, 7–16, reprinted in Burnyeat (2012), 21–35.
(1985). 'Sphinx without a Secret', *New York Review of Books*, 30 May 1985, 30–6, reprinted in Burnyeat (2012), 289–304.
(1997). 'First Words: A Valedictory Lecture', *Proceedings of the Cambridge Philological Society* 43, 1–20, reprinted in Burnyeat (2012), 305–26.
(2012). *Explorations in Ancient and Modern Philosophy*, vol. 2. Cambridge: Cambridge University Press.
Cairns, D. (1993). *Aidōs: The Psychology and Ethics of Honour and Shame in Ancient Greek Literature*. Oxford: Oxford University Press.
Carone, G. (1998). 'Socrates' Human Wisdom and *sophrosune* in *Charmides* 164c ff.', *Ancient Philosophy* 18, 267–86.
Caston, V. (2002). 'Aristotle on Consciousness', *Mind* 111, 751–815.
Chen, C.-H. (1978). 'On Plato's *Charmides* 165c4–175d5', *Apeiron* 12, 13–28.
Clark, J. (2018). 'Knowledge and Temperance in Plato's *Charmides*', *Pacific Philosophical Quarterly* 99, 763–89.
Coolidge, F. (1993). 'The Relation of Philosophy to σωφροσύνη: Zalmoxian Medicine in Plato's *Charmides*', *Ancient Philosophy* 13, 23–36.
(1995). 'On the Grounds for Aristocracy and the Rejection of Philosophy: A Reflection on Plato's *Charmides*', *Journal of Speculative Philosophy* 9, 208–28.
Cooper, J. (2004). 'Method and Science in *On Ancient Medicine*', in *Knowledge, Nature, and the Good: Essays in Ancient Philosophy*. Princeton: Princeton University Press, 3–42.
Corey, D. (2008). 'Prodicus: Diplomat, Sophist and Teacher of Socrates', *History of Political Thought* 29, 1–26.
Dancy, R. (2004). *Plato's Introduction of Forms*. Cambridge: Cambridge University Press.
Danzig, G. (2013). 'Plato's *Charmides* as a Political Act: Apologetics and the Promotion of Ideology', *Greek, Roman, and Byzantine Studies* 53, 486–519.
(2014). 'The Use and Abuse of Critias: Conflicting Portraits in Plato and Xenophon', *Classical Quarterly* 64, 507–24.
Davidson, D. (1973). 'Radical Interpretation', *Dialectica* 27, 313–28.
(2004). 'Expressing Evaluations', in *Problems of Rationality*. Oxford: Oxford University Press, 19–37.
Dean-Jones, L. (2003). 'Literacy and the Charlatan in Ancient Greek Medicine', in H. Yunis (ed.), *Written Texts and the Rise of Literate Culture in Ancient Greece*. Cambridge: Cambridge University Press, 97–121.
Dieterle, R. (1966). *Platons Laches und Charmides: Untersuchungen zur elenktisch-aporetischen Struktur der platonischen Frühdialoge*. (PhD dissertation, Freiburg).
Dorion, L.-A. (2004). *Platon: Charmide, Lysis*. Paris: Flammarion.
Dover, K. (1989). *Greek Homosexuality*. Cambridge MA: Harvard University Press.
Doyle, J. (2010). 'Socrates and Gorgias', *Phronesis* 55, 1–25.

Duncombe, M. (2020). *Ancient Relativity*. Oxford: Oxford University Press.
Dušanić, S. (2000). 'Critias in the *Charmides*', *Aevum* 74, 53–63.
Dyson, M. (1974). 'Some Problems Concerning Knowledge in Plato's *Charmides*', *Phronesis* 19, 102–11.
Ebert, T. (1974). *Meinung und Wissen in der Philosophie Platons*. Berlin: De Gruyter.
Edmonds, R. (2000). 'Socrates the Beautiful: Role Reversal and Midwifery in Plato's *Symposium*', *Transactions of the American Philological Association* 130, 261–85.
Effe, B. (1971). 'Platons *Charmides* und der *Alkibiades* des Aischines von Sphettos', *Hermes* 99, 198–208.
Evans, G. (1982). *The Varieties of Reference*. Oxford: Clarendon Press.
Faraone, C. (2010). 'A Socratic Leaf Charm for Headache (*Charmides* 155b–157c), Orphic Gold Leaves, and the Ancient Greek Tradition of Leaf Amulets', in J. Dijkstra, J. Kroesen, and Y. Kuiper (eds.), *Myths, Martyrs, and Modernity: Studies in the History of Religions in Honour of Jan N. Bremmer*. Leiden: Brill, 145–66.
Fine, G. (ed.) (2019). *The Oxford Handbook of Plato* (2nd ed.). New York: Oxford University Press.
Finkelberg, M. (2019). *The Gatekeeper: Narrative Voice in Plato's Dialogues*. Leiden: Brill.
Flamigni, G. (2017). *Presi per incantamento: Teoria della persuasione socratica*. Pisa: Edizioni ETS.
Francalanci, C. (2020). 'Love, Speech and Charm in Plato's *Charmides*: Reading the Dialogue through Emotions', in L. Candiotto and O. Renault (eds.), *Emotions in Plato*. Leiden: Brill, 186–98.
Frede, M. (1987). 'Philosophy and Medicine in Antiquity', in *Essays in Ancient Philosophy*. Oxford: Oxford University Press, 225–42.
  (1992). 'Plato's Arguments and the Dialogue Form', in J. Klagge and N. Smith (eds.), *Methods of Interpreting Plato and His Dialogues*. Oxford Studies in Ancient Philosophy supplement.
Garver, E. (2018). 'Charmides and the Virtue of Opacity: An Early Chapter in the History of the Individual', *Review of Metaphysics* 71, 469–500.
Gerson, L. (2013). *From Plato to Platonism*. Ithaca and London: Cornell University Press.
Gill, C. (2006). *The Structured Self in Hellenistic and Roman Thought*. Oxford: Oxford University Press.
Gonzalez, F. (1995). 'Self-Knowledge, Practical Knowledge and Insight: Plato's Dialectic and the Dialogue Form', in F. Gonzalez (ed.), *The Third Way: New Directions in Platonic Studies*. Lanham: Rowman & Littlefield, 155–87.
  (1998). *Dialectic and Dialogue: Plato's Practice of Philosophical Inquiry*. Evanston: Northwestern University Press.
Gordon, J. (2013). *Plato's Erotic World*. Cambridge: Cambridge University Press.

Gottesman, A. (2020). 'The *sōphrosynē* of Critias: Aristocratic Ethics after the Thirty Tyrants', in D. Wolfsdorf (ed.), *Early Greek Ethics*. Oxford: Oxford University Press, 243–61.

Hägglund, M. (2012). *Dying for Time: Proust, Woolf, Nabokov*. Cambridge MA: Harvard University Press.

Halliwell, S. (2000). 'The Subjection of Muthos to Logos: Plato's Citations of the Poets', *Classical Quarterly* 50, 94–112.

Halper, E. (2000). 'Is Knowledge of Knowledge Possible? *Charmides* 167a–169d', in Robinson and Brisson (eds.), 309–16.

Halperin, D. (1986) 'Plato and Erotic Reciprocity', *Classical Antiquity* 5, 60–80.

Hankinson, R. (1991). 'Greek Medical Models of Mind', in S. Everson (ed.), *Psychology*. Cambridge: Cambridge University Press, 194–217.

Hazebroucq, M.-F. (1997). *La folie humaine et ses remèdes: Platon* Charmide *ou De la modération*. Paris: Vrin.

Heitsch, E. (2000). 'Argumentationsschritte im *Charmides*', in Heitsch and von Kutschera, 7–34.

Heitsch, E. and Kutschera, F. von (2000). *Zu Platons Charmides*. Stuttgart: Franz Steiner Verlag.

Herrmann, F.-G. (2013). 'Dynamics of Vision in Plato's Thought', *Helios* 40, 281–307.

Hulme, E. (2022). 'Plato's Knowledge Vocabulary and John Lyons's *Structural Semantics*', *Oxford Studies in Ancient Philosophy* 61, 1–24.

Hyland, D. (1981). *The Virtue of Philosophy: An Interpretation of Plato's Charmides*. Athens, OH: Ohio University Press.

(2019). 'Socratic Self-Knowledge and the Limits of *epistēmē*', in Ambury and German (eds.), 45–62.

Irwin, T. (1995). *Plato's Ethics*. Oxford: Oxford University Press.

(1996). 'Art and Philosophy in Plato's Dialogues', *Phronesis* 41, 335–50.

(2019). 'The Platonic Corpus', in Fine (ed.), 69–91.

Joosse, A. (2018). '*Sōphrosunē* and the Poets: Rival Interpretations in Plato's *Charmides*', *Mnemosyne* 71, 574–592.

Kahn, C. (1988). 'Plato's *Charmides* and the Proleptic Reading of Socratic Dialogues', *Journal of Philosophy* 85, 541–9.

(1996). *Plato and the Socratic Dialogue: The Philosophical Use of a Literary Form*. Cambridge: Cambridge University Press.

Kaklamanou, E., Pavlou, M., and Tsakmakis, A. (eds.) (2021). *Framing the Dialogues: How to Read Openings and Closures in Plato*. Leiden: Brill.

Kamtekar, R. (2017). 'Self-Knowledge in Plato', in U. Renz (ed.), *Self Knowledge: A History*. Oxford: Oxford University Press, 25–43.

Ketchum, R. (1991). 'Plato on the Uselessness of Epistemology: *Charmides* 166e–172a', *Apeiron* 24, 81–98.

Kirk, G. (2016). 'Self-Knowledge and Ignorance in Plato's *Charmides*', *Ancient Philosophy* 36, 303–20.

Kosman, A. (1983). 'Charmides' First Definition: *Sophrosyne* as Quietness', in J. Anton and A. Preus (eds.), *Essays in Ancient Greek Philosophy*, vol. 2. Albany: State University of New York Press, 203–16.
  (2010). 'Beauty and the Good: Situating the *kalon*', *Classical Philology* 105, 341–57.
  (2014) 'Self-Knowledge and Self-Control in Plato's *Charmides*', in *Virtues of Thought: Essays on Plato and Aristotle*. Cambridge MA: Harvard University Press, 227–45, reprinted in F. Leigh (ed.) (2020) *Self-Knowledge in Ancient Philosophy: The Eighth Keeling Colloquium in Ancient Philosophy*. Oxford: Oxford University Press, 71–86.
Kraut, R. (2017). 'Plato', in E. Zalta (ed.), *The Stanford Encyclopedia of Philosophy*, Winter 2021 Edition, www.plato.stanford.edu/entries/plato/.
Kutschera, F. von (2000). 'Das Wissen des Wissens: Zur Argumentation in Platons *Charmides*, 164d4–175d5', in Heitsch and von Kutschera, 35–50.
LaBarge, S. (1997). 'Socrates and the Recognition of Experts', *Apeiron* 30, 51–62.
Laín Entralgo, P. (1970). *The Therapy of the Word in Classical Antiquity*. New Haven: Yale University Press.
Lampert, L. (2010). *How Philosophy Became Socratic: A Study of Plato's Protagoras, Charmides, and Republic*. Chicago: University of Chicago Press.
Lear, G. R. (2010). 'Response to Kosman', *Classical Philology* 105, 357–62.
  (2019). 'Plato on Why Human Beauty is Good for the Soul', *Oxford Studies in Ancient Philosophy* 57, 25–64.
Leigh, F. (2020). 'Self-Knowledge, Elenchus and Authority in Early Plato', *Phronesis* 65, 247–80.
Levine, D. (2016). *Profound Ignorance: Plato's Charmides and the Saving of Wisdom*. Lanham: Lexington Books.
Lewis, T. (1982–3). 'The Brothers of Ganymede', *Salmagundi* 58/59, 147–65.
Liske, M.-T. (1988). 'Absolute Selbstreflexion oder wertkritisches Wissen: Thesen zu Platons *Charmides*', *Theologie und Philosophie* 63, 161–81.
Luckhurst, K. (1934). 'Note on Plato *Charmides* 153b', *Classical Review* 48, 207–8.
Luz, M. (2001). 'Knowledge of Knowledge in Plato's *Charmides*', in K. Boudouris (ed.), *Greek Philosophy and Epistemology*, vol. 2. Athens: Ionia Publications, 100–10.
Martens, E. (1973). *Das selbstbezügliche Wissen in Platons Charmides*. Munich: Carl Hanser Verlag.
Mahoney, T. (1996). The *Charmides*: Socratic *sōphrosunē*, Human *sōphrosunē*', *Southern Journal of Philosophy* 34, 183–99.
McAvoy, M. (1996). 'Carnal Knowledge in the *Charmides*', *Apeiron* 29, 63–103.
McCabe, M. M. (2002). 'Developing the Good Itself by Itself: Critical Strategies in Plato's *Euthydemus*', *Plato Journal* 2, online.
  (2007a). 'Looking Inside Charmides' Cloak: Seeing Others and Oneself in Plato's *Charmides*', in D. Scott (ed.), 1–19, reprinted in McCabe (2015), 173–89.

(2007b). 'Perceiving that We See and Hear: Aristotle on Plato on Judgement and Reflection', in M. M. McCabe and M. Textor (eds.), *Perspectives on Perception*. Heusenstamm: Ontos Verlag, 143–77, reprinted in McCabe (2015), 283–309.

(2011). '"It goes deep with me": Plato's *Charmides* on knowledge, self-knowledge and integrity', in C. Cordner (ed.), *Philosophy, Ethics and a Common Humanity: Essays in Honour of Raimond Gaita*. Abingdon: Routledge, 161–80.

(2015). *Platonic Conversations*. Oxford: Oxford University Press.

(2017). *Seeing and Saying: Plato on Virtue and Knowledge*. Sather Lectures 1–6. Online.

(2019a). 'Plato's Ways of Writing', in Fine (ed.), 93–117.

(2019b). 'Ridicule and Protreptic: Plato, his Reader, and the Role of Comedy in Inquiry', in P. Destrée and F. Trivigno (eds.), *Laughter, Humor, and Comedy in Ancient Philosophy*. New York: Oxford University Press, 182–207.

(2021). 'Philosopher Queens? The Wrong Question at the Wrong Time', in E. Vintiadis (ed.), *Philosophy by Women: 22 Philosophers Reflect on Philosophy and its Value*. New York: Routledge, 112–21.

McCoy, M. (2005). 'Philosophy, Elenchus, and Charmides' Definitions of ΣΩΦΡΟΣΥΝΗ', *Arethusa* 38, 133–59.

McKim, R, (1985). 'Socratic Self-Knowledge and "Knowledge of Knowledge" in Plato's *Charmides*', *Transactions of the American Philological Association* 115, 59–77.

McPherran, M. (2004). 'Socrates and Zalmoxis on Drugs, Charms, and Purification', *Apeiron* 37, 11–33.

Méron, E. (1979). *Les idées morales des interlocuteurs de Socrate dans les dialogues platoniciens de jeunesse*. Paris: Vrin.

Mole, C., Smithies, D. and Wu, W. (eds.) (2011). *Attention: Philosophical and Psychological Essays*. New York: Oxford University Press.

Moore, A. (1997). *Points of View*. Oxford: Oxford University Press.

Moore, C. (2013). 'Chaerephon the Socratic', *Phoenix* 67, 284–300.

(2015). *Socrates and Self-Knowledge*. Cambridge: Cambridge University Press.

(2020a). *Calling Philosophers Names: On the Origin of a Discipline*. Princeton: Princeton University Press.

(2020b). '*Critias in Plato's Protagoras: An Opponent of agōn?*', in H. Reid, M. Ralkowski and C. Zoller (eds.), *Athletics, Gymnastics, and Agōn in Plato*. Sioux City: Parnassos Press, 67–86.

Moore, C. and Raymond, C. (2019). *Plato Charmides*. Indianapolis: Hackett.

Moran, R. (2001). *Authority and Estrangement: An Essay on Self-Knowledge*. Princeton: Princeton University Press.

Morgan, K. (2004). 'Plato', in I. De Jong, R. Nünlist and A. Bowie (eds.), *Narrators, Narratees, and Narratives in Ancient Greek Literature*. Leiden: Brill, 357–76.

(2021). 'Eros in the Platonic Frame', in Kaklamanou, Pavlou and Tsakmakis (eds.), 154–75.
Morris, T. (1989). 'Knowledge of Knowledge and Lack of Knowledge in the *Charmides*', *International Studies in Philosophy* 21, 49–61.
  (1993). 'Temperance and What One Needs in the *Charmides*', *Diálogos* 62, 55–72.
Moss, J. (2021). *Plato's Epistemology: Being and Seeming*. Oxford: Oxford University Press.
Müller, G. (1976). 'Philosophische Dialogkunst Platons (am Beispiel des *Charmides*)', *Museum Helveticum* 33, 129–61.
Murdoch, I. (1970). *The Sovereignty of Good*. London: Routledge & Kegan Paul.
Murphy, D. (2000). 'Doctors of Zalmoxis and Immortality in the *Charmides*', in Robinson and Brisson (eds.), 287–95.
  (2007). 'Critical Notes on Plato's *Charmides*', *Mnemosyne* 60, 213–34.
  (2014). 'More Critical Notes on Plato's *Charmides*', *Mnemosyne* 67, 999–1007.
Nails, D. (2002). *The People of Plato: A Prosopography of Plato and Other Socratics*. Indianapolis: Hackett.
Nehamas, A. (2007). 'Beauty of Body, Nobility of Soul: The Pursuit of Love in Plato's *Symposium*', in D. Scott (ed.), 97–135.
Nightingale, A. (1995). *Genres in Dialogue: Plato and the Construct of Philosophy*. Cambridge: Cambridge University Press.
North, H. (1966). *Sophrosyne: Self-Knowledge and Self-Restraint in Greek Literature*. Ithaca: Cornell University Press.
Notomi, N. (2000). 'Critias and the Origin of Plato's Political Philosophy', in Robinson and Brisson (eds.), 237–50.
  (2003). 'Ethical Examination in Context: The Criticism of Critias in Plato's *Charmides*', in M. Migliori and L. Napolitano Valditara (eds.), *Plato Ethicus: Philosophy is Life*. Sankt Agustin: Academia Verlag, 245–54.
O'Brien, L. (2020). 'Shameful Self-Consciousness', *European Journal of Philosophy* 28, 545–66.
Petre, Z. (2007). '"Zalmoxis, roi et dieu": Autour du *Charmide*', *Dacia* 51, 47–72.
Pichanick, A. (2005). 'Two Rival Conceptions of *sōphrosunē*', *Polis* 22, 249–64.
  (2016). '*Sōphrosunē*, Socratic Therapy, and Platonic Drama in Plato's *Charmides*', *Epoché* 21, 47–66.
Planeaux, C. (1999). 'Socrates, Alcibiades, and Plato's ΤΑ ΠΟΤΕΙΔΕΑΤΙΚΑ: Does the *Charmides* Have an Historical Setting?', *Mnemosyne* 52, 72–7.
Politis, V, (2007). 'The *aporia* in the *Charmides* about Reflexive Knowledge and the Contribution to its Solution in the Sun Analogy of the *Republic*', in F.-G. Herrmann and T. Penner (eds.), *Pursuing the Good: Ethics and Metaphysics in Plato's Republic*. Edinburgh: Edinburgh University Press, 231–51.
  (2008). 'The Place of *aporia* in Plato's *Charmides*', *Phronesis* 53, 1–34.
  (2015). *The Structure of Enquiry in Plato's Early Dialogues*. Cambridge: Cambridge University Press.
Press, G. (1993). 'Principles of Dramatic and Non-Dogmatic Plato Interpretation', in Press (ed.), *Plato's Dialogues: New Studies and Interpretations*. Lanham: Rowman & Littlefield, 109–27.

(2002). 'The *elenchos* in the *Charmides*, 162–175', in G. Scott (ed.), 252–65.
  (ed.) (2000). *Who Speaks for Plato? Studies in Platonic Anonymity*. Lanham: Rowman & Littlefield.
Rademaker, A. (2005). *Sophrosyne and the Rhetoric of Self-Restraint: Polysemy and Persuasive Use of an Ancient Greek Value Term*. Leiden: Brill.
Rappe, S. (1995). 'Socrates and Self-Knowledge', *Apeiron* 28, 1–24.
Rasmussen, W. (2008). *The Enigma of Socratic Wisdom: Resolving Inconsistencies in Plato*. Saarbrücken: VDM Verlag.
Raymond, C. (2018). 'Αἰδώς in Plato's *Charmides*', *Ancient Philosophy* 38, 23–46.
Redfield, J. (2011). 'Socrates' Thracian Incantation', in F. Prescendi and Y. Volokhine (eds.), *Dans le laboratoire de l'historien des religions*. Geneva: Labor et Fides, 358–74.
Reece, A. (1998) 'Drama, Narrative, and Socratic *erōs* in Plato's *Charmides*', *Interpretation* 26, 65–76.
Reshotko, N. (2006). *Socratic Virtue: Making the Best of the Neither-Good-Nor-Bad*. Cambridge: Cambridge University Press.
Robinson, T. and Brisson, L. (eds.) (2000). *Plato: Euthydemus, Lysis, Charmides. Proceedings of the V Symposium Platonicum*. Sankt Augustin: Academia Verlag.
Roochnik, D. (1996). *Of Art and Wisdom: Plato's Understanding of Techne*. University Park: Pennsylvania State University Press.
Rowe, C. (2007). *Plato and the Art of Philosophical Writing*. Cambridge: Cambridge University Press.
Rowett, C. (2018). *Knowledge and Truth in Plato: Stepping Past the Shadow of Socrates*. Oxford: Oxford University Press.
Rutherford, R. (1995). *The Art of Plato*. London: Duckworth.
Santas, G. (1973). 'Socrates at Work on Virtue and Knowledge in Plato's *Charmides*', in E. Lee, A. Mourelatos and R. Rorty (eds.), *Exegesis and Argument: Studies in Greek Philosophy Presented to Gregory Vlastos*. Assen: Van Gorcum, 105–32.
Schiefsky, M. (2005). *Hippocrates On Ancient Medicine: Translated with Introduction and Commentary*. Leiden: Brill.
Schirlitz, C. (1897). 'Der Begriff des Wissens zum Wissen in Platons *Charmides* und seine Bedeutung für das Ergebnis des Dialogs', *Jahrbucher für Classische Philologie* 43, 451–76 and 513–37.
Schmid, T. (1998). *Plato's Charmides and the Socratic Ideal of Rationality*. Albany: State University of New York Press.
Schmidt, G. (1985). *Platons Vernunftkritik, oder die Doppelrolle des Sokrates im Dialog Charmides*. Würzburg: Königshausen & Neumann.
Schofield, M. (2000). 'Approaching the *Republic*', in C. Rowe and M. Schofield (eds.), *The Cambridge Companion to Greek and Roman Political Thought*. Cambridge: Cambridge University Press, 190–232.
  (2006). *Plato: Political Philosophy*. Oxford: Oxford University Press.
  (2008). 'Ciceronian Dialogue', in S. Goldhill (ed.), *The End of Dialogue in Antiquity*. Cambridge: Cambridge University Press, 63–84.

(2013). 'When and Why did Plato Write Narrated Dialogues?', in E. Moutsopoulos and M. Protopapas-Marneli (eds.), *Plato, Poet and Philosopher*. Athens: Academy of Athens Research Centre on Greek Philosophy, 87–96.

Schultz, A.-M. (2013). *Plato's Socrates as Narrator: A Philosophical Muse*. Plymouth: Lexington Books.

Scott, D. (ed.) (2007). *Maieusis: Essays in Ancient Philosophy in Honour of Myles Burnyeat*. Oxford: Oxford University Press.

Scott, G. (2000). *Plato's Socrates as Educator*. Albany: State University of New York Press.

(2007). 'Introduction', in G. Scott (ed.), ix–xxxii.

(ed.) (2002). *Does Socrates Have a Method? Rethinking the Elenchus in Plato's Dialogues and Beyond*. University Park: Pennsylvania State University Press.

(2007). *Philosophy in Dialogue: Plato's Many Devices*. Evanston: Northwestern University Press.

Sedley, D. (2003). *Plato's Cratylus*. Cambridge: Cambridge University Press.

(2004). *The Midwife of Platonism: Text and Subtext in Plato's Theaetetus*. Oxford: Oxford University Press.

(2010). 'Plato's *Theaetetus* as an Ethical Dialogue', in D. Sedley and A. Nightingale (eds.), *Ancient Models of Mind: Studies in Human and Divine Rationality*. Cambridge: Cambridge University Press, 64–74.

(2019). 'The *Timaeus* as Vehicle for Platonic Doctrine', *Oxford Studies in Ancient Philosophy* 56, 45–71.

Smith, N. (2021). *Socrates on Self-Improvement: Knowledge, Virtue, and Happiness*. Cambridge : Cambridge University Press.

Solère-Queval, S. (1993). 'Lecture du *Charmide*', *Revue de Philosophie Ancienne* 11, 3–65.

Sorabji, R. (2006). *Self: Ancient and Modern Insights about Individuality, Life, and Death*. Oxford: Oxford University Press.

Sprague, R. (1992). *Plato Laches and Charmides*. Indianapolis: Hackett.

Stalley, R. F. (2000). 'Sōphrosunē in the *Charmides*', in Robinson and Brisson (eds.), 265–77.

Stern, P. (1999). 'Tyranny and Self-Knowledge: Critias and Socrates in Plato's *Charmides*', *American Political Science Review* 93, 399–412.

Stokes, M. (1997). *Plato: Apology*. Warminster: Aris & Phillips.

Sue, Y.-S. (2006). *Selbsterkenntnis im Charmides*. Würzburg: Königshausen & Neumann.

Szlezák, T. (1985). 'Charmides: Der Jüngling und der "schlechte Forscher"', in *Platon und die Schriftlichkeit der Philosophie: Interpretationen zu den frühen und mittleren Dialogen*. Berlin: De Gruyter, 127–50.

Tarrant, H. (2000). 'Naming Socratic Interrogation in the *Charmides*', in Robinson and Brisson (eds.), 251–8.

Taylor, A. E. (1949). *Plato: The Man and His Work*. London: Methuen.

Tigerstedt, E. (1977). *Interpreting Plato*. Stockholm: Almqvist & Wiksell.

Torres, J. (2021). 'Plato's Medicalisation of Ethics', *Apeiron* 54, 287–316.
Tsouna, V. (1997). 'Socrates' Attack on Intellectualism in the *Charmides*', *Apeiron* 30, 63–78.
  (2001). 'Socrate et la connaissance de soi : quelques interprétations', *Philosophie Antique* 1, 37–64.
  (2015). 'Plato's Representations of the "Socratics"', in U. Zilioli (ed.), *From the Socratics to the Socratic Schools*. New York: Routledge, 1–25.
  (2017). 'What is the Subject of Plato's *Charmides*?' in Y. Liebersohn, I. Ludlam, and A. Edelheit (eds.), *For a Skeptical Peripatetic: Festschrift in Honour of John Glucker*. Sankt Augustin: Academia Verlag, 34–63.
  (2022). *Plato's Charmides: An Interpretative Commentary*. Cambridge: Cambridge University Press.
Tuckey, T. (1951). *Plato's Charmides*. Cambridge: Cambridge University Press.
Tuozzo, T. (2001). 'What's Wrong with These Cities? The Social Dimension of *sophrosune* in Plato's *Charmides*', *Journal of the History of Philosophy* 39, 321–50.
  (2011). *Plato's Charmides: Positive Elenchus in a "Socratic" Dialogue*. Cambridge: Cambridge University Press.
  (2019). 'Two Faces of Platonic Self-Knowledge: *Alcibiades I* and *Charmides*', in Ambury and German (eds.), 30–44.
van der Ben, N. (1985). *The Charmides of Plato: Problems and Interpretations*. Amsterdam: Grüner.
Vlastos, G. (1987). 'Socratic Irony', *Classical Quarterly* 37, 79–96.
  (1991). *Socrates: Ironist and Moral Philosopher*. Cambridge: Cambridge University Press.
Vorwerk, M. (2001). 'Plato on Virtue: Definitions of ΣΩΦΡΟΣΥΝΗ in Plato's *Charmides* and in Plotinus *Enneads* 1.2 (19)', *American Journal of Philology* 122, 29–47.
Waugh, J. (2002). 'Questioning the Self: A Reaction to Carvalho, Press and Schmid', in G. Scott (ed.), 281–97.
Wellman, R. (1964). 'The Question Posed at *Charmides* 165a–166c', *Phronesis* 9, 107–13.
West, T. and West, G. (1986). *Plato Charmides*. Indianapolis: Hackett.
Williamson, T. (2007). *The Philosophy of Philosophy*. Oxford: Blackwell.
  (2018). *Doing Philosophy: From Common Curiosity to Logical Reasoning*. Oxford: Oxford University Press.
Witte, B. (1970). *Die Wissenschaft vom Guten und Bösen: Interpretationen zu Platons Charmides*. Berlin: De Gruyter.
Wolfsdorf (2008). *Trials of Reason: Plato and the Crafting of Philosophy*. Oxford: Oxford University Press.
Woolf, R. (2008). 'Socratic Authority', *Archiv für Geschichte der Philosophie* 90, 1–38, reprinted in P. Remes and J. Sihvola (eds.) (2008). *Ancient Philosophy of the Self*. New York: Springer, 77–107.
Zuckert, C. (2009). *Plato's Philosophers: The Coherence of the Dialogues*. Chicago: University of Chicago Press.

Index of Ancient Passages

Aristotle
  De Anima
    3.2, 425b12–17, 177

Critias
  B48, 51
  B53–73, 149

Heraclitus
  B5, 75
Herodotus
  4.94-6, 228
Hesiod
  Works and Days
    311, 146
Hippocratic corpus
  On Ancient Medicine
    9, 106
Homer
  Odyssey, 11, 36–7, 224
    16.205, 37
    17.347, 36
    17.578, 37
    19.535, 236
    19.562-9, 37

Plato
  Apology, 7, 12, 156, 158, 230
    21a, 8
    21a3, 35
    21a7, 157
    21b4, 156
    21b7, 156
    21b8, 156
    21c2–d8, 8
    32b–c, 57
    32c–d, 57
    34a, 11
    38b, 11
  Critias, 11

  Crito, 7
  Euthyphro, 7, 34
  Gorgias, 212
    456a–b, 97
    464b–466a, 209
    482a–c, 7
    484c, 46
  Laches
    201b2–3, 8, 119
  Laws
    4.719e–720e, 39
    4.721d–723b, 39
    4.722d–e, 39
    9.857c–e, 39
    10, 8
    10.888a, 39
    10.894a–896b, 8
  Lysis
    204b5–c2, 93
    204e10–205a2, 93
    206a1, 93
    206a–c, 137
    210e, 137
    210e3, 93
  Meno, 7–8, 15
    82b4, 112
  Parmenides, 6
    135d4, 23
    135d7, 23
    136a2, 23
    136c5, 23
  Phaedo, 6–8, 12
    59b, 12
    73a–b, 7
    100b1–3, 7
  Phaedrus, 8–9, 17, 143
    245c–e, 8
    251a5–7, 75
    252d6–e1, 75

Philebus
  38b–e, 218
Protagoras, 149
  336d–e, 11
Republic, 7, 9, 31
  4, 9
Sophist, 7
  263e–264a, 218
Statesman, 7, 9
Symposium, 17
  176d, 101
  217a–219d, 247
  220d–e, 47
  222a4, 75
  222b1–4, 247
Theaetetus, 7
  189e–190a, 218
Timaeus, 11
  17c–19b, 7
  72a4–6, 9
  72b3, 127

Xenophon
  Hellenica
    2.3.15-16, 55
  Memorabilia
    1.2.12, 55

General Index

Adamietz, J., 20
aporia, 51, 131–2, 182–6
attention, 62, 69–70, 75, 79–80, 92, 95, 101–2, 138, 141–3, 154–5, 170, 176, 222, 227, 234–5, 252

beauty, 17–26, 38–40, 45–52, 57, 60–2, 68–73, 78–84, 91–9, 102, 109, 113–16, 120–4, 128–9, 132–43, 145–7, 166, 217, 220–6, 247–8, 251–2, 254
belief (*doxa*), 77, 103–5, 108–10, 112, 156, 162–4, 175, 210–20, 223–5
benefit, 26, 96–7, 131, 145, 152–3, 165, 172–3, 182, 186–7, 197–203, 205–10, 218–25, 229–33, 236–45 see also goodness
body, 19, 22, 57, 60–5, 68–73, 76–92, 97–108, 114–15, 129, 138–40, 166, 195–6, 226–8, 243–4, 248, 251
Brown, L., 67

Chaerephon, 8, 10, 16, 22, 31, 33–5, 37, 39–40, 42–5, 57, 62–3, 69–70, 127, 156–7
charm, 22, 44, 48, 78, 82–3, 88, 91, 98–101, 104, 195, 230, 245, 248
Chen, C.-H., 20

doctors, 19, 22, 27, 36, 53, 78–97, 99, 105–8, 152, 189–96, 198–9, 202, 228–30, 243, 248

epistēmē (knowledge), 90, 165–7, 175, 179, 192, 195, 202, 206, 208, 210, 217–18
eros, 17, 59, 61, 68–73, 80–1, 84, 114, 133, 137, 142–3, 175, 188–9, 217, 247–8
erotics, art of, 19, 61, 76, 93–7, 102, 109, 133–7, 246–8, 251

family, 8–10, 38, 50–2, 96–8, 129, 171
focus *see* attention

goodness, 22, 26, 69, 82, 84, 114, 120, 128, 147, 151–4, 173, 187, 195, 208, 220–5, 228–9, 232, 235–45, *See also* benefit

Hesiod, 146–50, 153, 159–62, 198
Homer, 8, 11, 36–7, 53, 120–1, 146–9, 184, 198, 236

Irwin, T., 21, 32

Kahn, C., 9
kalon see beauty
knowledge *see epistēmē*
knowledge of knowledge, 87, 90, 131, 145, 170–4, 182–93, 197–8, 201–10, 213, 218–21, 225–8, 231, 234–9, 242
Kosman, A., 141

love *see* eros

medicine, art of, 19, 57, 69, 81–97, 103–9, 153, 165–7, 175–6, 189–93, 196, 205–6, 209, 228–30, 235–44
Moore, C. and Raymond, C., 234–5

Nehamas, A., 139–41, 227

Odysseus, 36–7, 53, 236
opinion *see* belief
Oracle, Delphic, 8, 125, 151, 156–61, 234

Penelope, 37, 53, 224, 236
perception, 103, 106–7, 177–81
Planeaux, C., 47
politics, 57–8, 191, 200–1
Press, G., 23

Santas, G., 21
Schiefsky, M., 106–7
Schofield, M., 138

Sedley, D., 8–9, 13
self-control, 80–1, 141, 143, 227
self-knowledge, 8, 18, 20, 42–3, 46, 64–7, 73, 142, 145, 153–9, 161–74, 183, 187–9, 201, 205–6, 210–13, 217–23, 226, 234
sight, 174–7, 180–1, 217
soul, 8, 18–26, 34, 48–9, 57, 60–1, 68–73, 76–115, 118–24, 128–39, 143, 163, 166, 175–6, 179–81, 185, 189, 193, 195–6, 217, 221, 227–30, 243, 246–9, 251, 254
soul-doctor *see* soul-medicine
soul-medicine, art of, 19, 22, 57, 61, 76, 89–97, 102–4, 108–9, 113, 117, 166, 196, 230, 248–52
Stalley, R. F., 20

Telemachus, 36–7, 121
testimony, 40–2, 85, 106
Thirty Tyrants, 10–11, 52–7, 246, 251
Thracian doctors *see* doctors
Tsouna, V., 150, 250

utopia, 198–202, 208, 227–9, 232, 236, 242–3

Vlastos, G., 7

war, 47, 69, 111
Waugh, J., 32
Williamson, T., 151–2

Xenophon, 34, 45, 55

For EU product safety concerns, contact us at Calle de José Abascal, 56–1°, 28003 Madrid, Spain or eugpsr@cambridge.org.

www.ingramcontent.com/pod-product-compliance
Ingram Content Group UK Ltd.
Pitfield, Milton Keynes, MK11 3LW, UK
UKHW021447090925
462724UK00024B/1320